William Angus Knight, William Minto

The Literature of the Georgian Era

William Angus Knight, William Minto

The Literature of the Georgian Era

ISBN/EAN: 9783337205140

Printed in Europe, USA, Canada, Australia, Japan

Cover: Foto ©Thomas Meinert / pixelio.de

More available books at **www.hansebooks.com**

THE LITERATURE

OF

THE GEORGIAN ERA

THE LITERATURE

OF

THE GEORGIAN ERA

BY THE LATE

WILLIAM MINTO, LL.D.

PROFESSOR OF LOGIC AND ENGLISH IN THE UNIVERSITY OF ABERDEEN

EDITED, WITH A BIOGRAPHICAL INTRODUCTION, BY

WILLIAM KNIGHT, LL.D.

PROFESSOR OF MORAL PHILOSOPHY IN THE UNIVERSITY
OF ST ANDREWS

WILLIAM BLACKWOOD AND SONS
EDINBURGH AND LONDON
MDCCCXCIV

PREFACE.

THE following Lectures by Professor Minto on *The Literature of the Georgian Era* were originally delivered, not to the Arts students whom he addressed in the University class-room, but to a special audience brought together in the Music Hall of Aberdeen, under the auspices of the Local Examination Committee of the Senatus Academicus. This will explain why some points are treated in greater detail than would have been necessary in addressing advanced students. As explained in the "Introduction," to Mr John H. Lobban belongs the credit—as he had all the labour—of looking up and copying out the illustrative extracts from the authors referred to, or criticised by his master.

In addition to these Lectures, and as a cognate Supplement, it has been thought expedient to publish three essays by Professor Minto, which were ready for press before his death, and were meant by him to be included in a work, to be entitled *Reconsiderations of some Current Conceptions about Eminent Poets.* Two of them are devoted to Pope, the former being a criticism of Mr Courthope's Biography, and the latter a noteworthy discussion on "The Supposed Tyranny of Pope." These were contributed to *Macmillan's*

Magazine in January 1890 and September 1888, and the right of reproducing them has been generously conceded by the owners of the copyright. The other, on Burns, has not been previously published. It was delivered as a lecture to the Philosophical Institution of Edinburgh. In reference to it—as Mr Lobban tells us—Professor Minto said that it was "most distinctly the best thing" he had ever written. The projected *Reconsiderations* would have included, amongst others, an essay on John Donne, two papers on Wordsworth,—originally contributed to *The Nineteenth Century,*—and another on "Matthew Arnold's Meliorism." As the last of these does not fall within the literature of the era included in the "Lectures" which follow, and the first belongs to a previous period, while Wordsworth has been discussed in the course of this volume, these papers are not included in the "Supplement."

W. K.

October 1894.

CONTENTS.

LECTURES.

CHAPTER I.

THE POSITION OF MEN OF LETTERS IN THE EIGHTEENTH CENTURY.

CHAPTER II.

POPE.

CHAPTER III.

POPE—*continued.*

CHAPTER IV.

POPE—*continued.*

CHAPTER V.

A GROUP OF EIGHTEENTH-CENTURY POETS.

CHAPTER VI.

POPE—*continued.*

CHAPTER VII.

POETRY BEETWEN POPE AND COWPER.

CHAPTER VIII.

DECLINE OF POETRY—THE NOVEL.

CHAPTER IX.

THE NOVEL.—*continued.*

CHAPTER X.

THE NEW POETRY.

CHAPTER XI.

SCOTTISH POETRY IN THE EIGHTEENTH CENTURY.

CHAPTER XII.

WORDSWORTH.

CHAPTER XIII.

WORDSWORTH—*continued.*

CHAPTER XIV.

WORDSWORTH (*continued*)—COLERIDGE—SOUTHEY.

CHAPTER XV.

CAMPBELL—MOORE.

CHAPTER XVI.

SCOTT.

CHAPTER XVII.

BYRON.

CHAPTER XVIII.

NOVELISTS FROM MRS RADCLIFFE TO BULWER LYTTON.

CHAPTER XIX.

SHELLEY AND KEATS.

SUPPLEMENT.

BIOGRAPHICAL INTRODUCTION.

In the year 1890, I asked Professor Minto to contribute a volume on *Logic, Inductive and Deductive*, to the series of "University Manuals" which I had organised some time previously, and was then editing. It was not completed till shortly before his death, but the proof had been revised by himself in all its details; and it seemed only loyal to his memory to send it to the press, in the exact form in which he left it.

It has now fallen to me to edit a volume of his Lectures, on the Literature of the Georgian Period; and, although they would have been greatly altered and recast, had he lived to see them through the press, it is now inexpedient to do more than correct clerical errors in transcription. Mr Lobban — who acted as Professor Minto's assistant for some time, and whose estimate of his Master will be found in a later page—has been good enough to go over these Lectures with the same end in view.

At the request of Mrs Minto, I agreed to edit this book, and to write a brief introductory sketch of my late friend. We differed on many points—philosophical, literary, political, artistic, and social—but I never knew any man with whom recognised differences counted for less, so far as per-

sonal esteem was concerned. Indeed, our differences en-
hanced my regard for him every time we met.

He was not only the most chivalrous of intellectual
opponents, but the most appreciative; and he had the
rare gift of presenting to those who differed from him the
very doctrine from which they dissented, and the kernel
of the position from which they stood aloof, in a non-
controversial and attractive manner.

I have never known a more genial, generous, or upright
man than Professor Minto. He never alluded to the points
on which men differed from him in reference to *ultimata*,
as expressed in their published writings; and, so far as
friendly intercourse was concerned, these differences were
as though they were not. He instinctively met every one
on his own level, sympathetically appreciating truth and
excellence wherever he found them. This characteristic
came out most notably in his comments on those who had
misconstrued, and even opposed him. I never heard him
say an unkind word of any opponent.

The first occasion on which we met was at a University
Extension Conference, which was being held in Glasgow,
and to which those representatives of the four Scottish
Universities who had interested themselves in the work,
as organisers or secretaries, &c., were invited. There
was one person in the room whom I did not know; and
he seemed to know no one present from Edinburgh, Glasgow, or St Andrews. But observing this silent man,
with a noticeable countenance, sitting in the background
and in a corner of the room, I went up to him, and
asked him what University he represented. As soon as
he had introduced himself, he was asked to help in the
organisation of a comprehensive plan of University Extension for Scotland at large. Aberdeen had, up to that
time, taken no active part in the movement; and Professor
Minto was the first to interest himself in it, which he did
with much ardour, offering many important suggestions.

He came to St Andrews, to discuss that and other things with me, and soon became an intimate friend.

I can never forget the days he spent at Edgecliffe, and my repeated visits to him afterwards at Aberdeen, our talks on Philosophy and Literature—far beyond the summer night and into early morning—in his house at Westfield Terrace, our golf-matches on the Links, and social intercourse with friends at the Club, or in his most genial home.

As I was a friend of his later years, it seemed appropriate to follow the plan which I pursued in the case of the late Principal Shairp of St Andrews, and to place together a series of photographic sketches—taken from opposite points of view—of the character, genius, and career of a remarkable man, by his earlier friends and more intimate pupils. These tributes have been rendered spontaneously, and given very cordially.

I do not feel it incumbent on me to characterise his work in Philosophy, or his contributions to Literature, in detail. It will suffice to record one or two things, which were written before these admirable character - sketches by others reached me.

I consider it not the least merit in Professor Minto's career that, while a man of letters *par excellence*—and for many years diverted from Philosophy to Literature by his work as a Journalist, and a critic of men and public measures—he succeeded, during his tenure of it, in making the Aberdeen Chair, with its dual claims, quite as distinguished in the department of Philosophy as in that of Literature. All students bear witness to this. His book on *Logic, Inductive and Deductive*, is as original and bright as that of any writer on the subject in Great Britain, during the last quarter of a century. In all probability his previous life as a journalist not only confirmed that rare capacity for work which distinguished him as an undergraduate, but fitted him for popularising an abstruse subject, and keeping his exposition of it free from the technicalities which have so often disfigured the treatment of Logic. The fact that he had been no mean power in the literary circles of the south gave a special weight to what he said from his academic chair; and while the bejants of the north found that they had before them, in the English Literature class, a Teacher, of whose achievements amongst his contemporaries it might be truly said—(although *he* would never have said it, nor thought it)—*pars magna fui*, the students of Philosophy found that they were being taught by an original mind, and not by a mere expositor of school Logic.

A wonderful critic of his *Logic* has complained of its "laxity of reference to Greek writers and to modern," and has added that the editor should have supplied a bibliography, and index, and notes, and references, &c. He has even doubted whether it should ever have had a place in such a Series! But the ways of reviewers are inscrutable. To none of the authors whom I asked to co-operate in this series of Manuals was it a greater satisfaction to me to delegate work, than to hand over this volume to Professor Minto; and its success, both in this country and in America, has been marked. It has a value of its own, which has already made it useful in University and College class-rooms, being one of the freshest and most stimulating books which our British philosophical literature has received for many years.

As a contribution to logical science, its Introduction will probably be welcomed generations hence, by students of the subject, when dry-as-dust logicians are forgotten. To be taught how to escape from illusion and fallacy of every kind, so as to get into the light of reality, is no small gain to the student of evidence; and there can be little doubt that Professor Minto's book—while a reflection of the work done by him, in the Logic class-room of Aberdeen, for thirteen years—will be found one of the best handbooks, introductory to the study of Philosophy, for those who cannot resort to a University, and for whose assistance these Manuals were originally designed.

In Philosophy, Minto was singularly open to light from every quarter. I often told him that he was more eclectic than I was. When discussing the ideal and the real in Philosophy or in Art, he always proved himself one of the most fair-minded of men, a reconciler of differences, and as ready to recognise merit from the most opposite quarters as any disciple of the school of *a priori* thought.

The range of his knowledge and culture was almost encyclopædic, as was that of his friend and rival, Robertson Smith; so that, like the late Professor Trail of Edinburgh —editor of the seventh edition of the *Encyclopædia Britannica*—he was probably the only man in the University who could have been trusted on an emergency to conduct the class of any one of his colleagues who might be accidentally laid aside from duty.

It is a noteworthy circumstance that, when it was finally determined to separate the subjects of Logic and Literature in the University of Aberdeen, a memorial was addressed to Professor Minto, signed by 350 of his former pupils, asking him to accept the Chalmers Chair of English Literature.

The lectures published in this volume, which have been printed from Professor Minto's own MSS., are a very inadequate index of the extent of his knowledge, or his critical insight into the more delicate problems which arise in the study of English Literature; but, as he meant to recast them with a view to publication, they are sent forth in the belief that they contain literary judgments which he would himself have ratified, in any subsequent work. At the same time, I believe that there are articles of William Minto's, I should not say buried, but — for the mass of readers—lost, in the *Encyclopædia Britannica, The Nineteenth Century,* and other magazines, which, in their critical vision, their wise insight, and felicitous appraisal of authors little known (or at least little read), are greatly superior to those put together in this volume for the first time. There are papers on Wordsworth, and other magnates in our great English hierarchy, which will be found as valuable to posterity as the critical notices of any of our modern reviewers. In addition, there are numerous Introductory Lectures delivered to his class,— such as those on "The English Language," on "The Usefulness of Plodding," on "Industry"; and others delivered to Literary Societies in the north, that on "K., B., and Q.," or three new novelists—(they were Kipling, Barrie, and Quiller-Couch),—which would adorn another volume of his remains.

As Minto's knowledge was not derived from secondary sources, his criticism was invariably at first hand. I was often struck with his knowledge of out-of-the-way authors. He could quote *The Day's Estival* as readily as he showed his knowledge of the writings of Thomas, ex Albiis. These delightful days at Aberdeen, when—after a round of the Links—we used to watch the fleet of boats going out from the harbour to the herring fishing, and talk of Metaphysics or of Literature, vividly recall to me how glad Minto was to be ultimately relieved from what became— to a temperament like his—the drudgery of editorship. I nevertheless believe that his training in the editorial chair, and his varied literary work in London, developed his unique fitness for the work he did at the University. It prevented him from ever being pedantic. It gave simplicity, piquancy, and diversity to his style; and to it is greatly owing the fact that, in all his subsequent expositions of the abstruser matters of Philosophy, he was untechnical, and even vernacular.

In the following brief sketch of his life, I avail myself of notes derived from several quarters.

William Minto was born at Nether Auchintoul, Alford, on the 10th of October 1845, the farm then occupied by his father. He was sent to Gallowhill school, near Alford, which he left in May 1854, going for six months to the parish school of Tough. In November 1854 his father entered upon the tenancy of the farm of Littlemill, Auchterless, and the son was sent to a private school at Bruckhills in the neighbourhood. Here he remained for two years, after which he went for a year to the Episcopal school at Fisherford, Culsalmond. In 1857 his parents removed to Huntly, where William was taught in the Gordon Schools, under a very able master, the Rev. John Macdonald, who gave him a thorough training in classics, as a preparation for the bursary competition at the University of Aberdeen. He cherished the memory of this teacher to the last, entertaining for him the greatest admiration and regard.

Before giving an outline of his College career, an explanation of the constant race between him and the late Robertson Smith, the distinguished Professor of Arabic at Cambridge, is desirable. He went to College in the winter of 1861-62, at the age of sixteen, his means of preparation being such as already indicated. Robertson Smith was more than a year his junior; and, by his father's arrangement as a matter of policy, was kept at home studying to the very utmost under himself, he being one of the best teachers of the day, accomplished both in mathematics and classics. The consequence was, that Smith carried off the first bursary with comparative ease, his Latin version being perfect, *sine errore*, in every respect—probably as good a version as a classical master could have produced. Minto, with his inferior advantages, was able to carry off the Moir bursary of £15. The disparity in years and means of training made the start of the two competitors necessarily unequal; and it was by an extraordinary strain of application that Minto was able, in a very short time, to equal, and even to surpass, Robertson Smith, in some of the subjects. At the end of the first year his work had been such that he took the 8th prize in Latin and the 2d in Greek. In English he only attained a third place in the order of merit.

Professor Bain writes: "In the English class one incident occurred which constituted the first occasion of my taking notice of his personality. I began in that year the system of setting in writing two essays a-week, and engaged an assistant to read them. The only person that I could find as an assistant to begin with, before I got advanced pupils of my own, was an assistant-librarian in the College. The out-of-door essays I made him examine and value, and also indicate errors, so that they might be returned. After giving them back one day, Minto came up to me at the end of the hour, and showed me his paper with some red ink marks under portions of it, which was the mode of indicating some error, or want of correctness. He asked me to tell him what that meant. I looked at it, and I found that there was really nothing to correct in the matter at all; and the incident showed me that the assistant was not to be trusted with the function of indicating errors, so as to enable me to return the essays; and from that time forward I ceased the practice."

In the Honours examinations Minto had a first in Classics, a second in Mental Philosophy, and a second in Mathematical Science—a triple honour, never before or since accomplished. As prizes, he carried off the Simpson in Greek and the Boxhill in Mathematics: he also obtained the Hutton prize (which was awarded for distinction both in Classics and in Philosophy)—the total money value of the prizes being £110.

He graduated as Master of Arts in 1865, and afterwards obtained the Ferguson scholarship in Classics, open to graduates of all the Scottish Universities.

In the session of 1865-66 he attended the Divinity Hall, and in the summer of 1866 went to Merton College, Oxford, where he obtained an exhibition of £80.

His experience at Oxford seemed to impress him with

the inexpediency of pursuing his studies there, and he resolved to leave it at the end of the year, which he did, without taking the Oxford degree. He seemed to think that to wait for a Fellowship at Merton would not be so advantageous to him as to go south to the metropolis, or to return to Scotland.

In the autumn of 1867 he was undecided as to his future; but, owing to his distinction in Science, as well as in Classics and Philosophy, an offer was made to him by Mr David Thomson, the Professor of Natural Philosophy in Aberdeen, to become his endowed assistant,—an office to which a salary of £100 a-year was attached. The engagement seemed to give satisfaction to both parties, and he entered upon its duties in the following November. The only thing doubtful was whether he had that sort of handicraft skill required in an assistant who had to take part in experimental work, and that of course remained to be tested. The engagement, however, came to an abrupt termination in December, the occasion being Minto's refusal to take part in the experiment of subjecting himself to an electric shock, so as to excite the laughter of the students, which he considered derogatory to his position as an assistant. It is unnecessary to discuss the details of this unfortunate affair, further than to say that he objected, and rightly, "to be made part and parcel of the class apparatus." When released from this post he was appointed temporarily by Professor Bain as his English class-assistant, and to give various aid in connection with certain books which he then had in hand. With this occupation Minto began his volume on *English Prose Composition*, which he wrote exclusively in Aberdeen, during the course of the next three years, having the resources of the University library at his command for the purpose. The work appeared in 1872.

During the four years which he now spent at Aberdeen, Minto was active in a variety of ways, in connection with

the University, although not one of its recognised officials.
He took a noteworthy part in the work of the University
Literary Society, which was founded in 1871, and of which
he was elected president in 1872. He was also an active
organiser in rectorial contests, although he had not himself a
vote. The election which occurred during his stay in
Aberdeen resulted in the return of Mountstuart Grant
Duff for the second time in 1869. There was a close
contest. The majority was a very narrow one—only 12;
indeed it was found that there was a tie of Nations, and the
Duke of Richmond and Gordon gave the casting-vote in
favour of Sir William Maxwell, who, seeing there was dissatisfaction with the mode in which the election had been
made, magnanimously declined to accept office, and allowed
Mr Grant Duff to be elected. Minto's influence was very
marked and powerful, so much so that but for him Mr
Grant Duff would have failed.

In 1872 there was a vacancy in the representation of the
University Council in the Court, and it was again due to
his untiring energy that the Rev. John Christie, minister of
Kildrummy, was elected.

In 1872 the examinership in Mental Philosophy at
Aberdeen became vacant, and Minto became a candidate.
His friends in the Court were the Rector, the Rector's
Assessor, and the Assessor to the General Council, all of
whom may be said to have owed their standing to his exer-
tions in their behalf at the different elections. His securing the appointment as Examiner was an important step in
his future career, being the beginning of his systematic
studies in Philosophy, while his other work was more
exclusively in connection with English Literature.

In the following year (1873) he left Aberdeen, and went
up to London to engage in literary work. He obtained a
post on *The Examiner* newspaper, and in its columns he
wrote, with special force and clearness, on John Stuart Mill,
on the occasion of his death in May 1873. His article was

one of a series of character-sketches on Mill, to which Herbert Spencer, Mr Frederick Harrison, Professors Henry Fawcett and Cairns also contributed. Later in that year *The Examiner* was purchased by Mr Peter Taylor, the Radical member of Parliament for Leicester. Mr Minto was selected as literary editor, and in 1874 as editor-in-chief. *The Examiner* had been started by Leigh Hunt in the earlier years of the present century. To it Charles Lamb, Shelley, Hazlitt, Haydon, and John Forster had contributed. It was edited for some time by M. Albany Fonblanque; but it had almost failed about the year 1870, when it was revived as the organ of philosophical Radicalism. It was, however, a literary as well as a political journal; and Mr Minto had very able coadjutors in both departments, such men as Mr John MacDonnell and Mr William A. Hunter being amongst them. With all its ability, however, *The Examiner* did not succeed. It had a very formidable rival in the ablest of all the weekly papers of Great Britain—*The Spectator.* Mr Taylor sold the property to Lord Rosebery, Mr Minto remaining co-editor along with Mr Robert Williams until 1878. When the paper was finally discontinued in 1880, Minto turned to purely political writing in *The Daily News.* He afterwards wrote in *The Pall Mall Gazette* (under the editorship of Mr John Morley), to which newspaper he was a regular contributor until he left London. While living as a journalist in London, Minto took a prominent part in political controversy, especially in connection with England's relations to the East, and the war in Afghanistan. He was one of the first to use a term which soon became current coin in political writing—the term "jingo." As he once told his students, " I am under the impression that I was the first to give the currency of respectable print to the chorus of the song, 'We don't want to fight, but by Jingo if we do,' and so forth," which was first made use of in an editorial article in *The Daily News.*

During his seven years in the metropolis, his literary, other than newspaper, work resulted in the publication of *Characteristics of English Poets*, in 1874, and *Defoe*, in the "English Men of Letters" Series, in 1879, besides miscellaneous contributions to various periodicals, such as *The Nineteenth Century*, *The Fortnightly Review*, *Macmillan*, *Blackwood*, and *The English Illustrated Magazine*. It may be noted that Mr Edmund Gosse was, for a time, the subeditor of *The Examiner*, and that Minto was the first to persuade Mr Theodore Watts to devote himself to literature.

He was early engaged by Professor Thomas Spenser Baynes, the late editor of the *Encyclopædia Britannica*, to contribute to its pages, and his contributions are to be found in most of the volumes of that Encyclopædia. In alphabetical order they were as follows: Byron, Chaucer, Dickens, Dryden, Fielding, Lytton, Mandeville, J. S. Mill, Minstrel, Moore, Poe, Pope, Reade, Scott, Sheridan, Sydney Smith, Smollett, Spenser, Steele, Sterne, James Thomson, Waller, Izaak Walton, Warton, and Wordsworth.

In 1880 Professor Bain retired from the Chair of Logic and English Literature in the University of Aberdeen, and Minto became his successor. In that year he married Miss Cornelia Griffiths, daughter of the Rector of Swindon, in Gloucestershire. When called to Aberdeen he devoted himself with rare assiduity to both branches of his Chair, although it was evident that the English section was what he liked best, and what he most excelled in. During the thirteen years that he held office in the University his literary activity was great. He published three romances: *The Crack of Doom*, which appeared first in *Blackwood's Magazine* in 1886, and was republished in three volumes in 1886; *The Mediation of Ralph Hardelot*, contributed to *The English Illustrated Magazine*, and published in bookform in 1888; and *Was She Good or Bad?* in 1889. In 1886 he brought out an admirable edition of Scott's *Lay of the Last Minstrel* for the Clarendon Press, with notes, and in 1891 an edition of *The Lady of The Lake*. In 1887 he edited a complete edition of Sir Walter's Poems for Messrs A. & C. Black. During his later years in Aberdeen he was also a frequent contributor to several of the London literary weeklies, notably to *The Bookman*. The posthumous volume on *Logic*, already referred to, contains the best part of his teaching in the Philosophical class-room of the University of Aberdeen.

In the Preface to that work he wrote:—

In this little treatise two things are attempted that at first might appear incompatible. One of them is to put the study of logical formulæ on a historical basis. Strangely enough, the scientific evolution of logical forms is a bit of history that still awaits the zeal and genius of some great scholar. I have neither ambition nor qualification for such a *magnum opus*, and my life is already more than half spent; but the gap in evolutionary research is so obvious that doubtless some younger man is now at work in the field unknown to me. All that I can hope to do is to act as a humble pioneer according to my imperfect lights. Even the little I have done represents work begun more than twenty years ago, and continuously pursued for the last twelve years during a considerable portion of my time.

The other aim, which might at first appear inconsistent with this, is to increase the power of Logic as a practical discipline. The main purpose of this practical science, or scientific art, is conceived to be the organisation of reason against error, and error in its various kinds is made the basis of the division of the subject. To carry out this practical aim along with the historical one is not hopeless, because throughout its long history Logic has been a practical science; and, as I have tried to show at some length in introductory chapters, has concerned itself at different periods with the risks of error peculiar to each.

An earlier work, issued the year before he died, the *Autobiographical Notes of the Life of William Bell Scott*, is a book of great value, as bearing on a wide circle of writers in Literature and Art. The varied information there contained as to such men as David Scott, Dante Rossetti,

Samuel Brown, Holman Hunt, Thomas Woolner, Carlyle, and others, is of the highest literary importance.

Minto's health was weakened before 1890. He often suffered from asthma, and in 1891 he was induced to try the effect of a sea-voyage in the Mediterranean, which refreshed him for a time. His academic and literary activity knew no intermission till he finally succumbed to a complication of ailments on the 1st of March 1893. Had he survived to see, and to profit by, the changes introduced by the University Commission into the curriculum of study at Aberdeen, he would have found in the new Chair of English a field for his energies, in which he would have probably enriched the Literature of his country in many ways. With a wide knowledge of philosophy, and a thorough-going philosophic discipline behind, he might have been expected to do as much as any of his contemporaries to advance the study of English in the land of his birth, and in his own *alma mater*, while the northern University would have felt his power in the consideration of all matters of academic policy.

Minto's death, although not altogether unexpected, was a shock, not only to the city of Aberdeen but to the country at large. Every Professor in the University, on hearing of it, made a sympathetic allusion to their common loss, and dismissed his class for the day. I extract the following account of his funeral from a local journal:—

A more inspiring ceremonial, and one that brought from their homes a more than usually large gathering of the public, of all ranks, has not been witnessed in Aberdeen than that which attended the funeral of Professor Minto yesterday. The obsequies were of a public character, and among the varied representatives that followed the mournful procession from Marischal College to Allanvale Cemetery there was a very large number of the deceased Professor's academical and other friends. The plate bore the inscription, 'William Minto, born Oct. 10th, 1845, died March 1st, 1893.' The coffin was carried to the grave on the shoulders of four shore porters. Long before the procession started from Marischal College, both sides of Union Street were densely lined with the populace, who waited patiently for nearly an hour to catch a last glimpse of the remains being carried to the grave. Funeral service was conducted in the Upper and Lower Halls, the professors, students, and varied University bodies assembling. The shop and dwelling-house window-blinds along the streets through which the procession passed were drawn down, and as the coffin passed the hats of spectators were respectfully raised all along the route. The weather was warm—very un-March like—and at intervals a bright sun shone, revealing the early breath of spring. As the *cortége* moved through the streets, the deep and solemn note of Victoria pealed at regular intervals from the tower of St Nicholas' steeple.

Dr W. Robertson Nicoll, the editor of *The Bookman* and other publications, sends me the following most appreciative paper:—

Minto was one of the most brilliant and industrious students Aberdeen University has ever known. He was one of three concerning whom a Professor said that none of them would ever see fifty. Their constitutions were not robust, and they were of eager, unresting temperament.

The natural thing for Minto would have been to enter at an English University, and he made the attempt. But it did not suit him, and after a short trial he also gave up Divinity. It was a bold step in these days to take up literature as a profession, but having made up his mind, he prepared himself with business-like thoroughness. He wrote articles and reviews in one of the Aberdeen newspapers (*The Herald*). Here, perhaps for the only time in his life, he occasionally gave rein to his great powers of sarcasm; but, for the most part, his criticisms were genial. He set himself to write books on literary history. In these he made the simple but unusual preparation of reading the authors he was to deal with. The result is that his *Manual* and his *Characteristics* are perhaps the most thoroughly original works of their kind. Minto did not, in the first instance, read criticisms of authors; he went to the fountainhead. In the case of some

authors — notably De Quincey — his research was of the most
elaborate kind.   At the time when his volume was published,
Minto probably knew more of De Quincey's work than any other
critic.   Another study he took pleasure in was that of Sir Roger
de Coverley.   He contended and proved that all that is amiable in
the character belongs to Steele.

While diligently occupied at this work, Minto found time to be
President of the University Literary Society—a body composed of
graduates and other members of the University.   As Vice-Presi-
dent, I had many opportunities of meeting him, and the association
ripened into intimacy.   Like all who really knew Minto, I soon
came to estimate his character even above his abilities.   I have
never known so equitable a mind.   Though a man of strong convictions and warm feelings, he was pre-eminently just, patient,
and generous.   He could make allowance for his bitterest opponents, and was quick to recognise the merits of those farthest
from him in opinion.   Even if he depreciated any man, he soon
began to recall redeeming traits.   This equitableness of temper
is what rises up and remains to me at every remembrance of
Minto.   He had also much *bonhomie*, and was singularly cour-
teous to every one.   In these gatherings of students he was seen at
his best, and it was his special delight to encourage and befriend
beginners.

When he went to edit *The Examiner* his old friends in Aberdeen followed his work with warm interest.   I am sure he has
never had justice done to his editorial ability.   *The Examiner*
was in low water, and in these days new ideas in journalism were
not favoured.   Possibly its politics were too advanced for readers
of the class it appealed to.   But Minto was in his way a great
editor.   He introduced the features which mark the new sixpenny
reviews—signed articles, stories, sketches, and miscellaneous para-
graphs.   For new writers he was always on the outlook, and Mr
Theodore Watts and Mr Edmund Gosse were among the young
critics he brought forward.   Dr Garnett's exquisite criticism was
often to be recognised.   For the work of woman he had a warm
welcome; Mrs Augusta Webster was one of many lady contributors.   But the comparative failure of the paper from a commercial standpoint discouraged him.   He had great pleasure in
thinking of his literary associations and friendships; but the

work of editing was to him "a disagreeable business," and he scarcely understood how any one could like it.

Of his career as a Professor others will speak. I believe he bridged the gulf which for long stretched so wide between Aberdeen students and their teachers. It was easy to see that his heart was in his work and with his pupils.

In later years I saw him frequently. Even when in delicate health and worried by controversies not of his seeking, he was what I had always known him—unalterably true to his convictions, generous in his judgment of opponents, unwearied in labour, and eagerly interested in literature—old and new. At our last meeting he talked of the writers who had influenced Dickens. I happened to say that John Poole, author of *Little Pedlington*, was the only novelist to whom, so far as I could see, Dickens owed anything. Minto replied that he believed he could trace marks of Theodore Hook in Dickens. He spoke of the lines—

In Vienna's fatal walls
God's finger touched him, and he slept—

in connection with the remark that the word "fatal" is incongruous with the sentiment that follows. He turned to his favourite theme, the young writers of the day. Most of them he met on his visits to London, and cheered them with his cordial praise. For Mr Barrie, whom he first met under my roof, he had a warm admiration, but I think he expected most from Mr Quiller-Couch. I sent him Mr Couch's poems for review in *The Bookman*, and it was, I believe, the last book read to him.   .   .

Minto's best work was done perhaps in literary history and criticism, and had he lived he would have given us a monumental book in this department. Nothing, however, could have increased the estimate of his character formed by all who knew him. The man himself was greater than any book he could have written.

Mr P. W. Clayden, the editor of *The Daily News*, sends the following note of Minto's connection with that newspaper:—

I am a little surprised to find how short his connection with us was. His first article appeared on the 14th of August 1878.

It was on Indian Finance. Here is the list of subjects on which he wrote in the first fortnight :—

Aug.	14.	Indian Finance.	Aug. 21.	The Eastern Question.
„	15.	Cyprus.	„ 22.	Batoum.
„	16.	The Eastern Question.	„ 23.	The Eastern Question.
„	17.	India.	„ 24.	The Government.
„	20.	The Eastern Question.	„ „	Election News.

He continued to write, chiefly on these subjects, till 1880, and his last article in *The Daily News* was on the 20th of May 1880. He also wrote some reviews, and occasional articles on literary subjects, as well as articles on the smaller topics which arise in the regular course of newspaper work. He acted during nearly the whole of this year and nine months as an assistant editor, attending at night twice a-week on evenings on which I was absent, and being with me when I took the editorship in Mr Hill's absence. My impression is that he never took quite kindly to the night-work. He was not a rapid writer, but his articles were distinguished for the fulness and accuracy of the knowledge they exhibited, and their forcible and clear argument. I always found him a most pleasant and trustworthy colleague. One result of that connection remains. We were wanting some one to write leaders on legal subjects, and Minto brought with him one day Mr Herbert Paul, now M.P. for South Edinburgh. Mr Paul showed great aptitude and capacity for the work, and has been more and more intimately associated with us ever since. During the time of Minto's connection with the paper I was busy at home in writing 'England under Lord Beaconsfield,' the notice of which in *The Daily News* was written by Minto. I find that my regular attendance at the office at night was then three times a-week, Minto being there on the other three nights. On any pressure arising I went on extra nights, and it was only on such nights and at the times when I was editing, that I was at the office at night with him. After he suddenly left in May 1880, we expected that he would come back again, as he had done on a previous occasion, but he did not. His leaving was entirely his own doing, and we all much regretted it. He was living then very near to me, and the break at the office made no break in our friendship. He was at once engaged on *The Pall Mall Gazette*, and I saw none the less of him. When he was sent to Aberdeen I greatly regretted his removal for my own sake, but rejoiced in it for him. He always came to see us down to the time of his last visit to London, and I always felt, to the end, that warm friendship for him which I had formed during the time we worked together at *The Daily News.* I do not think he was in his proper element in newspaper work. He was too fastidious as to style and treatment—using the word fastidious in its best sense —and was not entirely comfortable in the sort of rapid work which is required. His writing was perhaps a little too reflective for a daily paper—I mean that it necessarily took rather more time to produce than the more oratorical and dashing style of newspaper writing. It was the literary man, the scholar, the thinker, who was writing, rather than the busy politician. This literary character of his style was much valued. It is part of the tradition of *The Daily News* to cultivate that style. In his political views he was in hearty sympathy with the paper, though he always insisted on dealing with any topic on which he wrote in his own way, very often an original way.

The Rev. William L. Davidson of Bourtie, whose acquaintance I had the pleasure of making at Minto's house, and whose contributions to Philosophy and Literature are well known, writes thus :—

It is not easy to convey a correct impression of Professor Minto to those who were not personally acquainted with him ; and those who were fortunate enough to enjoy personal intercourse with him need no picture of mine. To me, Minto was a very choice friend. Our mutual acquaintance dates from the time that I was assistant to Professor Bain in the English and Logic classes at the University of Aberdeen, and Minto was associated with Professor Bain also in various literary productions. Minto's first work—that on the English Prose Writers—was then in course of formation ; and I quite well remember the care and energy that he expended on that book, and his intense desire to render it worthy of the subject and of the distinguished master under whose inspiration he wrote it. Meanwhile, although literature claimed his chief attention, politics had already begun to assert its hold over him. Even then, he was pronounced in his opinions—often dogmatic in asserting them in the presence of formidable opposition—and fast acquiring a firm grasp of those principles that he was, by-and-by, to apply with vigour as editor of *The Examiner*. In University matters he took a keen interest; and, though himself a graduate, was a moving spirit in the rectorial elections of those days. Socially, Minto was, at the date of which I speak, one of the most genial and pleasant of companions. He had then, and retained to the very close of his days, a *bonhomie* that was remarkable; and his intense enjoyment of the society of kindred souls, together with his abundant wit and humour, made him a universal favourite. I could record scenes and incidents that took place in Aberdeen, either in his own lodgings or in mine, in which he was a conspicuous figure, and which foreshadowed in no unambiguous way the man as he was soon to become. In particular, I recollect a striking reading and analysis of part of one of Massinger's plays, in his own room, which clearly disclosed the able and sympathetic critic that his work on the English Poets, later on, proved him to be. But these are sweet memories of the past, which are best kept to oneself.

For a number of years — indeed, during his whole stay in London, while he was attached to literature and journalism there —Minto's path and mine lay apart. Intercourse, however, was heartily resumed when he returned to Aberdeen in 1880, as Professor of Logic and English, in succession to Dr Bain, and continued to the end of his life.

I can now speak of him from that date, mainly in his professional and allied capacities.

The first thing that struck one in Minto, in his capacity of professor, was his deep interest in his students. His first concern was that, both in the English and in the Logic Class, each man should derive from the prelections the highest possible benefit that he was capable of receiving. As a consequence, he spared himself no pains in the preparation of his class lectures. Again and again have I found Minto, in his own house, busy over to-morrow's lecture—trying how best he could express, in vigorous phrase and with the apt illustration that was always at his command, the point that was to him perfectly clear, but which, he suspected, might present difficulty to the student. Lucidity was, in his eyes, the supreme virtue.

In this way he was ever ready to discuss with you obscure points in philosophy or in rhetoric, and to adopt whatever fresh light you might be able to throw upon the situation. He was particularly pleased if he could either find or have suggested to him some fresh historical aspect of the well-worn academic themes. Every year that passed found him deeper in his conviction of the power of the historical method in elucidating truth, and in bringing home its meaning to the learner. And this applied to his teaching of English as much as to his teaching of Psychology and Logic. I remember one day finding him in high spirits over the discovery he had just made, that the best way to make plain to his class the meaning of Humour was by inweaving the history of the word into his technical analysis, and accompanying with copious examples from literature. "Every man in his humour, you know," cried Minto, jubilant; "it was his humour to wear a coat with lappets," and so on. Allied to this was his keen appreciation of luminous definitions or of subtle distinctions between synonymous terms. I cannot forget the pleasure with which he received a little bit of phrasing of my own, which struck him as felicitous. I had gone to Aberdeen to address the youth of the city on Dr Murray's *New English Dictionary*, and, while there, was Minto's guest. "What's your subject?" he asked, on my arrival. I told him it was Dr Murray's Dictionary, and that I had entitled the lecture "Romance in Words." "Romance in Words!" he exclaimed, with a bright gleam of the eye, which never failed when his intellectual interest was awakened,—"capital! *that is the only proper definition of a dictionary.*" The same appreciation of word-distinctions marked his writings, and is one of the elements that makes his style so admirable.

A chief ground of Minto's great success as a teacher, and of his exceptional popularity with the students, lay in his juvenility of spirit and his boundless sympathy with youth. He was supremely fortunate in being able to put himself into the exact position of his audience, and thereby to carry them along with him. It is only another way of putting the same thing to say that, in teaching, he never forgot his own difficulties in student days in grappling with the subjects on hand; and, in setting himself with all his might to remove these, he was adopting the best plan of removing the difficulties of his hearers also.

Minto himself as a student, in his professorial days, is a theme that might well be elaborated. Vividly the picture rises of the Professor seated in his study, eagerly poring over some volume, or busily penning some disquisition, in full enjoyment of his pipe (for the harder he worked the harder he smoked); and then the pause, the sparkle in the eye, and forthwith some subtle criticism, or some apt Chaucerian quotation, or some comic remark, as the case might be; after that, relevant talk or discussion; and then resumption of the task. But Minto wrought too hard. Regardless of health, he sat, when not on College duty, almost day and night at his desk (for he burned the midnight oil far too profusely) for a number of years, with the briefest of holidays— elaborating theories, producing brilliant literary essays, dashing off critical reviews, writing novels, and shaping political speeches. Not even the strongest physical constitution could have stood it. But he laughed your warnings and advice to scorn, and waved you off with such a comic gesture that you almost forgave him, though you quite well saw that he was putting his resources to far too great a strain.

As an examiner, Minto was the embodiment of fairness. Scrupulous to a degree and painstaking, he never would allow partialities or personal predilections to weigh with him. This I can unreservedly testify, from my long association with him as examiner in Philosophy and English. While wishful to act impartially, he was also desirous that the examinee himself should feel that strict justice was being done to him. Hence his uniform readiness to go over their papers with students who had the misfortune to "go down" at an examination, and to show them frankly where and why they had failed, and how they might make up in the future. Many an unfortunate had reason to thank him for this kindly office.

As a host, Minto excelled. To see him at his best, you had to live with him under his own roof. Not only was his hospitality abundant, but his welcome was ever hearty and sincere. The stimulus, too, that you derived from discussion with him, and the enjoyment produced by his racy stories, his pleasantries and repartee, his sallies of genuine wit, were experiences never to be forgotten. Whether at the breakfast-table or at dinner, alike in the daytime and at the late hours of night, in his study, enveloped in a cloud of tobacco-smoke, Minto was always the same kind, bright, genial entertainer, rejoicing in you, and making you rejoice in him.

The last time I saw Minto was in my own house. He came to pay me a visit, of a few days' duration, in the middle of September 1892. As there were two other distinguished thinkers living with me at the same time, congenial spirits, he was in his best form intellectually, and in the height of enjoyment,—though, obviously, in very indifferent health. His enfeebled condition was to us a source of considerable anxiety; but he himself made light of it— for he was always heroic. Into the amusements, as well as into the discussions that went on, he entered heartily, and with no lack of his wonted vivacity; and it is a great satisfaction to me to know that he pronounced his last visit here to be one of the happiest moments of his life. Four months more, and he was gone. The news of his death brought to friends everywhere the sense of an irreparable loss; and learning mourned the departure of one who had done noble service for letters, and would have done even greater things had longer life been given him.

The following notes are from Mr P. Chalmers Mitchell, a student of Professor Minto's, and afterwards his friend :—

In the year that Professor Minto received his appointment as Professor, I joined the University of Aberdeen as a first year's student. I saw him for the first time at his inaugural lecture in the English class, which was then held later in the day than the other classes attended by students of the first year. It is no disrespect to the memory of the occupant of the Latin chair—the late Professor Black—or to the present distinguished Principal, who was then Professor of Greek, to say that I had left both their classes, unpersuaded, either by the bluff *bonhomie* of the one or by the urbane dignity of the other, into regarding Latin and Greek as anything but routine tasks. I entered the English class singularly untouched by the glamour of learning, although in the pleasant consciousness that a University was vastly better than School, because its day was several hours shorter; but in that English class-room I found a singularly pleasant man, not lecturing to a class, but sometimes sitting back in his chair, sometimes

leaning over his desk, and talking to a student, perched as I was
in a distant and disaffected back-row, about things that were
interesting.

Beforehand, I should have laughed at the suggestion that his
subject-matter *could* be made interesting. He was talking about
parsing, and analysis, and the derivations of words. In the matter
of parsing, it was obvious that any fool could do it; derivations
of words one had hitherto got up from lists before prize examinations; and in analysis, a succession of masters had each had a
separate whim in nomenclature. But in Professor Minto's hands
the derivation of words was so treated that a Dictionary became a
pageant of History, showing here the Crusaders dusty from the
Holy Land, bringing with them some new idea, some strange
animal or plant; or there, the prancing Normans introducing the
graces of chivalry or the subtleties of law. The parsing of words
was a tradition from the grammatical complexity of more primitive conditions of the language. The terminology of analysis was
as you pleased; the analysis itself was an anatomical display of
the vital organs, by which a sentence should convey its meaning.
I can see now that, in this first lecture, Professor Minto showed
the leading feature of his teaching. The information he gave he
did not offer for the direct acquisition of his pupils, as of intrinsic
value. What was given, was put before us as an illustration of
the vast interest of the field of knowledge, waiting for any of us
who cared to enter it. Incidentally we learned much, but chiefly
we learned how and why we were, for ourselves, to learn more.
In knowledge generally there were two special interests, the
picturesque and human interest of how our language, and our
Logic, came to be as they are; and the practical interest—clearly
separate from the other—of how best to use our language, or our
reasoning, for the purposes of to-day.

The bent of Professor Minto's teaching was specially marked in
his lectures upon Logic. I do not think that the technical subtleties of Formal Logic had much attraction for him. Certainly he
did not seek to stamp on the minds of his class the fantastic in-
genuities of ancient and modern schoolmen. His lectures upon
Formal Logic were lectures upon its evolution, and he sought to
show us how each stage in the development of Deductive Logic was
the abstract expression of an actual advance in man's power of

reasoning; and so we were spared the paradox which presents itself to the modern beginner in Deductive Logic. Although many processes of the "Science of Thought" seem but cumbrous methods of expressing the obvious, each method as unfolded by him had its explanation in the forgotten past. On the other hand, it was the practical use of Inductive Logic that Professor Minto chiefly insisted upon. In his exposition of this, he followed with rare appreciative sympathy, considering the varied interests of his life, the progress of the natural and physical sciences. As these notes must, from their brevity, be discursive, let me say that afterwards, when I knew him better, I was struck with his continued interest in subjects so remote from his own work as advances in Comparative Anatomy and Embryology. While on a visit to me at Oxford, in the summer before he died, two of the things that interested him most were some new preparations of fossil skulls in the University Museum, and a technical discussion on Weismann's views on heredity.

English Literature had so small a place in the curriculum for the degree of M.A., that Professor Minto could only give us twenty-five lectures on it. But, in that brief space, he so introduced us to the writers of our own tongue that their books became friends to us for life. In my own case, and in that of many others, I know that the most permanent impression we got at the University of Aberdeen was the love of English books, not for purposes of future analytic study, but simply as our friends throughout life. Recently, when we were talking about the proposed institution of a final honours school of English Literature at Oxford, I told him of what I had got from his own short course in Aberdeen. He said, in reply—what is specially worth remembering, now that so many schools of English Literature are practically accomplished facts—"I agree with those who think that English Literature might be made quite as severe an intellectual discipline as Greek or as Russian; but the point most easily lost sight of when it is turned into a discipline is that it is the readiest friend and the greatest comfort to the many who get their discipline in other subjects. You can get intellectual discipline from anything, but most people don't get much pleasure out of the things that were used to train their minds."

Not only was Professor Minto constantly accessible, and most ready to help and advise his students in every way; but he kept up friendly relations with many of them, and he was interested in them all, in their subsequent careers. The warm admiration I had for him, while I was a student, continued after I left the University; and I had the great good fortune to see him subsequently, on terms more intimate than are possible between teacher and pupil. It is perhaps only given to poets adequately to memorialise their dead friends. Nature makes other mortals more reticent, though reticence may be selfish; but I wish to say two things about Professor Minto. I wish to record the intense friendliness of his character. I do not only mean that he was the readiest of men to do good turns to others. All who knew him know that. But he had the rare virtue of seeing and believing only the best of other people. "What continually impresses me," he would say, "are what good fellows people are!" I have known no instance like him of the "charity that thinketh no evil." It was really difficult for him to believe that any of his acquaintances would do a mean thing, or an ill-natured thing, purposely. Of one or two people who had obviously done him an ill turn, I have heard him say, "Yes, I suppose he doesn't like me, but you know he is really a good fellow at heart;" and then he would give some practical instance of conduct to his credit.

The last thing I wish to set down is this. In no case, while I was a student, did I ever hear Professor Minto, in class or in private, touch upon any theological topic. Afterwards, even in intimate talk, he rarely spoke of ultimate questions of metaphysic, or belief. He had not the Scottish habit of strengthening his convictions by measuring them against those of others. But, in my rooms at Oxford, the last evening he was with me, and the last time I saw him, he took a book from my shelves and said, "One person I have to make good—viz., myself; but my duty to my neighbour is much more nearly expressed by saying, that I have to make him happy, if I may."

Mr John H. Lobban, who acted as Professor Minto's assistant in his latest years at the University, has sent me an appreciative estimate, which many Aberdeen students will be glad to read :—

In Mill's rectorial address to the students of St Andrews there is a passage which might, with great fitness, be applied to Professor Minto's work at the University of Aberdeen. "There is nothing," said Mill, "which spreads more contagiously from teacher to pupil than elevation of sentiment: often and often have students caught from the influence of a professor a contempt for mean and selfish objects, and a noble ambition to leave the world better than they found it, which they have carried with them throughout life." The tributes already paid by students are abundant evidence that Professor Minto exercised such an influence; but few students could have been fully aware of the thoroughness and scrupulous fairness with which he performed his duties as professor and examiner.

These qualities his assistants had necessarily excellent opportunities of observing, and I recollect how forcibly I was impressed by them when I had first to examine university papers under his supervision. In the case of one examination, where the time for correction was so limited that he divided the papers with me, Professor Minto had arranged a scheme of marking with such precision that, after doing a number of papers together, the possibility of a discrepancy between our respective estimates was reduced to a minimum. It was only after having tested some of my results that he felt justified, in fairness to the students, in leaving a number of papers entirely in my hands. One other instance of the same desire for scrupulous fairness I may record. One of a number of essays that I had to value was so atrociously written and marred by emendations that, actuated no doubt by a not unnatural impatience, I had marked it rather hardly. Although one of more than a hundred essays, it did not pass the Professor's eye; for when soon after I went to discuss them with him, he asked me with characteristic humour and courtesy if I would allow him to read an essay to me. As read by him it certainly was more than an average production, and as I saw the lesson he meant so courteously to convey I owned my error, and suggested a higher value, which he agreed to. He then laughingly told me that he had generally to impress his assistants with the moral that the matter of a student's paper should not be taxed for any blemish in its outward form.

As a lecturer, Professor Minto had a horror of "talking at large."

When using his lecture notes I was struck with the endless erasures and corrections in the manuscript. This was due to his passionate desire for clear thinking and clear expression. He once told me that, whenever he noticed any general inability on the part of his class to follow him, he at once reconsidered the passage, and strove with all his powers of language to put it in a way that would admit of no dispute. This was the explanation of the countless erasures, —the explanation, too, I imagine, of the unique way in which he could compel the unbroken interest of his students, no matter what the subject on hand. He desired, he told me, that his students should always get hold of something definite in every lecture, but few who reaped the advantage of that simplicity and clearness had any idea of the infinite pains and literary skill that produced them.

Of the thoroughness that permeated all his work I may adduce one example that fell under my notice. About a month before the Christmas vacation he had to deliver a historical lecture to a country audience. As he was loaded with other work, and even at that time far from strong, I suggested that he might save himself so much research by using some of his plentiful old material, which I argued would have been quite as acceptable to his audience. He humorously rebuked me for my base advice, saying that he had "still some regard for his literary conscience," and that he had become so interested in his subject that he had ceased to view it as a task. This I found to be no idle assertion, for in a conversation some days later, when talking over the subject of his lecture, he cited dates and quoted extensive passages from history with such absolute ease that I am convinced that, though as yet he had not put a word on paper, I got the bulk of the lecture, delivered with as much accuracy and grace of expression as did the audience that heard it read.

It is, however, of the period of his last illness that I can hope to add anything of interest to what has been already said by others. It seemed to me characteristic of Professor Minto that, when he was suddenly prostrated and unable to conduct his two classes, he did not bid me or even ask me to fill the breach. When summoned by him to consider what was to be done in the emergency, he suggested his proposal with the utmost delicacy; and it was only after I had expressed my willingness to try the

work that he accepted as a favour, what he would obviously have
been justified in regarding as a privilege conferred. During the
whole of his illness it is no hyperbole to say that he exhibited an
extraordinary triumph of will. It was his express wish that he
should know exactly what I lectured on from day to day, and
though racked with pain he discussed the work of both classes
with all his usual ardour. It was sometimes hard for me to realise
the extent of his illness, while he impressed upon me the important
points of some development in literature which he desired me to
emphasise. His rare powers of memory never failed him, and I
recollect how, while propped up in bed, he would quote illustrations for the English lectures from Chaucer or Pope, unravel one
of Marlowe's or Shakespeare's plots, or explain some far-fetched
conceit in Donne. It seemed to me infinitely pathetic to hear
him in broken words, but feigning something of that joyous ring
of voice with which his students will always associate their
memories of Chaucer, assuring me that John Donne deserved the
epitaph :—

> Here lies a king that ruled, as he thought fit,
> The universal monarchy of wit.

It was, however, on the occasion of his attempt to resume work
for the second time that his mental heroism was most apparent.
He told me repeatedly that he felt it to be his only chance of recovery, and that if he could not lecture he might surrender all hope.
Doubtless this feeling was genuine, but I saw that he was prompted
also by the desire to relieve myself of at least half the work. I
was present in his anteroom, when he literally staggered into the
classroom to deliver his last lecture ; and I can conceive no greater
effort of will than that which enabled him to triumph over his pain,
and to deliver a brilliant lecture on the decline of the Elizabethan
drama.

Of the value of his own literary work he was ever dubious. On
more than one occasion during his illness he spoke hesitatingly of
what he had written as not "half good enough for publication,"
and the only time I remember him speaking with confidence of his
unpublished work was, curiously enough, the last occasion on which
he spoke to me of literary matters. Asking me whether I saw my
way clear to the end of the session, he begged me to do all the

justice I could to the lecture on Burns, repeating, with unusual emphasis, that his lecture on Burns, formerly delivered at Edinburgh, was "most distinctly the best thing" that he had ever written.

It would be an injustice to Professor Minto's memory, and one specially unpardonable for me to commit, were I not to record the appreciation he had of the sympathy extended him by his students. It will always be a pleasure for the English and Logic students of 1892-93 to know that Professor Minto repeatedly said that nothing had ever touched him more deeply than the way in which the students had reciprocated the feelings he had always entertained for them.

During the past eighteen years it has fallen to my lot to suggest many distinguished men for the St Andrews honorary degree of Doctor of Laws; but there is no one whom I ever proposed with greater satisfaction than Professor Minto.

The spontaneous tributes borne to him after his death in the Aberdeen University Magazine—*Alma Mater*—alike by students and professors, were more significant of the work he did, and of the esteem in which he was held, than the tributes recorded of any other Scottish teacher at the close of this century. From *Alma Mater* of March 1, 1893, the following extracts may be made:—

The first notice in *In Memoriam* is entitled "Vale!" In it the following occurs:—

The highest tribute we can pay to Professor Minto's memory is to say that he was the students' friend. With that disinterestedness and that perseverance which we must ever identify with his life, he has often pleaded our cause when we least knew it; and in his contact with the members of his own classes, his genial manner, his winning expression of face, and above all his kindly word, stand out even more strongly than his more immediate teaching. If there was ever a man who touched the heart of studentdom, that man was William Minto. His life was a living emblem of the power of sympathy. He felt for us and with us, and naturally enough we came first to respect and then to love him. In the words of Alfred Tennyson, he was "most a man," and, while we reverenced his intellect and gloried in his fame, it was for his manliness, his human nature, that we loved him. "His students almost adored him," said a press writer, in commenting on his death, and there is no exaggeration in the statement. To the outside world he was known for the fame of his mental powers, to us rather for his unfailing courtesy of manner, his rare loveliness of spirit. It was no mere precept that he gave when he told us to do our best to leave one small corner of earth the better for our being in it, for was not this his own constant endeavour? Of his devotion to duty one can scarcely speak, for had it been less, we cannot but feel that he might have been with us to-day. When public spirit, kindliness of disposition, and intellectual force unite to make a man and a teacher, who is brought into contact with those whose characters have in great measure to be formed, need we wonder that his removal should leave a gap which it seems wellnigh impossible to fill, and make the unspoken thought of every student in Aberdeen University to-day, "Without you, William Minto, our world seems lonesome"!

Mr H. J. C. Grierson, Professor Minto's successor in the Chair of English Literature, wrote :—

"PARMENIDES, MY MASTER PARMENIDES!"

Professor Minto has passed away, and with him a gifted and inspiring teacher. Some who have spoken of him have done so from the position of those who knew his great predecessor, and could compare the two. We knew only the one, and found in him the one true teacher of our experience.

Perhaps it is for this reason that we cannot draw the usual distinction between his teaching of literature and of philosophy. It may be that in the former he had done more original and valuable work, but it was in his Logic class that, for my own part, I first felt his full power as an instructor, and caught the spirit of his method. Dr W. L. Mackenzie has said justly that that method was historic, but it was also dialectic in the Socratic sense of the word. He realised to no small extent that the truest function of the teacher was not to fill the mind with information from without, but to elicit its own latent thoughts and faculties and interests. I have had occasion to compare his method with that of other lecturers in Logic, and it has deepened my sense of its value. He began with no abstract definitions, and he uttered no dogmatic statements, but he led us easily, and acquiescing with him at each step, from the simplest facts of our everyday consciousness to a realisation of the great problems of truth and reality.

In fact, the spirit of Professor Minto's philosophic teaching and literary criticism recalls the spirit of the greatest of teachers and critics, the Socrates that we know in Plato. It pursued the same inquiring method, it subjected to the same searching criticism all traditional dogmas, it glowed with the same enthusiasm for truth, and the best expression of truth.

Nor in other respects was he unlike that great teacher. Like him he loved young men, and met them with openness and freedom from all assertion of superiority. When but Bajans we were "gentlemen" to him, with opinions of our own, and minds to be appealed to; and when we came to know him personally we found the same openness, and a close personal interest in our lives and futures. He discussed with us, he planned with us, he laughed with us—and we loved him; but now, like Socrates, he is taken from us, when our esteem and affection were still growing, and we know not when we shall behold him again. "The hour of departure is come: we go our ways—I to die, you to live; but whose lot is the happier is hidden from all save God."

The following recollections are by his colleague, Professor W. M. Ramsay:—

It is not an easy task that the editors of *Alma Mater* have proposed to me; but I will try, at their request, to perform it, however inadequately and imperfectly. To describe on the moment a character so marked, so powerful, so self-contained and complete, so independent and individual, so true to his friends, so difficult for his enemies, is beyond my poor powers. I can only try to relate what I actually saw of William Minto, and the impression he made on me in old times, and this may perhaps help to give some shadow of his personality. At this moment I should like, as far as possible, to avoid anything that should rouse any feeling except sympathy.

When I entered College, Minto was Assistant Professor of Natural Philosophy, and it is a curious proof of the ignorance of University business and University life that used to characterise some Bajans, that I never, during that winter, heard a word about the great controversy in which he was involved. It was not till years had passed that I came to know what had occurred. After more than twenty years had passed, I found out the facts by consulting the files of the Aberdeen papers; and then I learned for the first time how splendidly the late Principal Pirie had advocated his cause in the Court. My ignorance at the time will therefore serve as an excuse for passing over the subject; but no one could refrain from alluding to the moral triumph which he gained in the long-run over those who had defeated him—so far as worldly appearance went—at the time. Few men in my time have had such a hard trial as he had, when, at the conclusion of a most brilliant University career, crowned with a Ferguson Scholarship, his *alma mater* closed her gates against him for an action which at the present time would be applauded and approved by all. We should now look on it as a proof of innate delicacy and gentlemanly spirit, if there could possibly arise an occasion to provoke it—which, with the tone that now rules in University life, is, I believe, impossible. In truth, there has been a great improvement in the standard of public feeling within the last twenty-five years, and I hope we should now make better use of his genius than of old.

It was not till the end of my fourth year at College that I first knew Minto, and our acquaintance began in connection with the recently founded Literary Society, to which, after a time, I had the honour of proposing that he should be admitted as an honorary member. His name was already familiar to me, for in the course of my third year he had matriculated as a student, and had taken an active part in the re-election of Sir M. E. Grant Duff as Lord Rector. I was sometimes quoted as a sad example of the students whom he had perverted to vote against the cause of Classics; but, in reality, I never to my knowledge saw him during that year, much less listened to his alluring speeches in public or in private.

"Bitter constraint and sad occasion dear" impelled me even then, when I had only vague blind yearnings after ancient literature, to vote as I have always done against the misdirection of classical studies, debasing them to be fetters, instead of wings, for the free modern spirit. It was our common study of modern literature that first brought us together as lovers of the "romantic" side in that literature, as believers that the aim and crown of all literary education is to understand and appreciate the spirit of our own age. We approached literature from quite opposite sides, and we differed widely on many points of thought and life—not points of mere detail, but ideas which we believed with our whole heart to be of infinite importance, and on behalf of which he at least was ready to die—yet our differences of view never interfered with our friendship ; and when we met, after years of separation, the old feelings remained as strong as ever.

Very soon after he joined the Literary Society, we elected him to the office of President, which fell vacant opportunely ; and there can be no doubt that the success of the young society was greatly due to the skill and knowledge which he brought to our aid.

After seeing a great deal of him in 1871, I lost sight of him for years, till we met accidentally on a London steamboat pier in 1879 ; and we continued to meet during my occasional visits to London, until I disappeared into the wilds of Asiatic Turkey in the spring of 1880. Before I went out he offered to do his best to procure the acceptance of letters from Turkey by the great London morning paper with which he was at the time connected. I fully intended to avail myself of his advocacy, but time was too short and life too busy for letter-writing, and only one or two brief notes passed between us, until the spring of 1886, when I received a letter from him telling that the Humanity Chair here would shortly be vacant, and advising me to be a candidate. I am glad now to say publicly, as I have often said to him, that I owe my appointment to this letter, and to the timely information which it gave me. But for his letter, I should have been ignorant, till it was too late, about the impending vacancy, and about various other facts which it was essential to know.

In the abundant opportunities I have since then had of observing Minto, the quality that most struck me was his thoroughness. Everything I have ever seen him do was done with the same devotion : he brought his whole powers of mind, and often (as I saw with alarm) his whole powers of body, to the work. The minute estimate of the capacities and faults of all his students which I have seen noted down in his books—apparently as a regular practice—astonished me : they resembled the sketches which professional readers of character are ready to supply to customers. He did not merely estimate numerically the value of each examination paper, he also estimated it qualitatively as an index of the candidate's moral and intellectual character.

That he persistently overworked himself I often observed, and often remonstrated with him about it—always to be met with the laughing reply that I was myself a worse instance of the fault. The chill which brought on the last illness was, I think, attributed by him to a game at curling during the Christmas vacation; but it seemed to me that quite as great mischief was done in December at a meeting of Faculty in the icy Senatus-room, where he sat for more than two hours at the head of the table, till he was obviously chilled to the marrow. When the meeting was over, he came to the fire saying, "I might as well go to my grave as do this sort of thing again." I have often pitied the wretched candidates for Honours and Scholarships who are compelled to shiver for three hours at a time in that room, which is generally as cold as a Roman Church on the Aventine in winter. By the time a few more have suffered from it, a new Senatus-room may be ready in Marischal College.

There is one quality which beyond all others rouses my admiration, and that quality Minto had in a remarkable degree—I mean courage. I can worship even mere physical courage, which it is nowadays the fashion to despise (especially among those who have never needed or seen or felt it); but the splendid moral courage which he showed seems to me almost the greatest quality in human nature. He never flinched a hair's-breadth from the opinion he believed in, however unpopular or even dangerous it might be : he always supported a friend if the world was against him.

As a critic and scholar, he was only coming to full consciousness of his powers and freedom in using them ; and there is good reason to think that the future work, which (had fate been kinder to us) he would have done as the first Professor of English in this University, would have been his best work, and, I think, would have taken permanent rank among the finest in its kind. His genius matured slowly, partly from its natural character, partly from the distractions and variations of occupation in which his life had been spent. Truly, I think, the University might have gained by wise treatment much more from him than it did.

The Faculty of Arts has lost him who was not merely the titular head, but also by a combination of fine qualities the mainstay of its reputation, both in Aberdeen and before the world. The University has lost its clearest-headed and ablest administrator: in every question that emerged he recognised at a glance what was the solution, and urged it with unhesitating energy. His quick insight was due to the fact that he never was governed by a calculation of selfish or narrow advantages: in every case he judged upon the same general principles. He lived and fought for an ideal of freedom and honesty, in the ultimate triumph of which he had the most unfaltering confidence. In this lay his strength and the secret of his perfect frankness and freedom from affectation. He worked, not for himself, not even for his family, but for his cause. He had nothing to conceal, but rather gloried in openly stating his real aims; and many believe, as I do, that, had not his policy been so often thwarted, our University would be to-day far stronger than it is.

In *The Bookman* of April 1893 Mr A. T. Quiller-Couch wrote :—

Were I to confess how seldom we met and how slight was our correspondence, your readers would think it highly presumptuous of me to write about Professor Minto, and that to call him a friend was almost indecent. Yet on one point, at any rate, they would be wrong. It is a fact that we never wrote a line to each other; yet from time to time, and by every common friend, he sent messages that were valuable beyond telling to a young man just beginning to write. But Minto's sympathies were always with the young; and, indeed, on the first occasion that we met this was rather trying. In my father's house the talk might run on statesmen, divines, or men of science; but men of letters were the great men. Other callings were well enough, but writers were a class apart, and to belong to it was the choicest of ambitions. I had grown up in this habit of mind, and have not yet entirely out-grown it; so that the prospect of seeing Minto and listening to him fluttered me, as no doubt it flutters a young curate to dine with his bishop. He would not let me worship, however; would not even let me listen; but seemed only anxious to hear about my own endeavours and prospects. I think this forgetfulness of self was native in him and incurable. Certainly, though I admired him as much as ever, he had won a very much warmer feeling in the inside of half an hour; and from that time was constantly adding to the load of kindness which now can only be repaid by mourning his loss and remembering his wise counsel and encourage-ment. No other critic has given me the tithe of that counsel or a hundredth part of that encouragement. And when I say that all this was bestowed at every opportunity from the date of our first and only intimate conversation to the time of his death,—that even on his death-bed he tried to do me a last service in the old fashion, —it will be allowed that my burden of obligation is heavy indeed.

I cannot believe that the newspapers and reviews have done justice to his memory. They praise him as a good man and a sincere lover of letters; but the quality of his work, and especially of his critical work, has received too little attention. For it was of the rarest. Whatever his subject, Minto seemed to approach it with a mind absolutely clear of prejudice; to take it up with the single desire of exploring it in his reader's company, and to handle it with a modest self-effacement that may explain the slightly ne-glectful attitude of a generation eager to be obtruded on by "strik-ing personalities." In the same way, though he was one of the few men left who could construct a long English sentence, and fit it with well-proportioned members, and make it walk upon legs, his style was so temperate and business-like, so admirable as a means to an end, and so naked of ornamentation, that it too often passed unnoticed. We must be "striking" in these times, or we are naught; but this writer never learned to use his theme as a stalking-horse for his own wit. He had an insatiable interest in literature; but this interest was scientific as well as sympathetic; and he handled criticism scientifically. On the whole, his method was that of Sainte-Beuve, and though there are many more showy, a better has yet to be invented. The others may please for a while; but in the end we shall sigh for temperance, modesty, restraint, the virtues that are above fashion, and never, never tire ; and where temperance, modesty, and restraint are valued we may be confident that Minto will not be forgotten. In a series to which all the best critics of his generation contributed, his monograph on Defoe stands out as a bright example of the way in which criticism should be written ; and its excellence in comparison with the majority grows clearer as time goes on—a sure test. But whether in his writings or his life, Minto was a man in whose company it was good to be, and to remain.

The following appeared in *The Westminster Gazette* of March 2, 1893 :—

QUHAT SAY THEY?

IN MEMORIAM WILLIAM MINTO. OBIIT MARCH I.

It was his constant care to make his subject, whether literature or the high and dry sands of metaphysics, as far as possible, a mirror of the life we live.

> The hand that led our pilgrim bands
>   These byegone years
> To England's wondrous lettered lands,
>   Its kings and seers,
> No more shall smooth the rugged way—
>   'Tis cold this day.

> In misty metaphysic maze
>   . He shed a light,
> That cleared away the hanging haze
>   And darkening night.
> But ne'er again shall he we weep
>   Our footsteps keep.

> Was it with Chaucer's dukes and dames,
>   Or saintly Bede ?
> Was it with Hamiltonian aims,
>   Or rigid Reid ?
> The byegone age was lit with life,
>   Its flux and strife.

> And still, he brought our restless times
> 　　Within his ken—
> A Barrie or a Kipling's rhymes
> 　　Would charm his pen.
> The dainty genius of a "Q"
> 　　　Was brought to view.
>
>
> Then, oft indeed a budding bard,
> 　　As yet unknown,
> Who found the way to glory hard,
> 　　He'd gladly own;
> The future way to fame was cleared
> 　　　The tyro cheered.
>
>
> The ravelled skein of logic-lore
> 　　We saw unwound;
> The trials of the path no more
> 　　The journey bound.
> Ah, who again shall lift the thorn
> 　　　As him we mourn! ·
>
>
> Can we, to-day immersed in gloom,
> 　　This guide forget,
> Although by very Crack of Doom
> 　　We seem beset—
> A halting tribute this, that sings
> 　　　Our king at King's.

In the same paper, *The Westminster Gazette*, of March 11, 1893, Minto's friend, Mr Richard Le Gallienne, writes as follows :—

PROFESSOR MINTO.

> Nature, that makes Professors all day long,
> And, filling idle souls with idle song,
> Turns out small Poets every other minute,
> Made earth for men, but seldom puts men in it.

> Ah ! Minto, thou of that minority
> Wert man of men ; we had deep need of thee !
> Had Heaven a deeper ? Did the heavenly Chair
> Of earthly Love wait empty for thee there ?

I may perhaps be allowed to repeat, at the close of this introductory and biographic sketch, that there is ample and most valuable material for a sequel volume of Minto's work, including his numerous *Encyclopædia Britannica* articles, his papers on John Donne, Wordsworth, and Matthew Arnold, as well as those delightful lectures which he gave to literary and other Societies in Scotland.

WILLIAM KNIGHT.

St Andrews, *June* 1894.

THE LITERATURE OF THE GEORGIAN ERA

CHAPTER I.

THE POSITION OF MEN OF LETTERS IN THE EIGHTEENTH CENTURY.

DECLINE OF ROYAL PATRONAGE—WHY IS THE GEORGIAN ERA A DISTINCT LITERARY PERIOD?—CONDITION OF POETRY DURING THE CENTURY, AND VIEWS OF ITS CRITICS AS TO THE MEANING OF NATURE.

THE combined reigns of the four Georges may possibly be thought an arbitrary and artificial section of literary history to choose as a subject for a course of lectures. What had the four Georges to do with literature? is a question that naturally occurs when they are proposed as the figureheads of a literary period; and the answer must be that they had little or nothing to do with literature, beyond occasionally furnishing in their illustrious persons fairly good themes for the humorist and the satirist. If you read Thackeray on the four Georges, you will see that these reigns supplied ample materials both for the laughing philosopher and the weeping philosopher. But neither of the first two Georges cared for literature, or did anything directly to encourage literature, and it was perhaps as well that they let it alone. Matters mended a little under the second two. George IV. had an interview with Dr Johnson, the record of which is one of the best known passages in Boswell's 'Life.' But this was after Dr Johnson's fame was fully established. The most conspicuous instance of royal patronage of literature in these reigns—patronage that really helped a rising man—occurred in the first year of this century, when the Prince, who afterwards became George IV., put down his name among the subscribers to Thomas Moore's translation of Anacreon, and admitted the youthful poet to the honour of personal acquaintance. Moore was overjoyed at this piece of good fortune; and well he might be, for it greatly helped him in his career of fashionable popularity. In a sense it may be said that literature owes the anacreontic lays of Tom Little to royal favour; and this is its only obligation to the favour of the four Georges — an obligation that cannot be thought of with altogether unmingled gratitude.

The Georges did little or nothing for literature. But though it looks like a paradox, this fact, so far from being a reason against choosing their reigns as a literary period, is one of the reasons why the accession of the dynasty constitutes a material point of departure for a historical survey. There is a certain interest in seeing how literature prospered when it was no longer sunned by the royal countenance, and what new influences came in to compensate the loss. Up to the time of the first George every eminent man of letters had received direct encouragement from the Court. In the fourteenth and fifteenth centuries literature was almost entirely dependent on royal favour, and there was always some member of the royal family who took a warm interest in letters. In the time of Edward III. Chaucer was patronised by John of Gaunt, taken into the royal household, and rewarded with lucrative public appointments. Gower undertook his most celebrated poem at the personal request of Richard II. One of the first cares of Henry IV. when he usurped the Crown was to remember and provide for the wants of his father's old favourite, the poet of the 'Canterbury Tales.' The ladies of this royal house connected their memories with all that was best in the literature of the time. Lady Jane Beaufort, granddaughter of John of Gaunt, inspired the author of the 'King's Quhair.' Her niece, the Countess of Pembroke, mother of Henry VII., was the principal promoter of learning in her generation. Margaret, the sister of Edward IV., who married the Duke of Burgundy, encouraged Caxton in the literary enterprise which led to the introduction of printing into England. Another Margaret, daughter of Henry VII., by her marriage with James IV. of Scotland, gave a new tone to the poetry of the Scottish Court. I need not give examples of the influence of the Court in literature during the sixteenth and seventeenth centuries. The circle of education began to widen very rapidly after the introduction of the printing-press, and the creative faculty was brought within the reach of many and diverse incitements to produce; capitalists pressed forward eager to divine and satisfy the new demands; but among the diverse influences on literary production, one was always conspicuous, the influence of the Court. Even when, as in the case of the great Shakespearian dramatic literature, writers did not receive their first impulse from the Court, the Court hastened to put the seal of its approbation on the new product. It was an entirely novel and unprecedented situation when the throne was filled by a king who could hardly speak a word of English, and who was entirely destitute of interest in English or any other literature; and it cannot but be interesting to examine what effect, if any, this circumstance had on literary production. At an earlier stage of literary history, in an earlier state of civilisation, the withdrawal of royal patronage would have been like the withdrawal of the sun from the solar system. Did it produce any perceptible effect on the literature of the eighteenth century? It did not: the centre of literary life and heat had shifted; where, then, are we to look for this centre?

The mere fact that the personal tastes of the king and his intimate circle ceased to have any directing influence on literature, would alone make the Hanoverian accession a notable literary epoch. But this event affected literature much more profoundly in another way—namely, by putting an end to a long period of political uncertainty. The settlement of the long-vexed question of the succession to the Crown made a change in the position of the man of letters that can only be described as a revolution. A long explanation is required to enable you to understand the full significance of this change, unless you happen to be versed in the history of the period. First, you must take notice of the means by which public opinion in those days was appealed to. There was no reporting of political speeches; there were no daily newspapers with leading articles; everything was done by means of occasional pamphlets in prose or verse. Nowadays, if you wish to know the minds of the leaders of opinion, you read the magazines and the leading articles in the newspapers. But in the time of Queen Anne, and for half a century before, the work of expressing and enlightening opinion was carried on by means of pamphlets. Whenever the public mind was excited on any question—a war, or a parliamentary election, or a great commercial enterprise, or a disastrous calamity—swarms of such pamphlets poured from the press; and if the public excitement ran high and the pamphlet was effectively written, it was sold in the shops and hawked about the streets in thousands. Next, you must take notice of the character of the great political question of the time,—the succession to the kingdom. From the Revolution of 1688 to the accession of George I. the succession was uncertain. The nation was divided into two great parties of Whig and Tory, the one eager to keep out, the other to bring back, the exiled family of Stewarts. Cartloads of pamphlets were written to work on the public mind for the one purpose or the other. It is difficult for us in these days to understand the intense, absorbing, passionate character of the political struggles that went on while the succession lay in dispute and uncertainty. A few years ago there was not a little excitement in this country over the Eastern Question. There were public meetings and speeches and articles without end; sides were taken with considerable earnestness and warmth. But the heat of a struggle is always in proportion to the importance for the combatants of the issue at stake; and no issue raised then could come home to the electors with one-tenth of the force of the momentous question, who should be king of the country. The power of the Crown was great in those days; and the leaders in the dispute about the succession fought with the fierce earnestness of men whose whole fortunes are bound up with the issue. Their properties, and even their lives, were at stake as well as their political power. If they took an active part on one side or the other, degradation, impoverishment, exile, even death might follow upon failure. Triumph meant honours, wealth, and power; defeat might mean forfeiture of their estates and banishment. Such were the high stakes for which the leaders were playing; and for the common people also the political struggle was intensely exciting. It was in great part a religious question with them; encouragement, toleration, persecution, awaited their doctrines and forms of worship, according as a Protestant or a Papist filled the throne; and their feelings were thus profoundly interested. No such issues hang upon political struggles now, and the passion of the conflict, however earnest and determined, can never reach the same pitch of absorbing intensity.

This, then, being the state of things, the leading combatants deeply in earnest, the public mind quick and susceptible, every incident closely watched and sharply taken advantage of, and pamphlets the recognised means of working on public opinion, what was the effect on literature? The political situation had a direct and immediate effect on the position of men of letters. The man who could write pamphlets, whether in prose or in verse, at once became a person of importance. Men of letters were sought after, caressed, rewarded—we must not say bribed—as they had never been before by ambitious politicians and grasping Ministers. Versifiers were in especial demand, and, of course, the patrons were met half-way. Young gentlemen at the Universities, with an elegant knack of versification, celebrated birthdays and battles, and even party triumphs in Parliament, and sent their effusions to the powerful, in the hope of being rewarded by solid appointments in the public service, of course irrespective of special fitness. The splendid successes of a few helped to crowd this avenue to fame and fortune. You all know the story of Addison and his poem on the battle of Blenheim: how the Lord Treasurer Godolphin complained to Lord Halifax of the poor quality of the poems generally written on such occasions, how Halifax said that he knew of a young poet who could do better, how a nobleman was sent to Addison's garret in the Haymarket to solicit his services, and how munificently the poet was recompensed with public appointments. This story is familiar, but it is only the most striking one of scores of a similar kind in Johnson's Lives of the Poets of that time. Addison himself, earlier in his career, when he was fresh from the University, was rewarded with a pension of £300 for a poem on the Peace of Ryswick. Lord Halifax, the patron who helped him to the favour of the Crown, himself owed his first advancement to literature. When plain Charles Montagu, he had co-operated with Prior in writing the political satire of 'The Town Mouse and the Country Mouse.' He was afterwards introduced to King William with the words: "Sir, I have brought a *mouse* to wait on your Majesty." "You do well to put me in the way of making a *man* of him," the king is said to have replied, and forthwith ordered him a pension of £500. Montagu's collaborator, Prior, was made secretary to an embassy. The political hits in his tragedy of 'Tamerlane' obtained for Rowe an under-secretaryship in the Treasury; Hughes obtained a place in the office of Ordnance for an ode on the Peace of Ryswick; Dr Blackmore's indirect compliments to the king in his 'Prince Arthur' procured him a knighthood and the post of royal physician. And so on and so on throughout the reigns of William and Anne. Places of all kinds in the gift of the Ministers of the Crown were freely distributed among men of letters, without the slightest regard to any qualification except their power of making men and measures popular by direct and indirect panegyric.

The effect of this extensive patronage on the *character* of Queen Anne poetry, on the poetry as poetry, we shall try to trace afterwards; meantime, I wish to make clear the position of men of letters before the accession of George I., and how completely this position was changed by the settlement of the disputed succession. Observe that the patronage of literature was not disinterested. The great office of the best literature is to elevate, strengthen, gladden, and purify human life, to expand the soul, to quicken the fancy, to enlarge the understanding, to lift the mind out of the narrow round of personal concerns and enable it to command a wider horizon. It was not to enable men of letters to fulfil this mission that the Ministers of King William and of Queen Anne lavished places and pensions on them. It was purely as party writers that they were patronised, as brilliant political pamphleteers, useful rhetorical panegyrists and biting satirists; and when the need for their services passed away, the fountains of patronage were dried up. Very soon after George's accession, it was apparent that the golden age was at an end. The batch of Whig poets who had remained faithful during the Tory Ministry of Queen Anne's last four years—Addison, Steele, Rowe, Tate, Tickell, and other minor celebrities—were munificently provided for in the first blush of the Whig triumph, but this was practically the last of the system. When Sir Robert Walpole got the reins of power firmly in his hands, and settled down into his policy of establishing the dynasty by peaceful measures, he saw that the poets, powerful enough agents in a time of warlike excitement, could be of little service to him, and he turned the golden stream from the Royal Treasury in another direction. Another circumstance helped to destroy the influence of the brilliant occasional writer, the rapid development of the periodical press, of newspapers and political journals. This was almost coincident with the accession of George I. There had been newspapers in the land from the time of the great Civil War, and regular political periodicals were established in the reign of Queen Anne, the first being Defoe's celebrated 'Review'; but the chronicling of news and the expression of opinion were distinct functions, left to different organs. Such sheets as the 'Flying Post' and the 'Mercury' gave nothing but news; the 'Tatler' and the 'Spectator' were confined to social essays; the 'Examiner' and the 'Whig Examiner,' 'Mercator' and the 'British Merchant' were purely political journals. The newspapers strictly so-called were not impartial; they were in the pay of different parties, and their intelligence was garbled in different interests; but they expressed no opinions, and it was only by the manipulation of news that they sought to influence the opinions of their readers. The "leading article," or "letter introductory" as it was at first called,—a prefatory dissertation intended to lead the readers to certain conclusions—was the invention of the acute genius of Defoe early in the reign of George I. From that time various news-journals began to retain a letter-writer, as the writer of leading articles was then called, and journalism became a distinct occupation. Much of the public money that had gone in the reign of Queen Anne to the occasional pamphleteer now found its way to the pockets of the professional journalist. It was a corrupt time, measured by our modern ideas of literary independence. Walpole, a hard unsentimental man of business, who believed in paying for services directly in solid cash, is said to have paid £50,000 in ten years to the literary supporters of his Administration; and one of them, Arnall, a journalist whose name you will find in no history of literature, boasted that he had received in three years no less a sum than £10,997, 6s. 8d. When we compare Walpole's system of securing literary support for his measures with that prevalent in the time of Queen Anne, we are compelled to admit that the great political patrons of the earlier period, Somers and Halifax, and Oxford and Bolingbroke, did have some respect for literature as literature, and took a certain pride in playing the *rôle* of Mæcenas, altogether apart from their sense of the political advantages of having men of letters on their side.

The great change effected in the position of men of letters at the accession of George I. is, then, a solid reason for beginning a literary survey from that date.   But the reign of the four Georges really owes its completeness as a literary period to an accident. It so happened that Pope's masterpiece, the 'Rape of the Lock,' was published in its complete form in the first year of the first George; while the last year of the last George witnessed the publication of his first volume of poëms by our late Poet-Laureate, Lord Tennyson.   We thus find at the beginning of our period the leader of one great school of poetry in the full blaze of his reputation; and at the end the dawn of another great luminary and the foundation of a new school.   What had poetry gained in the interval—an interval containing the splendid poetic achievements of the first quarter of the nineteenth century, with the great names of Wordsworth and Coleridge, and Scott and Byron, and Keats and Shelley?   At first sight it might seem as if there had been only a full circle revolution of a fixed wheel, an oscillation of a pendulum to and fro,—as if Poetry had only moved from the elaborate artistic care of Pope to the freedom and spontaneity of Wordsworth and Byron, and back to the elaborate art of Tennyson.   But there was a real progression.   Tennyson embodies new poetic ideals in his art, and these ideals were conceived and shaped in the interval between him and Pope.   The age of Wordsworth and Byron was not only a season of great creative energy, but also a season of vivid and searching criticism. Not only were new masterpieces produced, but new life was given to the discussion of the first principles of the art of Poetry.   And not only were the technicalities of poetry discussed — publicly discussed — by some of the leading masters in the art, the principles of diction, metre, imagery, and general construction, as had been done by hundreds of writers on the art of Poetry from Aristotle and Horace down to the Duke of Buckingham and Mr Hayley, but new topics were introduced, and chief among them the nature of the poetic faculty and the principles on which rank should be assigned to poets in their various degrees as spiritual benefactors of mankind. Wordsworth led the way both in creation and in criticism. Wordsworth was by no means the most popular poet in his generation; he had by no means the most powerful influence on the public, but he had unquestionably of all men in his generation the greatest influence on men of letters, on the producers of poetry. It is, to use the language of political economy, among the manufacturers and not the consumers of poetry that his influence is to be traced, and upon them it was enormous. For us, as students of poetry, the most significant and instructive fact in the reign of the four Georges is the gradual rise of the reputation of Wordsworth, and the gradual fall of the reputation of Pope. About the close of the reign of George IV. the reputation of Wordsworth had reached its zenith; the reputation of Pope, supreme and unchallenged throughout the eighteenth century, had fallen to its nadir. We may fairly take Macaulay's essay on Byron, published in 1831, as marking the triumph of the Wordsworthian school. This essay, written with all the energy of Macaulay's brilliant rhetoric, laid hold of what had before been little more than an esoteric doctrine, and spread it far and wide over the public mind. Macaulay danced a sort of breakdown over the prostrate body of the great poet of the eighteenth century. He concentrated and emphasised all that had been said in disparagement of Pope. Pope had no imagination in the highest sense; he had no correctness in the highest sense; he was a painstaking slave to artificial rules; his poetry was like a trimly kept garden, with smooth-shaven grass, flower-beds in geometrical figures, symmetrical walks and terraces, and pillars and urns and statues, and trees and hedges clipt into unnatural shapes. Hundreds of writers since Macaulay have repeated his comparison of Pope's poetry to a trim garden, and have said after him that such poetry could be enjoyed only in an age of hoops and periwigs. For the last fifty years Macaulay's vigorous caricature has dominated the public opinion about Pope. Pope's faults have been put in the foreground; his merits have been admitted grudgingly; his admirers have been obliged to adopt an apologetic tone.

Pope, then, was the hero of the first part of our period, and the dethroned idol of its closing years, knocked from his pedestal and rolled in the dust. Ought he to be set up again? Not all the king's horses, nor all the king's men, could restore him to the place that he once occupied in public estimation, side by side with the greatest men in literature. But, on the other hand, there can be no doubt that the reaction against him in public estimation was carried much too far. His rank in public estimation—I wish to lay emphasis on that expression; for, paradoxical as it may seem, I believe that among the few who make poetry a serious study— and there were such men in the eighteenth century as well as in the nineteenth (Macaulay cannot be included in the number)— there has been no substantial oscillation of opinion about the merits of Pope. They have felt that his range of subjects was limited, and that his power of expression was not of the very highest, but that within his limits and the measure of his power, his execution was of unrivalled brilliancy. Wordsworth and Coleridge felt and acknowledged this, if not as heartily at least as explicitly as Byron and Campbell. It is true that Wordsworth and Coleridge and other disciples had not the same full sympathy with Pope's subject-matter, and consequently were less hearty in their acknowledgment of his excellences, and more disposed to dwell upon his defects. Byron, who had tried his hand at satire, was more forward to acknowledge the brilliant point and masterly condensation of Pope's work. But they were in substantial agree- ment intellectually. They knew equally well where Pope's strength lay, and where his weakness lay. They knew the master's hand, and they drew the line at its limitations. There was no such nice discrimination, however, in the public estimation of the poet, based upon the treatment of him by poetical and critical authorities. The general easy-going reader who does not, in Wordsworth's language, make poetry a study, knows no middle station between good and bad, between admirable and the reverse. He either ad- mires heartily or he is wholly uninterested and contemptuous. And in so far as he is influenced by authority, he is apt to be wholly led away by what is put in the foreground, to look at this only, and neglect the qualifications ranged in the middle distance and the background. Thus it happened that when Wordsworth's school, who put Pope's defects and limitations in the foreground, became the leaders of critical opinion, the hero of the eighteenth century was thrown from his pedestal in public estimation. It is a most difficult thing to gauge public opinion; but a very fair test of it, as regards either men or measures, is to be found in the attitude of moderate advocates. If moderate advocates are apologetic and conciliatory, the man or the measure, we may be sure, does not stand high in the estimation of the public addressed. Now, applying this principle in the case of Pope, we find that in the eighteenth century, before his poetry had passed through the crucible of the Wordsworthian school, such a moderate critic as Joseph Warton had to be cautious in hinting at defects; whereas in recent years such temperate admirers as Mr Carruthers or Mr Mark Pattison have to guard themselves carefully against the charge of putting Pope's merits too high. Such incidents as these are significant of Pope's changed position between the accession of the first George and the demise of the last. He had fallen immeasurably in public estimation, and he was rated much below his deserts.

Now, although it is impossible ever to restore Pope to the position he once occupied, it is our business here to try to obtain just ideas about poets, and to sweep away from our minds all artificial impediments to the enjoyment of various kinds and degrees of excellence in poetry—to clear our minds of prejudice and look at poets fairly for ourselves. The disciples of Wordsworth and Coleridge, in their wholesale condemnation of the poetry of the eighteenth century, have fixed in the public mind a great many erroneous conceptions. We shall endeavour to see for ourselves, taking them one by one, what manner of men the eighteenth-century poets were, what aspirations they had in their art, and how their aspirations were limited by their personal character and circumstances, and by the circumstances of their times, especially by the ruling traditions of poetry in their respective generations.

A very common impression about the poets of the eighteenth century is that they lived in slavish subjection to a set of narrow and exclusive rules of criticism; that they had no love for nature, either in scenery or in human affections or passions—a finicking race of artists, conventional and artificial, shuddering at Shakespeare as a wild and irregular genius, or, as Voltaire called him, an untutored savage. Now if, with these prepossessions in your minds, you take up any eighteenth-century poet of rank, from Pope down to Hayley, one of George III.'s laureates, who represents the low-water mark of eighteenth-century poetry, and if you read the language in which they speak of nature and of Shakespeare, you will open your eyes in astonishment. Take, for example, the following passage :—

"A tree is a nobler object than a prince in his coronation robes. Education leads us from the admiration of beauty in natural objects to the admiration of artificial or customary excellence. I do not doubt but that a thorough-bred lady might admire the stars because they twinkle like so many candles on a birthnight."

This is an extract not from Wordsworth, but from Spence's record of the conversation of Pope, of the poet whose poetry is compared to an artificial garden, and whose narrow and exclusive authority stifled the imagination of the eighteenth century. The irony of Macaulay's comparison of Pope's poetry to an artificial garden lies in the fact that Pope had more to do than any one else in destroying the fashion of artificial gardening in England, not merely by his ridicule of it but by leading the new fashion of landscape-gardening, in which a closer attempt is made to reproduce natural beauties. But, at least, it will be said, Pope spoke disparagingly of Shakespeare. Read the preface to his edition of Shakespeare, for he took some trouble in editing Shakespeare, and you will see. It is true he once remarked to Spence that "it was mighty simple in Rowe to write a play professedly in Shakespeare's style—that is, professedly in the style of a bad age." But we must remember what it was in the style of Shakespeare's age that he considered bad. The particulars that he specified as faults were such as have universally been considered faults of style, and such as no writer has ever tried to imitate without making himself ridiculous. For example, Pope said that "Shakespeare generally used to stiffen his style with high words and metaphors for the speeches of kings and great men : he mistook it for a sign of greatness. This is strongest in his early plays ; but in his very last, his 'Othello,' what a forced language has he put into the mouth of his Duke of Venice." Now it was probably not from mistaking it for a mark of greatness that Shakespeare stiffened his words in the speeches of great men, but because his audience expected it, because the stage demanded it; still, whatever the reason, take any great man's speech in Shakespeare where the situation is not filled with passion, and I think you will agree with the eighteenth-century critic that no style could be more intolerably bad. Do you ever at the theatre now listen to such speeches as those of the Duke of Venice, and what impression do they make upon you?

No: though Pope often heard his own age described as the Augustan age of English poetry, in which the art had been carried to a perfection unattained before, he was by no means insensible to the greatness of his great predecessors, Chaucer, Spenser, Shakespeare, and Milton. His conversations with Spence[1] afford abundant evidence of his catholicity as well as of his delicacy of judgment; and if we pass from Pope to his successors in the eighteenth century, we find that we cannot number disrespect for Shakespeare among the causes of their poetic degeneracy, and that Nature was often in their mouths, if not in their hearts, as the great original from which the poet ought to draw. Their adoration of Shakespeare is not exceeded by the most reverential and least critical member of the New Shakespeare Society. Take Akenside, for example. When in 1749 a French company played by subscription at Drury Lane, Akenside penned a most spirited remonstrance, which he put in the mouth of Shakespeare. He imagined our great poet insulted by this invasion of his domain.

> " What though the footsteps of my devious Muse
> The measured walks of Grecian art refuse,
> Or though the frankness of my hardy style
> Mock the nice touches of the critic's file;
> Yet what my age and climate held to view
> Impartial I surveyed, and fearless drew.
> And say, ye skilful in the human heart,
> Who know to prize a poet's noblest part,
> What age, what clime could e'er an ampler field,
> For lofty thought, for daring fancy, yield?

---

[1] Observations, Anecdotes, and Characters of Books and Men.   By the Rev. Joseph Spence.

> I saw this England break the shameful bands
> Forged for the souls of men by sacred hands;
> I saw each groaning realm her aid implore;
> Her sons the heroes of each warlike shore:
> Her naval standard (the dire Spaniard's bane)
> Obey'd through all the circuit of the main.
> Then too great Commerce, for a late found world,
> Around your coast her eager sails unfurled.
> New hopes, new passions, thence the bosom fires,
> New plans, new arts, the genius thence inspires;
> Thence every scene which private Fortune knows
> In stronger life, with bolder spirit, rose."

Take next Gray, who is sometimes spoken of as the crowning instance of the artificial poetry of the eighteenth century. How far he was from being the victim of a narrow and exclusive taste in literature we shall see afterwards. He was one of the pioneers of the romantic movement; he was a minute observer and an enthusiastic worshipper of nature; and he carried his admiration of artless poetry so far as to find beauties even in Lydgate, whom few of the admirers of early English poetry have even the patience to read. For Shakespeare his enthusiasm was unbounded; the poetry of his own age seemed poor and starved in comparison. "But," he says in a metrical letter to his illustrator Bentley, in which he sighs for the artist's grace, and strength, and quick creation—

> "But not to one in this benighted age
> Is that diviner inspiration given,
> That burns in Shakespeare's or in Milton's page,
> The pomp and prodigality of heaven."

Gray visited Switzerland and Scotland, and the Lake District; and wrote enthusiastic descriptions of the scenery in letters to his friends. He vied with Wordsworth in the sincerity of his passion for the Cumberland Lakes; with Scott in his love for the Scottish Highlands. "I am," he wrote, "charmed with my expedition; it is of the Highlands I speak; the Lowlands are worth seeing once, but the mountains are ecstatic, and ought to be visited in pilgrimage once a year. None but these monstrous children of God know how to join so much beauty with so much horror. A fig for your poets, painters, gardeners, and clergymen, that have not been among them; their imagination can be made up of nothing but bowling-greens, flowering-shrubs, horse-ponds, Fleet ditches, shell-grottoes, and Chinese rails."

I might multiply quotations to show that neither Shakespeare nor Nature was undervalued by the poets of the generation after Pope's. If their poetry was limited in amount and narrow in quality, it was not for want of a taste for better things. Criticism, in short, was busy preparing the way for the reception of a new race of poets by augmenting dissatisfaction with the poetry of the time, and creating a taste for something different. We see this spirit two generations after Pope, even in the works of the weak and amiable Hayley. Hayley was not a self-satisfied driveller; he was painfully conscious of his own weakness, feeling, as he said himself—

> " Whene'er I touch the lyre
> My talents sink below my proud desire."

We must not look upon him as a failure, owing to the benumbing influence of narrow criticism. He repudiated critical authority in most valiant words. He denounced the " Classic Bigot " and " System's Haughty Son " as earnestly as the blindest disciple of the Lakers :—

> "Thou wilt not hold me arrogant or vain,
> If I advise the young poetic train
> To deem infallible no Critic's word ;
> Not even the dictates of thy Attic Hurd :
> No ! not the Stagyrite's unquestioned page,
> The Sire of critics, sanctified by age !
>
> .   .   .   .   .   .
>
> How oft, my Romney, have I known thy vein
> Swell with indignant heat and gen'rous pain,
> To hear, in terms both arrogant and tame,
> Some reas'ning Pedant on thy Art declaim ;
> Its laws and limits when his sov'reign taste
> With firm precision has minutely traced,
> And in the close of a decisive speech
> Pronounc'd some point beyond the Pencil's reach,
> How has thy Genius, by one rapid stroke,
> Refuted all the sapient things he spoke !
> Thy Canvas placing, in the clearest light,
> His own Impossible before his sight !
> O might the Bard who loves thy mental fire,
> Who to thy fame attun'd his early lyre,

> Learn from thy Genius, when dull Fops decide,
> So to refute their systematic pride !
> Let him, at least, succeeding Poets warn
> To view the Pedant's lore with doubt or scorn,
> And e'en to question, with a spirit free,
> Establish'd Critics of the first degree !"

It was in the revival of the grand Epic that Hayley saw a possible future for Poetry, and Mason seemed to him the destined hero of this regeneration.

> " Ill-fated Poesy ! as human worth,
> Prais'd, yet unaided, often sinks to earth ;
> So sink thy powers ; not doom'd alone to know
> Scorn, or neglect, from an unfeeling Foe,
> But destin'd more oppressive wrong to feel
> From the misguided Friend's perplexing zeal.
>
> . . . . . .
>
> What ! is the Epic Muse, that lofty Fair,
> Who makes the discipline of Earth her care !
> That mighty Minister, whom Virtue leads
> To train the noblest minds to noblest deeds !
> Is she, in office great, in glory rich,
> Degraded to a poor, pretended Witch,
> Who rais'd her spells, and all her magic power,
> But on the folly of the favouring hour ?
> Whose dark, despised illusions melt away
> At the clear dawn of Philosophic day ! "

He examines the received opinion that supernatural agency is necessary to the Epic, and denounces and derides all systematic rules. A great Epic might be achieved if the subject were taken from British history.

> " By some strange fate, which rul'd each Poet's tongue,
> Her dearest Worthies yet remain unsung.
> Critics there are, who, with a scornful smile,
> Reject the annals of our martial Isle,
> And, dead to patriot Passion, coldly deem
> They yield for lofty Song no touching theme.
> What ! can the British heart, humanely brave,
> Feel for the Greek who lost his female slave ?
> And shall it not with keener zeal embrace
> Their brighter cause, who, born of British race,
> With the strong cement of the blood they spilt,
> The splendid fane of British Freedom built ? "

Liberty, brooding over this neglect, invites Mason to undertake the task.

> " Justly on thee th' inspiring Goddess calls ;
> Her mighty task each weaker Bard appalls ;
> 'Tis thine, O Mason ! with unbaffled skill,
> Each harder duty of our Art to fill ;
> 'Tis thine in robes of beauty to array,
> And in bright Order's lucid blaze display
> The forms that Fancy, to thy wishes kind,
> Stamps on the tablet of thy clearer mind.
> How softly sweet thy notes of pathos swell,
> The tender accents of Elfrida tell ;
> Caractacus proclaims, with Freedom's fire,
> How rich the tone of thy sublimer Lyre ;
> E'en in this hour, propitious to thy fame,
> The rural Deities repeat thy name :
> With festive joy I hear the sylvan throng
> Hail the completion of their favourite Song."

I think I have quoted enough to show you that the eighteenth-century poets were not, on principle at least, enamoured of trimness and primness in art, or insensible to the wild irregular strength and beauty of nature. They did not of set choice and with deliberate acquiescence confine themselves to a low range of imagination, looking up from their comfortable artificial gardens with supercilious or cynical contempt on the loftier flights of poetry. If the age was comparatively barren of the higher poetry, the explanation is not to be found in the predominance of narrow and exclusive critical theories.

CHAPTER II.

POPE.

If you take a cursory glance at the list of Pope's works and their
subjects, you will see that they fall naturally into three divisions
or periods: (i.) The poems by which he acquired his reputation,
his "Pastorals," his "Windsor Forest," his "Essay on Criticism,"
his "Rape of the Lock,"—all written during the reign of Queen
Anne; (ii.) his translations of Homer, by which he enlarged his
reputation and his fortune, his principal occupation during the
reign of George I.; (iii.) the satirical and moral poems, with
which he crowned his reputation, and seriously compromised his
character. This is an obvious division, apparent on the surface;
and if you look deeper, you will find that there is more justification for it than there generally is. There is often a disadvantage
in dividing the works of an artist into periods; it is often misleading. You are apt to imagine that at each period a complete
transformation has passed over the style or the spirit of the
man's work; that he has become a new creation, working with
entirely different aims and powers; and that the work of each
period is sharply marked off from that of every other. There is a
tendency in this way to break up and disperse the individuality of
the man, to confuse his identity. Now the artist is himself in all
periods; in any period he is more like himself than like anybody

else ; any two periods of his work have more in common with each other than they have with any period of another man's work, supposing him to be a great artist, an artist of marked and masterful individuality. It only happens that some men at certain stages come under new influences from without, or new impulses from within, the effect of which is distinctly traceable in their work, though not to the extent of blurring their individuality. This happens more or less to all men, but it is only when the new influence becomes for the time paramount that there is any advantage in separating the whole productions of a man's lifetime into periods. When the development has been slow and equable, as in the case of Chaucer, or Shakespeare, or Gray, or Wordsworth, or Tennyson, when the course of the poet's activity has received no violent and sudden bent from new circumstances or new impulses, there is no advantage in dividing his work into periods.

In the case of Pope circumstances did interfere materially with the direction of his poetic labours, and two important epochs or turning-points can be distinctly specified. The first was when his early successes transferred him from the influences of his father's family and his home circle of acquaintances to the very different world of London society, when boyish ambitions and enthusiasms underwent a transformation. If these ambitions had been allowed free play, he would not have translated Homer. This was a money-making enterprise, instigated by the worldly spirit that then passed into him from new and fashionable acquaintances. The second epoch was when his independence had been secured by the success of his translations, and he was free to follow the guidance and stimulation of his friends Arbuthnot, Swift, and Bolingbroke, and abandoned his powers to the service of personal and party strife.

Pope was born in the year of the Revolution, 1688. His father, who was a London merchant, retired from business in that year, and went to live at Binfield in Windsor Forest. The most influential fact in Pope's family circumstances was the religion of his father, who was a Roman Catholic. This probably influenced the father in retiring from business when the Catholic James II. was driven from the throne and the Protestant William took his place. Further, it influenced the education of Pope in two ways. The public schools were closed to him, and he received very little regular education. He was taught to read by an aunt, the widow of the portrait-painter Cooper, who left him at her death, when he was five years old, all her "bookes, pictures, and medalls sett in gold or otherwise." At the age of eight he was taught the rudiments of Latin and Greek by the family priest; then he was sent for a time to a little school at Twyford, near Winchester, in Hampshire, then for a time to another in Marylebone, then to a third at Hyde Park Corner in London; then he read for a time under the care of another priest; but at the age of twelve he was left entirely to his own resources. This desultory education, leaving him to read at will, was probably an advantage for a studious boy, who could not remember when he began to make verses of his own invention, who compiled a play for his schoolfellows before he was twelve, and had such a veneration for poets and poetry that as a small schoolboy he ventured into Will's Coffee-house that he might have the pleasure of seeing and hearing Dryden, the greatest English poet then living. These little facts show how precocious Pope was, both in poetic sensibility and in ambition. When his father, who was probably anxious for his health, took him from school in London to live at home in the Forest, he plunged with delight into a miscellaneous course of reading in poetry, and he not only read but imitated. His school education had been too scrappy to make him expert in construing foreign languages; he could barely construe Tully's Offices, he says, when he left school; but in the course of the previous century all poets of note—Greek, Latin, Italian, and French—had been translated into English verse, and with the help of these translations the ardent student had no difficulty in mastering the sense. "Mr Pope," Spence says, "thought himself the better in some respects for not having had a regular education. He (as he observed in particular) read originally for the sense, whereas we are taught for so many years to read only for words." Nor, although the boy was left entirely free to read what he pleased, was he left altogether without friendly guidance. Here, again, the family Catholicism was serviceable to him; it was an advantage to belong to a proscribed sect. The members of such a sect always hold much more closely together without distinctions of rank; distinctions of rank and station are levelled by their common political disabilities. Hence it happened that Catholic families in the neighbourhood, of good position and literary culture, who would probably not have visited the retired linen-draper if he had belonged to the established religion, made the acquaintance of him and of his precocious son, and helped the latter with encouragement and advice in his reading and in the first flights of his genius. In particular, Sir W. Trumbull, a retired diplomatist, living at Easthampstead, within a few miles of Binfield, made a companion of the boy, and directed him to the study of the French critics. Through another Catholic family, the Blounts of Mapledurham, one of whom, Mrs Martha Blount, was his attached friend in his last years, Pope made the acquaintance of Wycherley and Henry Cromwell, and through them of Walsh and Granville, all poets and keen critics of literature.

Thus, while Pope's sensibilities were still fresh, and his whole nature docile and pliable, he was guided into the very middle of the literary current of his time, and left to paddle at his own sweet will in backwaters and eddies. The eager and ambitious boy was, in fact, stimulated to the very utmost of his powers, and directed to strive with all his energies after what was then considered literary excellence by the highest authorities. We can see in his early efforts traces of a clear-sighted purpose, while trying to do what was then certain of winning applause, to choose subjects that had not been already appropriated by great poets, and in which success was still open to all comers. It was then a critical maxim that the highest work of which the human mind was capable was a great epic, and many treatises had been written in French and in English, in prose and in verse, on the principles of epic poetry. Sir Richard Blackmore, while Pope was at school, had attempted an epic on the subject of Arthur. It was a ponderous failure. Pope began an epic about the age of twelve. The subject was mythological, the hero being Alcander, a prince of Rhodes. It was, he told Spence, "about two years in hand." In later life he considered that it was better planned than Blackmore's, though equally slavish an imitation of the ancients; but he never published it, and it was finally burnt by the advice of Atterbury. Even in his boyhood Pope had judgment enough to understand that his powers were not yet sufficiently mature for original composition, and he resolved to perfect them in the first place by imitations of his predecessors. Walsh advised him that there was one praise yet open to English poets, the praise of correctness. In Pope's boyhood, the most successful poetical publication had been Dryden's translation of Virgil. What Dryden had translated, Pope did not presume to meddle with. Dryden was his hero, his model, his great exemplar. But he proceeded to take translations of classics by less eminent poets, and try to improve upon them. With this ambition he translated the first book of the 'Thebaid' of Statius, whom he considered the most eminent Latin epic poet next to Virgil, several of Ovid's 'Heroic Epistles,' and a considerable part of the 'Metamorphoses,' besides passages from Homer. It was one of Pope's vanities to try to give the impression that his metrical skill was even more precocious than it was; and we cannot accept his published versions of Statius and Ovid as evidence of his proficiency at the age of fifteen or sixteen, the date, according to his own assertion, of their composition, though they were not published for several years afterwards. But it is ascertained matter of fact that, by the time he was sixteen, his skill in verse was such as to astonish veteran critics like Wycherley and Walsh, and that his verses were handed about in manuscript, and admired by men who were then in the foremost walks of letters.

Pope spent eight or nine years in this arduous and enthusiastic discipline, reading, studying, experimenting, poetry his only business and idleness his only pleasure, before anything of his appeared in print. In these preliminary studies he seems to have guided himself by the maxim, formulated in a letter to Walsh, July 2, 1706, that "it seems not so much the perfection of sense to say things that have *never* been said before, as to express those *best* that have been said *oftenest*."[1] His first publication was his "Pastorals." Jacob Tonson, the bookseller, had heard these pastorals highly spoken of, and he sent a polite note to Pope asking

---

[1] " True wit is Nature to advantage dressed,
What oft was thought but ne'er so well expressed."

that he might have them for one of his miscellanies. They appeared, accordingly, in May 1709, at the end of a volume containing contributions from Philips, Sheffield, Garth, and Rowe. We can see how Pope was induced to make his first essay in Pastorals. Dryden's translation of Virgil's Eclogues had drawn attention to this species of composition. Walsh had written a critical preface to Dryden's translation, in which he laid down the rules of pastoral poetry, and severely trounced M. Fontenelle, a fashionable French writer of pastorals, for his violation of the rules.

This artificial species of poetry has been almost universally ridiculed as tedious and insipid from the time of Pope to the present day. It is not worth while to waste much time over it; but as it is often condemned hastily, and in ignorance of what it proposed to attempt, it is only justice to Pope, and it may be of some interest, to consider what were the aims of the pastoral poet as conceived by Pope and Walsh. They did not pretend to imitate any incidents in the lives of actual shepherds. Theocritus did this, and Allan Ramsay. But the shepherds of Pope and Walsh were avowedly the shepherds of the golden age, when the best of men were employed in shepherding,—men, as Walsh says, " of learning and good-breeding." These shepherds were assumed to be men of the most delicate and gentle feelings, living a life of simplicity and calm tranquillity, never agitated by harsh and violent passions. Any tender feeling that ruffled their lives was softened and subdued by the steady repose and quiet placid beauty of their surroundings, and the mute sympathy of nature with their woes. Realise the still and tranquil beauty of this ancient pastoral world, and you will admit that it was a fine conception. The poets of this world did not trouble themselves to argue that such a world ever really existed; they admitted that it never existed except as a beautiful fiction. Such was the conception of this species of poetry held by a school of critics among whom Pope had personal friends. You will find it set forth at length in Walsh's preface to Dryden's translation of Virgil, in which minute rules are deduced for bringing details into harmony with this general design. Now this being the aim of the ideal pastoral, to give lyric expression to the joys and the sorrows, the loves and the griefs, of imaginary beings in imaginary circumstances, I think you will see that many of the criticisms passed on Pope's " Pastorals " are beside the mark. He has been censured for not doing what he could not have done without being inconsistent with his original design. Mr Elwin, for example, Pope's truculent editor, who has examined every line in Pope with inveterate hostility, but apparently never lifted his eyes from details to consider Pope's work as a whole, says: "Originality was impossible when Pope's only notion of legitimate pastoral was a slavish mimicry of classical remains. Had he drawn his materials from the English landscape before his eyes, from the English characters about his doors, and from the English usages and moods of thought in his own day, he would have discovered a thousand particulars in which he had not been anticipated by Greeks and Romans. He neglected this inexhaustible territory, and bestowed so little attention upon the realities around him, that, though his descriptions are confined to the barest generalities, they are not unfrequently false."

If Pope had acted on this advice, no doubt he might have written a much more generally interesting poem, with more of flesh and blood and passion in it, but it would not have been the kind of poem that he intended to write. Johnson's criticism is more to the point when he says that the pastoral form of poetry is "easy, vulgar, and therefore disgusting; whatever images it can supply are long ago exhausted; and its inherent improbability always forces dissatisfaction on the mind." This is strong criticism, but perfectly fair. Johnson was thinking more particularly of elegiac pastoral poetry—poems in which poets lamented the death of friends under the fiction that they were shepherds; and he condemned this kind of poetry as a whole, partly because it gave an air of affectation to the poet's grief, and partly because there was nothing new to be said. He fully recognised what the poet intended to do, but held that it was not worth doing. The same criticism had been passed on occasional pastoral elegies by Steele in the 30th number of the 'Guardian' (April 15, 1713). Steele complained that they were too much on one plan :—

" I must, in the first place, observe that our countrymen have so good an opinion of the ancients, and think so modestly of themselves, that the generality of pastoral writers have either stolen all from the Greeks and Romans, or so servilely imitated their manners and customs as makes them very ridiculous. In looking over some English pastorals a few days ago, I perused at least fifty lean flocks, and reckoned up an hundred left-handed ravens, besides blasted oaks, withering meadows, and weeping deities. Indeed, most of the occasional pastorals we have are built upon one and the same plan. A shepherd asks his fellow, ' Why he is so pale? If his favourite sheep hath strayed? If his pipe be broken? Or Phyllis unkind?' He answers, ' None of these misfortunes have befallen him, but one much greater, for Damon (or sometimes the god Pan) is dead.' This immediately causes the other to make complaints, and call upon the lofty pines and silver streams to join in the lamentation. While he goes on, his friend interrupts him, and tells him that Damon lives, and shows him a track of light in the skies to confirm it, then invites him to chesnuts and cheese. Upon this scheme most of the noble families in Great Britain have been comforted ; nor can I meet with any right honourable shepherd that doth not die and live again, after the manner of the aforesaid Damon."

There is not room for much variety in such poetry, the personages of which are simple people with few interests and few cares. Undoubtedly Milton's "Lycidas," *apropos* of which Johnson made his sweeping condemnation, is an exception to the general lameness of these pastoral elegies. The exquisitely sweet and rich music of his verse would have redeemed the most trite and easy of conceptions. But the pastoral elegy was so common in the years between Milton and Johnson, that the critic might have been pardoned a strong expression of his weariness of the poem, though this criticism of Milton is one of the aberrations of his generally sound judgment of poetry and generally true feeling for poetic excellence. At least he must be allowed to have confined his criticism to the kind of poetry which the author intended to produce. He did not censure him because he had not done what he could not have done without deviating into another kind of poetry. To have put into the golden age the manners of country folk as they were to be seen near his own doors, would not have been an excellence. That the imaginary manners of a fanciful golden age can never possess deep human interest, is of course true enough, and Pope's " Pastorals " cannot claim a high rank as poetry. Johnson's criticism of them shows his usual good sense and sanity. "To charge these pastorals," he says, "with want of invention is to require what was never intended. The imitations are so ambitiously frequent, that the writer evidently means rather to show his literature than his wit. It is surely sufficient for an author of sixteen not only to be able to copy the poems of antiquity with judicious selection, but to have obtained sufficient power of language and skill in metre to exhibit a series of versification which had in English poetry no precedent, nor has since had an imitation."

Johnson remarks upon "the close thought" shown in the composition of the "Pastorals": "Pope's 'Pastorals' are not, however, composed but with close thought; they have reference to the times of the day, the seasons of the year, and the periods of human life." "Windsor Forest" is more open than the "Four Pastorals" to the charge of incongruously and incorrectly mixing up heathen deities with modern circumstances, archaic conventional fancies with modern realities. There is a cold artificiality about such lines as these:—

> "See Pan with flocks, with fruits Pomona crown'd;
> Here blushing Flora paints th' enamel'd ground;
> Here Ceres' gifts in waving prospect stand,
> And nodding tempt the joyful reaper's hand."

Pan and Pomona, and Flora and Ceres have little life for their few English readers. Still, after discounting such lines, and the extravagant praise of Granville, and the ludicrous comparison of Queen Anne to Diana, there are many beautiful passages. Pope's observation of nature was admitted by Wordsworth, and his microscopic fidelity is remarked on by M. Taine. "Every aspect of nature," says Taine, "was observed; a sunrise, a landscape reflected in the water, a breeze amid the foliage, and so forth. Ask Pope to paint in verse an eel, a perch, or a trout; he has the exact phrase ready; we might glean from him the contents of a Gradus."

We may remark, as illustrating the close connection of one literary event with another, and the way in which literary influences are handed down, that the same craze for Pastorals which produced Pope's juvenile exercises, by one impulse after another, sending out waves in all directions as from a centre of disturbance in a pool, gave us the poetry of Burns. Kindled by the theories and the practice of the English wits and poets, Allan Ramsay wrote real pastoral poetry, exhibiting the customs, the dress, the games, the domestic sorrows, the loves, and the lives of real shepherds. And the "Gentle Shepherd" awoke the genius of Burns. This great result may excuse us for dwelling so long on Pastoral poetry in the reign of Queen Anne.

Pope professed to have written both his "Pastorals" and "Windsor Forest" in 1704 or 1705, at the age of sixteen, only adding to the latter the passage about the Peace. Probably he had retouched them, as they lay by him. It was part of his vanity to pretend to have been even more precocious than he was, a foible that has been severely commented on.

These "Pastorals" led to one of the first of Pope's celebrated literary quarrels, which is often referred to as an example of his irritable jealousy and subtle underhand proceedings. This has been discussed at great length and in a spirit of bitter hostility to Pope by Mr Elwin—at great length, and yet with the omission of important circumstances, if his object was to prove that Pope was the aggressor.

In the volume of Tonson's Miscellanies in 1709, in which Pope's "Pastorals" appeared, the first place was occupied by a set of Pastorals by Ambrose Philips—"Namby Pamby"—in every way inferior to Pope's. Four years afterwards, on April 6, 1713, appeared in the 'Guardian,' edited by Steele, the first of a series of papers on Pastoral Poetry—discussing pastoral poets from Theocritus downwards, and stating the principles of the art. Really these papers were a covert puff of Philips. Modern pastoral poets were ridiculed for introducing Greek rural deities, Greek flowers and fruits (hyacinths and Pæstan roses), Greek names of shepherds (Damon and Thyrsis, and so forth), Greek sports and customs, and religious rites. They ought to make use of English rural mythology, hob-thrushes, fairies, goblins, and witches; they should give English names to their shepherds; they should mention flowers indigenous to English climate and soil; and they should introduce English proverbial sayings, dress, and customs. All excellent principles, afterwards followed by Allan Ramsay. But the 'Guardian' proceeded to cite Philips as an English poet who had fulfilled these conditions, and consequently established for himself a place side by side with Theocritus, and Virgil, and Spenser. Philips was the eldest born of Spenser. Pope was never mentioned as a pastoral poet, though a few lines were quoted from one of his imitations of Chaucer.

Now Pope was bitterly angry at this, and he took what Mr Elwin considers a mean revenge. He sent to Steele a paper professing to be a continuation of the papers on Pastoral Poetry, reviewing the poems of Mr Pope by the light of these principles. Ostensibly Pope was censured for breaking these rules, and Philips was praised for observing them. It was a most cutting piece of irony, passages being cited from Philips where he had complied with all the precepts of the 'Guardian,' and yet had written the most insipid commonplace. Pope himself, though ostensibly condemned, was really exalted, being described in one place as having "deviated into downright poetry."

When the paper was sent to him, Steele, misled by the opening sentences, was at first unwilling to publish a direct attack on Pope, and asked Pope's leave to print it, which was graciously granted.

Elwin severely condemns this as a mean, spiteful, underhand trick, and declares that Pope's vanity made him the aggressor. I own to having some sympathy with the fun of the thing; but, apart from that, I don't think that Mr Elwin has made out that Pope was the aggressor. In spite of his laboured argument, he has omitted several cardinal circumstances, allowing, as is his custom, a few points to carry him away, while he does not look at the whole.

The papers in the 'Guardian' were really a covert attack on Pope. What were the circumstances? Pope's "Windsor Forest," a pastoral, appeared in the beginning of March. It contained a eulogy of the Peace of Utrecht, the great achievement of the Tory Ministry, to which Steele and Addison and the Whig coterie were far from friendly. A few weeks afterwards appeared a series of papers on Pastoral Poetry, in which Pope was studiously ignored, and a feeble poetaster, his rival in that kind of poetry, extravagantly lauded. I should call that mean and underhand, and Pope's method of retaliation strikes me as simply highly ingenious and amusing, and not unfair. A magnanimous man would have passed by the slight without notice; but if a man did condescend to notice it, as Pope did, his crime was not of a very black dye. He only hoisted the enemy with their own petard.

CHAPTER III.

POPE—*continued.*

OUR starting-point to-day, the "Essay on Criticism," was published in 1711, midway between the "Pastorals" and "Windsor Forest." An excellent rule occurs at l. 253:—

> "Whoever thinks a faultless piece to see,
> Thinks what ne'er was, nor is, nor e'er shall be.
> In ev'ry work regard the writer's end,
> Since none can compass more than they intend."

What was Pope's end? He wrote the "Essay on Criticism" for the entertainment of the cultivated people, men and women of wit and learning in his time, who were greatly interested in the art of poetry. It belongs to the class of poems called Didactic, but the object of such poems is not instruction, even when they state and illustrate rules of conduct. The object of poetry is to give immediate pleasure. When Virgil wrote his 'Georgics,' his object was not to lay down practical rules for the husbandman, but to present a beautiful picture of country life. Darwin's 'Botanic Garden' was meant, not to serve the same purpose as lectures on botany, but to give pretty pictures of plants and their habits. So in Pope's "Essay on Man," his object is not to write an ethical or theological treatise, but to give pointed and brilliant expression to certain views of man's character, of his position in the universe, and of his destiny. This might be indirectly instructive, by furnishing people with striking and easily remembered reflections as maxims of conduct, but the poet's primary purpose was to charm and delight by the novelty of his expression.

In the "Essay on Criticism" his purpose is less lofty—he did not strive to lead his readers into the same lofty region of delightful emotion. His purpose was simply to condense, methodise, and give as perfect and novel expression as he could to floating opinions about the poet's aims and methods, and the critic's duties to

"What oft was thought but ne'er so well expressed."

He was keenly interested in the subject himself, as day by day he read and meditated on it in his quiet home at Binfield; and so were his acquaintances. He took for granted that the town, the coffee-houses, and the drawing-rooms would also be interested: and he was not disappointed. The work excellently served its primary purpose of giving pleasure to the town.

He expounded many commonplaces so admirably, so perfectly, so happily, that ever since they have been quoted in the form he gave them, *e.g.* :—

"Fools rush in where angels fear to tread."—l. 625.

"The bookful blockhead, ignorantly read,
With loads of learned lumber in his head."—l. 612.

"Good-nature and good-sense must ever join.
To err is human; to forgive, divine."—l. 525.

"True ease in writing comes from art, not chance,
As those move easiest who have learn'd to dance."—l. 362.

"Expression is the dress of thought."—l. 318.

"'Tis not a lip, or eye, we beauty call,
But the joint force and full result of all."—l. 245.

"A little learning is a dang'rous thing."—l. 215.

"From vulgar bounds with brave disorder part,
And snatch a grace beyond the reach of art."—l. 152.

Now a writer who makes expressions by means of smart epigram, startling instances, and brilliant illustration his chief aims, and chooses topics of knowledge and opinion rather than feeling, is not, strictly speaking, a poet, even if he writes in verse. We do not call him a poet, but a rhetorician. We call a man a poet who touches our feelings by means of words, as a painter or a sculptor does by painted canvas or chiselled stone. But rhetoricians in verse are capable of giving us much delight, by presenting our beliefs in new and unexpected lights, and this was what Pope did in his "Essay on Criticism." We do not always find ourselves in agreement with the opinions expressed, but the expression is always vivid and often most felicitous.

Johnson criticises Pope's precept regarding the use of "representative metre," as stated in the lines :—

> " 'Tis not enough no harshness gives offence,
> The sound should seem an echo to the sense.'

"This notion," says Johnson, "has produced, in my opinion, many wild conceits and imaginary beauties. All that can furnish this representation are the sounds of the words considered singly, and the time in which they are pronounced."

Here he makes the mistake of assuming that the rhythm is determined solely by the number of accented and unaccented syllables—by the pauses and the syllables in and out of accent. He quotes a passage in which the numbers are the same as in Pope's translation of Homer's description of Sisyphus rolling the stone up the hill. In the description of Sisyphus the sound seems adapted to the sense, and yet here is another set of verses in the same number, which do not convey the same feeling of effort. Johnson argues that the reason must be, simply that the subject is different; the numbers are the same, but the meaning being different, we estimate the sound by the meaning. "The mind often governs the ear, and the sounds are estimated by their meaning." Johnson forgets that the quantity of the vowels and the difficulty of the consonants affect the rhythm.

If I am to spend so much time over Pope's early poems, how am I to cover in twenty lectures the poetry of the four Georges? I can, of course, in such a short course, attempt only to give you some idea of the leading artistic aims of poetry in that period, the poetic ideals, what the poets tried to do, what we are to look for in their poetry, and how they came to have these aims. And upon these inquiries we get much light from these early poems of Pope, because they were written under the direct influence of the arbiters of good taste in writing in his time.   In the "Essay on Criticism" he puts these standards of good taste into brilliant words, and so helped to perpetuate their influence.   But their influence was exerted in many forms that could not be put into words, because the men of the time were not conscious of them.

One of the favourite ways of accounting for the barrenness of the eighteenth century is to say that the poets, influenced by Pope, were subject to narrow and exclusive rules of criticism, that they were slavishly subservient to the ancients, writing only according to these precedents, and that, consequently, their poetry was dull and artificial and wanting in nature.   I believe this to be a shallow theory, held in entire ignorance of the great forces that control and shape the poetry of living generations of men.   Reverence for the ancients, more particularly for the Roman ancients, Virgil and Horace, was undoubtedly an influence in the time of Pope; but it was only a slight influence then, and in the subsequent generations of the century it was not an influence at all.

Let us see what exactly was meant by this subservience to the ancients.   At first sight it would look as if Pope had no reverence for the ancients, but proposed to himself quite an independent standard—namely, Nature :—

> " First follow Nature, and your judgment frame
> By her just standard, which is still the same :
> Unerring Nature still divinely bright,
> One clear, unchang'd, and universal light,
> Life, force, and beauty must to all impart,
> At once the source, and end, and test of Art.
> Art from that fund each just supply provides ;
> Works without show, and without pomp presides."

But, if we read on, we come upon several passages that seem to betray a slavish admiration for the ancients :—

> " You then whose judgment the right course would steer,
> Know well each Ancient's proper character ;
> His fable, subject, scope in ev'ry page ;
> Religion, country, genius of his age ;
> Without all these at once before your eyes,
> Cavil you may, but never criticise.

> Be Homer's works your study and delight,
> Read them by day, and meditate by night;
> Thence form your judgment, thence your maxims bring,
> And trace the Muses upward to their spring.
> Still with itself compar'd, his text peruse,
> And let your comment be the Mantuan muse.
> When first young Maro in his boundless mind
> A work t' outlast immortal Rome designed,
>
> .   .   .   .
>
> Nature and Homer were, he found, the same.
> Convinced, amaz'd, he checks the bold design;
> And rules as strict his labour'd work confine,
> As if the Stagirite o'erlook'd each line.
> Learn hence for ancient rules a just esteem;
> To copy Nature is to copy them."

Again, in speaking of the breach of these rules, he declares:—

> "But though the ancients thus their rules invade
> (As kings dispense with laws themselves have made),
> Moderns, beware! or if you must offend
> Against the precept, ne'er transgress its end;
> Let it be seldom, and compell'd by need;
> And have, at least, their precedent to plead.
> The critic else proceeds without remorse,
> Seizes your fame, and puts his laws in force."

The case now seems very strong for Pope's subservience to the ancients. This is strengthened by looking at the general scope of his works. He spent ten years in translating Homer; ten more in professedly imitating Horace.

But look a little deeper, and you will see that Pope craftily qualifies his subservience to the ancients. Their rules must be observed, but then their rules are very vague and general; there is much in the poet's art that they cannot teach; and even if they are broken, success justifies the transgressor:—

> "Some beauties yet no precepts can declare,
> For there's a happiness as well as care.
> Music resembles poetry, in each
> Are nameless graces which no methods teach,   ⎫
> And which a master-hand alone can reach.   ⎬
> If where the rules not far enough extend
> (Since rules were made but to promote their end),

> Some lucky license answer to the full
> Th' intent propos'd, that license is a rule.
> Thus Pegasus, a nearer way to take,
> May boldly deviate from the common track ;
> From vulgar bounds with brave disorder part,
> And snatch a grace beyond the reach of art."

This is surely a sufficient declaration of independence. Obey their rules when it suits you.

But then Pope goes on to allow this license only to the ancients. "Moderns, beware," he says, and for this interdict on the moderns he is severely censured by Mr Elwin. If Mr Elwin had had a little more nimbleness of spirit, and consequently been able to understand the quick and subtle wit and sly humour of Pope, he might have seen that Pope was here laughing in his sleeve at mechanical critics :—

> " I know there are, to whose presumptuous thoughts
> Those freer beauties, ev'n in them, seem faults.
>
> .   .   .   .
>
> Most critics, fond of some subservient art,
> Still make the whole depend upon a part :
> They talk of principles, but notions prize,
> And all to one lov'd folly sacrifice.
>
> .   .   .   .
>
> Thus critics of less judgment than caprice,
> Curious not knowing, not exact but nice,
> Form short ideas ; and offend in arts
> (As most in manners) by a love to parts."

Pope, then, left himself full liberty to depart from the ancients when he chose—and he took it. Even his translation of Homer was a very free translation. "A very fine poem, Mr Pope, but it is not Homer," was Bentley's remark. His imitations of Horace are among his most original poems, according to Pattison ; and everybody will agree that they are most original.

Pope's submission to the ancient masters was not slavish or subservient. He studied them as great masters ought to be studied when they are not read simply for enjoyment. He studied them with a mind open to receive impulse and suggestion from their example.

Were Pope's eighteenth-century successors slavishly submissive to the ancients ? Pope died in 1744, when there was more than

half of the century to run.   I will not weary you with quotations,
but I could quote many passages from Akenside, Gray, Churchill,
to show that Pope's successors exalted Shakespeare, who broke
many of Aristotle's rules,

> "Above all Greek, above all Roman fame."

I have quoted already one passage from Hayley, late in the century,
feeblest of poets, to show how little they were repressed by the rules
of the ancients.   Valiant protestation of contempt for rules is not
always a sign of strength, but I don't think it was the rules of the
ancients that kept down eighteenth-century poetry.   A mechanical-
minded ecclesiastical place-hunter—Mason—tried to write tragedies
on the Greek model and failed.   Was it wit?   An outrageous
admiration for brilliant expression, for highly polished epigram?
Well, even Pope did not consider that wit was everything :—

> "Some to *conceit* alone their taste confine,
> And glitt'ring thoughts struck out at ev'ry line ;
> Pleas'd with a work where nothing's just or fit ;
> One glaring chaos and wild heap of wit.
> Poets, like painters, thus unskill'd to trace
> The naked nature and the living grace,
> With gold and jewels cover ev'ry part,
> And hide with ornaments their want of art.
>
> .   .   .   .   .   .
>
> Others for *language* all their care express,
> And value books, as women men, for dress :
> Their praise is still,—the style is excellent ;
> The sense they humbly take upon content.
> Words are like leaves ; and where they most abound,
> Much fruit of sense beneath is rarely found."

And after Pope we do not have much wit.   There is nothing better
than the coarse vigour of Churchill and the ribald buffoonery of
Wolcot (Peter Pindar).

I don't think we can say that the eighteenth century failed in
poetry because the energies of its verse-makers were directed to
rhetorical brilliancy.   Hayley and Mason and Darwin, the leading
poets in the boyhood of Wordsworth and Coleridge and Scott,
were not rhetorically brilliant ; their rhetoric was ineffective ; they
were simply dull ; and we can hardly say that they failed as poets

because they tried to be rhetoricians. They would probably have been dull in any case.

Another way of accounting for the eighteenth-century barrenness is to ascribe it to the monotony of the versification. Macaulay speaks as if every aspiring poet thought couplets the only permissible form. Pope used only the couplet, and, it is often said, brought it to such mechanical perfection that any versifier after him could turn out smooth, and finished, and melodious couplets, with as much ease as a machine cuts wood into blocks of a given size. Pope imposed restrictions upon himself; such as that each couplet must end with a break in the sense, that an extra syllable must be admitted only in one place, and that the metrical pauses must fall only in certain places. The eighteenth-century poets followed him till the world became weary of heroic couplets.

This theory also will not bear examination. Couplets are not necessarily monotonous, witness Chaucer's "Knight's Tale," Marlowe's "Hero and Leander," Keats's "Endymion," Swinburne's "Tristram and Iseult." Monotony in the case of the couplet does not arise from the poet putting himself under strict conditions. We do not find Pope's couplets monotonous, if we are interested in the subject. He leaves himself room enough for variety within his limits.

The poems of Hoole, and Hayley, and Mickle, and Mason, and Darwin are monotonous in rhythm, not because they wrote couplets, but because they wrote bad couplets, and would have been equally monotonous if they had written in any other stanza. No doubt writing in a strictly fettered rhythm imposes a greater strain upon the poet; but if he has power to stir our feelings profoundly, the regularity of the rhythm, keeping the passion of his theme within bounds, gives him a stronger hold upon us. If there is no intense life in what he has to say to us, there is of course nothing to moderate; and he will not interest us any the more whatever gymnastic feats he performs in the way of rhythm, any more than a musician can hold us spellbound by flourishes from top to bottom of the scale.

Besides, the eighteenth-century poets did not, as a matter of fact, enslave themselves to the couplet as the only permissible form.

It was not slavish submission to the ancients, nor to the heroic couplet, nor to the demand for rhetorical brilliancy, that kept so much of the poetry at a low level. We are only scratching on the surface of an explanation when we adopt any such theory. Nor will it do to say that the eighteenth century was an age of prose; that its mission was to form the prose style of English literature. We wish to know why it was an age of prose—why it adopted this mission. Nor will it do to say that it held a false theory of poetic diction. We wish to get at the feeling that made them satisfied with their conventional diction as the right thing.

We must look away from such details if we are to understand the eighteenth century, and look at poetic productions as wholes. Take the works of the leaders of the great poetic revival of this century—Wordsworth, Scott, Byron. In what broad respects do they differ from all the works of the eighteenth century? The form of their poems, in a large sense of the word, is new, and their vein of feeling is new. They treat new themes in a new way, and with a new spirit. Above all, they give serious expression to their own personal emotions. Consider the new form of the "Lay of the Last Minstrel," the first genuinely popular poem, interesting to all classes, between the time of Queen Anne and the nineteenth century—a metrical romance regularly constructed, with perfect unity of action, incidents all helping forward the progress of the story through various complications to a *dénouement*. No such poem had ever been written before; it was a new form in poetry—classical regularity of form, combined with romantic freedom of accident. Then the spirit of the poem—the serious epic treatment of the necromancing lady of Branksome Hall, the Goblin page, the wizard, and the bold moss-trooper. We have nothing like this in the eighteenth century. In Pope's time such personages would either have been burlesqued or treated with affected respect, such as a grown-up person would use towards fairies and hobgoblins in telling stories about them to a child. Taken as a whole, in form and spirit, the "Lay" was a new thing in literature. The same may be said of "Childe Harold." Here also we find a new kind of epic, such as the general writers on epic poetry had never contemplated,—the hero of which is not a mythical king like Prince Arthur, or a personified virtue moving

in Faeryland like Spenser's Red Cross Knight, or Guyon, or Britomart, but a modern man moving in modern scenes. Wordsworth
also is new in form as well as in spirit. No poet before him had
dared to shut himself up in the country and choose, as the subject
of his verse, his own personal emotions and reflections as aroused
by the moving spectacle of sky and mountain and glen, and the
homely life of ordinary rustics. He wrote a kind of pastoral
poetry that had not been legislated for by the technical lawgivers
of the art.

The serious expression in new forms of intense and generous
personal emotion is a broad characteristic of the nineteenth-
century revival. Now we can understand why the poets of the
eighteenth century failed in the artistic expression of serious and
generous feeling. The main defects of their poetry can be traced
to one source—the character of the audience for whose judgment
they had respect, by whose ideals they were controlled, who were
to them the arbiters of taste. The standard of taste in the time
of Queen Anne, and till near the end of the century, was a self-
consciously aristocratic and refined society, self-conscious of their
superior manners and superior culture, and disposed to treat the
ways of the vulgar with amused contempt. This, I think, can be
shown to be at the root of the striving after wit and the respect
for established models, and the false theory of poetic diction in
serious poetry. Fear of being vulgar, fear of being singular,—
these were the real nightmares that sat upon eighteenth-century
poetry.

CHAPTER IV.

POPE—*continued.*

I AM not sure that you all followed what I said in my last lecture
about the influences that formed the poetic ideals of the eighteenth
century. By the poetic ideals of a generation I mean the ideas
prevalent among those interested in poetry as to what poetry
should be—the sentiments that they wish to find in poetry,—the
intellectual, or moral, or emotional cravings for which they seek
satisfaction in poetry. But, you may ask, How can this be said
to make poetry? Is it not the poet who makes the poetry? Yes;
but he makes it in harmony with—or, if he is a defiant man, in
antagonism to—the poetic ideals of the men with whom he mixes
and for whom he writes. You have heard of the spirit of the age—
an intangible something that sets its mark upon all the works of a
generation of men, their books, their architecture, their dress, their
commercial enterprises, their institutions. What I mean by the
poetic ideal is the working of this spirit upon poetry. I am inclined to think myself that people sometimes speak of this spirit
of the age in too unqualified terms, as if everything came under
its influence. Now many things escape its influence, as you recognise when you speak of things or persons being behind the age;
it is only the most distinctive products of the age that feel its shaping, its generative force. And besides, there may be more than
one spirit in a generation, each with its own range of influence,
handed down, it may be, from past times, and kept alive by sym-

pathy with them, or engendered by the peculiar circumstances of the circle of people whom it pervades. Go into churches of widely different sects, for example, and you seem to breathe different atmospheres—a different spirit pervades them ; the "full force and joint result" of ornament and ritual and sermon is somehow different. You might find it hard, if you fixed on details, to say where the difference lies ; the same sermon that is preached in one might have been preached in the other ; the same hymns might have been sung ; yet we feel under the influence of a different spirit. And further, these various churches have probably less in common with each other, though they mix in the same age, than they have with the churches of past ages, each of them perpetuating a traditional spirit of its own, and perhaps making it a point of honour to keep that unchanged.

The same holds in poetry. A poet writes under the influence of a certain spirit, a certain social medium, which shapes and colours what he writes. To discover this we must look not only at the general character of his age, but also at the character of his immediate audience, of the circle in which he moves. We must study his relations with them, whether they are relations of harmony, as in the case of Pope, or relations of antagonism, as in the case of Byron. And we can't expect to get at this subtle spirit by studying isolated details, and arguing about them. My object in last lecture was to impress this fact upon you in the case of eighteenth-century poetry. There is a something in the spirit of eighteenth-century poetry which the critics of this century, broadly speaking, do not like. They complain that the eighteenth century is barren of true poetry. And they often set to work to account for this by fastening on details of form, and diction, and imagery, and metre. Some say the barrenness is due to subservience to ancient rules, others to an exclusive ambition after witty expression, others to a slavish attachment to one kind of metre.

Now, in the first place, I think they exaggerate the barrenness of the century. It is often spoken of as if there were no good poetry then, whereas it was only comparatively deficient in certain kinds. And, in the second place, we do not satisfactorily account for the deficiency in certain kinds, if we look at details by themselves. We must look at them in connection with the spirit of the society for which Pope wrote. The spirit of this society accounts not only for much that was in Pope's poetry, but also for much that was in the two following generations, because the traditions of this society were maintained after Pope's time, its spirit was transmitted as the dominant spirit in literature till the end of the century. There were revolts against it in the poetry of Thomson and Dyer, and Gray and Collins, and Burns and Cowper, but, on the whole, it maintained its hold. Its supremacy was not, indeed, shaken till Wordsworth and Byron raised the standard of rebellion, and the majority at once in fact, and gradually in open avowal, went over to them.

The society that imposed the laws of taste in poetry in Pope's time was, as I said, an aristocratic society, self-consciously so, as it could hardly fail to be when high and low, rich and poor, were marked off from each other by such conspicuous differences of dress and manners, as they moved about in their daily life. It was not only self - consciously but superciliously aristocratic. Sympathy with the simple feelings of unfashionable folk was rare in those days. Now in such a society one ruling motive—except, of course, among persons of natural hardihood or assured position in it—is fear of vulgarity, resulting in a disposition to treat as vulgar whatever is done by people outside the pale of fashion. Many details might be urged against this view, but I think it must be allowed that this is a very prevalent motive.

Let us see, then, how this prevalent motive would operate on poetry, supposing the poet to be under its influence. It would affect both his choice of subjects and his manner of treating them. Nature, Pope said, is "at once the source and test of art." But Nature is a vague term, which each person interprets as meaning his own nature, and that must always be interpenetrated by the spirit of a man's social surroundings, the spirit prevalent among his companions. The Nature from which Pope chose his themes was either human nature, as he saw it in fashionable society, or human nature so treated as not to offend their susceptibilities. Pope's conception of Nature did not lead him to go, like Wordsworth, to simple country-people for his subjects, and for his diction to " the natural language of man in a state of intense emotion." " True wit," he said—by wit meaning poetic expression—is " Nature to advantage dressed." This casual metaphor in the "Essay on Criticism" takes us nearer to the centre of Pope's ideal of poetic expression, which was also the ideal of his age, than any other single passage in his writings.

Let us take an example of what a refined contemporary of his, writing in the 'Guardian' about Philips's "Pastorals," considered the dressing of Nature to advantage :—

"I will yet add another mark, which may be observed very often in the above-named poets, which is agreeable to the character of shepherds, and nearly allied to superstition, I mean the use of proverbial sayings. I take the common similitudes in pastoral to be of the proverbial order, which are so frequent, that it is needless and would be tiresome to quote them. I shall only take notice upon this head, that it is a nice piece of art to raise a proverb above the vulgar style, and still keep it easy and unaffected. Thus the old wish, ' God rest his soul,' is finely turned—

> ' Then gentle Sidney liv'd, the shepherd's friend ;
> Eternal blessings on his shade attend.' "

So easy a metamorphosis as this Pope would have despised, for the poetic dress of nature is esteemed according to the poet's originality and ingenuity in constructing it. Pope, on the contrary, would have required such an expression as only a man of genius could devise after much toil. In a 'Treatise on the Art of Sinking in Poetry'—one of the miscellanies published conjointly by Pope, Swift, and Arbuthnot—you will find that Pope ridicules simple expressions and the raising of language above the vulgar style, enforcing his opinion by specimens of bathos culled from the poets of the time : *e.g.*, "Who knocks at the door ?" becomes when *raised above the vulgar*—

> " For whom thus rudely pleads my loud-tongued gate,
> That he may enter ?"

or Theobald's elevation of "Open the letter" into the sounding line, "Wax ! render up thy trust."

If you look at Pope's poetry closely, you find that though he avoided easy elevations he did think it necessary to use language which now seems affected and insincere. In this you see him influenced by the spirit of his age. In his "Messiah," published in the 'Spectator' (May 14, 1712), and considered by critics of the time to be a very fine poem and an improvement on Isaiah, whose prophecy we think grand in its simplicity, we clearly see this influence at work. For example, in Isaiah (xli. 19) we have, "I will set in the desert the fir tree, and the pine, and the box tree together," while Pope describes the change as follows:—

> "Waste, sandy valleys, once perplex'd with thorn,
> The spicy fir and shapely box adorn."

For Isaiah's phrase "the sucking child" Pope has got "the smiling infant," and the whole poem is full of similar examples. So, too, we find many examples of bad taste in his translation of Homer, for Pope considered it necessary through the whole of that work to dress Homer to advantage for the fashionable society of Queen Anne's time.

That society would have ridiculed Achilles weeping by the side of Thetis, and accordingly Pope "elevates" the passage thus:—

> "Far in the deep recesses of the main,
> Where aged Ocean holds his watery reign,
> The goddess-mother heard. The waves divide ;
> And, like a mist, she rose above the tide :
> Beheld him *mourning* on the naked shores ;
> And thus the sorrows of his soul explores."

Pope has not rendered the touching simplicity which Homer achieves without infringing, to our modern ideas, on the dignity of his heroic characters. In the case of minor poets of the time this elevation of diction is not always achieved with the same taste that Pope—master of language—showed. In the translation of the 'Odyssey,' in which Pope was assisted by two coadjutors, the magnifying of the incidents is less skilfully managed and the affectation becomes more apparent. We may cite for this purpose that passage in the sixth book of the 'Odyssey' where Odysseus discovers Nausicaa and her maidens at the stream. The affectation in the poetical translation is apparent when we compare it with the prose version by Butcher and Lang: "Then they took the garments from the wain, in their hands, and bore them to the black water, and briskly trod them down in the trenches, in busy rivalry. Now when they had washed and cleansed all the stains, they spread all out in order along the shore of the deep, even where the sea, in beating on the coast, washed the pebbles clean. Then having bathed, and anointed them well with olive oil, they took their midday meal on the river's banks, waiting till the clothes should dry in the brightness of the sun. Anon, when they were satisfied with food, the maidens and the princess, they fell to playing at ball, casting away their tires, and among them Nausicaa of the white arms began the song." Very different this from the grandiloquent version by Brome, which Pope approved by using it as his own :—

> " Then emulous, the royal robes they lave,
>   And plunge the vestures in the cleansing wave
>   (The vestures cleans'd, o'erspread the shelly sand,
>   Their snowy lustre whitens all the strand !).
>   Then with a short repast relieve their toil,
>   And o'er their limbs diffuse ambrosial oil ;
>   And while the robes imbibe the solar ray,
>   O'er the green mead the sporting virgins play
>   (Their shining veils unbound). Along the skies,
>   Toss'd, and retoss'd, the ball incessant flies,
>   They sport, they feast ; Nausicaa lifts her voice,
>   And, warbling sweet, makes earth and heaven rejoice."

With the primitive enjoyment described by Homer the poet did not evidently sympathise. The character either of the poet or of his audience was at fault : either the poet was insensible to the charms of such passages, or his audience would have considered them coarse. When the Queen Anne poets wrote for the stage— which must appeal to the sympathies of a wider circle—and not for fashionable society, you find that the art of simple writing was not lost. Half-consciously the poets wrote differently for different audiences. True, Addison's " Cato " is a splendid example of the stilted style of the period, but there are here and there decided exceptions.

Gay's songs, in plays addressed, as plays must be to succeed, to a wider circle than the fashionable society of the time, show that the art of simple writing was not lost. In " 'Twas when the seas

were roaring" (from "What d'ye call It ?" 1715), and in "Black
Eyed Susan," occur such lines as these :—

> "Cease, cease, thou cruel ocean,
>   And let my lover rest.
> Ah, what's thy troubled motion
>   To that within my breast ?"

> "So the sweet lark, high poised in air,
>   Shuts close his pinions to his breast
> (If chance his mate's shrill cry he hear),
>   And drops at once into her nest."

Gay had more of a gift for simple, fluent, easy, melodious song
than any of his contemporaries. Yet, even in these, there is a
touch of burlesque, an accent of insincerity in the poet's assumed
sympathy with the simple feelings of simple folk. In his "Pastorals" Gay made broad fun out of the superstitious ignorance
and coarse sentiments of rustics : he had no eye, as Wordsworth
had, for their higher modes of feeling ; he saw only the rude defects incident to the hardness and narrowness of their lives, and
these amused him. They amused fashionable people, and Gay,
a fat, good-natured, simple-hearted man, petted and caressed and
pensioned by great people all through his literary life, quite fell
in with their humour.

There is one kind of poetry, mock-heroic or heroic-comical, for
which the elevated Queen Anne style is peculiarly suited — in
which its affectation and insincerity are not felt as faults, because
affectation and insincerity are part of the humour in which the
poet writes. Pope's poetic diction is seen in one of its happiest
applications in the "Rape of the Lock," where trivial incidents,
and little anxieties and interests, and pretty frivolities are purposely treated as matters of vast moment. Here, also, he found
a theme well within the interests of his audience. I presume that
you have all read this charming poem, and have learnt from your
edition of it how it originated in a young lord's cutting off a
lock of a lady's hair ; how this led to a coolness between the two
families ; how Pope was asked to write a poem on the subject, to
smooth over the quarrel ; how the poem appeared in 1712, and was

expanded before 1714 to the form in which we have it. It is a different sort of theme from the technical essays, and the translations and imitations of Virgil and Ovid and Chaucer, in which Pope had hitherto exerted himself,—a theme directly suggested by the fashionable life of the time, by human nature as it lived and moved in the society of Queen Anne's days. Pope had a model in Boileau's "Lutrin," a model as regarded the form, but the subject was fresh and new; it came to him from breathing life, and was not laboriously sought.

Pope has been charged with gross impoliteness in writing such a poem; indeed, M. Taine found in it a coarseness akin to Swift's. "Pope," wrote M. Taine, "dedicates his poem to Mrs Arabella Fermor with every kind of compliment. The truth is, he is not polite; a Frenchwoman would have sent him back his book, and advised him to learn manners; for one commendation of her beauty she would find ten sarcasms upon her frivolity. . . . In England it was not found too rude. Mrs Arabella Fermor was so pleased with the poem that she gave away copies of it. . . . But the strangest thing is, that this trifling is, for Frenchmen at least, no badinage at all. It is not at all like lightness or gaiety. Dorat, Gresset, would have been stupefied and shocked by it. We remain cold under its most brilliant hits. Now and then at most a crack of the whip arouses us, but not to laughter. These caricatures seem strange to us, but do not amuse. The wit is no wit: all is calculated, combined, artificially prepared; we expect flashes of lightning, but at the last moment they do not descend. . . . We say to ourselves now that we are in China: that so far from Paris and Voltaire we must be surprised at nothing; that these folks have ears different from ours; and that a Pekin mandarin vastly relishes kettle-music. Finally, we comprehend that even in this correct age and this artificial poetry, the old style of imagination exists; that it is nourished as before, by oddities and contrasts; and that taste, in spite of all culture, will never become acclimatised; that incongruities, far from shocking, delight it; that it is insensible to French sweetness and refinements; that it needs a succession of expressive figures, unexpected and grinning, to pass before it; that it prefers this coarse carnival to delicate insinuations; that Pope belongs to his country, in spite of his classical polish and his studied elegancies; and that his unpleasant and vigorous fancy is akin to that of Swift."

This poem, which English critics of all schools agree in praising as a masterpiece of light, airy, gay extravagance—*marum sal*, as Addison called it—strikes M. Taine as a piece of harsh, scornful, indelicate buffoonery. For him it is a mere succession of oddities and contrasts, of expressive figures, unexpected and grinning,—an example of English insensibility to French sweetness and refinement. What especially offends his delicate sense is the bearishness of Pope's laughter at an elegant and beautiful woman of fashion. Pope describes with a grin on his face all the particulars of the elaborate toilet with which Belinda prepared her beauty for conquest, and all the artificial airs and graces with which she sought to bewitch the heart of susceptible man. The Frenchman listens without sympathy, without appreciation, with the contemptuous wonder of a well-bred man at clownish buffoonery. He sees nothing to laugh at in a woman's spending three hours over her toilet. Is she not preparing a beautiful picture for him? She cannot do this without powders and washes and paint-pots. What is there to laugh at in this? It is a mere matter of fact. The entire surrender of the female heart to little artifices for little ends does not strike him as ludicrous. His delight in the finished picture, the elegant graceful captivating woman, hallows every ingredient used in the making of it. It is not polite to laugh at a woman.

CHAPTER V.

A GROUP OF EIGHTEENTH-CENTURY POETS.

BETWEEN the end of Pope's second period and the beginning of his third a new poet appeared, of a very different vein.

It was in the last year of the reign of George I. that this fresh and powerful voice made itself heard in literature. A respectable clergyman of literary tastes, Mr Whatley, chanced to take up a volume of poems lying on the counter of Millan the publisher. The poems had been published for some weeks, but had attracted no attention. As he turned over the leaves Mr Whatley's attention was roused; before he laid the book down attention had developed into enthusiasm, and he rushed off to the coffee-houses to proclaim the discovery of a new poet.

The new poet was James Thomson, a young man of twenty-six, just as old as the century, who had been born and bred in very different circumstances from Pope, and whose poetry consequently derived its tone from very different influences. Consider the life of Thomson up to the time when "Winter," the first of his poems on the 'Seasons,' was published in 1726, and you will see that a very different strain was to be expected from him. His father was a minister in the Scotch Lowlands—minister of the parish of Southdean in Roxburghshire. The extraordinary death of this gentleman, when his son was in his eighteenth year, is significant both of the superstitious atmosphere in which the poet was edu-

cated and of the sensitiveness of the organisation that he inherited.
There was a ghost in the parish of Southdean, and the minister
was sent for to lay it; but no sooner had he begun his exorcism
than it seemed to him that he was struck on the head with a
ball of fire, and he never recovered from the shock. A man of
such susceptibility and overpowering vividness of imagination
was fitting father to a poet. He had literary neighbours also,
like Pope's father, who encouraged his boy in verse-making.
There was Mr Riccarton, minister of the neighbouring parish
of Hobkirk, who wrote a poem on Winter, and is shown by that
fact to have been likely to give the author of the 'Seasons' an
early bias towards the vein of sentiment and reflection that
afterwards took possession of him. A neighbouring laird, Sir
W. Bennet of Chesters, also took notice of the schoolboy, invited
him to spend his summer holidays at his house, and being himself an amateur of poetry, encouraged him to compose verses.
Thomson's juvenile verses must have been very clumsy compared with Pope's. We have a specimen of them, published in
the 'Edinburgh Miscellany' in his twentieth year, when he
had completed his course of studies in Arts in the University
of Edinburgh, in which, while the language is rough, there is
a certain force and freshness of vision, an air of sincere delight
in country scenes, evidences of unaffected loving observations of
country sports. There is a story told of Thomson's unwillingness
to leave Tweedside for the University. He was sent to Edinburgh on horseback with a servant, but was back before the servant, saying he could study as well on the braes of Sou'dean
as in Edinburgh.

To Edinburgh, however, Thomson had to go, and the whole
family removed there on the father's sudden death. He was
a student in Divinity till 1724, and in October of that year
was severely reproved by the Professor for the exuberance of
his imagination in an exercise lecture on the 119th Psalm. In
March 1725, armed with introductions from an aristocratic friend
of his mother's, the Lady Grizel Baillie, he went in quest of
Fortune to London, where a college friend of his, David Mallet,
was already settled as tutor in the family of the Duke of Mon-
trose. Thomson also obtained a tutorship — in the family of

Lord Binning, son-in-law of his Edinburgh patroness—but held it only for a few months.

It seems to have been in the neighbourhood of Lord Binning's house at Barnet that the idea of writing a poem on Winter first took shape in Thomson's mind. The approach of winter in 1725 found him in circumstances in which he needed all the consolations of a warm imagination. His mother had died a few weeks after he parted from her at Leith, and he was himself in pecuniary straits, with but little prospect of realising the hopes with which he had come to the capital. Read the opening lines of "Winter" with this knowledge of the poet's circumstances, and you will see how natural it was that such thoughts should come into his mind, as he walked to and from his country lodging, with eyes that had long been accustomed to watch changes in the sky and on the face of the earth— turning to them now for relief from his own cheerless-looking future. Very different this from the situation of the artist Pope, for whom poetry was not a consolation for desperate circum- stances, but a business pursued with ease and deliberation.

> "See, Winter comes, to rule the varied year,
> Sullen and sad, with all his rising train ;
> Vapours, and clouds, and storms. Be these my theme.
> These ! that exalt the soul to solemn thought
> And heavenly musing. Welcome, kindred glooms,
> Congenial horrors, hail ! with frequent foot,
> Pleased have I, in my cheerful morn of life,
> When nursed by careless Solitude I lived
> And sung of Nature with unceasing joy,
> Pleased have I wander'd through your rough domain ;
> Trod the pure virgin-snows, myself as pure ;
> Heard the winds roar, and the big torrent burst ;
> Or seen the deep-fermenting tempest brew'd
> In the grim evening sky. Thus pass'd the time,
> Till through the lucid chambers of the south
> Look'd out the joyous Spring, look'd out and smiled."

Descriptive poetry it seems to me—*i.e.*, poetry descriptive of inanimate nature—must always be more or less dull unless we have some clue to the mood of the poet. The description then lives for us as an expression of the writer's ruling emotion ;

it acquires human interest. Of course the human interest of Thomson's descriptions is not always due to the colours thrown upon them by his own hopes and fears for himself; it is only passages here and there that have a direct biographical interest. The gloomy notes of the opening of his poem on Winter are only significant of the mood in which he began the poem; once fairly absorbed in his subject, he seems, as it were, to have been carried on the wings of imagination far above and away from the anxieties of his own life, up into sublime contemplation of the great forces of Nature, and into warm sympathy with the human hardships and enjoyments, horrors and amusements, peculiar to the season. When Thomson is called a descriptive poet, it must be remembered that he not merely describes Nature with the minute fidelity of a landscape painter; it is always Nature in its relation to man: the ways and the feelings of man have even greater interest for him than the changing appearances of sky and earth and sea. The secret of his extraordinary popularity is that he describes in sonorous and dignified verse not only what all men must see as long as the seasons endure, but also what all men must feel as long as they are affected by the changes of the seasons, and have hearts to feel for one another's joys and pains.

The poem of "Winter," published in the spring of 1726, leapt at once into popularity. Two editions were exhausted in a few months. The freshness of the poem must have helped it greatly with the fastidious coffee-house critics of the time. Nobody since Milton had handled blank verse with such power. The subject also was fresh; no poet since Milton had lighted on such a theme for sublimity of imagination and breadth of human interest. It came to Thomson quite spontaneously; from his own hardships to the general hardships of all living things in winter, and the efforts of man to make the most of the gloomy season, was a natural transition; and coming to him as a happy thought, the subject was treated with genuine enthusiasm. And if we look at the general structure of the poem, we see another thing that must have struck the critics of the time as a novelty. It was an innovation upon the classical structure. It does not follow any predetermined scheme or plan, beyond beginning with the storms of early winter, and ending with the thaw that heralds the approach of spring. The poet leaves himself free to digress wherever casual associations may lead him.

The best way of giving an idea of Thomson's method and style will be to follow the course of this his first, freshest, and most powerful poem. He begins, as I have said, after a short introduction, with a description of the black skies, heavy rains, and floods of early winter :—

> "Then comes the father of the tempest forth,
> Wrapt in black glooms. First joyless rains obscure
> Drive through the mingling skies with vapour foul ;
> Dash on the mountain's brow, and shake the woods,
> That grumbling wave below. The unsightly plain
> Lies a brown deluge ; as the low-bent clouds
> Pour flood on flood, yet unexhausted still
> Combine, and, deepening into night, shut up
> The day's fair face. . . .
> Wide o'er the brim, with many a torrent swelled,
> And the mix'd ruin of its banks o'erspread,
> At last the roused-up river pours along :
> Resistless, roaring, dreadful, down it comes
> From the rude mountain, and the mossy wild,
> Tumbling through rocks abrupt, and sounding far ;
> Then o'er the sanded valley floating spreads,
> Calm, sluggish, silent ; till again, constrained
> Between two meeting hills, it bursts away,
> When rocks and woods o'erhang the turbid stream ;
> There gathering triple force, rapid and deep,
> It boils, and wheels, and foams, and thunders through."

Then follows the description of a storm, preceded by an invocation to the winds, in the style of personification now obsolete. It is obsolete ; not so the description of the storm itself. There is a real picture before his mind's eye as he describes ; and he is intent above everything in bodying forth this picture to his reader. Heightening the effect at the end by the addition of superstitious horrors may be said to be conventional :—

> " Ye too, ye winds ! that now begin to blow
> With boisterous sweep, I raise my voice to you.
> Where are your stores, ye powerful beings ! say,
> Where your aërial magazines reserved,
> To swell the brooding terrors of the storm ?

> In what far distant region of the sky,
> Hush'd in deep silence, sleep you when 'tis calm ?
> . . . . Red fiery streaks
> Begin to flush around.   The reeling clouds
> Stagger with dizzy poise, as doubting yet
> Which master to obey ; while rising slow,
> Blank, in the leaden-colour'd east, the moon
> Wears a wan circle round her blunted horns.
> . . . . The cormorant on high
> Wheels from the deep, and screams along the land.
> Loud shrieks the soaring hern ; and with wild wing
> The circling sea-fowl cleave the flaky clouds.
> . . . .
> Meanwhile, the mountain billows, to the clouds
> In dreadful tumult swell'd, surge above surge
> Burst into chaos with tremendous roar,
> And anchored navies from their station drive,
> Wild as the winds across the howling waste
> Of mighty waters.   . . .
> The whirling tempest raves along the plain ;
> And on the cottage thatch'd, or lordly roof,
> Keen-fastening, shakes them to the solid base.
> Sleep frighted flies ; and round the rocking dome,
> For entrance eager, howls the savage blast.
> Then too, they say, through all the burdened air,
> Long groans are heard, shrill sounds, and distant sighs
> That, utter'd by the demon of the night,
> Warn the devoted wretch of woe and death."

Then he imagines the storm to subside at midnight, and gives his midnight reflections :—

> " Nature's king, who oft
> Amid tempestuous darkness dwells alone,
> And on the wings of the careering wind
> Walks dreadfully serene, commands a calm ;
> Then straight, air, sea, and earth are hush'd at once.
> . . . .
> Now, while the drowsy world lies lost in sleep,
> Let me associate with the serious Night,
> And Contemplation, her sedate compeer ;
> Let me shake off the intrusive cares of day,
> And lay the meddling senses all aside."

Next comes his famous description of a snow-storm, followed by his touching narrative of the shepherd lost in the snow :—

" As thus the snows arise ; and foul, and fierce,
All Winter drives along the darken'd air ;
In his own loose-revolving fields the swain
Disaster'd stands ; sees other hills ascend,
Of unknown, joyless brow ; and other scenes
Of horrid prospect shag the trackless plain.   .
Nor finds the river, nor the forest, hid
Beneath the formless wild ; but wanders on
From hill to dale, still more and more astray ;
Impatient flouncing through the drifted heaps,
Stung with the thoughts of home ; the thoughts of home
Rush on his nerves, and call their vigour forth
In many a vain attempt.
 . . . .   Down he sinks
Beneath the shelter of the shapeless drift,
Thinking o'er all the bitterness of death,
Mixed with the tender anguish Nature shoots
Through the wrung bosom of the dying man ;
His wife, his children, and his friends unseen.
In vain for him the officious wife prepares
The fire fair-blazing and the vestment warm ;
In vain his little children, peeping out
Into the mingling storm, demand their sire
With tears of artless innocence.   Alas !
Nor wife, nor children, more shall he behold,
Nor friends, nor sacred home.   On every nerve
The deadly Winter seizes ; shuts up sense ;
And, o'er his inmost vitals creeping cold,
Lays him along the snows, a stiffened corse,
Stretched out, and bleaching in the northern blast.
 .   .   .   .
And here can I forget the generous band,
Who, touched with human woe, redressive searched
Into the horrors of the gloomy jail ?
 .   .   .   .
Ye sons of Mercy ! yet resume the search ;
Drag forth the legal monsters into light,
Wrench from their hands Oppression's iron rod,
And bid the cruel feel the pains they give."

The thought of this pathetic incident leads him to reflect on the broad contrast between rich and poor ; and there next appears in his poem the first notable reference in our literature to the great humanitarian movement for reforming the horrors of prison life, with which the name of Howard is associated.   Winter scenes at home lead to winter scenes on the Alps, on the Pyrenees and the Apennines, and he draws a thrilling picture of the bands of wolves that prowl over the snowy wastes. Then he passes to his own ideal of enjoyment in winter, in a retreat

"between the groaning forest and the shore,"

with chosen books and chosen friends. Next he takes up winter enjoyments in the village and in the city, pausing by the way to denounce gaming, and eulogise Lord Chesterfield. From this he returns to a description of Nature under frost, and games on the ice; this leads him to winter in the Arctic regions, the life of the Laplanders, the fate of Sir Hugh Willoughby the Arctic explorer, and the romantic career of Peter the Great. Then follows the thaw, and the concluding reflections on human destiny.

The best of Thomson's 'Seasons' is undoubtedly "Winter," though "Autumn" probably surpasses it in technical skill. He wrote more slowly and laboriously after his first success; and there are more frequent traces in his other seasons of deliberate imitation of Virgil's 'Georgics,' and deliberate search for good descriptive topics. "Summer," the longest, appeared in 1727; "Spring" in 1728; and "Autumn" in 1730. The 'Seasons,' as now printed, contain many later revisions and additions, in some of which he had the assistance of Pope.

The best way to read these poems is not to read them through, but to take the argument and pick out any theme that strikes you as interesting. You will thus best appreciate the "bold description and the manly thought" to which the poet laid claim. Avoid "Spring," and his tedious description of the golden age, and the influence of the season on birds and beasts, and fishes and men.

Between 1730 and 1748 Thomson produced little worthy of remembrance. His song "Rule Britannia" appeared in 1740, in a masque of "Alfred," written by him in conjunction with David Mallet. The 'Castle of Indolence' was published in the last year of his life.

The 'Seasons' remained Thomson's great achievement. It was a striking but not inexplicable fact that contact with London literary society, to which he was at once admitted on the success of " Winter," paralysed his poetic faculty, or at best robbed it of half its strength. He had written with comparatively unconscious freedom before, with the victorious joy of reaching and even surpassing his brightest ideals of poetic achievement ; contact with a more critical society, and more exacting standards of literary finish, seems to have bred self-distrust. In compliance with the taste of his new companions, he became more ambitious of displaying his learning, and chose topics in which it was easier, than in the description of the 'Seasons,' to show an acquaintance with history and political philosophy. He used his metrical power also in the service of politics. His first political venture, " Britannia," published in 1729, when the nation was intensely excited over attempts by Spain to challenge our then newly-won dominion of the seas, was immensely popular. But it owed its success to its opportuneness, rather than to its power, though its strains were ardent and vigorous enough. We are apt perhaps to underrate the force of Thomson's patriotic verses, from forgetting that he did much to foster the national sentiment, and was the original author of many expressions that have since become the commonplace expressions of that sentiment. Some lines sound like very hackneyed stump declamation, but they had more heart and meaning in the mouth of the poet of the first generation of British ascendancy, when Britain, consolidated by the union of the Kingdoms, and by the Treaty of Utrecht, acknowledged victor in the protracted struggle for the empire of the seas and of the new worlds, was glowing with the intoxication of newly-acquired power. But Thomson's next and much longer political poem, " Liberty " (1734), in which he narrated the career of this goddess, and described the glories that she created in Greece and Rome before fixing her home in Britain, fell flat, though the composition of it was his chief labour for three years. This was the poem which Johnson owns he could not finish ; and about which a contemporary wit remarked that the poet " had taken a *liberty* which was not agreeable to *Britannia* in any *season.*" Thomson also wrote for the stage, but without success, his one memorable triumph being the song of " Rule Britannia." Although Thomson published sometimes by subscription, he made but a poor income out of his poetry, and he was unfortunate in his sinecures. Lord Chancellor Talbot, whose son he had accompanied as tutor to Italy, made him Secretary of Briefs in the Court of Chancery, and he held this office for rather more than three years (December 1733 to February 1737), losing it on the death of his patron. The Prince of Wales gave him for some years a pension of £100, but withdrew it in a pet. From 1744 till his death he held the sinecure office of one of the Commissioners for the Leeward Islands.

Thomson must be acknowledged to be one of the greatest of our minor poets—*i.e.*, of those that are ranked next to the great names of Chaucer, Spenser, Shakespeare, Milton, Wordsworth, and Byron. He holds this place in virtue of his vigour of imagination, his broad manly sentiment, the individuality of his verse, and the distinction of his subject. These have given him a remarkable and enduring popularity. And measured by his influence on succeeding literature, his is by far the greatest figure among minor poets. Both in his use of blank verse, and in the easy discursive general structure of his poems on the Seasons, he had many imitators, the most eminent of whom was the poet Cowper. And his influence reached into our own century. It was most marked on Wordsworth ; and the fact, just put on record by Mrs Richmond Ritchie (Miss Thackeray), that Thomson's 'Seasons' was the first poetry known to Tennyson in his boyhood, enables us to understand whence our Laureate received the impulse to his minute observation of Nature and country life.

A word or two on another poet, also nourished by influences outside Pope's circle, but, unlike Thomson, never brought within that circle, John Dyer. He was the son of a Welsh solicitor, but abandoned the law himself for painting and poetry, and in his early manhood apparently wandered about South Wales as an itinerant painter, rhyming as he went. He was born in the same year with Thomson, and his first and best poem, "Grongar Hill," appeared in Lewis's 'Miscellany' in 1726, in the same year with Thomson's "Winter." It is a sweet little descriptive poem, in the four-accent measure of Milton's "L'Allegro," as pure and fresh and clear in its vision of natural objects as anything written by any of the Lakers, and exquisitely musical in its numbers. It is Wordsworthian also in its moralising :—

"And see the rivers how they run
Through woods and meads, in shade and sun !
Sometimes swift, sometimes slow,
Wave succeeding wave, they go
A various journey to the deep,
Like human life, to endless sleep !
Thus is Nature's vesture wrought
To instruct our wandering thought ;
Thus she dresses green and gay,
To disperse our cares away.
Ever charming, ever new,
When will the landscape tire the view !
The fountain's fall, the river's flow,
The woody valleys, warm and low ;
The windy summit, wild and high,
Roughly rushing on the sky !
The pleasant seat, the ruin'd tower,
The naked rock, the shady bower ;
The town and village, dome and farm,
Each give each a double charm,
As pearls upon an Æthiop's arm.
  See on the mountain's southern side,
Where the prospect opens wide,
Where the evening gilds the tide,
How close and small the hedges lie !
What streaks of meadows cross the eye !
A step, methinks, may pass the stream—
So little distant dangers seem :
So we mistake the picture's face,
Eyed through Hope's deluding glass ;
As yon summits soft and fair,
Clad in colours of the air,
Which, to those who journey near,
Barren, brown, and rough appear :
Still we tread the same coarse way ;
The present's still a cloudy day."

In the course of his wanderings as a painter, Dyer went to Rome, and on his return in 1740 published a poem called "The Ruins of Rome." It is in blank verse, most musical in its rhythm, and exquisitely delicate and precise in phrase and epithet ; but its declamatory apostrophes and exclamations strike us now as somewhat antiquated ; and its moralising vein of melancholy sentiment may be said to have been superseded for this century by Byron's stanzas in "Childe Harold" on the ruins of Athens.

The following lines on Modern Rome will sufficiently illustrate his treatment of blank verse :—

> " Behold by Tiber's flood, where modern Rome
> Couches beneath the ruins : there of old
> With arms and trophies gleamed the field of Mars :
> There to their daily sports the noble youth
> Rush'd emulous ; to fling the pointed lance ;
> To vault the steed ; or with the kindling wheel
> In dusty whirlwinds sweep the trembling goal ;
> Or wrestling, cope with adverse swelling breasts,
> Strong grappling arms, close heads, and distant feet ;
> Or clash the lifted gauntlets ; there they formed
> Their ardent virtues ; in the bossy piles,
> The proud triumphal arches ; all their wars,
> Their conquests, honours, in the sculptures live.
> And see from every gate those ancient roads,
> With tombs high verg'd, the solemn paths of Fame !
> Deserve they not regard ? "

On his return to England Dyer entered the Church, and reappeared seventeen years later with another poem, also in blank verse, "The Fleece." The first lines will give you an idea of the subject :—

> " The care of sheep, the labours of the loom,
> And arts of trade, I sing."

This poem, and Somerville's "Chase," a didactic poem on hunting (1735), may be numbered among the discursive didactic poems called into being by the success of Thomson's 'Seasons.' Where Dyer treats of soils, and pastures, and breeds of sheep, and prohibitive legislation against the export of wool, and fulling, and weaving, and dyeing, and the foreign trade in wool, he becomes more technical than most readers of poetry are prepared for ; but intermixed with these technicalities are some of the most exquisite passages of description in the language. You can easily get at them by means of the argument. If all the four books had been like these, we could understand Akenside's saying "that he would regulate his opinion of the reigning taste by Dyer's 'Fleece' ; for if that were ill-received, he should not think it any longer reasonable to expect fame from excellence."

CHAPTER VI.

POPE—*continued.*

AS A SATIRIST AND MORALIST—FAILURE IN EPIC POETRY—'THE DUNCIAD'
—'ESSAY ON MAN.'

WE have to deal to-day with Pope as a satirist and a moralist. His 'Dunciad' (1728), his 'Essay on Man' (1732-34), 'Moral Essays' (1735), and his 'Imitations of Horace' (1733-37) were the great literary events of the fifteen years after the publication of Thomson's 'Seasons,' and showed the author in a new vein. They were a series of surprises as far as Pope was concerned,— works that his previous performances had not prepared the public to expect.

Pope's translation of Homer and his editions of Shakespeare occupied him till 1725, when he had reached the age of thirty-seven, and was in the maturity of his powers, with an independence secured by the enormous profits of his Homer. Then began the third period of his literary career. The works that he then produced, and which I have already enumerated, are his greatest works in point of literary power. But why did he not then produce works of more permanent and universal interest? Why did he not then return to his youthful scheme of writing a great epic? The critics of this century have refused Pope a place by the side of Milton, because his subjects were of inferior quality, appealing to a lower range of human emotion, and incapable from their very nature, however excellent the treatment of them, of being made the subjects of equally great poetic achievements. Now Pope, as we have seen, was fully possessed of the idea that a great epic was the greatest work that a poet could accomplish; why, then, when he was free to choose, did he not undertake such a work?

To answer this, we have to look both to Pope's character and to his circumstances. He toyed with the idea of writing a great epic. He told Spence that he had it all in his head, and gave him a vague sketch of the subject and plan of it, but he never put any of it on paper. This indecision was partly due to his character and partly to his circumstances. Partly he shrank from the labour, and partly he was turned aside by circumstances to other labours which fully occupied his energies. One reason why great epics are rare is that the composition of them, in addition to imaginative genius and genius for rhythmical expression, demands an intellectual staying power and energy of will such as are rarely found in human beings with or without the poet's special gifts. Reflect for a moment on the intellectual force that a poet must exert in writing a tragedy. To give moving expression to a single tragic situation; to imagine and body forth in language that all men feel to be true to nature the changes of passion in the heart of one character in one of the scenes in 'Macbeth,' or 'Hamlet,' or 'Othello,' so that not a line shall ring false, requires no ordinary intellectual concentration; but to exhibit in a succession of scenes, each profoundly wrought out, a progression of events towards a tragic catastrophe, bringing many agencies to bear, and assigning to each its right influence, giving voice to many and various passionate emotions, sustaining at every moment and gradually deepening the interest of the hearer, observing the hundred conditions of tragic effect,—this puts an immensely greater strain on the strength of intellect and will. Unless the poet goes right by a sort of instinct, borne along in a rapturous delight with each triumphant step, he must collapse; but instinct in this case is only another name for intellect, one, however, that can hold in its grasp at once and satisfy at once the conflicting claims of a multitude of conditions which a weaker intellect can grasp only one by one, and can never fully reconcile because it can never bring them all together. It may be doubted whether the strain is equally great in epic, because the difficulties do not occur with the same cumulative importunity; they admit of being vanquished, if not singly at least in smaller detachments. Still even in epic the strain is such as few men in the history of literature have proved equal to, though multitudes have tried. Now Pope, as you know, was not constitutionally a strong man. I am not here speaking of muscular strength, but of constitutional strength. His life, as he said, in the prologue to his 'Satires,' was one long disease. It has always been a matter of wonder that, to use Mr Leslie Stephen's phrase, he got as much work out of his frail body as he did. One of the secrets of his endurance was that he worked in comparative tranquillity. He avoided the stress and strain of complicated designs, and applied himself to designs that could be accomplished in detail,—works of which the parts could be separately laboured and put together with patient care, into which happy thoughts could be fitted, struck out at odd moments, and in ordinary levels of feeling. Even the work of translating the 'Iliad,' a very different work from creating an epic, weighed very heavily on his spirits. After he was fairly committed to it, he told Spence he was often under great pain and apprehension. "I dreamt often," he said, "of being engaged in a long journey, and that I should never get to the end of it."

This shrinking from sustained intellectual strain, to be prolonged day after day for weeks or months or years—for a great epic cannot be written in a day—was probably one of the reasons why Pope did not attempt an epic, though he liked to think over subjects. The hero of the one that he had planned was the legendary Brutus, the Trojan coloniser and name-father of Britain, the invention of the fertile romances of the twelfth century. Pope proposed to describe how he established civil and ecclesiastical order in England—a theme, you will observe, that could have been treated in cold blood. We have probably not lost much from his never having carried out this design. It may be doubted whether he had the intellectual strength for a great epic, though in the "Eloisa and Abelard" he showed himself capable of dealing powerfully with a single tragical situation.

But now to consider the circumstances that diverted him from attempting such an epic as he was capable of, and led him into the walks of satire, in which for keenness and brilliancy of point he has never been surpassed. Imitating the epic style, we must ask our Muse of Literary History, "Tell me, O Muse, what dire offence moved the great Pope to make war upon the little dunces.

Who were the dunces, and what had they done to provoke his ire, so that he spent some years in composing an elaborate poem designed to subject them to everlasting ridicule?"

"The history of the 'Dunciad,'" Johnson says in his 'Life of Pope,' "is minutely related by Pope himself, in a dedication which he wrote to Lord Middlesex in the name of Savage." According to this account, the origin of the poem was very simple. Pope and one or two of his intimate friends, notably Swift and Arbuthnot, were great connoisseurs of good poetry, and one of their favourite amusements—they had formed a little club for the purpose in the reign of Anne, fifteen years before the publication of the 'Dunciad '—was to make fun of bad poetry. With this view the intimates had together composed a 'Treatise on Bathos, or the Art of Sinking,' in which they collected and invented superlative specimens of mixed metaphors, preposterous similes, and generally of the bombast and extravagance and inanity of bad poetry, and classified bad poets according to their eminence in the various arts of debasing instead of elevating their subjects. These specimens of the bad they ascribed to various letters of the alphabet, most of them taken at random. Well, no sooner was the treatise published than the infatuated scribblers proceeded to take the letters to themselves, and in revenge to fill the newspapers with the most abusive falsehoods and scurrilities they could possibly devise. "This gave Mr Pope the thought that he had now some opportunity of doing good, by detecting and dragging into light these common enemies of mankind," who for years had been anonymously aspersing almost all the great characters of the age. Their persistent attacks upon himself had given him a peculiar right to their names—and so he wrote the 'Dunciad.'

It might seem, then, that the Muse of History had nothing to tell; but she is an inquisitive Muse, and she has not remained satisfied with Mr Pope's account. If the letters of the alphabet were distributed at random among imaginary bad poets, it is the most singular chance on record that they happened so often to correspond with the initials of poets and poetasters of the time. The gods of the literary Olympus, playing at the Art of Sinking, were not quite so innocent in their amusements as Pope pretended; they were rather like the little boys in the fable throwing stones at the frogs, and they had no right to assume virtuous airs when the frogs protested and retaliated. It is, besides, fatal to the strict accuracy of Pope's account that the book of 'Miscellanies,' containing the treatise on the Bathos, was published in 1727, while Pope, from his letters to Swift, is known to have been engaged on the 'Dunciad' in 1726, and from internal evidence is conjectured to have begun it several years earlier. In extreme opposition to Pope's account is another history of the affair, adopted by those who take the worst view of his character, and will have it that he was essentially vindictive and malignant. This view is that Pope's motives for writing the 'Dunciad' were purely spiteful and personal; that as soon as his hands were free from his translation of Homer, and his independence secured by the profits of that work, he proceeded to settle old scores with those who had not spoken as favourably as he liked about his poetry. There is strong justification for this view in the fact that the most prominent persons ridiculed in the 'Dunciad' can be shown to have given him offence. Theobald or Tibbald, the original hero of the poem, had criticised his edition of Shakespeare, as he thought, insolently. Cibber, in whose favour Tibbald was subsequently deposed,—the 'Dunciad' received many alterations and additions after its first issue,—had ridiculed a play in which Pope in his earlier days had some share, and had retaliated on the first mention of his name in the 'Dunciad.' Dennis was an old enemy. Lintot, the publisher, had accused him of unfair practices in the division of the profits of the 'Odyssey,' which proved less successful than the 'Iliad.' And so on. You will find the details in any edition of the 'Dunciad,' most fully in the recent edition by Mr Courthope, who has succeeded Mr Elwin in the task begun by Croker. Indeed, it was not denied by Pope that the men satirised had previously attacked him; it was openly avowed, and specimens of their attacks were prefixed to his own complete edition: it was these attacks, he said, that had given him a right to make use of the names of his assailants.

Was it, then, personal spite, the vindictiveness of wounded vanity, as some critics think, or was it, as he professed himself, "the thought that he had now some opportunity of doing good," that moved Pope to write the 'Dunciad'? The truth probably lies between the two views. Both motives may have operated, as well as a third not so obvious,—an unscrupulous love of fun, and delight in the creations of a humorous imagination. Certainly, to represent the ' Dunciad ' as the outcome of mere personal spite is to give an exaggerated idea of the malignity of Pope's disposition, and a wrong impression of his character. He was not a morose, savage, indignant satirist, but airy and graceful in his malice, writing more in fun than in anger, revengeful, perhaps, and excessively sensitive, but restored to good-humour as he thought over his wrongs by the ludicrous conceptions with which he invested his adversaries. We do not feel the bitterness of wounded pride in his writings, but the laughter with which that pride was consoled. He loved his own comic fancies more than he hated his enemies. His fun at the expense of his victims was so far cruel that he was quite regardless of their sufferings, probably enjoyed them ; but it was an impish and sprite-like cruelty, against which we cannot feel any real indignation, because it is substantially harmless, while its ingenious antics never fail to amuse. And in extenuation of the cruelty, I see no reason to reject Pope's own plea that he never took the aggressive, although Mr Elwin has attempted at great length to show that this could not be maintained. In the "Epistle to Dr Arbuthnot," which is Pope's most elaborate defence of himself as a satirist, he pretends to greater magnanimity and lofty tranquillity of mind than any merely human being can possess, and which he himself was undoubtedly far from possessing, being really extravagantly sensitive to criticism. Still, undue weight may be given to stories illustrating how keenly Pope felt criticisms when first they were communicated to him, and how long after an offence had been committed he seized an opportunity of repaying it. Granting the truth of these stories, I should still contend that Pope soon recovered his equanimity after the first quick anger was past, and that there was little or no bitterness in his heart when he took his revenge, and that he reconciled this revenge with a moral purpose—the chastisement of men worthy of chastisement. The Epistle to Arbuthnot, I believe, really represents his permanent attitude of mind, the stable condition in which his mind rested when it had recovered from any passing derangement of its equilibrium.

It has been said that to thoroughly enjoy the 'Dunciad,' one would have to give as much time to the study of it as the author gave to its composition. That, of course, is an exaggeration; still, to appreciate the full force of every hard hit and sly pinch, even with the help of Mr Courthope's ample commentary, would doubtless require long and laborious study. If you have leisure for it, it might be worth while, because in the process you would get an intimate knowledge of political and literary life in London in Pope's time, and it is always interesting to know how people lived in circumstances different from our own. This is one of the most harmless ways of indulging that love of gossip which is deeply rooted in most human beings.

But without mastering all the details, we may enjoy the 'Dunciad' simply as a work of humorous imagination, the only drawback being the tendency of the author's imagination to carry him into physically disgusting incidents. Pope's original design seems to have been to describe the progress of Dulness from ancient times to his own generation, ascribing all the disasters that happened to learning, such as the burning of the Library of Alexandria and the irruption of the Goths into the Roman empire, as due to the settled and resolute hostility of this goddess, bent upon restoring the dominion that she held while the intellectual world was still in chaos. In this history he could find opportunities for ridiculing the so-called dunces of his own time by describing them and their works as instruments in the hands of the goddess Dulness for accomplishing her purpose. This was probably the germ, the first thought, of the poem; so that the third book, from l. 70 onwards, was probably the first part thought of, if not actually the first composed. But the germ grew in Pope's mind; and now this history of the reign of Dulness upon earth appears only as a prophecy made to the hero of the poem. Book I. describes the abode and the surroundings of Dulness in mock-heroic style, but with real splendour of imagination; the goddess sits wreathed in clouds in a certain part of the city of London, with her Prime Ministers and all the products of her leaden inspiration round her. Then the hero, Colley Cibber, is described offering prayers and sacrifices to the goddess. She hears him and carries him off to her sacred dome, and anoints and proclaims him King of the

Dunces. Book II. describes the games held in honour of his coronation, a burlesque of the heroic custom. Much of this you had better skip; but towards the end there is an account of a reading match among critics that is very amusing. Book III. is chiefly occupied with a vision of the progress of Dulness. After the games the king falls asleep in the lap of the goddess, and visits in his dreams—after the manner of Ulysses in the 'Odyssey' and Æneas in the 'Æneid'—the nether regions, where he meets Settle, a dull poet of the previous generation. Settle talks to him, and takes him to the top of a mountain, whence he shows him the past triumphs of the empire of Dulness, then the present, and lastly the future. Book IV. was added by Pope many years afterwards (in 1742), and professes to be the completion of the prophecies in Book III. The goddess sits in state, surrounded by her flatterers and parasites; various public bodies appear by deputation before her, and report progress. The conclusion is intensely comical; in the middle of a gracious speech from the throne her majesty yawns, and the whole world follows suit and sinks into slumber:—

> "More she had spoke, but yawn'd.   All nature nods:
> What mortal can resist the yawn of gods?
> Churches and chapels instantly it reached
> (St James's first, for leaden G—— preached);
> Then catch'd the schools; the hall scarce kept awake;
> The convocation gap'd, but could not speak:
> Lost was the nation's sense, nor could be found,
> While the long solemn unison went round;
> Wide, and more wide, it spread o'er all the realm;
> Ev'n Palinurus nodded at the helm;
> The vapour mild o'er each committee crept;
> Unfinished treaties in each office slept;
> And chiefless armies dozed out the campaign;
> And navies yawned for orders on the main."

Apart from the mere personalities of the poem, most of the Dunces satirised are types that reappear in every age. On this ground some critics claim for the poem a universal utility, and praise Pope for having rendered permanent service in the warfare of true literature against counterfeit. This fantastic Pope showed himself perfectly sensible that, in so far as concerned the annihila-

tion of Dunces, his work had been written in vain. Even of the
men ridiculed by name, Pope says :—

> " You think this cruel ? take it for a rule
> No creature smarts so little as a fool.
> Who shames a scribbler? breaks one cobweb thro',
> He spins the slight, self-pleasing thread anew :
> .   .   .   .
> Throned in the centre of his thin designs,
> Proud of a vast extent of flimsy lines,
> Whom have I hurt? has Poet yet, or Peer,
> Lost the arch'd eyebrow, or Parnassian sneer ? "

And if this was true of the Dunces expressly ridiculed, who is
likely in after-generations to take their characters to himself?
Mr Courthope specifies three classes of Dunces in the poem : the
authors of personal scurrilities in the journals of the day, who
took great liberties with eminent names, in the same coarse vein
in which Pope replied to them; the party journalists, whom Pope,
as a member of the Opposition, considered to be in ministerial
pay; and pedantic scholars, antiquaries, and naturalists. In the
pursuit of ridicule, Pope was not particular about truth to nature,
and there are two men in particular whose place in the 'Dunciad'
has generally been considered absurd, Cibber and Bentley, the
great classical scholar. Cibber was a popular actor, and he protested that his greatest enemy could not call him dull; he was
nothing, if not lively. But Pope did not mean by *dull* the opposite
of lively. Dulness, he says in his lines about Cibber—

> " Dulness with transport eyed the lively dunce,
> Remembering she herself was pertness once."

It is not indeed easy to say what he did mean by dull, except un-
interesting to himself. The story is told of him that he once fell
asleep at his own dinner-table when the Prince of Wales was talking to him about poetry. With such a man the Dull must have
been a very wide category. I am afraid he would have considered
the critical study of the 'Dunciad' insufferably dull, if it had
been written by anybody but himself. It would seem indeed
as if, in the end, he had come to much the same conclusion as
Thackeray in his 'Book of Snobs.' When Thackeray had carefully

studied all the varieties of snob, he could not resist the humorous conclusion that he might after all be a snob himself. And something of the same humour seems to me to have crossed Pope's mind before he had completed his 'Dunciad.' It is a dull world, and we are all dunces more or less.

We have left little time for Pope's remaining works—the 'Essay on Man,' the 'Moral Essays,' and the 'Satires' and 'Epistles.' As regards the origin or suggestion of them, they are as much due to the influence of Bolingbroke as the 'Dunciad' was to Swift and Arbuthnot. Then there are the theological and moral controversies. One little circumstance that has not been remarked probably contributed to set Pope at work in this new direction. In the year in which he finished his 'Odyssey,' Young, afterwards the author of 'Night Thoughts,' published a satire called 'The Universal Passion, or The Love of Fame.' It is a very unequal production, but it was immensely popular for a time. This may have excited Pope's emulation, more particularly seeing that the satirist—Pope having then been engaged for ten years on Homer —asked, Why slumbers Pope?

As regards the substance. If you wish to make a study of the 'Essay on Man,' which professes to furnish in verse a system of natural theology, I would recommend you to Mark Pattison's edition. Moral maxims tend to become antiquated. Pope's are old enough to be commonplace, but not old enough to be quaint. In the 'Moral Essays' the one you may perhaps find the most interesting is that on "The Characters of Women." His standpoint is stated with perfect candour in the opening lines :—

> "Nothing so true as what you once let fall,
> 'Most women have no characters at all,'
> Matter too soft a lasting mark to bear,
> And best distinguished by black, brown, or fair."

And again in the lines :—

> "In men, we various ruling passions find ;
> In women, two almost divide the kind ;
> Those, only fix'd, they first or last obey,
> The love of pleasure, and the love of sway."

In these statements Pope repeats a commonplace of his day, and if objection be taken to them we must bear in mind that we are not to look in satire for sober, strict truth, but rather for brilliant paradoxes. The theory of a Ruling Passion is probably a correct one, and it has been misunderstood by adverse critics. Macaulay, in his essay on Mme. D'Arblay, calls it a silly notion, his own theory being that each man is a compound of desires often at war with one another, one having the ascendancy sometimes, and sometimes another, each uppermost by turns like the spokes of a running wheel, or the sails of a windmill, or balls playing in a fountain. Where is Shylock's ruling passion? he asks. Or Othello's? or Henry V.'s?

The theory is declared to be at variance with the diversity of nature. Rightly understood, it was not so. Its advocates only contended that, however various might be the passions of mankind, however often they might come in conflict, still there was one before which, when it came to a fight, every other yielded. Understanding the theory in this way, we should have no hesitation in saying that Shylock had a ruling passion—the hatred of a persecuted race for its persecutors. Even his love of money gives way before this, as his affection for his daughter gives way before his love of money. The strength of his ruling passion is indeed indicated by its triumph over the passion next to the throne when the two come in conflict. He has few opportunities, only one indeed in the course of the play, of obtaining substantial gratification for it; that one he eagerly and fiercely seizes on.

It cannot, of course, be said that such a passion is the key to all the mysteries of a man's nature; that is, of course, a rhetorical expression. But a knowledge of it may be a clue to the secret of a man's deviations from the rules of ordinary prudence or ordinary good feeling. It is seldom that one overgrown propensity swallows up all the rest. True; but unless this is the case, the character attracts no interest, because it possesses no singularity, nothing to distinguish it from the mass of mankind, whose ruling passion is selfishness tempered by sympathetic impulse, and fear of what people will say and do. That this is the right interpretation of the theory, you can prove by taking Pope's examples. It explains a man's singularities,—gives unity to his peculiarities as distinguished from others.

CHAPTER VII.

POETRY BETWEEN POPE AND COWPER.

GLOVER—JOHNSON—COLLINS—THE POET AND THE ORATOR—GRAY.

I PROPOSE to-day to run rapidly over the poetry of the forty years, roughly speaking, between Pope and Cowper, Crabbe and Burns, dwelling more particularly on the poetry of Gray and Collins. This period is generally and justly regarded as one of the most barren in our literature. The poems that have any interest, except for the antiquary, are few and far between. Collins and Gray wrote very little, very much less than any poets of equal rank in literature,—the one dying young, and the other composing at rare intervals. Small as their poetry is in amount, it stands out above the level of the time, owing to its originality and individuality: all the others may be roughly classed as imitators either of Pope or of Thomson, or of both.

If we look at the works of the young poets who ventured to publish during the last years of Pope's life, what principally strikes us is that, with the exception of Gray and Collins, the ablest of them were guided in their aims by the poetical ambitions of Queen Anne society. One youth, a London merchant, Richard Glover, was bold enough to attempt what Pope shrank from, the composition of a great epic. The subject was taken from Greek history, but the poet throughout had an allusive eye to contemporary politics. This reference to practical affairs was thoroughly in the Queen Anne spirit, when the poets, as I explained to you, being intimate companions of public men, took sides in party conflicts, and kept in view the assistance of their friends at least as much as the satisfaction of the poetical aspirations of their readers. Glover's hero was Leonidas, the Spartan king who sacrificed himself at Thermopylæ to hold in check the Persian invaders of Greece; and the grasping tyrant Xerxes was the great enemy against whom the hero had to contend. But Glover the poet was an ally of the politicians opposed to Sir Robert Walpole, and one of the accusations against this Minister, urged most persistently by the Opposition to drive him from power, was that he truckled to the power of Spain, meekly negotiating and compromising British interests when a true patriot would have had recourse to war. Hence when Glover wrote in denunciation of the power of Persia, it was the power of Spain that he had in his mind's eye; and when he eloquently expounded through Spartan senators the true duty of a patriot, the readers were expected to apply this as an argument against Sir Robert Walpole. "The plan and purpose of 'Leonidas,'" it was said, "is to show the superiority of freedom over slavery, and how much virtue, public spirit, and liberty, are preferable both in their nature and effects to riches, luxury, and the insolence of power." Incidentally the poet found opportunity to discuss many of the burning questions—treatment of the non-combatants in war, superiority of a citizen army over mercenaries. 'Leonidas' had thus great temporary popularity. Viewed simply as an artistic production, its great novelty was that, although professing to be a great epic, it had no supernatural machinery. "Never was an epic poem," Lord Lyttelton wrote, "which had so near a relation to common-sense. He has neither fighting gods nor scolding goddesses; neither miracles nor enchantments; neither monsters nor giants in his work; but whatever human nature can afford that is most astonishing, marvellous, and sublime." The metre of the poem was blank verse, modelled on Thomson's. But in the laboured descriptions of scenery he is much less definite in his pictures than Thomson; in fact, Glover's descriptions show all the faults of the conventional style.

> " The plain beyond Thermopylæ is girt
> Half round by mountains, half by Neptune laved.
> The arduous ridge is broken deep in clefts

> Which open channels to pellucid streams
> In rapid flow sonorous. Chief in fame,
> Spercheos, boasting once his poplars tall,
> Foams down a stony bed. *Throughout the face*
> Of this broad champaign, numberless are pitched
> Barbarian tents. Along the winding flood
> To rich Thessalia's confines they extend.
> They fill the vallies, late profusely blest
> In Nature's vary'd beauties."

Then after enumerating the shrubs, flowerets, ivy, lawn, poplar-groves torn up, cut down, trampled by the barbarian invaders, he goes on :—

> " Yet unpolluted, is a part reserved
> In this deep vale, a patrimonial spot
> Of Aleuadian princes, who, allies
> To Xerxes, reign'd in Thessaly. There glow
> Inviolate the shrubs. There branch the trees,
> Sons of the forest. Over downy moss,
> Smooth walks and fragrant, lucid here and broad,
> There clos'd in myrtle under woodbine roofs
> Wind to retreats delectable, to grots,
> To silvan structures, bow'rs, and cooling dells
> Enliven'd all and musical, with birds
> Of vocal sweetness, in relucent plumes
> Innumerably various. Lulling falls
> Of liquid crystal, from perennial founts
> Attune their pebbled channels."

However long you study this description you will not be able to realise any landscape that was definitely before the poet's vision when he wrote: there is a certain vague framework of scenery, but when the poet comes to details, he puts us off with conventional oft-repeated phrases for natural grandeurs and beauties— the laving Neptune, arduous ridges, pellucid and sonorous streams, winding floods, Nature's varied beauties, downy moss, retreats delectable, grots, silvan structure, bowers, and cooling dells. The poet, in short, only gives us musical phrases for what the senses find in nature, thus dressing these charms to advantage; there is nothing in his landscapes of the life that the human imagination in moments of excitement is apt to ascribe to the face of Nature. Read the Prologue to Act iv. of " Henry V." and you will understand the difference.

There is one poem of Glover's — "London, or the Progress of Commerce"—that illustrates the fashionable poetical style of the Queen Anne time,—the prevalent idea as to how Nature was to be dressed to advantage. As a London merchant, Glover no doubt felt his heart swell within him as he looked at the bustle of many nations on the London wharves, and saw ships from many distant regions crowding up the Thames. How did he give expression to this exaltation of mind? He could not present the coarse and vulgar details of trade to a fine Queen Anne gentleman; he asks his reader to look at them through a fine allegorical veil, transports us to the regions of mythology, and gives a long narrative of a love affair between the sea-god Neptune and the nymph named Phœnice, the guardian spirit of the Phœnicians. The beautiful nymph Commerce was the offspring of this Union. This is the poet's way of relating the prosaic fact that the Phœnicians were the first great traders by sea; and the events in the subsequent history of Commerce are given as incidents in the life of the nymph Commerce, from her cradle and her nursery till the time when she fixed her abode in Great Britain.

Among the followers of Pope in Satire there is only one name of distinction, Samuel Johnson, afterwards the great prose moralist, critic, and lexicographer. The critic made his mark in literature by a poem; but he is one of the exceptions to the saying that the critics are the men who have failed in literature, for his imitation of Juvenal was a success. It was natural that Johnson should choose Juvenal as his model while Pope adopted the style of Horace. Horace was the gay light-hearted satirist of the foibles of the literary and fashionable society of Rome; whereas Juvenal took a more stern and gloomy view of life, lashed the vices of his age in a spirit of moral indignation, contrasted the miseries of the poor with the ostentatious splendour of the rich in Roman society, and denounced heartlessness, dishonesty, sycophancy, — all the vices of a wealthy and showy civilisation,—with bitter and unsparing scorn. There was nearly as much difference between them as between Tom Moore and Carlyle. Pope, himself in easy circumstances, and the friend of noblemen and statesmen, naturally had most sympathy with Horace's view of life; while Johnson, then living in London, as Carlyle describes him, on fourpence halfpenny a-day, and earning a precarious livelihood as a bookseller's drudge, as naturally thought of Juvenal as a model, and resolved to apply to modern circumstances the sarcasms of this satirist on the Roman metropolis.

"Slow rises worth by poverty depressed,"

is one of the lines in Johnson's "London." He had fitter experience of the fact in the insolence and indifference of busy employers, too closely occupied with other affairs to have time, if they had had the insight, to detect his great talent. As far as versification goes, Johnson proved himself an apt pupil of Pope; nobody since has equalled him in combining Pope's terseness with Pope's smoothness. And in one respect Johnson even might be said to have surpassed Pope, if Pope's object had been merely to imitate the ancient Roman. Johnson is at more pains to find exact modern parallels to the ancient situations, and is always felicitous in the turn he gives to Juvenal's phrases. But the truth is that he went to work rather as a scholar than as a satirist. Indignation at the vices satirised was much less a motive with him than the scholar's ambition to make a clever adaptation of the original. Hence although his "London" attracted some attention, and Pope, always generous as well as right in his judgments of genuine literary merit, prophesied that the author would not long remain unknown, there was little real vitality in the poem. It was really an imitation, owing much of its interest to the original, and often appearing destitute of motive when not read in connection with the original. Pope's so-called imitations, on the other hand, are equally interesting to the reader whether or not he is acquainted with Horace; the reader perhaps may get additional pleasure from observing the cleverness of the parallel, but the satire has independent point and relish. There is more of Johnson's genuine sentiment in the "Vanity of Human Wishes," another imitation of Juvenal, published ten years later.

For eminence in poetry, novelty and distinction are first requisites; and during Pope's closing years the only poets that began to show capability of poetic work that should be at once distinctive in power or spirit and high in quality, were Gray and Collins. The great novelty of their work as compared with Pope's was that it was lyrical; they wrote mostly in that form of poetry which is called the Ode.

You are doubtless familiar with some, at least, of Gray's poems. You all know the "Elegy." But the "Elegy" was not the work on which he most prided himself, or upon which he would have desired his rank as a poet to be adjudicated. It was instantaneously, and has always since been popular, but he considered that the popularity was due to the subject as much as to the art of the poet. The "Ode on the Distant Prospect of Eton College," the "Hymn on Adversity," the "Progress of Poesy," and "The Bard," were his masterpieces in point of artistic construction. It may increase your interest in them if I point out a few respects in which these lyrics differ from other lyric poetry in our language—*i.e.*, poetry in which the poet gives expression directly to emotion, instead of describing outward nature, or narrating events, or putting words into the mouths of characters whose actions are represented on the stage.

But, perhaps, I had better speak of Collins first, as he is less known, and there is one poem of his which I can confidently recommend to you as certain to yield you the highest delight, if you take the trouble to master its intricate harmonies. Of his life there is little to be told, and that little is painful. Born in 1721, and educated at Oxford, he went to London in 1744, the year of Pope's death, as a literary adventurer, at a time when only one man, and that Pope, had succeeded in making literature a profitable profession. He had not Johnson's endurance, or his practical talents; a youth—strange phenomenon for those who take the conventional view of the eighteenth century—of fantastic imagination, with not a little of the temperament of Shelley, delighting, as Johnson puts it, "to rove through the meanders of enchantment, to gaze on the magnificence of golden palaces, to repose by the waterfalls of Elysian gardens." Two years before he went up to London he had published a volume of poems, 'Persian Eclogues,' Persian Pastorals, reconciling, as you will observe, the taste of the time for pastorals with the inclination of his own fancy towards the gorgeous East. For such a man the booksellers had little employment; and as he had but scanty means of subsistence except by his pen, he gave way in the struggle for existence: he bore up for a little against clouds that he felt to be gathering on his reason, was confined for some time in a madhouse, and died at the age of thirty-nine, in the year of Burns' birth, 1759.

Collins is best known by his Ode on "The Passions," but incomparably his finest and most distinctive work is the "Ode to Evening." The superior popularity of "The Passions" is easily explained. It might be recited at a penny reading, and every line of its strenuous rhetoric would tell; every touch would be at once appreciated. But the beauties of the "Ode to Evening" are of a much stronger kind, and the structure of it is infinitely more complicated:—

" If aught of oaten stop, or pastoral song,
    May hope, chaste Eve, to soothe thy modest ear,
        Like thy own solemn springs,
        Thy springs, and dying gales;

    .   .   .   .

Now air is hush'd, save where the weak-ey'd bat,
With short, shrill shriek flits by on leathern wing,
    Or when the beetle winds
    His small but sullen horn,

As oft he rises 'midst the twilight path,
Against the pilgrim borne in heedless hum:
    Now teach me, maid compos'd,
    To breathe some softened strain,

Whose numbers, stealing through thy darkening vale,
May not unseemly with its stillness suit,
    As musing slow, I hail
    Thy genial lov'd return!

    .   .   .   .

While Spring shall pour his showers, as oft he wont,
And bathe thy breathing tresses, meekest Eve!
    While Summer loves to sport
    Beneath thy lingering light:

While sallow Autumn fills thy lap with leaves,
Or Winter, yelling through the troublous air,
    Affrights thy shrinking train,
    And rudely rends thy robes:

> So long, regardful of thy quiet rule,
> Shall Fancy, Friendship, Science, smiling Peace,
>   Thy gentlest influence own,
>   And love thy favourite name !"

It gains nothing from being read aloud. It is a poem to be taken into the mind slowly; you cannot take possession of it without effort. Give a quiet evening to it; return to it again and again ; master the meaning of it deliberately part by part, and let the whole sink into your mind softly and gradually, and you will not regret the labour. You will find yourselves in possession of a perpetual delight, of a music that will make the fall of evening for ever charming to you. Difficulty is not necessarily a virtue in a poem, but neither is it necessarily a defect. The poet who fixes a rare and evanescent mood in harmonious rhythm and imagery, thus making it a permanent possibility for the human race, cannot always build his new and delightful home for the imagination out of common materials, and the workmanship with which he adorns it may be curious and intricate. Such a pleasure-house is often built up by abstruse workings of the imagination, in regions far above the prosaic level, and the spirit must shake off its natural slothfulness before it can rise with the poet and enter into and take possession of the home that he has made for it.

A distinction has been drawn between the poet and the orator. The poet, it has been said, is essentially an egotist, expressing what he feels without caring how it may affect others ; whereas the orator is essentially a sympathetic man, always considering the effect of his expression upon others, striving to look at what he says from their point of view, or, as Mr Gladstone once put it, receiving from his audience in a vapour what he gives back to them in a flood. I confess that I don't attach much value to such distinctions. They are always half-truths. Nearly everything that has been said by poets in the way of general truth about poetry is not even quarter-truth, because each puts his own prac- tice as if it were a universal rule. All poets express their own emotions, more or less, and all poets are more or less influenced by their audience. Still the degree in which they are self-centred, or liable to be disturbed by outside influence, constitutes a marked difference in character, and, properly qualified, this distinction between the poet and the orator serves to illustrate the difference between Collins and Gray. It is this difference that Mr Swinburne has in his mind when he says that, "as a lyric poet, Gray is unworthy to sit at the feet of Collins," and that "there was but one man in the time of Collins who had in him a note of pure lyric song, a pulse of inborn music irresistible and indubitable"—namely, Collins himself. Comparatively speaking, Collins sang to gratify his own feelings, beginning when the impulse was on him, and leaving off when he was satisfied; Gray considered in what mood his song would find his audience, how he could seize their attention, how sustain and increase it, and how leave them deeply impressed at the end. Gray, in short, wrote with a deliberate eye to the effect to be produced on his reader.

Even in the "Elegy," which reads like a spontaneous outburst of feeling, this is apparent if you look at the construction of it. You will find a regular symmetrical division in it, an arrangement of facts such that the reader, though he passes from one train of thought to another, is not kept too long in one mood, not wearied by reflections in the same vein. The variety is studied and carefully proportioned. Gray deliberately suppressed one stanza, because to have put it in would have made too long a parenthesis :—

> "There scattered oft, the earliest of the year,
> By hands unseen are show'rs of violets found ;
> The redbreast loves to build and warble there,
> And little footsteps lightly print the ground."

The stanza is beautiful in itself,—some have gone so far as to say that it contains purer poetry than any of the stanzas that were retained ; but Gray decided that it would be out of proportion, and sacrificed it.

In the "Eton College," again, the change from emotion to emotion, the balance of the parts, the pathetic humour of the conclusion, which recalls and binds together and suffuses the whole, must strike everybody who reflects for a moment on the construction of the poem. The effect of the whole, and of each part as contributing to the whole, has been elaborately calculated—elaborately, and yet with such vividness of emotional insight that there is no trace of labour. Stanza follows stanza as if by spontaneous growth, and the concluding reflection arises as if by irresistible suggestion.

It has been made a point of distinction between Gray and the lyric poets of this century, Wordsworth and Byron more particularly, that in their lyrics they express purely personal emotion, feelings peculiar to themselves. They take us into confidence, as it were, about their own concerns, and invite our sympathy, which we cannot give unless we sympathise with their characters. Gray, on the other hand, suppresses himself, and strives to interpret emotions that all men must feel in presence of the subject of his verse. This is certainly true of the "Elegy" and the "Ode on Eton College." These are not expressions of individual feeling, like Byron's "Farewell to England," or some of Wordsworth's "Solitary Reaper"; they express melancholy and humorous reflections common to all mankind, as common as the fact of death and the heedless enjoyment of the present by the young.

But it is dangerous to generalise about poets. The emotions to which lyrical expression is given in the "Progress of Poesy" and the "Bard" are as purely individual as the most singular of Wordsworth's meditations on rustic life. Johnson's criticisms of these wonderful wonders of wonders, as he called them, are savage and unsparing. Sometimes this is attributed to personal jealousy. It is a superficial view, and unjust to the great critic. It is true that Johnson manifests a good-humoured contempt for Gray's character. We can easily understand this when we consider the circumstances of the two men. Gray was a Fellow of a College in Cambridge, precise, finicking, and reserved in manner. The dignified little man had few intimates; he was a great reader, a scholar of marvellously wide range, reputed the most learned man in Europe. But, as Johnson saw and said, he did very little with his learning. Five or six poems was not a great result of so much reading. We can easily understand that the indefatigable producer under difficulties, the sturdy, strenuous, companionable giant of Bolt Court, Fleet Street,—a very different locality from Peterhouse, Cambridge, —would have little sympathy with such a man. Beneath Gray's reserved exterior there was great depth of feeling; and with all his minute scholarship, he was a man of large and comprehensive views. Constitutional melancholy and self-distrust seem to have been the secrets of his small amount of production.   But this was not known fully to the world till after his death.   He never spoke out during his life.   Any apparent injustice done him by Johnson was due to a want of knowledge that was not possible to Johnson when he wrote.   And as regards the Odes, we can understand Johnson's want of sympathy without ascribing any part of it to personal jealousy.   They appeal really to scholars and historians. The Greek motto fixed to the "Progress of Poesy" signifies that they are vocal only to the initiated.   There is not a line that is not charged with a historical allusion.   So marvellous is the rhythm that single stanzas may be read with delight; but the significance of the whole demands study.   The substance of them is a series of ecstatic visions of historical events,—of the personal emotions felt by a historian who was also a man of feeling and imagination.   The "Bard" is full of alliteration and personification, and exemplifies the rhetoric of Gray.   There is a quick transition, when the Bard foretells the accession of the House of Tudor and the glory of Elizabeth :—

> " ' But oh ! what solemn scenes on Snowdon's height
>   Descending slow their glitt'ring skirts unroll.
> 'Visions of glory, spare my aching sight,
>   Ye unborn Ages, crowd not on my soul !
>   No more our long lost Arthur we bewail.
>   All hail, ye genuine Kings, Britannia's Issue, hail !'
> ' In the midst a Form divine ;
>   Her lyon-port, her awe-commanding face,
>   Attempered sweet to virgin-grace.
>   What strings symphonious tremble in the air,
>   What strains of vocal transport round her play !
>   Hear from the grave, great Taliessin, hear ;
>   They breathe a soul to animate thy clay.
>   Bright Rapture calls, and soaring, as she sings,
>   Waves in the eye of Heav'n her many-colour'd wings.' "

CHAPTER VIII.

DECLINE OF POETRY—THE NOVEL.

WALPOLE'S CRITICISM—WHY THE WANT OF POETRY WAS NOT FELT—DIARY OF A LADY OF QUALITY—RISE OF THE NOVEL—'PAMELA'—CONNECTION WITH MAGAZINE LITERATURE—FIELDING—HISTORICAL NOVELS—'THE CASTLE OF OTRANTO.'

I GAVE some account in my last lecture of the great poets of the middle part of the eighteenth century. Why there was such a scarcity of good poetry during that period is a question that admits of great diversity of opinion : that there was a scarcity of it is a matter of fact, and it was felt at the time. In this as in most other social facts there were probably several causes at work. One of these causes is very plainly hinted at in a contemporary letter by a very shrewd observer, Horace Walpole, second son of the great Prime Minister. Writing to his friend Sir Horace Mann in 1742, he said : "If you did amuse yourself with writing any-thing in poetry, you know how pleased I should be to see it, but for encouraging you to it, d'ye see, 'tis an age most unpoetical ! 'Tis even a test of wit to dislike poetry; and though Pope has half-a-dozen old friends that he has preserved from the taste of last century, yet I assure you the generality of readers are more diverted with any paltry prose answer to old Marlborough's secret history of Queen Mary's robes. I do not think an author would be universally commended for any production in verse, unless it were an ode to the Secret Committee, with rhymes of liberty and property, nation and administration."

This is in effect to say that, in the opinion of Horace Walpole, fashionable society was too much occupied with politics to have any interest to spare for poetry. To understand how this was possible, we must remember that political power was then confined to a very narrow circle. It was not, as you are aware, till nearly a century afterwards that the middle classes, the commercial classes, obtained a share of political influence. The men who had any chance of a voice in the management of the affairs of the nation were the men whose wives and daughters constituted polite society in the metropolis—"the town," as they called themselves. And intrigues were incessantly going on to keep Ministers on or put Ministers out, in all which the wives and daughters took a keen interest. The affairs of the State were the affairs of the town, and had an exclusive absorbing and personal interest that they no longer possess for any single section of the community now. Hence the literature that had most direct interest for the town was political, and a damaging attack on a Minister, a piece of scandal or argument, whether in prose or in verse, was apt to eclipse any production that depended for its effect on the interest peculiar to poetry.

The absorbing interest in politics among those who were at the time the chief patrons, promoters, and consumers of literature was probably one of the causes of the poetic barrenness of the middle of the eighteenth century. This political interest was fed and nourished by the press, with a regular supply, weekly, bi-weekly, and daily.

Among the other things that may be mentioned as taking the place of poetry among the enjoyments of a life of leisure at this time is the stage. Queen Anne and her Ministers exerted themselves to purify and reform the stage. Under Charles II. ladies went to the theatre masked, and things were spoken that were not very fit for them to hear. Queen Anne prohibited the wearing of masks, and instituted a moral censorship of plays, insisting that everything intended for public performance should first be submitted to the Lord Chamberlain. That official was not so particular as he is now, but there was a marked improvement in the morality of plays. The theatre took a more important place among fashionable amusements. It has not, I think, been remarked that the dreariest period in the poetic annals of the eighteenth century

is almost exactly coincident with the career of David Garrick.
You will see how a powerful counter-attraction at the theatre,
such as would occupy the serious attention of intellectually disposed people, would diminish the demand for poetry, and rob the
poet of that devoted sympathy in the absence of which he cannot
work with full power, if you consider for a little how people of
leisure at that time distributed their day. There is an amusing
paper in the 'Spectator,' No. 323, which professes to give the
diary of a lady of quality. It is of course a caricature, but it
gives us an idea of the arrangement of a fashionable day, of the
hours that were kept by fashionable people :—

"*From three to four.*—Dined. Mrs Kitty called upon me to go to the
Opera before I was risen from table.

"*From dinner to six.*—Drank tea. Turned off a footman for being rude
to Veny.

"*Six o'clock.*—Went to the Opera. I did not see Mr Froth till the beginning of the second act. Mr Froth talked to a gentleman in a black wig.
Bowed to a lady in the front box. Mr Froth and his friend clapped Nicolini
in the third act. Mr Froth cried out Ancora. Mr Froth led me to my
chair. I think he squeezed my hand.

"*Eleven at night.*—Went to bed. Melancholy dreams. Methought
Nicolini said he was Mr Froth."

The morning was spent in reading, if there was anything to
read, playing with pets, seeing to the dressmaker, shopping,
going to church, the mid-day service at St Paul's, where the
music was good, being especially fashionable. Half-past two
or three was the dinner-hour. After dinner was the time for
making calls or walking in the Mall; and in the evening there
were public entertainments and private assemblies. There was
probably then a greater separation than exists now in the
social amusements of men and women :. after dinner the men
went to the coffee-houses if they did not go to the play, and
the women went to tea-parties, where throughout the greater
part of the century card-playing was the chief alternative to
scandal and other small talk. The theatres opened at five o'clock,
and the entertainment lasted till nine. You will thus see that
the theatre filled an important gap in the day ; and that when it
was the rage, it was likely to absorb not a little of fashionable
interest. Under Garrick, revivals of Shakespearean plays were

the great theatrical events; earlier in the century, revivals of
Dryden. The morning was the chief time for reading. Addison's
lady of quality on two of her mornings read Dryden's "Aurungzebe,
or the Indian Emperor"; if she had lived thirty years later, she
would probably have spent the same time over Shakespeare. Can
you wonder that such solemn ponderosities as Johnson's "London "
or " Vanity of Human Wishes," or such intricate harmonies and
sublimities as Collins's " Ode to Evening " or Gray's " Progress of
Poesy," failed to arrest general attention when the vacant hours
of the morning could be spent in reading the thrilling scenes of
"Richard III." or "Othello," and the evening in seeing Shakespeare's heroes impersonated by the most original modern actors?
The town naturally yielded to the greatest attraction, and there
was no body of readers outside this fashionable society in whose
sympathy the poet might find nourishment.

Two kinds of literature, then, imperatively claimed a portion of
the hours available for reading in the reigns of the first Georges,—
political journals and plays. People in society were bound to read
these, because they were talked about; and not to know them or
appear to know them was to have nothing to say, or no grace in
listening. And there was a third kind which became prominent
in the second ten years of George II.'s reign, about the time when
Pope published the last of his Satires. This was the novel. New
forms of literature, as I have before said, always have the advantage in freshness and force of interest over old forms. The novel
appeared in a new form with Richardson's ' Pamela ' in 1740.
About the time when Horace Walpole wrote the letter from which
I quoted at the beginning of the lecture, ladies at Ranelagh Gardens, then one of the fashionable resorts, were holding up to each
other their copies of ' Pamela,' to show that they had in their possession the most popular book of the day. The industrious antiquarian has cast doubt upon the literal truth of this story, pointing out that Ranelagh Gardens were not opened to the public till
eighteen months after ' Pamela ' had begun to run through many
editions. Vauxhall, however, was open, if Ranelagh was not, and
the incident may have been observed there. At any rate, the fact
expressed by the story is true enough, that ' Pamela ' was at once
and universally popular. In January 1741, the editor of the

'Gentleman's Magazine' wrote as follows: "Several encomiums on a series of Familiar Letters, published but last month, entitled 'Pamela, or Virtue Rewarded,' came too late for this Magazine, and we believe there will be little occasion for inserting them in our next; because a Second Edition will then come out to supply the Demands of the Country, it being judged in town as great a sign of want of curiosity not to have read 'Pamela,' as not to have seen the *French* and *Italian* Dancers." This testimony is almost as quaint and significant as the story about Ranelagh Gardens. Books must be new in form as well as in substance before they create such a *furore* as that indicates. There has been nothing like it in my time. The nearest approach I recollect is J. R. Green's 'Short History of the English People.' Fashionable ladies carried it about with them on their visits to country-houses.

Richardson has long received the honour of being regarded as the founder of the English Novel, but of late it has been customary to go a little further back, and trace the beginnings of the novel in the papers by Addison and Steele in the 'Tatler' and the 'Spectator.' The novel, it is said, was developed, not created, by Richardson. Now this is hardly fair to the ingenious printer, if it is meant to deny him the credit of having invented or stumbled upon a new species of composition—the novel of manners, stories in which the characters are drawn from ordinary domestic life, and of which the interest lies in picturing how they affect one another and how they are affected by circumstances. It is true that the novel was developed and not created; but it is not more true of Richardson's novel than of any other new species of composition, such as Marlowe's tragedy, or Scott's romantic tale, or Byron's personal epic. All alike are developed, not created, in the sense of having many affinities with the kind of literature immediately anterior to them. Thus in the novel of manners there are two elements—there is a description of ordinary character and there is plot-interest—*i.e.*, there is a story. Both of these elements are found in the generation before Richardson, but not in combination. It was he who combined them in his novel of manners, and therefore is he entitled to the praise of having invented a new species of composition.

You will find abundant descriptions of manners in the 'Spectator,' and many delicate studies of character. Whoever wishes to get a living knowledge of the Queen Anne time must give evenings to the 'Spectator,' and observe the incidents that are pictured as occurring in the shops and the streets and the places of amusement, at balls and tea-tables and dinner-tables, and the private sanctuaries where fine ladies issue adorned for conquest. The quiet 'Spectator' penetrated everywhere. Especially in the letters from fictitious correspondents—from Jenny Simper, Aurelia Careless, Betty Cross-stitch, Constantine Comb-brush, Florinda, Corinna Jeraminta, Jack Courtly, Toby Rentfree, Will Cymon, Dick Lovesick, and so forth—you will find many happy studies of manner and character, many of the touches of nature that make all the world kin. But there is no story to weave the detached studies together. We learn how Jenny Simper—being, as she described herself, a young woman with her fortune to make—went to church, and was much aggrieved because the clerk of the parish, an ex-gardener, wreathed the pews so thickly with evergreens that she could not make eyes at the desirable baronet during the service; but it had not occurred to anybody to make a heroine out of Jenny Simper, or a hero out of the baronet, or a story out of incidents within the probabilities of ordinary life. There were stories to read in the days of Queen Anne; there have been stories from the very beginning of literature; but they were of a different kind from the stories told in novels of manners. There were, in the first place, the great long-winded romances, full of amazing adventures, heroes of superhuman strength and courage and generosity, and heroines of surpassing beauty and constancy. The sceptical spirit had banished them from polite society in town, but they still lingered in the country and in the less enlightened strata of middle-class life, and, on the whole, perhaps did good with all their unreality, through their high standard of ideal conduct. There were stories of another kind, stories of fashionable intrigue, to which the name of novel was sometimes given—stories that served no good purpose. Finally—though this was not in the reign of Queen Anne, but in the reign of her successor George I.—there came the novels of adventure and crime—the invention of Defoe.

Richardson did not invent stories any more than he invented the description of manners, but that does not in the least detract from the originality of his invention of the domestic novel,—a story of incidents all within the area of possible occurrences in everyday life. The idea of writing such a story came to him by accident. He was an industrious and prosperous printer,—a stout, rosy, vain, prosy little man, not at all the sort of man that might be expected to be a fashionable novelist. Of poor parentage, he had been apprenticed to a London printer; had spent some years as a press-reader or proof-corrector—not a bad position for acquiring a knowledge of literature; had married his master's daughter, and acquired an extensive business. When he was near the age of fifty some bookseller friends of his, struck perhaps by his excellence as a letter-writer, had suggested to him that he should compose a "familiar letter-writer"—"a little volume of letters in a common style, on such subjects as might be of use to those country readers who were unable to indite for themselves." In his youth, as it happened, Richardson had had a singular experience in the way of writing letters for others. Three young women who could not write had employed him, when he was a boy of thirteen, to conduct their correspondence with their sweethearts, which he did, he tells us, much to the satisfaction of his employers, and without betraying their confidence. This may have been known to the booksellers who suggested his writing a volume of model correspondence. At any rate, he undertook the task. But having a genius for story-telling, it occurred to him, as he turned the project over in his mind, that he might tell a story in a series of letters, which would serve equally well as models for letter-writing, and at the same time cultivate the principles of virtue and religion in the minds of the youth of both sexes. Accordingly, he chose a country girl, Pamela, in the service of a young squire, Mr B., and made her relate in letters to her friends her experiences from day to day and week to week in very trying circumstances. Friends write to advise Pamela in her difficulties, and so the story is carried on with most circumstantial minuteness, Pamela describing with the most careful exactness every particular of what happens to her, and adding her own reflections, surmises, and appeals for approbation and advice. The effect of this method is that, if you have any sympathy with the heroine, you get intensely interested in her perplexities; the very fulness of the details, and the close truth to nature with which the novelist follows every turn in the girl's thoughts, compel you to read on. No one can read over a few scenes from Richardson without feeling that he is a master of his art; but few people now, I imagine, read any of his novels through. It was otherwise in his own generation, when readers had more in common with the thoughts and sentiments of his voluminous descriptive letter-writers. The fame of 'Pamela' made Richardson a great personal favourite, especially with ladies. Several ladies of quality made a pet of him, deluged him with confidences, and urged him to write more; and under their flattering encouragement he produced 'Clarissa Harlowe,' a model of every virtue in higher life, and 'Sir Charles Grandison,' his ideal of a perfect gentleman. 'Clarissa' is universally acknowledged to be his masterpiece. An anecdote was given by Macaulay which shows how entrancing the story may become to readers once fairly caught by the current of it. He took the whole eight volumes with him when he was in India to a hill-station during the hot season, and lent the first volume to the Governor's wife. She read it and lent it to the Governor's secretary, and went to Macaulay for the second. Thus the whole eight volumes passed from hand to hand, and for a week or more the whole station was in a ferment over the fortunes of Clarissa, the readers anxiously waiting their turn for the successive volumes. Richardson is long-winded and prolix to a degree, but that, in spite of all his faults of style, he had the art of interesting his own generation was abundantly proved, and apparently his greatest novel is still capable in favourable circumstances of exerting its spell.

A much more brilliant writer, though a less minute anatomist of ebbs and flows and cross-currents of feeling, was Richardson's great successor and caricaturist, Henry Fielding. Two men more unlike than these two pioneers of the modern novel could not be conceived. Richardson's experiences were all of business life and quiet domestic life. In his voluminous correspondence with lady friends after his sudden leap into fame, which seems not to have disturbed in the least the even tenor of his habits, we have minute pictures of the circumstances in which he wrote his books—sometimes in his backshop in Fleet Street, sometimes in an arbour in his garden at Hammersmith, reading what he had written to the young ladies of his family, talking with them over his characters, judging from their criticisms as the story went on whether he had produced the effects intended. Fielding was a much less domesticated character—a high-spirited, mirth-loving roysterer, the son of a younger son of a noble family, who, when his scanty allowance ran short, or was not paid at all, tried to subsist by writing for the stage and the journals, organised a company of his own, started more than one journal of his own, married a wife and spent her small fortune in a year or two, read for the bar, and obtained an appointment as a police-magistrate, never contriving to make both ends meet, yet never losing his cheerfulness or his generous temper. With all his wit and keen powers of observation, Fielding was probably too much hurried and pressed with the cares and enjoyments of his happy-go-lucky life from day to day to be capable of striking out a new path in literature; and it was by an accident that he fell into the track of the humble tradesmanlike printer, and then discovered a rich field for his genius. When 'Pamela' became the rage, there was much in the sentiment of it that appealed to Fielding's sense of the ludicrous, and he resolved to write a parody. Beginning in this spirit, he wrote a few chapters, more eminent for wit than for delicacy, and then practically abandoned the design of burlesquing Richardson, and went on to describe life as he had seen it in the course of his varied experience, and characters as they presented themselves to his own mind and heart. The life that he described was not always the highest in point of morality, and his characters were not always spotless; but there is this to be said for him as a moralist, that he threw no sentimental halo over vice, that he honoured true worth in manhood and in womanhood, that his Parson Adams, his Squire Allworthy, and his Amelia, are among the most lovable characters in fiction, and that no satirist ever exposed meanness, hypocrisy, and kindred vices with healthier scorn and ridicule. Apart from the substance of his work, his method was very different from Richardson's. He discarded the epistolary way of telling his story. The comic epic was his model. Hence Byron called him the "prose Homer of human nature." And he does not leave his characters to reveal themselves, as the so-called dramatic novelist does,—as Dickens does, for example,—in what they do and say. He makes a running commentary on their conduct as he goes along; button-holing you, as Thackeray puts it, while he conducts you through his picture-gallery, and discoursing familiarly about the creatures of his imagination.

I cannot here enter upon an elaborate criticism of Richardson and Fielding. I wish only to show you their places in literature as the originators of a new species of composition, which, while it was fresh and new, and practised by masters of their art, helped to push poetry out of a foremost place in the minds of the reading public. I would recommend you to read what is said about Fielding by Thackeray in his 'Lectures on the Humourists,' and by Mrs Oliphant on Richardson. I will not dwell upon the immediate successors of these pioneers, Smollett, Sterne, and Goldsmith, but pass on to a novel of a new kind, produced twenty-five years after Richardson's 'Pamela,' Horace Walpole's 'Castle of Otranto.'

It would almost seem as if, after twenty years of the new kind of fiction inaugurated by Richardson, including the masterpieces of Fielding and Smollett and Sterne, the literary appetite began to pine for something new, and to hark back to the old fare of supernatural romance. You must not suppose that the old-fashioned stories were at once extinguished by the new style; they were only pushed into the background, relegated, perhaps, to a less fastidious class of reader. If you look at the lists of published books in old numbers of the 'Gentleman's Magazine,' you will see that publishers still found readers for scandalous stories, for romances such as the 'Adventures of Telemachus,' and for more or less fictitious biographies of eminent criminals. But it was only novels of the new kind that made a conspicuous mark among readers in the height of literary fashion—till the 'Castle of Otranto' appeared, which was professedly an attempt to com-

bine the supernatural incidents of the old romance with the truth
to nature in dialogue and character introduced by the new novel.

It was Horace Walpole's opinion that in the novels of everyday
life, Nature had cramped Imagination. There had been plenty of
invention, but it was invention of scenes such as might occur in
common life: the novelists had excluded themselves from the great
resources of fancy. He thought that, for the sake of greater variety,
the fancy should be left free to "roam through the boundless realms
of invention," and thus have an opportunity of creating more interesting situations. But he freely admitted that it would never
do to go back to the condition of the old romances, in which everything was unnatural,—in which not only the incidents were improbable, but the conduct of the personages in the face of those
incidents fantastic, their language absurdly inflated, their sentiments preposterous. He proposed, therefore, a compromise between the two. He was to have liberty to defy the rules of
probability in the incidents, but he was to bind himself to adhere
to probability in what he made his characters feel and say and do
in the improbable emergencies. Their lot was to be cast in a land of
wonders, of strange apparitions, and miraculous occurrences, but
they were to comport themselves as human beings might be expected to do in the circumstances.

Constructed deliberately on this plan, the 'Castle of Otranto'
founded a new school of fiction. It is called a Gothic Romance,
and the scene is laid in a Gothic castle, with a labyrinth of vaulted
passages beneath it, one of which, by a trap-door, communicates
with a church in the neighbourhood. Manfred, the Prince of
Otranto, is the central figure in the story, a bold and unscrupulous man, though not without redeeming traits in his character.
The title to the principality has been in his family for only two
generations before him, and the title of his grandfather was more
than doubtful. The last prince of the rightful line was Alfonso
the Good, who died in the Holy Land; the Marquis of Vicenza
was the nearest heir, but Manfred's grandfather had forestalled him,
and was powerful enough to keep him out of his own. There was
a mysterious prophecy that Manfred's line would keep possession
till the house had become too small for its rightful owner. Now

naturally there was one point about which Manfred had a morbid anxiety—the preservation of his line. His wife Hippolyte had borne him but two children, a boy and a girl. The boy was a puny sickly child, but Manfred determined to marry him to the only daughter of the rival claimant, the Marquis of Vicenza. He obtained this Lady Isabella from her guardians during her father's absence in the Holy Land, and the supernatural part of the story begins with the preparations for the wedding. The wedding party is assembled in the chapel of the castle, when, to Manfred's intense impatience, it is discovered that the boy-bridegroom—he was only fifteen—is missing. A servant is sent in haste to his apartments on the other side of the court. The servant returns staring, speechless, and foaming at the mouth. Manfred and his retainers rush into the court, and find the poor boy mangled and bleeding, crushed to death by a gigantic helmet of black steel with huge black plumes. The helmet is a hundred times as big as any ever made for mortal man, and the plumes are in proportion, and seemed to fill the courtyard as with a black forest. Manfred is astounded, but, in the depth of his grief and wonder, he has presence of mind enough to say, "Take care of the Lady Isabella "—for a purpose which appears presently. Nobody can tell where the helmet has come from, but in the midst of their conjectures a young peasant remarks that it is exactly like in every respect but size to the helmet on the head of the black marble statue of Alfonso the Good in the church. Manfred flies into a passion. Some of his servants rush to the church, and find that the helmet from Alfonso's statue is gone. The cry is raised that the young peasant, who is a stranger in the place, is a necromancer, and that it is he who, by his black art, has compassed the death of the young prince. Manfred orders him to be confined in the helmet, to starve to death unless his familiars supply him with food. Then Manfred proceeds to carry out a suddenly-formed resolution. The supernatural thwarting of his purpose has maddened him. He will divorce his wife and marry Isabella himself. He sends for Isabella and broaches his design to her. She is horrified. He lays hands on her. Then the plumes on the helmet outside in the courtyard are violently agitated, and rustle against the window accompanied by a low hollow sound. "See," Isabella cries, "Heaven itself declares against your wicked purpose!" "Heaven nor Hell shall prevent me!" he says. At this instant one of the pictures on the wall, the portrait of his grandfather, heaves a deep sigh, and presently walks out of its frame on to the floor.

These examples will give you some idea of how Walpole effected his proposed reconciliation of reality and romance. The only real importance of his work is that it marks a new point of departure from the novel as conceived by Richardson and Fielding.

CHAPTER IX.

THE NOVEL—*continued.*

AT the close of last lecture I mentioned that Walpole's 'Castle of Otranto' founded a new school of novels, the novels of supernatural incident.   It was also the first to direct the attention of novelists to the great wealth of materials for their craft that might be found in feudal times, lawless turbulent characters, unbridled passions, and picturesque costume and architecture.   The very year after the 'Castle of Otranto' was published, there appeared what I take to be our first *Historical Romance*, 'Longsword, Earl of Salisbury.' I only know the work from the description of it in the 'Monthly Review' of the time,—I have never been able to get sight of the book itself.   It is never mentioned in our literary histories, as far as I know.   According to the 'Monthly Review,' it made an attempt to follow historical truth; "the truth of history was artfully interwoven with entertaining fictions and interesting episodes."   This could not be said of the 'Castle of Otranto,' which, although the scene was laid in feudal times, had no basis in actual historical fact.   'Longsword,' then, seems to have been the first anticipation in species, if not in quality, of Scott's historical romances.

But, indeed, it would give a wrong impression of the way in which the public mind is gradually prepared for the reception of a writer of genius, and the atmosphere created in which he finds vital sustenance, to ascribe the initiative in any new kind of writing absolutely to one man or one work. I remarked in my last lecture on the injustice of denying to Richardson the praise of inventing the modern English novel of manners. I pointed out at the same time how he had predecessors in one essential feature of this new literary form. But it is possible that, owing to the emphasis I was obliged to lay on his originality, I induced you to think of him as standing out more prominently from his compeers and predecessors, more sharply marked off from his age, than he really was. The individual is great in literature, but he does not create out of nothing; the soil is prepared for him, and the materials gradually accumulated which he seizes upon and turns to new shapes. Individuals take new departures, take the lead in new expeditions into the untried and unexplored; but the ways and means for the expeditions are first accumulated by the co-operation of many. Thus the 'Castle of Otranto' and 'Longsword' were new departures; but about the time when they were made there was a general harking back to the customs and the literature of the middle ages. A year after the publication of Walpole's romance, 1765, Bishop Percy published his famous 'Reliques of Ancient English Poetry'; and, a few years before, Macpherson had produced first his 'Fragments' of ancient Gaelic poetry, and then his pretended translation of the Ossianic epics, 'Fingal' and 'Temora.' The study of medieval antiquity was, in fact, becoming a very general pursuit among the learned when Walpole took the lead in introducing the sentiment of it into prose fiction.

It was some years before Walpole had an eminent successor in his own peculiar walk of romance, flavoured with supernatural or quasi - supernatural incident. The next conspicuous romance of this species was Mrs Radcliffe's 'Mysteries of Udolpho,' published nearly thirty years later. Meantime, in 1778, a conspicuous mark was made by a novel in the Richardson school of domestic fiction, a novel that arrested and sustained universal attention in the literary world amidst the crowd of writings that poured from the press. This was Miss Burney's 'Evelina,' and it was the first of a long series of triumphs for the sex in this branch of literature. In the fifty - five years between Sterne's 'Tristram Shandy' and Scott's 'Waverley' the chief honours in novel-writing were carried off by women—Miss Burney, Mrs Radcliffe, Miss Edgeworth, and Miss Austen. The names that became classic during this interval were all names of women.

Miss Burney was the first woman to achieve first-rate distinction in the modern novel, thirty-eight years after Richardson had led way into the new form. But you are not to suppose that during that long period women had abstained from trying a kind of writing for which women have such special qualifications in their keen eye for manners, their quick sense of the ridiculous, and sharp insight into character. Very soon after the invention of the novel, circulating libraries were also invented; novel-reading became a passion, and novel-writing one of the few money-making branches of literature. As early as 1752, the 'Monthly Review,' a monthly organ of literary criticism started in 1748, complained of the labour of reading the multitude of novels submitted to its judgment. They spring up like mushrooms every year, every work of merit producing a swarm of imitators. In 1755, a witty writer in the 'Connoisseur' proposed to establish a literary factory, and of course the manufacture of novels was to be a prominent part of the business, an eminent cutter-out being retained for the plot and leading adventures, with numerous assistants competent to fill in details. To supply the eager needs of the circulating library, many translations were also made from the French, the novels of Marivaux and Mme. Riccoboni being special favourites. Such being the demand for novels, as soon as this delightful form of literature was invented, women were well to the front both as translators and as original authors. There was Mrs Charlotte Lennox, for example, a lady with a literary career of nearly half a century, which began very prosperously but ended rather unhappily, the old lady, who for so long had supported herself by miscellaneous work with her pen, being under the necessity of writing after her powers had fallen off. She was one of the great Johnson's favourites, and the success of her first novel, 'Harriet Stuart,' in 1751, was celebrated by a supper at the Devil Tavern, where the mighty "Rambler" crowned her with laurel. Her next work, the 'Female Quixote,' in 1752, was a still greater success. It certainly is a very amusing book. It describes the adventures of a beautiful young lady, whose father, a powerful Minister, having retired from the world in disgust at his fall from office, kept her in complete seclusion in the country. Here the young lady, finding a complete collection of the fantastic romances to which I have referred as being fashionable in Queen Anne's time, accepts in all seriousness their ideals of heroism and love and the proper behaviour of lovers, models her lonely life with her maids after the fashion of the romantic heroines, and keeps her mind constantly occupied with expectations of romantic adventures. Encountering a stranger in one of her rides, she takes him for a desperate lover come to carry her off by force, and behaves as romantic princesses do in such circumstances, orders her servants to secure and disarm the unfortunate man, and treats his protests as signs of villainous duplicity. She takes one of her father's gardeners for a prince in disguise, and is hardly disabused of her fancy when the young man is cudgelled by the head gardener and dismissed, being caught in the act of stealing carp from a fish-pond. Her father wishes to marry her to a cousin, whom he invites to his castle to make her acquaintance with this object; but she is deeply offended with the young man because he does not make love in the high-flown manner of romantic chivalry, and instead of serving her faithfully and humbly for several years before, with faltering voice and devout reverence he begs the unutterable favour of kissing her hand, and blurts out a declaration of love after a few weeks' acquaintance. As you may suppose, many capital situations occur before Arabella is enlightened as to the difference between the ways of real life and the ways of seventeenth-century romance. The story is rather wire-drawn, but full of humour. Johnson continued a friend to the authoress to the last, and wrote proposals for printing a quarto edition of her works in 1775; and it would seem that, with all her various literary industry, Mrs Lennox needed such services as old age came upon her. She would seem to have been not particularly amiable in private life, if we are to believe Mrs Thrale's judgment (recorded in Mme. D'Arblay's 'Diary'), that everybody admired Mrs Lennox, but nobody liked her. Miss Fielding, the sister of the novelist, also wrote several novels, and in the opinion of Richardson, who was not a little jealous and spiteful towards his rival and caricaturist, showed a more intimate knowledge of the human heart than her (gifted) brother. This was not the general opinion, though an admirer wrote of her that "Miss Fielding was one of those truly estimable writers whose fame smells sweet, and will do so to late posterity, one who never wrote

     'One line which dying *she* would wish to blot,' "

—a compliment that could hardly be paid to Henry Fielding.

Another female novel-writer, whose fame has been kept green by the fame of her children and great-grandchildren, was Mrs Frances Sheridan, the authoress of 'Sydney Biddulph' and 'Nourjahad,' and the mother of Richard Brinsley Sheridan. In the opinion of Charles James Fox, 'Sydney Biddulph' was the best of modern novels, and Johnson wept over it, and complimented the authoress by telling her that he doubted whether "on moral principles she had a right to make her readers suffer so much." It is a curious circumstance that precisely the same complaint of carrying the sufferings of a heroine to an intensely painful pitch, harrowing the reader with continuous and unrelieved and undeserved distresses, might be brought against more than one of the powerful novels of her great-grandaughter, the Hon. Mrs Norton, especially against 'Stuart of Dunleath.' The 'Memoirs of Sydney Biddulph' appeared in 1761, and Mrs Sheridan was undoubtedly the most eminent female novelist before Miss Burney; although, according to Mrs Barbauld, Mrs Brooke, another indefatigable novelist and translator, whose 'Lady Julia Mandeville' was republished in Mrs Barbauld's collection, was the "first female novel-writer who attained a perfect purity and polish of style."

You will see, then, that women had not been idle in the new field of literature before Miss Burney produced her 'Evelina,' though this lady was the first to take rank with the masters of the art. "She," says Macaulay, "first showed that a tale might be written in which both the fashionable and vulgar life of London might be exhibited with great force and with broad comic humour, and which yet should not contain a single line inconsistent with rigid morality, or even with virgin delicacy. She took away the reproach which lay on a most useful and delightful species of composition. She vindicated the right of her sex to an equal share in a fair and noble province of letters." This is true in the main, as is generally the case with Macaulay's broad and vigorous rhetoric, only it is a trifle exaggerated. All the female novelists that I have mentioned were unexceptionable in point of morality, as much so as Miss Burney. Macaulay was probably thinking of the female novelists of a much earlier period when he praised Miss Burney for her delicacy—of Mrs Behn and Mrs Manley and Mrs Haywood. There was no lack of purity in the 'Female Quixote,' and 'Sydney Biddulph' would compare favourably in this respect with Victorian novelists. And for more than thirty years before the appearance of 'Evelina' her sex had taken an equal share with men in novel-writing, at least in point of quantity. It was the masterly natural freshness of the character-drawing, the clear unencumbered vivacity of the incidents, the frankness of the humour—in a word, the originality, the absence of literary artificiality, that signalised 'Evelina' as a work of genius, and set everybody talking about the new writer. Miss Burney was not the first woman novelist, but she was the first with a distinct vein of her own who wrote with her eyes on the subject and not on any established model of approved style. Macaulay is more exact when he speaks of the great force and broad comic humour with which Miss Burney de-picted vulgar as well as fashionable life. It was the picture of vulgar life—life in a would-be fashionable tradesman's family—that specially attracted notice in an age when the fashionable world had been described to death in hundreds of periodical essays and novels. We happen to have preserved for us a good deal of the talk that went on about 'Evelina' in the first months after its appearance when it was all the rage. Miss Burney published it anonymously, not even her own father knowing who was the author; and she recorded in her diary, which is almost as delightful as her novels, what she heard people saying about the book and its characters. It was the vulgar characters that were particularly commented on and admired. The position of the heroine Evelina was such as to bring her in contact with various classes. Her origin was mysterious, but she had been brought up by a clergy-man in the country, and when she was seventeen she was brought out in London society by a lady who knew her mother's history. Thus in the first part of the story we have descriptions of the rustic beauty's experiences at a ball, an opera, a ridotto, a visit to

Ranelagh Gardens, a visit to the Pantheon. The girl's timidity, the scrapes she falls into in consequence, and her encounters with an empty fop, an enamoured but unscrupulous baronet, and an accomplished, noble-minded, high-bred lord, who of course eventually marries the heroine, are described in a vein of the most exquisite comedy. In Lord Orville Miss Burney succeeded in drawing what Richardson attempted in Sir Charles Grandison—a perfect gentleman, who is at the same time not the least of a prig. Evelina's ignorance and timidity get her into scrapes, but these are nothing to the troubles caused by a terrible relation on the mother's side, a vulgar Frenchwoman, her grandmother, Mme. Duval, who very soon turns up. The scenes between this most amusing harridan and her friend's husband, Captain Mirvan, a salt of the oldest school, are boisterously farcical. The old tar hates the French, and conceiving a violent animosity against Mme. Duval, makes it his chief amusement to draw the old hag, as he puts it, putting her into violent passions, insulting her in every way imaginable, devising practical jokes at her expense. One of these—in which he and the baronet, who for interested reasons is his ally, disguise themselves as highwaymen, drag her roughly from her carriage, and leave her with her legs tied in a ditch, first tearing off her false hair—has uncomfortable consequences for Evelina, for her grandmother insists upon taking possession of her, and carries her off to the society of certain poor relations in the city. The Braughton family and their lodger, Mr Smith, were the great hit of the book. Mr Braughton, the father, was a silver-smith in Snowhill, a close-fisted money-making tradesman, but his girls were quite fine ladies, and their radiant vulgarities, their squabbles with their rude brother Tom, their contempt for their country cousin Evelina, their respect for the great Mr Smith, made excellent sport for the fashionable readers of Miss Burney's novel. It amused them vastly to see all the foibles and artificial distinc-tions of polite society travestied by these lower animals. There is Mr Smith, in particular, the first-floor lodger, a city clerk with an immense conceit of superiority to the vulgar herd round him, a sort of pinchbeck master, who patronised Evelina and introduced her to all the glories of a Hampstead ball, where Mme. Duval, the

French grandmother, danced a minuet to the grinning admiration of all beholders. Mr Smith, in the fine tambour waistcoat of which he was so self-conscious, was the delight of Miss Burney's readers. "The Holborn beau for my money," laughed Dr Johnson to Miss Burney; "O you sly rogue, you character-monger." The adventures of Evelina with the Braughtons are conceived in the spirit of the liveliest farcical invention. When Miss Burney comes to her third volume and the unravelling of her plot, which contains not a few ingenious surprises, she becomes more conventional and sentimental, but nothing could be better than the freshness of incident and humorous character-drawing of the first two volumes. It says something for the humanity of the time that Captain Mirvan was generally considered to have gone too far in his baiting of the old Frenchwoman Mme. Duval and the silly fop Mr Lovel. This should be remembered when a certain episode in the third volume is quoted as an example of the brutality of manners among the upper classes. Two young men of the period staying at a fashionable country house, in their passion for betting, got up a race of a hundred yards between two poor old women who can hardly walk; and when one of the hobbling old things falls and hurts herself so badly that she can do no more, her backer swears at her and urges her on with unfeeling cruelty, the whole company standing by to enjoy the fun. We should bear in mind that such conduct was as abhorrent to the general sentiment of Miss Burney's time as it is to the general sentiment of our own time. It was not upon such incidents that the popularity of Miss Burney's 'Evelina' was founded.

It was a matter of wonder to Miss Burney's contemporaries how a writer who showed such an intimate knowledge of high life could at the same time have acquired the knowledge of vulgar middle-class life shown in her portraits of the Braughton family. The explanation lay in the peculiar position of the authoress's father. She was the daughter of Dr Burney, a man of considerable celebrity in his time, an intimate of the Johnson and Reynolds circle, author of a 'History of Music,' and the most fashionable music-master of his generation. His high place in his profession made him a man of note in Continental schools of music, and foreign singers coming to England made a point of coming with an introduction to Dr Burney. And while they were negotiating an engagement in London, the strangers frequently gave a taste of their quality in Dr Burney's drawing-room. There is, besides, a sort of freemasonry among artists, which makes them willing to render any little service they can to the good-natured and popular in the brotherhood. Hence all the world was eager to come to Dr Burney's musical parties, where they could always hear the newest and most distinguished things in music; and on the evenings when Mrs Burney received, the music-master's humble house in St Martin's Street was beset with fashionable carriages. The quite demure little daughter, who sat shy and silent in company while her brain was teeming with comic fancies, and, as is often the way with shy demure people, boiled over with comic reminiscences to her sisters when the visitors were gone, had thus excellent opportunities of studying the ways of the fashionable world. But Dr Burney was not a proud man. He allowed his children to play with the children of a wigmaker in the adjoining houses. And among these humbler acquaintances, Miss Burney picked up that acquaintance with life in a different plane of society which made the fortune of her first novel.

Sometimes it is said now that 'Evelina' was overrated in its day. It is impossible not to acknowledge that she painted manners and habits with sprightliness and fidelity, but it is said that "when she rises from manners and habits to paint feelings, we see little but indecision on the one hand or exaggeration on the other." This is all very true, and yet Miss Burney was undoubtedly a novelist of the first rank. Undoubtedly she would be overrated if she were put on a level with Richardson as an analyst of feeling, or Fielding as a humorist, or George Eliot as a scientific investigator of cause and effect in emotional changes, or any other novelist in the walk in which his special strength lies. But there are varieties of excellence, all equally admirable of their kind, and Miss Burney was pre-eminent in her special kind, because she attempted only what she was qualified to perform. In her first two novels, 'Evelina' and 'Cecilia,' there was nothing written against the grain, simply because it was supposed to be the right thing for a novel: she did not follow the fashion of her time in long-winded sentimental reflections or fine-spun analysis of feeling. The truth is that her writing, after her first four years of authorship, was a failure, because in 'Evelina' and 'Cecilia' she had exhausted all that was fresh in her observation of manners, and assumed thereafter a point of view that was not natural to her.

The next pre-eminent work of fiction after Miss Burney's novels was the 'Mysteries of Udolpho,' published in 1794, and also written by a woman. It was not a novel—a story of real life and character—but a romance. In the preface, in which Horace Walpole had acknowledged the authorship of the 'Castle of Otranto,' while claiming the credit of having invented a new species of romance, he modestly admitted that he was sensible of his own inability to give full effect to his conception, and expressed a hope that he had paved the way for "men of brighter talents," superior to himself in the imagination and the exhibition of the passions. This good wish was not fulfilled for nearly thirty years, and was then fulfilled by a woman of brighter talents, Mrs Radcliffe. She adopted Walpole's idea of giving the imagination freer play in the invention of incidents than the novelist could do if he kept to the manners of modern life. But she adopted his idea with an important difference as regarded the licence of improbability that he allowed himself. It is curious to note how the licence that Walpole sought for the imagination was gradually abridged by those who caught up his idea and followed in his track. The most successful of his imitators before Mrs Radcliffe was another woman, Clara Reeve, a very industrious authoress, who produced what she called, after Walpole, a Gothic Romance, the 'Old English Baron,' in 1777. But Mrs Reeve, though she owned him as a master, declined to be led by him in one particular; she thought that he went too far with his supernatural improbabilities. Statues that drop blood—swords that take a hundred men to lift—pictures that groan and walk out of their frames—struck her as needlessly wild inventions, calculated to shake the reader's faith in the story and give it a grotesque and ridiculous

air, such as a nursery tale has for a grown man. Accordingly Mrs
Reeve drew the line at ghosts. There is a haunted wing in the
castle of the old English baron, and there is an heir wrongfully
kept from his inheritance, and brought up as a peasant's son ; but
for the punishment of the wrongdoer and the restoration of the
defrauded youth to his own, the only supernatural machinery
employed is the ghost of a murdered man. Thus far Mrs Reeve
abridged the licence for the supernatural allowed by the authority
of Walpole, and Mrs Radcliffe imposed on herself a still stricter
self-denying ordinance. She abjured the supernatural altogether,
and yet contrived to keep her readers from first to last in an
atmosphere of mysterious excitement and superstitious dread.
There are no supernatural agents in her tales—neither wizard nor
spectre ; everything that happens is carefully explained as being
due to natural causes ; yet we are kept in a flutter and fever of
excitement as much as if evil spirits and good spirits were constantly at work around us. The situations are eerie ; she puts us
in scenes where we are liable to the invasion of superstitious
panic, in dark forests and lonely castles, with long echoing cor-
ridors and secret passages and rooms shut up because they are
believed to be haunted ; she surrounds us with turbulent, desperate,
unscrupulous characters. Unaccountable sounds are heard when our
feelings are deeply interested in the fate of hero or heroine, voices
where no speaker is visible, strains of music in lonely places where
it seems all but impossible that any musician should be ; there are
unaccountable apparitions and marvellous disappearances. There
is generally some mystery afloat ; when one has been cleared up
we are not suffered long to breathe freely before we are caught in
the toils of another. Yet all the time only human agents are at
work ; there is nothing improbable except the extraordinary combination of circumstances, nothing supernatural except in the
superstitious imaginings of the personages of the story. Everything that seemed as if it must be the work of spirits is carefully
and fully explained as the story goes on. Mrs Radcliffe has been
censured for these explanations, as if they were a mistake in point
of art, destroying the illusion and making us ashamed of ourselves
for having been imposed upon. This censure I can regard only as

an affectation, unless when it comes from a convinced believer in
ghosts.   Such persons might resent the explanation as casting
doubts upon their cherished belief.   But for other people I can
see nothing that could be gained by leaving the mysterious incidents unexplained, except by the authoress, who would undoubtedly have saved herself an immense deal of trouble if she
had made free use of ghosts and other supernatural properties,
whenever she required them, without taking any pains to explain
how the facts occurred.   I read the story myself with a double
interest; I enjoy the excitement of superstitious wonder and awe
while the illusion lasts, and when the mystery is cleared up, and
the excitement is gently subsiding, I am in a mood to get additional enjoyment from reflecting on the ingenuity of the complication that gave to the illusion for the moment the force of
truth.   Yet it was no less a person than Sir Walter Scott that set
the fashion of objecting to Mrs Radcliffe's explanations.   If we
were to inquire curiously into the objection, we should probably
find that the inquiry led us into one of the differences between
classical art and romantic art.   Mrs Radcliffe, although in the
main a disciple in the school of romantic art, yet paid homage to
classical art in her efforts to explain the strangest occurrences by
accidents within the limits of human possibility; and a thorough-
going romanticist like Sir Walter Scott might be inclined to reprobate this concession.   Yet one great leader of romantic art
in France, George Sand, followed Mrs Radcliffe's example, and
in her 'Consuelo' and 'Comtesse de Rudolstadt' accounted for
many strange and apparently supernatural occurrences by human
agency.

It was justly remarked by Mr George Moir, in his treatise on
Romance, that Mrs Radcliffe has in later times been most unjustly
made to bear the sins of her imitators.   "The truth is," he says,
"that the sarcasms which have been directed against the puerile
horrors of Mrs Radcliffe ought justly to have been confined to the
extravagances of her successors, who imitated her manner without
either her imagination or her judgment, and conceived that the
surest means of producing effect consisted in pressing the springs
of the terrible as far as they would go.   In the hands of these

imitated imitators, the castles became twice as large and ten times
as perplexing in their architecture; the heroine could not open
an empty drawer without stumbling on a mysterious manuscript
written by her father or her mother; nor leave her room to take a
twilight walk, of which heroines are always strangely fond, without stumbling on a nest of banditti; the gleam of daggers grew
more incessant; the faces of the monks longer and more cada-
verous, and the visits of ghosts so commonplace that they came at
last to be viewed with the same indifference by the reader as they
were of old by honest Aubrey or less honest Dr Dee."

CHAPTER X.

THE NEW POETRY.

COWPER—HIS ALLEGED REVOLUTION OF POETRY.

In my last two lectures on the novels of the eighteenth century, I tried to show you how much the public mind was occupied with this new kind of literature. Poetry was for the time pushed aside. You will now, I trust, understand that it is a very inadequate explanation of the small amount of poetry that was written between Pope and Wordsworth, and of the poorness in quality of much of that small amount, to say that the poets of the period were hampered by a slavish subservience to classical models. There is abundance of evidence that would-be poets, on the contrary, strained after originality. Even before Pope died, Matthew Green, a poet of whimsical and dainty vein, who wrote with great sprightliness of humour and lightness of touch, made it his boast that he was no imitator :—

> "Nothing is stolen : my Muse, though mean,
> Draws from the spring she finds within ;
> Nor vainly buys what Gildon sells,
> Poetic buckets for dry wells."

The truth is, that Pope's perfect success was not encouraging to imitators; there was no chance of fame except in a different kind, and the mood of readers, delighted and fully occupied with prose fiction, was such as to chill poetic genius by the most blighting of all influences, indifference. The public was dancing to a different tune, and the poet sat silent with a feeling that he must pipe in vain. Now and again Poetry made a violent struggle to get a hearing and a following, as when Churchill, the satirist, in the sixties of the century, throwing all the refinements of Queen Anne satire to the winds, laid about him with rude, furious, distempered force. He made a noise in his time, but when interest in the ephemeral subjects of his boisterous abuse and fierce invective had passed away, his verse had not sufficient intrinsic merit to command readers. Churchill certainly was no bigot to classical rules, no victim to smooth and easy couplets. The next poet to make a popular and enduring mark gained his readers by accommodating his verse to an easy, familiar, discursive prose style, with which the great body of readers were for the time enchanted.

It is usual to speak of Cowper as a "reformer of poetry, who called it back from conventionality to nature," and as the herald of Wordsworth and Byron. Universally this new movement is spoken of as a revolt against the authority of Pope; and as it took place simultaneously with the French Revolution, or nearly so, this revolt is regarded as one of the signs of the revolutionary temper of the time. Now, there can be little doubt that the intense excitement and ferment produced by the French Revolution and the career of Napoleon affected the poetry of the time. But it gives an essentially wrong impression to speak as if the struggle of the French people with a corrupt aristocracy and royalty stimulated the poets of England to take up arms against their poetic tyrant, and depose him with anger and contumely. We can hardly speak of deposing a tyrant when there is no tyrant to depose. And it is the merest fiction, the most unsubstantial shadow of a metaphor, to describe Pope as tyrannising over English poetry at the close of the eighteenth century. A poet can tyrannise only as the temporary vicegerent of the poetic spirit, and the poetic spirit itself had no dominion over the affections of the English people at this time. Pope's deposition had, in fact, been accomplished by the coming to power of prose fiction. There had been a period of anarchy in poetry; every poet had been doing that which was right in his own eyes, struggling desperately after something new, catching at straws like a drowning man, and there had been no poet of sufficient eminence to establish a general empire. There was nobody to revolt against when Wordsworth appeared; the throne was vacant, open to any comer powerful enough to establish his right by poetic might.

But Cowper, it is said, called poetry back from conventionality to nature. He pioneered Wordsworth in discarding the poetic diction sanctioned by the Queen Anne critics, their "heightened" expression, their vain endeavours to dress nature to advantage. That is to say, Cowper's diction is more like the language of prose. But was this a revolt against the tyranny of Pope? It seems to me more accurate to describe it as a submission to the tyranny of the novel-writers and pleasant discursive prose-essayists. Cowper himself began his literary career as an essayist and writer of light trifling verses in the style of Prior and Green; and it was by applying this same style to more serious subjects that he made a beginning in the so-called revolution. The worst of the revolution explanation of the great movement that Cowper is said to have heralded, an explanation so easy and simple and thought-saving, is that it radically misrepresents the sources of the revolution, and puts out of sight the real continuity of the literary history of the eighteenth century. It would lead us to suppose that the simpler diction, the discursive method, the prevalence of narrative by which the new poetry was characterised, were adopted out of antagonism to Pope; whereas really the new poetry was enriched by the prose-essayists and novelists, as these had themselves received benefits from the Queen Anne poets. There had thus been a substantial gain in literature from generation to generation, and real progress, real development. It was not, as the revolution explanation would import, that the Queen Anne style had been discarded in the third or fourth generation as an entirely false ideal, as a wasteful venture in a wrong direction, an unprofitable divergence from the true paths of imaginative literature. The prosemen of the middle forty years of the century were helped by the brilliant epigrammatic poets of the Queen Anne time; and the poets of the following generation received light and leading in their turn from the prosemen of the generation before them. Cowper, the herald of Wordsworth, may perhaps be described as a reformer of poetry, but it is more significant of his historical position to describe him as an essayist in verse.

In the numerous biographical and critical sketches of Cowper, among which the latest, Mr Goldwin Smith's and Mrs Oliphant's, may be mentioned as perhaps the best, sufficient attention has not been paid to Cowper's literary work in his early manhood, before his first madness and his conversion to Evangelical Christianity, the events which are rightly regarded as the mainsprings of the poetry now associated with his name, "Table Talk," "The Task," and the "Occasional Poems." The work of his early manhood, while he was still a buckish and briefless barrister, is generally mentioned; but it is slurred over as if it were of no consequence in his history, as if it were a thing that had nothing in common with the productions of his regenerate days. It can be shown, I think, that, in so far as merely poetic qualities are concerned, this early work was quite as revolutionary or unrevolutionary as the poems of his pious old age.

With the main outlines of Cowper's life you are, I daresay, familiar. He was the son of a country clergyman, the grandson of a Justice of the Common Pleas, the grand-nephew of a Lord Chancellor. After passing through Westminster School, he was apprenticed to an attorney, and had as his fellow-apprentice the famous lawyer who afterwards became Lord Thurlow. The youths spent their time, he tells us, "in giggling and making giggle," both in the attorney's office and in the house of Cowper's uncle, where dwelt a cousin with whom he was in love. Emancipated from the attorney's office, and called to the bar, Cowper took chambers in the Temple, and lived a gay and idle life, trusting to family influence for a sinecure, and doing no sort of work in his profession. It was during this period that he wrote the poetry and prose which has, I think, been unduly neglected in dissertations on his career. He belonged to a literary set. Two of his Westminster school-fellows, Bonnell Thornton and Colman the dramatist, conducted for two years (from January 1754 to September 1756) a very popular periodical in the style of the 'Spectator,' the 'Connoisseur.' Cowper was an occasional contributor. The gaiety of these young Templars may be judged from the fact that seven of the old Westminster boys formed a coterie, to which they gave the name of the Nonsense Club, in which the fun of giggling and making giggle was continued. There Cowper lived till he reached the age of thirty-two, when a long-expected sinecure, in the gift of his kinsman Major Cowper, was ready for his occupancy. This was the clerkship of the Journals of the House of Lords. There were two sinecures in Major Cowper's gift, and it would seem that through some indecision or change of purpose on the poet's part, suspicion was aroused about the nominee, and it was resolved that he should be examined as to his competency before the bar of the House of Lords. Cowper was horror-struck at the prospect; fiddled excitedly for some months with preparations for the ordeal; then on the day before attempted to commit suicide, and was found to be out of his mind. It is idle to speculate upon the causes of this catastrophe. Madness is often puzzling to the most skilful doctors, making inquiry at the time and in full possession of minute circumstances that we desire in vain to know in a historical case. Mere fright at a public examination would not have driven Cowper mad if he had had no predisposition to madness. But a small circumstance may suffice to upset a man of nervous, susceptible, irresolute temperament, when his natural feebleness of will has been increased by want of occupation, and his health deranged by want of exercise. The only premonitory symptoms of Cowper's madness is found in a poem, written nine years before the catastrophe (in 1754), in which he speaks of being driven to poetry

> " to divert a fierce banditti
> (Sworn foes to everything that's witty)
> That, with a black infernal train,
> Make cruel inroads in my brain,
> And daily threaten to drive thence
> My little garrison of sense."

"The fierce banditti which I mean," he adds, "are gloomy thoughts led on by spleen." The spleen in those days was the supposed physical source of hypochondria; a melancholy and despondent person was said to be suffering from the spleen. Matthew Green wrote a poem on the spleen, and the banishment of its depressing influence by wholesome laughter—

> "To cure the mind's wrong bias, Spleen,
> Some recommend the bowling-green ;
> Some hilly walks ; all exercise ;
> Fling but a stone, the giant dies.

> Laugh and be well.   Monkeys have been
> Extreme good doctors for the Spleen ;
> And kitten, if the humour hit,
> Has harlequin'd away the fit."

Unfortunately Cowper was too much frightened at the prospect of appearing before the Lords to take the excellent advice of his favourite poet.   He was confined for eighteen months in a lunatic asylum, where his reason was restored, it would seem, by such a judicious regimen as might have averted the malady if it had been · employed in time.

Cowper returned to sanity, strange to say, in a blaze of religious rapture.   His physician, Dr Cotton, was a pious man, a writer of hymns, and used to hold religious conversations with his patients —an ill-advised thing, as Mr Goldwin Smith remarks, if Cowper's madness had been religious mania.   In the poet's case religion was not the malady, but an element in the cure.   One morning in the summer of 1765, after a visit from his brother, he rose with a new sense of health; at breakfast on the bright summer morning felt still better; on a sudden impulse took up the Bible, from which he had shrunk in dull despair during his illness, and all in a moment was filled with an ecstatic conviction that he had made his peace with God and was again in his right mind.   In Cowper's tender, sensitive, dependent spirit, with an imagination ever running swiftly towards intolerable horrors, and a will much too feeble of its own strength to arrest this tendency, the doctrines of Evangelical Christianity found a congenial subject.   It was one of those instantaneous conversions which Wesley and his disciples believed to be a moment in the history of every true believer.   The doctor was at first suspicious of this sudden change in his patient, but his doubts were soon removed.   Cowper had really recovered, and found in his ecstatic faith the stay and support that his dependent spirit required.

It is doubtful whether the recovery would have been permanent —it was never permanent in the sense of being securely fixed against accident, but it is doubtful whether it would have been as permanent as it was—had not a fortunate chance thrown him in the way of the Unwin family when he was discharged from the asylum.   Mrs Unwin was a woman born to be the support of such a man ; gentle in her ways, so as never to wound his tenderly fastidious taste; unaffectedly pious, so as to comfort him in his doubts and fears, and confirm his ecstasies with the sweetness of her sympathy ; yet with all this of a cheerful temper, and always ready to laugh with a hearty genuine ring at the sallies of his exuberant humour. There never was a more perfect compatibility of temper. Mr Unwin was alive when they first met, and the poet was admitted as a lodger into their parsonage; but they continued to live together at Olney after his death, Mrs Unwin tending him and humouring him with unfailing gentleness and self-sacrifice. There was no thought of marriage between them ; their love was not the love of lovers. Much has been written, and not a little insinuated, about the relationship between Cowper and Mrs Unwin; but I think Mrs Oliphant is right in her interpretation of the poet's character, that he belonged to a class of men celibate by nature, born to be dependent on the tender ministrations and affectionate companionship of women, yet as near as may be devoid of passion. Mrs Unwin was seven years older than the poet, and neither her son, with whom he corresponded, nor his relatives, who were greatly pleased with the happiness he had found, seem ever to have dreamt of regarding the gentle rescued lunatic as a dangerous lover.

Much less fortunate for Cowper was his relationship with an overwhelming Evangelical enthusiast, Mr Newton, the vicar of Olney, the converted captain of a slaver. It was at his instance that Mrs Unwin and the poet settled at Olney, to be near him. He took possession of them after Mr Unwin's death, and no priest ever exercised authority with more arbitrary confidence. Occupation was what Cowper wanted, and Mr Newton found him occupation in regular spiritual exercises, in visiting the sick in body and in mind, and in writing hymns. For some time Cowper was happy in the vocation thus found for him, but the strain was too much ; his mind again gave way, and for five years he remained moody, dejected, and full of capricious insane fancies. Gentle Mrs Unwin found for him during this period an occupation in which he took a childish delight, making chairs and tables for her, and cages, baskets, and hutches for his pets, of whom he collected a great number about him, having at one time " five rabbits, three hares, two guinea-pigs, a magpie, a jay, and a starling; besides two goldfinches, two canary birds, and two dogs." When the long fit passed off, Mr Newton again set him to work upon hymns, and the 'Olney Hymns' were published in 1779, fourteen years after the poet's first recovery.

I mention this period to show you how long the poet was in finding his true vocation—the employment in which he enjoyed a full measure of happiness. "I never received a little pleasure in my life," he once said; "if I am delighted, it is always in the extreme." His letters show that under Newton's dictatorship he was often happy, but it was by fits and starts. It was a fortunate thing for him when this strenuous spiritual director left Olney, and could overawe him only by letter. Not long after his departure, Mrs Unwin, with her quiet penetrating insight, devised an employment for him in which he found four years of unclouded happiness. She had observed that he was never so completely drawn away from himself as when he was writing, and in the November of 1780 she suggested to him that he should attempt a poem of some length, and gave him as a subject the "Progress of Error." The poet was now in his native element, not perfectly suited with a subject, but still more at liberty to indulge his quick imagination than he could have been in the composition of hymns. He set to his new employment with delight, and produced in quick succession the "Progress of Error," "Table Talk," "Truth," "Expostulation," "Hope," "Charity," "Conversation," and "Retirement." Mr Newton from a distance expressed doubts about the new departure, but the poet pacified him with the idea that his verses might be the means of attracting to the true faith some whom the truth in its naked severity was apt to repel. Wesley chose lively popular airs for his hymns, on the principle that it was not well that the devil should have all the best tunes; and Newton apparently tolerated Cowper's moral satires, as he called them, from a similar motive.

The "Moral Satires" were published in 1782, and were rather coldly received by the critics. It was otherwise with his next publication, a work begun under a different influence, an influence that was like a renewing of the poet's youth. The casual reader who has heard in a vague way of Cowper's relations with devoted women, generally couples Mrs Unwin and Lady Austen together as two pious Methodist ladies who sacrificed themselves to cheer the gentle poet's melancholy. But the two women were very different in character, and the poet's acquaintance with the one had a very different course from his acquaintance with the other. The one by her patient, forbearing, sympathetic companionship did most for his happiness; the other in a brief angel's visit did most for his reputation. Mrs Unwin was his household friend and slave for more than thirty years; Lady Austen was his gay and sparkling playfellow for less than three. Lady Austen's settlement in Olney was a bright interval in Cowper's long residence there, which, with all his fitful Evangelical enthusiasm, he could not help feeling to be a monotonous imprisonment when he remembered the bustling variety of his ten years' life in the Temple. He spoke of Olney, after she left, and after she awakened his memories of other days, as a "moral Bastille." She was a woman of the world, very different from the quiet Puritanic country clergyman's wife; the widow of a baronet, who had lived much in Paris, handsome, vivacious, full of talk and high spirits. "She is a lively agreeable woman," Cowper wrote to Newton immediately after his first interview with her—he had chanced to see her shopping in Olney with her sister, one of Mrs Unwin's few intimates in the place, and had requested Mrs Unwin to ask her to tea. "She has seen much of the world, and accounts it a great simpleton, as it is. She laughs and makes laugh, and keeps up a conversation without seeming to labour at it." Lady Austen was charmed with the poet, and the poet was charmed with Lady Austen. She brought back to him breezy sketches of the world from which he had so long been secluded. She romped with the playful old boy of fifty, playing battledore and shuttlecock with him, whilst Mrs Unwin played on the harpsichord. She told him diverting stories, among others the adventure of John Gilpin, which kept him awake with laughter for a whole night, and for which he rewarded her by turning it into verse. But above all, his "Moral Satires" being now completed and published, she suggested to him that he should write a poem in blank verse, and when he asked her for a subject, laughingly named the sofa on which she sat. This was the origin of the series of poems called the "Task," composed in a much gayer and more discursive mood than the "Moral Satires."

It was the "Task" that made Cowper's reputation, and it was inspired by a revival, under Lady Austen's companionship, of that more mundane spirit to which he had long been a stranger. This alone would make it worth while to look back and see what his writing was like while he was still a young "buck," as the phrase then went, living in chambers in the Temple, and giggling and making giggle at his uncle's house in Southampton Row. We have seen what the Methodist spirit did for him. It inspired the 'Olney Hymns' and the "Moral Satires," and neither of these performances made the great world outside the Evangelical circle feel that a new poet had arisen in England. This achievement was reserved for the "Task," written during the temporary resuscitation of a half-disused way of looking at the world, written in a gayer mood, and therefore it is of interest to look at the tone and style of Cowper's first writing, before he came under Methodist influence.

Cowper contributed three papers to the 'Connoisseur' in March, April, and May 1756, Nos. 111, 115, 119. If we did not know that they were Cowper's, they would strike us as extremely clever and idiomatically written imitations of Addison, the great exemplar of periodical essayists at the time. Knowing that they are Cowper's, and induced thereby to scrutinise them more closely, we have no difficulty in detecting the peculiar note of playfully extravagant humour with which we are familiar in the "Task." The first of the papers is an absurd description of "the delicate Billy Suckling, the contempt of the men, the jest of the women, and the darling of his mamma,"—a picture of an impossible young milksop who fancies himself a buck. Neither then nor afterwards was Cowper capable of drawing human character from life; his uncontrollable sense of fun pushed him into comic exaggerations that seem rather silly to people less easily tickled. The fun of the second paper, a letter from an old bachelor, Christopher Ironside, describing his persecution by young ladies, is equally extreme but not so obvious; and may perhaps be taken as throwing some light on the kind of romping that went on between Cowper and his cousins in Southampton Row:—

"The female part of my acquaintance entertain an odd opinion that a Bachelor is not in fact a rational creature—at least, that he has not the senso of feeling in common with the rest of mankind; that a Bachelor may be beaten like a stock-fish; that you may thrust pins into his legs, and wring him by the nose; in short, that you cannot take too many liberties with a Bachelor. I am at a loss to conceive on what foundation these romping philosophers have grounded their hypothesis, though at the same time I am a melancholy proof of its existence, as well as of its absurdity.

"A friend of mine, whom I frequently visit, has a wife and three daughters, the youngest of which has persecuted me these ten years. These ingenious young ladies have not only found out the sole end and purpose of my being themselves, but have likewise communicated their discovery to all the girls in the neighbourhood; so that if they happen at any time to be apprised of my coming (which I take all possible care to prevent) they immediately despatch half-a-dozen cards to their faithful allies, to beg the favour of their company to drink coffee and *help tease* Mr Ironside. Upon these occasions my entry into the room is sometimes obstructed by a cord, fastened across the bottom of the door-case; which, as I am a little near-sighted, I seldom discover till it has brought me on my knees before them. While I am employed in brushing the dust from my black rollers, or chafing my broken shins, my wig is suddenly conveyed away."

In the last of these papers there are comic descriptions of the behaviour of various characters when in possession of a secret— all in the same strain of simple childlike exaggeration. At this period Cowper scribbled a great deal more than he printed. These three papers in the 'Connoisseur' are specimens of the early practice by which he acquired the mastery of comic description that appears occasionally in the "Task"—the abundance of detail, and the felicity of phrase. It was in writing prose essays and prose letters that Cowper acquired the copious, easy, familiar diction that entitles him to rank with poetic reformers. Cowper is often referred to as an example of a man whose fancy and imagination blossomed late in life, because he was fifty before he acquired reputation as a poet. That a man much tried by physical suffering should, in the evening of his days, take up his pen and write poetry with a serious purpose, trying thereby to catch trifles which could not be caught in any other way, has a look as of inspiration. This no doubt has contributed to perpetuate the delusion. But it will not bear examination.

Cowper not only wrote prose with exquisite grace and skill in his youth, but his manner as a verse-writer was also fully formed before he was thirty. At the age of seventeen he wrote some work — heroic blank verse in imitation of Philips's "Splendid Shilling"—that shows, even in the opinion of Southey, the same character as the blank verse of the "Task," written when he was more than fifty. That he read little poetry, in fact confined his reading to Milton after his first attack of madness, is unduly insisted on, if the meaning is to prove that his poetry came fresh out of a mind unacquainted with what had been done before, and consequently having no relation with preceding literature. It must be remembered that Cowper was thirty-two before madness first overtook him, and that all through his early manhood he led a life of perfect leisure, his only employment being to read and write for his own amusement.

Very soon after the "Task" was completed, Cowper lost the pleasant company of the "fair" who had "commanded" it. A certain mystery hangs over the cause of Lady Austen's sudden departure from Olney. There was obviously some disturbance in the harmony of the happy family, and there has been much speculation as to the cause. "What else was to be expected?" many people ask. Mrs Unwin naturally became jealous of Cowper's attentions to her gay and fashionable rival, and he, having to choose between them, was bound in honour to stand by his lifelong companion and nurse. No other result was to be expected when two women were attached to one man. This is the easiest explanation, but it has the defect of not suiting what we know of the characters of the three persons concerned. Strange to say, or rather it would be strange to say if we were not aware of the extent to which men of reputation are idolised, nobody has thought of putting any of the blame on the poet, if blame there was in the matter. The rupture must have been brought about either by Lady Austen's grasping eagerness to have more than her fair share of the poet's attentions, or by Mrs Unwin's unreasonable jealousy. It seems to me much more likely that the coolness which led to Lady Austen's departure arose between Cowper and herself, and that the long-suffering patient Mrs Unwin had nothing to do with it; that it was not strained relations between the two ladies, but strained relations between one of them and the poet, that broke up the alliance. Whether Lady Austen was in love with Cowper or not, is a question we have no means of deciding. It is not unlikely. Men incapable of feeling passion themselves may not be incapable of inspiring passion in others. Lady Austen afterwards married a Frenchman of letters, M. de Tardiff, and Cowper, though much older than her, being fifty when she made his acquaintance, besides being a poet, had a boyish playfulness of temper and a quickness of wit not without their charm. Whether in love with him or not, Lady Austen certainly sought his society, though a great liking for the ministrations of Mr Scott, the curate, was her ostensible reason for taking a house in Olney. Now Cowper, though gentle, affectionate, and playful, would seem to have had his full share of the invalid's fretful, exacting, and capricious selfishness, and it is quite conceivable that Lady Austen, by no means so patient and self-denying a woman as Mrs Unwin, may simply have tired of his exactions and caprices. If we read between the lines of one of his letters to his cousin, Lady Hesketh, this explanation is almost forced upon us. "On her first settlement in our neighbourhood," Cowper writes, " I made it my own particular business (for at that time I was not employed in writing, having published my first volume and not begun my second) to pay my *devoirs* to her ladyship every morning at eleven. Customs very soon become laws. I began the 'Task,' for she was the lady who gave me the Sofa for a subject. Being once engaged in the work, I began to feel the inconvenience of my morning attendance. We had seldom breakfasted ourselves till ten ; and the intervening hour was all the time I could find in the whole day for writing, and occasionally it would happen that the half of that hour was all that I could secure for the purpose. But there was no remedy. Long usage had made that which was at first optional a point of good manners, and consequently of necessity, and I was forced to neglect the 'Task' to attend upon the Muse who had inspired the subject. But she had ill-health, and before I had quite finished the work was obliged to repair to Bristol." The sprightly Muse, with all her stability of temper, sense of religion, and seriousness of mind, must soon have become disagreeably conscious of the difference between the forced attendance of a wayward and irritable invalid with his thoughts elsewhere, and the effusive *camaraderie* with which he sought her company in the bright days of their first companionship.

> " O Love ! it is a pleasant thing
> A little time, while it is new."

Mrs Unwin might not have resented the change, but Lady Austen was not Mrs Unwin, and she "repaired to Bristol." We might have understood the cause of the separation better if the lady had kept Cowper's letter of farewell, but she was so dissatisfied with it that she threw it in the fire—tempted, perhaps for once in her life, to believe that Methodism was cant. Lady Austen was too exacting, or Cowper was too exacting; anyhow, they could not get on together—any explanation you please except that Mrs Unwin was jealous. To entertain this explanation for a moment is to commit the most senseless outrage on the memory of a gentle self-denying woman, who bore with all the crazy poet's selfish whims and caprices, and watched over him with more than a mother's love till her own mind gave way under the strain.

CHAPTER XI.

SCOTTISH POETRY IN THE EIGHTEENTH CENTURY.

THE ELEVATION OF A DIALECT INTO A LITERARY LANGUAGE—INFLUENCE
OF OLD BALLADS—WATSON'S COLLECTION—ALLAN RAMSAY—THE EASY
CLUB—'THE GENTLE SHEPHERD'—SONG-WRITERS—SKINNER, ETC.—
FERGUSON—BURNS.

If the eighteenth century was a comparatively barren period in English poetry, it was otherwise in Scotch poetry. It witnessed in Scotland an extraordinary phenomenon, the elevation of a dialect by the genius of one man to a place among literary languages.

People have almost ceased wondering that a ploughman should have proved himself capable of great work in literature, but it is still customary to speak of Burns as an uneducated man. Now we may lay it down as an axiom that, whenever a man does great work of any kind, he has been specially educated for it, if not by the deliberate care of parents or his own deliberate choice, by a still greater schoolmaster, Accident. When we find any apparent exception to this rule, we may be sure that there is something wrong with our conception of education. Burns is an apparent exception only when we take education to mean instruction in school and college. But this course of instruction has never yet been in our country a literary education, an education for the man of letters. It has been at best but an education for certain professions and for a scholarly career. Neither school nor college, as they were in the days of Burns, could have contributed one iota to his efficiency as a poet. For his work as a poet he had received from early youth the best possible education. I mean as regards the purely technical or literary qualities of his verse. As regards the feelings that he expressed, the character that is reflected in his poetry, though the feelings are in the main healthy and the character in the main noble, we may think that circumstances might have been a more perfect schoolmaster. But his literary education was as perfect as could be desired. What a poet above all needs is an easy command of the language in which he writes, and the early training of Burns was excellently fitted to give him this.

For two generations before Burns wrote there had been throughout Scotland an unbounded enthusiasm for song-writing in the native dialect. The movement began early in the century among a knot of idle lairds, younger sons, and Writers to the Signet in Edinburgh; but in the course of a very short time it became universal throughout the country. Men and women of all ranks took part in it, from the bold, black-eyed, lucky Isabel Pagan, who kept an alehouse in Ayrshire, to the accomplished Lady Anne Lindsay, daughter of the Earl of Balcarres. Judges of the Court of Session, scions of noble houses, ministers, farmers, gardeners, shepherds,—no one thought himself too high to condescend or too humble to aspire. All were ambitious of trying their hand at a rhyme in the vernacular. There is no example in history of a literary movement so widely diffused, perhaps because up to that time there had been no example of a whole people through all its ranks educated to read and write. Miscellany after miscellany poured from the press collecting the effusions of the wonderfully miscellaneous herd of writers; and these collections were conned in moorland bothies and kitchen firesides as ardently as in libraries and drawing-rooms. It was in this school that Burns received the literary education that fitted him for his work in life. He was nourished on two generations of poetry; taught by its mistakes, warned by its affectations, inspired by its enthusiasm, stimulated by its successes. He had a large body of literature before him in the same kind that he attempted; in this he was steeped to the lips. But how was the unlettered ploughman to distinguish between good and bad? In this his own strong sense, clearness of insight, and warm passionate nature kept him right. He applied with merciless, unfaltering severity one touchstone—commonplace enough, in words at least, to the critics of the time—truth to nature. Pope's praise of Nature—

> " Unerring Nature, still divinely bright,
>   One clear, unchanged, and universal light,
>   Life, force, and beauty must to all impart
>   At once the source and end and test of Art "—

a eulogy that Burns had by heart—was accepted and applied by him to the letter. And in applying this test of truth to Nature to enable him to distinguish between good and bad, genuine and affected, in the work of his predecessors, and to guide him in the execution of his own, the peasant had a decided advantage over men of higher social rank, because the nature that the Scotch poets of the eighteenth century sought to interpret was rustic nature. It was no wonder that a ploughman bore off the laurel crown from all competitors in this keen race for poetic fame. Who but a real country swain was to be expected to be supreme in pastoral lyrics ? The songs of Burns would have been much more miraculous if he had been anything but a ploughman.

Akin to the vulgar error of wondering at Burns as an un-educated poet, is the error of regarding Scotch vernacular poetry as purely indigenous, a growth out of the hearts of the people, gradually perfecting itself and taking shape unaffected by any influence from without. Between the reigns of James VI. and Queen Anne there was no poetry of note written in Lowland Scotch. It had its roll of distinguished names while the Jameses reigned in Scotland—the first James himself, Henryson, Dunbar, Lindsay, Montgomery; but it ceased to be a literary language when the Court was removed from Holyrood. The poets went with the Court; the singing birds with the hands that caressed and fed them, the hearts that were cheered and the fancies that were humoured with their songs. For a hundred years the Muse of Scotland was mute. Immediately after the union of the king-doms there was a revival of poetry in the Lowland Scotch. That this revival was fostered by the growing prosperity of the country, and the rise of a new class of wealthy patrons, is highly probable ; but it is a very common opinion that the new growth of fancy and imagination which these men encouraged was entirely spontaneous, uninfluenced either by the earlier Scotch poetry or by the poetry of the southern centre of civilisation ; that it was the offspring of the teeming fancies of unsophisticated men, innocent of any literature but the Bible and the Shorter Catechism.

The error is natural enough, if we think of the Scotch poetry of the eighteenth century as peasant poetry, written by peasants for peasants, artless jets of song, most of them rude, imperfect, disfigured by make-weight epithets and make-shift rhymes, an irregular and uneven stretch of poetry, redeemed from ephemeral insignificance only by the semi-miraculous genius of one of the peasant poets. None the less is it an error to regard this poetry as of entirely spontaneous generation. If it is worth writing about, it is worth inquiring into ; and when we inquire closely into its beginning, we see that, like all the literary growths, it had its seed-time as well as its harvest. The seeds of the new poetic vegetation which so rapidly overspread the country came from the old Scotch poetry of the sixteenth century, and as it grew slips were grafted on it from plants that were flourishing at the time in the poetic gardens of England. In plain language, poetry was revived in Scotland by reprints of the old Scotch poetry, and the new Scotch poets studied the English poets and critics, and in the first instance at least translated into their vernacular and applied to their own circumstances the ideas that they found in their approved masters. The truth is, that the peasant poetry of Scotland, so far from being spontaneous in the sense of being unconditioned by previous literature, is one of the few unambiguous and decided examples of the influence of critical ideas on creative literature.

The leader of the poetic revival in Scotland was Allan Ramsay, but the work that marks the beginning of better days was Watson's 'Collection of Choice Scots Songs, Ancient and Modern,' published in 1706, when Ramsay was a young man of twenty. He had been bred in the country, or near Hopetoun Mines in Lanarkshire, of which his father was manager ; but his father dying when he was a child, and his mother marrying again, he had been sent to Edinburgh at the age of fifteen, and apprenticed to a wigmaker. Watson's Collection was the first poetry he read. He was charmed with it ; took to repeating snatches of it ; and from humming it over,

began to feel an impulse to make verses himself. It was thus
that the ingenious wigmaker received his first impetus—

> "Then emulation did me pierce,
> Whilk ne'er since ceased."

Soon after chance threw him in the way of more learned amateurs, and brought him into the full stream of Queen Anne literary
influences.   There were modern as well as ancient poems in
Watson's Collection.   Among the ancient pieces were Dunbar's
"Thistle and Rose," and the humorous poem of which the authorship is disputed between James I. and James V., "Christ's Kirk
on the Green."   Among the modern contributors was William
Hamilton of Gilbertfield, the "Willie" who, according to the
song, was a "wanton wag," a roystering young Jacobite lieu-
tenant, who formed himself apparently on the poetic ideal of
the Restoration,—a Scotch Etherege or Rochester.   The young
wigmaker made his acquaintance, probably in the way of business;
but, on the basis of their common interest in poetry, the acquaintance became more intimate, and Ramsay was admitted a member
of a club to which Hamilton belonged along with other choice
spirits of literary leanings and Jacobite political faith.   The fact
that Ramsay, though his family had come down in the world,
could trace his descent from a younger son of an Earl of Dalhousie,
probably helped, along with his social and poetic gifts, to secure
him admission to this Easy Club, as it was called.   That the Easy
Club, which was broken up by the Rebellion of 1715, had a literary
as well as a political basis, is shown by the circumstance that the
members of it assumed fancy literary names; and the bent of
Ramsay's literary homage at the time is indicated by his choice for
himself of the name of Isaac Bickerstaff, then famous as Steel's
pseudonym in the 'Tatler.'   Ramsay made himself so popular in
the Easy Club that he was appointed its Poet-Laureate, and by a
formal minute adjudged "a gentleman."

Through these Jacobite gentlemen, Ramsay's friends and patrons
of the Easy Club, with leanings to the good old times of the
Stuarts and a disposition to scoff at Puritans as their natural and
hereditary enemies, the spirit of the Restoration passed into the
peasant poetry of Scotland to do battle with the austere spirit of

the Kirk. It is a striking illustration of the vitality of ideas and their directive power over conduct that the Cavalier ideal, transmitted through Ramsay, took possession of the warm temperament of Burns, and worked out in him the incontinent irregularities that made shipwreck of his life. Ramsay himself was too cool of temper to be made a victim in like manner : convivial, quick-witted, libertine enough in theory, a welcome guest at the drinking bouts then fashionable, ever ready to help in driving dull care away with a jest or a song, he was yet sufficiently master of himself to combine poetry with an eye to business. He prospered as a wigmaker ; he set up as a bookseller ; he published two poetical miscellanies by which he made some money. He had none of Burns's over-scrupulous and fantastic objection to taking payment for his songs ; he published them in broadsheets as he wrote them ; and it is said to have been a custom with the good wives of Edinburgh to send one of their children with a penny for Allan Ramsay's latest. " Renowned Allan, canty callan," was described by a sour critic as a " convivial buffoon " ; but though he ruined himself late in life by building a theatre which the magistrates would not allow him to open, he was, like his contemporary Pope, a good man of business. Ramsay's own conduct was not mastered by the ideal of reckless generosity and self-indulgence to which he gave expression in his poems ; but none the less he had great influence in connecting poetry with ostentatious and swaggering profligacy in the minds of the peasant poets of Scotland.

The pleasure-loving side of Ramsay's temperament was encouraged and expanded by his connection with the Easy Club ; and it was in this connection also that in all probability he received the suggestion of the work that is his only enduring title to fame —the 'Gentle Shepherd.' We have no positive evidence that he conceived fully the idea of writing such a work at this time,—the memoirs of his life are exceedingly scanty ; but it is all but certain that he was at this time put on the road that led him to this pastoral poem—the first genuine pastoral poem that had appeared in European literature between the time of Theocritus in the third century B.C. to the eighteenth century. This conclusion is irresistible when we look at the chief events in English literature during the three years of Ramsay's membership of the Easy Club.

He was a member of the Club from 1712 to 1715. The kind of poetry that was most in vogue at the time was pastoral poetry. We have already seen how general had been the discussion of this kind of poetry for some years. During the existence of the Easy Club, interest in the topic had received a fresh stimulus from the publication of Pope's 'Windsor Forest' and Ambrose Philips's 'Pastorals.' For the purpose of puffing Philips and depreciating Pope, there was a series of articles on Pastoral Poetry in the 'Guardian,' which doubtless were read by Isaac Bickerstaff's double in the Easy Club. Everybody who had any pretension to literary fashion read Steele and Addison's periodicals, and the members of the Easy Club were keen and ardent amateurs of poetry, not a little self-conscious of poetic ambition. To puff Philips and depreciate Pope was the prime purpose of these articles in the 'Guardian,' and this purpose was cleverly defeated by the stratagem of the poet whose reputation was in danger; but unintentionally and by the way the articles served a more important purpose—namely, guiding Allan Ramsay into a kind of poetry exactly suited to his talents. One of the papers in the 'Guardian' reads now like a recipe for Allan Ramsay's great pastoral; the 'Gentle Shepherd' might be said to have been made from it as from a prescription, so exactly in the scheme and accessories does the poet follow the advice of the critic. "Paint the manners of natural rustic life," said the critic to the poet, "not the manners of artificial shepherds and shepherdesses in a fictitious golden age; use actual rustic dialect; instead of satyrs and fauns and nymphs, introduce the supernatural creatures of modern superstition." This was what the essayist in the 'Guardian' advised, and what Ramsay with happily appropriate genius did. I know no other instance in literature where a poet has carried out the ideas of a critic so perfectly. Ramsay pottered for a little with pastoral dialogues of the old artificial school, in which he made Steele and Pope discourse in the character of shepherds about the deaths of Addison and Prior,—a fancy rendered all the more absurd by his making these two shepherds discourse in the Scotch dialect. But he soon abandoned these affectations, and produced his drama of real rustic life in 1725. Its repute was instantaneous and widespread. Edition after edition was produced; it was said that the

'Gentle Shepherd' was almost as common a book in the houses of the Scotch peasantry as the Bible. Amateur companies were organised in country parishes to act it. Even to this day, it is said, such companies exist and perform occasionally in the south of Scotland. The fame of the 'Gentle Shepherd' spread beyond Scotland. It probably furnished the hint of the 'Beggar's Opera' to Gay; so that if Ramsay owed something to the critical ideas of his English contemporaries, he may be said to have repaid the debt.

The songs interspersed through the 'Gentle Shepherd,' which is rather an operetta than a drama, are not the best part of it. I cannot say that I think highly of Ramsay's gifts as a song-writer. His genius was not lyrical. His songs, even the best of them, strike me as smirking and affected, entirely destitute of genuine lyric rapture. We have only to place his "Auld Lang Syne," or his "Nanny O," by the side of Burns's words to the same airs to feel how empty they are of lyric sincerity and force,—how artificially, mechanically, and laboriously they have been put together.

> "How joyfully my spirits rise,
>   When dancing she moves finely—O ;
> . I guess what heaven is by her eyes,
>   Which sparkle so divinely—O.
> Attend my vow, ye gods, while I
> Breathe in the bless'd Britannia,
> None's happiness I shall envy,
> As long's ye grant me Nanny—O."
>   —RAMSAY.

> "Her face is fair, her heart is true,
>   As spotless as she's bonny—O ;
> The opening gowan, wat wi' dew,
> Nae fairer is than Nannie—O.
> Come weel, come woe, I care na by,
> I'll tak' what Heaven will sen' me, O ;
> Nae ither care in life have I
> But live and love my Nannie—O !"
>   —BURNS.

The inferiority of Ramsay is still more manifest when we look at his "Auld Lang Syne." The opening lines have a ring of insincerity that pervades the whole song :—

> " Should auld acquaintance be forgot,
>   Tho' they return with scars ?
> These are the noble hero's lot,
>   Obtained in glorious wars.
> Welcome, my Varo, to my breast,
>   Thy arms about me twine,
> And make me once again as blest
>   As I was lang syne."

There are two lines in Ramsay's " Farewell to Lochaber " that seem to be conclusive against his claim to a respectable place among song-writers. A soldier bidding farewell to his sweetheart is a well-chosen lyrical theme ; Ramsay had abundance of poetical intelligence, and is often happy in his choice of themes. And the opening lines, when sung to the beautiful air, are undeniably simple and touching :—

> " Fareweel to Lochaber, fareweel to my Jean,
>   Where heartsome wi' thee I hae mony days been."

But presently come the two lines which strike an absurdly false note, and turn the plaintive soldier into a burlesque impostor :—

> " These tears that I shed they are a' for my dear,
>   And no' for the dangers attending on weir."

Fancy a departing soldier explaining that he weeps not because he is afraid of the enemy, but because he is sorry to leave his sweetheart ! *Qui s'excuse, s'accuse.* The girl, if she had a particle of spirit, would have laughed, and set him down at once as a transparent humbug. No man capable of writing a good song with any deep sentiment or passion in it could have passed such a preposterous insincerity as that. No ; " renowned Allan, canty callan," had not the lyric gift. His strength lay in humorous description and portraiture ; in arch, sly, " pawky " fun. The portrait of him by his son is a speaking likeness of the poet as we know him through his works ; it is a keen, slyly humorous face, the face of a man with a quick sense of the ridiculous, and a firm touch in the exhibition of what amuses him, but it is not the face of a lyric poet.

If we except the songs, which, as I have said, are of rather unequal merit, we cannot but admire the manner in which Ramsay embodied the idea so casually suggested by the English critic. As is usually the case in such matters, several places are claimants for the honour of being the scene of the poem, but probably New-hall in Peeblesshire conforms most to the poetic descriptions. The plot is slender, but not more so than we should expect in such an operetta, and the scenes are connected with no little dramatic skill. The bulk of the story narrates the pastoral loves of Roger and Jenny, and of Patie, the Gentle Shepherd, and Peggie, a shep-herd's niece. Sir William Worthy, a somewhat priggish but not unamiable knight, is the presiding genius; in Patie he recognises his son, and in Peggy his niece, and the faithful lovers receive his blessing. Bauldy, Madge, and Mause supply what comic element there is, but the humour is of a quiet, subdued order, never ap-proaching the rollicking fun of Burns. The light, bantering con-versation between Peggy and Jenny is admirably done, and the spirited eulogy of Patie by his sweetheart is a good example of the style of language that Ramsay considered most suited to a Scottish pastoral :—

> "Sic coarse-spun thoughts as thae want pith to move
> My settled mind, I'm o'er far gane in love.
> Patie to me is dearer than my breath ;
> But want of him I dread nae other skaith.
> There's nane of a' the herds that tread the green
> Has sic a smile, or sic twa glancing een.
> And then he speaks with sic a taking art.
> His words they thirle like musick thro' my heart.
> How blythly can he sport, and gently rave,
> And jest at feckless fears that fright the lave !
> Ilk day that he's alane upon the hill,
> He reads fell books that teach him meikle skill.
> He is—but what need I say that or this?
> I'd spend a month to tell you what he is !
> In a' he says or does there's sic a gait,
> The rest seem coofs compar'd to my dear Pate.
> His better sense will lang his love secure !
> Ill nature heffs in sauls that's weak and poor."

In a prologue for the 'Gentle Shepherd' on the occasion of one of its presentations on the stage, the poet declared—

> "Tho' they're but Shepherds that we're now to act,
> Yet, gentle audience, we'd not ha' ye mistake

> And think your entertainment will be rude.
> Most men and all the ladys think it good ;
> Our Pastoral Author thinks so too, but fears .
> The diction may offend some nicer ears.
> This we regard not, therefore will proceed
> To act the blithesome life that shepherds lead."

Now, it is just this fact, that Allan Ramsay did not "regard" those "nicer ears," that constitutes his main literary importance. He is worthy to be called the pioneer of Burns, because he had the sense and ability to combat victoriously the theory of men like Beattie, who held that the Scottish language was incapable of being made the vehicle of literary expression.

Half a century elapsed between the publication of the 'Gentle Shepherd' and the boyhood of Burns, and meantime the impulse given by Ramsay and the ingenious gentlemen and ladies who co-operated with him in his publications had diffused itself all over the country. We had our group of singers here in the North : George Halket, the author of "Logie o' Buchan"; Alexander Ross, the author of the "Fortunate Shepherdess"; Priest Geddes, author of "Lewie Gordon" and the "Wee Wifiekie"; and greatest of them all, indeed one of the greatest of Scotch song-writers, John Skinner, the author of "Tullochgorum" and the "Ewie wi' the crookit Horn." In "Tullochgorum," especially, there is a wonderful rapidity and spirit in its music,—an indefinable something that manifestly proclaims Skinner to be the fellow-countryman of William Dunbar and Burns :—

> " What needs there be sae great a fraise
>   Wi' dringing dull Italian lays ?
>   I wadna gie our ain Strathspeys
>   For half a hunder score o' 'em.
>   They're dowf and dowie at the best ;
>   Dowf and dowie, dowf and dowie,
>   Dowf and dowie at the best,
>   Wi' a' their variorum ;
>   They're dowf and dowie at the best,
>   Their allegros and a' the rest ;
>   They canna please a Scottish taste,
>   Compar'd wi' Tullochgorum."

These are lines that, both for their music and their sentiment, were likely to appeal to Burns, and it is no surprise, therefore, to find

Burns writing words so laudatory as these: "I regret, and while I live I shall regret, that, when I was in the North, I had not the pleasure of paying a younger brother's dutiful respect to the author of the best Scotch song ever Scotland saw—'Tullochgorum's my delight.' There is a certain something in the old Scotch songs, a wild happiness of thought and expression, which peculiarly marks them, not only from English songs, but also from the modern efforts of song-wrights, in our native manner and language. The only remains of this enchantment, these spells of the imagination, rest with you."

It is remarkable that the Northern song-writers were all educated men — in the popular sense of the word educated—schoolmasters and clergymen. In the south of Scotland poetic ambition was more universal. Then the middle years of the eighteenth witnessed something like the palmy days of the Troubadours of Provence in the thirteenth century, when every hamlet had its laureate. We cannot wonder that the genius of Burns should have been excited by such surroundings, and that very early in life falling in love, and knowing of neighbouring bards who addressed verses to the objects of their affections, he was moved by an ambition to show that he also was a song-writer. Thousands of little bards at that time limited their aspirations to fame within the parishes in which they were born. That the ambition of Burns took a wider range was due partly to the masterful strength of his nature—that of course is an indispensable condition of wide-reaching ambition; but partly also to peculiar circumstances in his life that fostered his ambition and kept it from being quenched in his hard struggle for bare existence as the son of a poor farmer. Where other young men in his rank of life, like young men with a turn for versification in higher ranks of life, were eager only to gain the admiration of the women, and establish a reputation for cleverness with the men among whom they were born, Burns from a very early period aspired to make the streams of his native country as famous as the classic Ilissus and the silver-winding Thames:—

> "E'en then a wish, I mind its power,
>   A wish that to its latest hour
>   Shall strongly heave my breast;

> That I for poor auld Scotland's sake,
> Some useful plan or book could make,
> Or sing a sang at least " ;

and again in a poem showing more definitely the latitude of his ambition :—

> " Ramsay and famous Fergusson
> Gied Forth and Tay a lift aboon ;
> Yarrow and Tweed, to monie a tune,
> Owre Scotland rings ;
> While Irwin, Lugar, Ayr, and Doon,
> Naebody sings.
>
> Th' Ilissus, Tiber, Thames, and Seine,
> Glide sweet in monie a tunefu' line ;
> But, Willie, set your fit to mine,
> And cock your crest ;
> We'll gar our streams and burnies shine
> Up wi' the best ! "

And the natural greatness of mind that prompted this ambition was not without special influences to keep the flame alive. Had Burns been educated as other local rhymers were, he might have remained, like them, content with local fame, ignorant of the great world outside, hungering for no applause beyond his own small circle, because he was unaware of anything more to be desired. But the education of Burns was different from that of other local rhymers, and had carried him to spiritual altitudes, the views from which were bounded by a much wider horizon.

In common with all the other young men of the time, rich and poor, Burns had the advantage for a poet of living in a poetical atmosphere ; but he had the further special advantage of coming under personal influences that helped powerfully to give his work the quality of greatness. His want of school and college instruction was fully compensated by the exceptional tastes, abilities, and literary interests of his father and his schoolmaster. We may truly say, I think, that for his special training as a poet—for the literary part of it, that is to say—the happiest accident of his life was his contact with Mr Murdoch, who, when a youth of eighteen, was employed by William Burness, and one or two of his neighbours, to teach their children. That this young schoolmaster was a man of no ordinary vigour, flexibility, and breadth of interest, was shown by his subsequent career. He went to London, and made a living as a teacher of French, an extraordinary feat for a young country Scotchman; and gained such repute as a teacher, though he ultimately ruined his prospects by intemperate habits, that at one time he had as a pupil in English no less a person than M. Talleyrand. We can hardly over-estimate the lift above provincial commonplace that was given to the future poet by his contact with a man of such activity and range of mind. Mr Murdoch was greatly attracted by the character of William Burness—for so the father spelt his name; and attracted also by the character and abilities of the boys, he took a warm interest in them, and gave an unusual turn to the reading of the family, introducing them to authors not ordinarily within the knowledge of a peasant's household. Robert Burns was but a small boy when Murdoch was engaged as a teacher to the combined families; but when he was a youth of fifteen or sixteen the young man chanced to be appointed English teacher in the Ayr Academy, and the elder Burness, always eager to get education for his sons, sent Robert for a short time to board with him. Charmed with the aptness of his pupil, with his manly character, his enthusiasm for knowledge, and his powerful grasp of intellect, Murdoch did his utmost to give a bent to his studies. It was only for a short three weeks that Burns could be spared from the work of the farm, where he was already doing the work of a man; but during that time, so eager was the pupil to learn, and so willing was the master to communicate, that, as Murdoch afterwards stated, he and his boarder were hardly a moment silent—the one inquiring, the other answering and expounding. Among other things, Murdoch gave him a start in learning French, to such effect that Burns afterwards by himself acquired such a knowledge of the language that he was able to read it with ease. He was rather proud, in fact, of the accomplishment, and fond of airing scraps of French in his correspondence. But this knowledge of French was the least of the benefits Burns derived from this inspiring and stimulating teacher.

Looking at his life till he was twenty-two or twenty-three, we find, from a memorandum-book which he kept, the extent of his reading, and we may safely say that there were very few young men at that time in any rank whose acquaintance with the poets of the previous century was so great. He had read most of the English poets, including Shakespeare, Pope, Shenstone, Allan Ramsay, and collections of Scotch songs; and he not only read them, but pondered over them. His habit was always to carry a book in his pocket, in which way he is said to have worn out two copies of Mackenzie's 'Man of Feeling.' This gives us a clue to his mode of mental application. He took a rigorously critical attitude. We can imagine him reading over his songs, then turning the work over in his mind and judging with his perfect taste whether it was true to nature. Burns was wont to take his own songs to pieces; word by word, line by line, stanza by stanza, all passed under review, and were critically pronounced on by their author. There could be no greater misconception than to regard Burns as an uneducated poet. This idea has made shipwreck of many a promising poet, or at least of many a youth capable of becoming a pleasing versifier, for they get the idea that it is derogatory to poetic genius to take intellectual labour over their verses. They are under the idea that Burns produced songs without considering whether they were good or bad. We may be sure that no amount of genius will produce perfect art, unless the man of genius will bestow intellectual labour on it. A perfect poem, such as many of Burns's lyric gems are, can no more be written without labour than can a statue be carved out of stone.

CHAPTER XII.

WORDSWORTH.

CONNECTION WITH PREVIOUS POETRY—SKETCH OF LIFE—LYRICAL BALLADS.

FROM the phrases that are generally used about nineteenth-century poetry, one would expect to be conscious of a great and sudden change in passing into it out of the poetry of the eighteenth century. Were the new poets not inspired with the spirit of the French Revolution? Did they not rise in their might, glowing with a noble spirit of independence, and fling the poetic traditions of their fathers to the winds? Pope with his mechanical couplets, his passion for epigrammatic condensation, his fear of going beyond classical example, was sitting on poetry like a nightmare when the French Revolution broke out; and the English Muse, fired by this great modern example of insubordination, would bear him no longer, cast off her Old Man of the Mountain, and roamed greatly, daring wherever Fancy or Imagination tempted, with all the fearless ardour of new-found liberty. Such is the language in which the new movement is often spoken of, and if we accept it literally, we should expect to find somewhere between the old poetry and the new a sudden discontinuous break: we should expect, as we followed the history of our literature, to encounter all of a sudden the signs of a great and complete transformation such as might be made on the face of nature by an earthquake or a deluge. But no such catastrophic spectacle is presented to the historic eye. A great change took place, but it was an easy gradual transition, a quiet evolution of new things, not a fierce upheaval and sweeping away of old things as worthless rubbish and a triumphant reconstruction upon entirely new lines. We must not ignore the fact that there was a change because we cannot put our finger upon the exact moment when the change occurred; but it is equally unhistoric to be misled by the character of the tremendous political event of the time into ascribing a similar character to the grand new season of poetry that opened with the nineteenth century.

The hold of the Queen Anne style on literature, as we have seen, relaxed gradually; the sentiments that it embodied gradually palled from custom on the class for whom Pope wrote; longings for new excitements gradually made themselves felt; and gradually also the class whose taste had dominated Queen Anne literature lost their supremacy in the world of art. The prosemen of the last sixty years of the century were, as I have already indicated, the chief literary agents of the transformation that gradually evolved itself, year by year, ten years by ten years, now moving quickly, now moving slowly. The novelists and the romancers educated the taste of the public for new subjects and for a new style,—for subjects of more various human interest, and a style less condensed and elaborate, more free and discursive. Pope's readers had little taste for romantic marvels or for domestic pathos; the romancers and the novelists accustomed the public to such imaginative food, and so prepared the way for Scott and Wordsworth. Even the Byronic spirit had its prototype in prose.

Wordsworth's preface to his 'Lyrical Ballads' in 1798 is a great landmark in the history of poetry, because it woke people up to a consciousness of the change that had taken place, and compelled critics to define their position in the face of that change. This preface, and the volume with which it is connected, we must consider at length; but in the first place let us look at Wordsworth's early life, and at the poems written by him before the 'Lyrical Ballads.' In these early poems we shall see how gradual was his transition from the poetic style of his predecessors, notwithstanding the revolutionary note of his famous preface.

To some of Wordsworth's admirers it might appear a sort of

sacrilege to try and trace the growth of his poetic style, because he has himself in the "Prelude" written his poetic autobiography. "The Growth of a Poet's Mind" is the sub-title of this wonderful poem, in which flashes of poetic rapture are so strangely mixed with prosy moralisings and pragmatic dogmas about education. Seeing that the poet has given the history of his own mind, it is to his worshippers as final as the Koran to a good Mohammedan; and any presumptuous attempt to add to it might be treated by them as the books in the Alexandria Library were treated by the Caliph Omar. · They might say: If your essay contains anything not to be found in the "Prelude," it is wrong; if it contains what is already to be found there, it is superfluous. But it is possible to go beyond the revelation of the "Prelude" without contradicting it, or merely bringing to light what is useless and superfluous. It is the growth of his mind, of his feelings, of his impassioned love for Nature, that is there recorded; not the growth of his poetic art, of his aims and methods as an artist: and these are interesting to us, if we wish to see him in his right relations with his predecessors. His early poems furnish more valuable clues for this inquiry than the "Prelude," which is rather an imaginative interpretation of his youth than a literal record. And we have other clues besides in his singularly matter-of-fact prose notes on the circumstances in which he composed his early poems.

The chief incidents in Wordsworth's early life were taken down from his own dictation. He was the son of one of Sir James Lowther's land-agents, whose headquarters were at Cockermouth, and of the daughter of a mercer in Penrith. His early boyhood till the age of nine was spent partly at Cockermouth and partly at Penrith, both beautifully situated little towns in Cumberland. From nine to seventeen he was at a boarding-school in Hawkshead, another romantically situated little town in the north of Lancashire. His mother died when he was seven years old and his father when he was thirteen; but his uncle, in whose guardianship he was left, although Lord Lonsdale had borrowed all his father's money and refused to pay it back— the repayment not being made till the old lord's death many years afterwards—his uncle kept both him and his brother at school, and sent them both to Cambridge, the poet entering in 1787, his seventeenth year. Wordsworth took his degree in 1791, travelled for some time in France and Italy, lived for a few years in London, thought of the Church as a profession, thought of journalism as a profession, but finally decided to retire to his native valleys and live on his small inheritance, devoting his days to "plain living and high thinking." He was nearly thirty when he took this determination, and he persevered in it to the end of his days in 1850, with the addition to his means of plain living of a Commissionership of Stamps in 1813, and a pension of £300 in 1842.

Such is the bare outline of Wordsworth's life. What were the ruling circumstances that co-operated with inborn genius to make him the poet that he was? Read the "Prelude" and you will find that his own answer is simply Nature—the mountains and the mists, and the leaping sounding cataracts of the valleys where he lived in youth. This is how he describes his feelings in his school-days at Hawkshead :—

> " I would walk alone
> Under the quiet stars, and at that time
> Have felt whate'er there is of power in sound
> To breathe an elevated mood, by form
> Or image unprofaned ; and I would stand,
> If the night blackened with a coming storm,
> Beneath some rock, listening to notes that are
> The ghostly language of the ancient earth,
> Or make their dim abode in distant winds.
> Thence did I drink the visionary power ;
> And deem not profitless those flecting moods
> Of shadowy exultation ; not for this,
> That they are kindred to our purer mind
> And intellectual life ; but that the soul,
> Remembering not, retains an obscure sense
> Of possible sublimity, whereto
> With growing faculties she doth aspire,
> With faculties still growing, feeling still
> That whatsoever point they gain, they yet
> Have something to pursue."

And again :—

> " 'Twere long to tell
> What spring and autumn, what the winter snows,
> And what the summer shade, what day and night,

Evening and morning, sleep and waking, thought
From sources inexhaustible, poured forth
To feed the spirit of religious love
In which I walked with Nature.   But let this
Be not forgotten, that I still retained
My first creative sensibility;
That by the regular action of the world
My soul was unsubdued.   A plastic power
Abode with me; a forming hand, at times
Rebellious, acting in a devious mood;
A local spirit of his own, at war
With general tendency, but, for the most,
Subservient strictly to external things
With which it communed.   An auxiliar light
Came from my mind, which on the setting sun
Bestowed new splendour; the melodious birds,
The fluttering breezes, fountains that run on,
Murmuring so sweetly in themselves, obeyed
A like dominion, and the midnight storm
Grew darker in the presence of my eye:
Hence my obeisance, my devotion hence,
And hence my transport.
                              Nor should this, perchance,
Pass unrecorded, that I still had loved
The exercise and produce of a toil,
Than analytic industry to me
More pleasing, and whose character I deem
Is more poetic as resembling more
Creative agency.   The song would speak
Of that interminable building reared
By observation of affinities
In objects where no brotherhood exists
To passive minds.   My seventeenth year was come!
And, whether from this habit rooted now
So deeply in my mind, or from excess
In the great social principle of life
Coercing all things into sympathy,
To inorganic natures were transferred
My own enjoyments; or the power of truth
Coming in revelation did converse
With things that really are, I, at this time,
Saw blessings spread around me like a sea.
Thus while the days flew by, and years passed on,
From Nature and her overflowing soul
I had received so much, that all my thoughts
Were steeped in feeling: I was only then

> Contented, when with bliss ineffable
> I felt the sentiment of Being spread
> O'er all that moves and all that seemeth still ;
> O'er all that, lost beyond the reach of thought
> And human knowledge, to the human eye
> Invisible, yet liveth to the heart ;
> O'er all that leaps and runs, and shouts and sings,
> Or beats the gladsome air ; o'er all that glides
> Beneath the wave, yea, in the wave itself,
> And mighty depth of waters."

At Cambridge he attended little to the studies of the place. "He began residence at seventeen," says Mr Myers, "and his northern nature was late to flower. There seems, in fact, to have been even less of visible promise about him than we should have expected; but rather something untamed and insubordinate, something heady and self-confident—an independence that seemed only rusticity, and an indolent ignorance which assumed too readily the tones of scorn." But his mind was not idle :—

> "Oft when the dazzling show no longer new
> Had ceased to dazzle, ofttimes did I quit
> My comrades, leave the crowd, buildings and groves,
> And as I paced alone the level fields
> Far from those lovely sights and sounds sublime
> With which I had been conversant, the mind
> Drooped not ; but there into herself returning,
> With prompt rebound seemed fresh as heretofore.
> At least I more distinctly recognised
> Her native instincts : let me dare to speak
> A higher language, say that now I felt
> What independent solaces were mine,
> To mitigate the injurious sway of place
> Or circumstance, how far soever changed
> In youth, or to be changed in after years.
> As if awakened, summoned, roused, constrained,
> I looked for universal things ; perused
> The common countenance of earth and sky :
> Earth, nowhere unembellished by some trace
> Of that first Paradise whence man was driven ;
> And sky, whose beauty and bounty are expressed
> By the proud name she bears—the name of Heaven.
> I called on both to teach me what they might ;
> Or, turning the mind in upon herself,

> Pored, watched, expected, listened, spread my thoughts,
> And spread them with a wider creeping ; felt
> Incumbencies more awful, visitings
> Of the Upholder of the tranquil soul,
> That tolerates the indignities of Time,
> And, from the centre of Eternity
> All finite motions overruling, lives
> In glory immutable. But peace ! enough
> Here to record that I was mounting now
> To such community with highest truth—
> A track pursuing, not untrod before,
> From strict analogies by thought supplied,
> Or consciousnesses not to be subdued.
> To every natural form, rock, fruit, or flower,
> Even the loose stones that cover the highway,
> I gave a moral life : I saw them feel,
> Or linked them to some feeling : the great mass
> Lay bedded in a quickening soul, and all
> That I beheld respired with inward meaning.
> Add that whate'er of Terror or of Love
> Or Beauty, Nature's daily face put on
> From transitory passion, unto this
> I was as sensitive as waters are
> To the sky's influence in a kindred mood
> Of passion ; was obedient as a lute
> That waits upon the touches of the wind.
> Unknown, unthought of, yet was I most rich—
> I had a world about me—'twas my own ;
> I made it, for it only lived to me,
> And to the God who sees into the heart."

Now how were the poet's sensibilities thus keenly awakened to the glories and the beauties of Nature ? What first made him alive to the joy of poring over every shade of colour, every minute variation of form in natural things, and seeking in them, with never-ending satisfaction, images of human life in its manifold relations ? And what influences governed his expression of what he saw and felt ? The "Prelude" is silent on these points. It merely chronicles the phases of his delight in looking and imagining. There was in Wordsworth to the last not a little of that untamed rustic egotism which Shakespeare caricatured in Holofernes and Sir Andrew Aguecheek ; the egotism which, owing to slight contact with other human beings, is never tired of contemplating the strangeness of its own moods. " I am a fellow of the strangest mind in the world," said Sir Andrew, and in these words expressed an undying characteristic of the isolated man who seldom makes comparison of his own mind with the minds of his fellow-creatures. Wordsworth's distinction lay not in what he felt, but in the play of his imagination on what he felt. He magnifies the strangeness of his absorption in Nature by representing it as a mysterious inexplicable feat, originating he knew not how, but present with him from his earliest years, and gaining no strength but from its own impetus. "The 'Prelude' is a work of good augury for human nature," Mr Myers says, in commenting on the poem. "We felt in reading it as if the stock of mankind were sound. The soul seems going on from strength to strength by the mere development of her inborn power." The "Prelude" is a noble poem, but this particular feature of it I should consider a weakness and not a strength. No man can stand alone; the aspiration to do so is as inhuman as the achievement is impossible. The soul that seeks to isolate itself from its fellows must infallibly harden and wither.

When, however, we turn to his early poems and to his prosaic notes and illustrations of them, we can see clearly enough the continuity of his descent from the great poets who had written before him.

The "Evening Walk" and the "Descriptive Sketches" were published in 1793. Commenting many years afterwards on the couplet—

> "And fronting the bright west, yon oak entwines
> Its darkening boughs and leaves in stronger lines,"

he says: "This is feebly and imperfectly exprest; but I recollect distinctly the very spot where this first struck me. It was on the way between Hawkshead and Ambleside, and gave me extreme pleasure. The moment was important in my poetical history, for I date from it my consciousness of the infinite variety of natural appearances which had been unnoticed by the poets of any age or country, so far as I was acquainted with them; and I made a resolution to supply in some degree the deficiency. I could not at that time have been above fourteen years of age." There was more then than mere disinterested delight in the poet's contemplation of Nature; mingled with that delight was a poet's ambition, and the joy of having found an untrodden track. And he did not qualify himself for this self-imposed mission by mere indolent gazing and dreamy pursuit of the thick-coming fancies that crowded his mind, while his eye drank in what Nature presented to him. If the "Prelude" had been intended as a plain historical narrative of the growth of a poet's mind, it would have been strange that he does not mention in the description of his Cambridge life an incident that connects him with the poet Gray. He studied Italian then, and his teacher was Gray's friend. It was not, however, from the Italian poets that he caught the rhythm of his early style. You will have no difficulty in detecting his poetical masters if I read you a passage or two from the "Evening Walk" and the "Descriptive Sketches" :—

> "Sweet are the sounds that mingle from afar,
> Heard by calm lakes, as peeps the folding star,
> When the duck dabbles 'mid the rustling sedge,
> And feeding pike starts from the water's edge,
> Or the swan stirs the reeds, his neck and bill
> Wetting, that drip upon the water still ;
> And heron, as resounds the trodden shore,
> Shoots upward, darting his long neck before.
> Now, with religious awe, the farewell light
> Blends with the solemn colouring of night ;
> 'Mid groves of clouds that crest the mountain's brow,
> And round the west's proud lodge their shadows throw,
> Like Una shining on her gloomy way,
> The half-seen form of Twilight roams astray ;
> Shedding, through paly loopholes mild and small,
> Gleams that upon the lake's still bosom fall ;
> Soft o'er the surface creep those lustres pale,
> Tracking the motions of the fitful gale.
> With restless interchange at once the bright
> Wins on the shade, the shade upon the light.
> No favoured eye was e'er allowed to gaze
> On lovelier spectacle in faery days."

Or again :—

> "Once, Man entirely free, alone and wild,
> Was blest as free—for he was Nature's child.
> He, all superior but his God disdained,
> Walked none restraining, and by none restrained :
> Confessed no law but what his reason taught,
> Did all he wished, and wished but what he ought.

> As man in his primeval dower arrayed
> The image of his glorious Sire displayed,
> Even so, by faithful Nature guarded, here
> The traces of primeval Man appear ;
> The simple dignity no forms debase ;
> The eye sublime, and surly lion-grace :
> The slave of none, of beasts alone the lord,
> His book he prizes, nor neglects his sword ;
> Well taught by that to feel his rights, prepared
> With this ' the blessings he enjoys to guard.' "

The former of these passages reminds one of Goldsmith as forcibly as of Pope, but in the latter Pope alone is clearly the model. There is an evident effort after balance and condensed expression, but it is not executed with nearly the perfection and terseness of the Popian couplet. The imitation is, however, sufficiently apparent to be well worth noting as an interesting link between the two poets.

Wordsworth's next publication was the 'Lyrical Ballads,' in 1798. The volume was published in conjunction with Coleridge. Coleridge visited Wordsworth in the summer of 1797, when he had resided with his sister at Racedown in Dorsetshire. By this time Wordsworth had written his poem "Guilt and Sorrow" in the Spenserian stanza ; his tragedy of "The Borderers"; and the description of the "Ruined Cottage." I mention these poems because it is a significant fact that every poem written by Wordsworth up to the time of Coleridge's visit, while they show considerable poetic power, gave little indication of distinctive individual genius. This visit seems to have had a wonderfully quickening and awakening effect on Wordsworth's nature. The two young men were charmed with one another, and Wordsworth removed to Alfoxden in Somersetshire to enjoy his friend's companionship. During the year that followed he produced much, and what he produced bore a distinctive mark, as if the radiant restless vitality of the more variously gifted man had stirred his more sluggish northern nature to its depths, stimulated him to put forth his full powers, and made him feel in the exercise of them a confident sense of mastery. It may truly be said that Wordsworth hardly knew what was in him till the companionship of Coleridge widened the horizon of his aims.

The volume published at Bristol in 1798 contained Coleridge's "Ancient Mariner"; the rest of the volume was by Wordsworth. In the authorised edition of his works no chronological order is followed; they are classified according to subjects; and it is important, if we would understand the controversy that has been raised round Wordsworth's name, that we should pick out and read together the poems that were published together in 1798. "We are Seven" is now included among the "Poems referring to the period of Childhood" (No. x.); "The Complaint" (21), "The Last of the Flock" (22), "The Idiot Boy" (31), and "Her Eyes are Wild" (37), among the "Poems Founded on the Affections"; "The Reverie of Poor Susan" (13), "The Thorn" (23), "Lines above Tintern Abbey" (26), among "Poems of the Imagination"; "Expostulation and Reply" (1), "The Tables Turned" (2), "To my Sister" (5), and "Simon Lee" (6), among "Poems of Sentiment and Reflection"; "Goody Blake and Harry Gill," among "Miscellaneous Poems."

When these poems are read together, we begin to understand why such a shout of derision was raised by the critics against the 'Lyrical Ballads,' and why they impressed so deeply those who were not repelled by their strangeness. The poet's personality was powerfully expressed in them, and he was a markedly different kind of person from any that had before presented himself as a poet. His humour was a strange kind of humour and his seriousness ran in an unusual vein, and humour and seriousness were strangely intermixed. The public found subjects that they were accustomed to consider too vulgar and common for poetry treated apparently with pathetic intention, but in so grotesque a way as only to make them laugh at the attempt on their tender feelings. There was, indeed, one poem in the volume, the "Lines written above Tintern Abbey," in which a fresh theme was handled with a power that nobody could be insensible to. If all had been like this, the acknowledgment of Wordsworth's greatness would not have been checked and held back by astonishment at the grotesque strangeness of the lyrical ballads, to which the title of the volume challenged special attention. This was the poem in which he first gave expression to his impassioned worship of Nature:—

" Five years have past ; five summers, with the length
Of five long winters ! and again I hear
These waters, rolling from their mountain springs
With a soft inland murmur.—Once again
Do I behold these steep and lofty cliffs,
That on a wild secluded scene impress
Thoughts of more deep seclusion ; and connect
The landscape with the quiet of the sky.
The day is come when I again repose
Here, under this dark sycamore, and view
These plots of cottage-ground, these orchard-tufts,
Which at this season, with their unripe fruits,
Are clad in one green hue, and lose themselves
'Mid groves and copses.   Once again I see
These hedgerows, hardly hedgerows, little lines
Of sportive wood run wild ; these pastoral farms,
Green to the very door; and wreaths of smoke
Sent up, in silence, from among the trees !
With some uncertain notice, as might seem
Of vagrant dwellers in the houseless woods,
Or of some Hermit's cave, where by his fire
The Hermit sits alone.
                              These beauteous forms,
Through a long absence, have not been to me
As is a landscape to a blind man's eye :
But oft in lonely rooms, and 'mid the din
Of towns and cities, I have owed to them,
In hours of weariness, sensations sweet,
Felt in the blood, and felt along the heart ;
And passing even into my purer mind,
With tranquil restoration :—feelings too
Of unremembered pleasure : such, perhaps,
As have no slight or trivial influence
On that best portion of a good man's life,
His little, nameless, unremembered acts
Of kindness and of love.   Nor less, I trust,
To them I may have owed another gift,
Of aspect more sublime ; that blessed mood,
In which the burthen of the mystery,
In which the heavy and the weary weight
Of all this unintelligible world,
Is lightened :—that serene and blessed mood,
In which the affections gently lead us on,—
Until, the breath of this corporeal frame,
And even the motion of our human blood,
Almost suspended, we are laid asleep

In body, and beeome a living soul :
While with an eye made quiet by the power
Of harmony, and the deep power of joy,
We see into the life of things.   If this
Be but a vain belief, yet, oh ! how oft—
In darkness and amid the many shapes
Of joyless daylight ; when the fretful stir
Unprofitable, and the fever of the world,
Have hung upon the beatings of my heart—
How oft, in spirit, have I turned to thee,
O sylvan Wye ! thou wanderer thro' the woods,
How often has my spirit turned to thee !
    And now, with gleams of half-extinguished thought,
With many recognitions dim and faint,
And somewhat of a sad perplexity,
The picture of the mind revives again :
While here I stand, not only with the sense
Of present pleasure, but with pleasing thoughts
That in this moment there is life and food
For future years.   And so I dare to hope,
Though changed, no doubt, from what I was when first
I came among these hills ; when like a roe
I bounded o'er the mountains, by the sides
Of the deep rivers, and the lonely streams,
Wherever Nature led : more like a man
Flying from something that he dreads, than one
Who sought the thing he loved.   For Nature then
(The coarser pleasures of my boyish days,
And their glad animal movements, all gone by)
To me was all in all ;—I cannot paint
What then I was.   The sounding cataract
Haunted me like a passion ; the tall rock,
The mountain, and the deep and gloomy wood,
Their colours and their forms, were then to me
An appetite ; a feeling and a love,
That had no need of a remoter charm,
By thought supplied, nor any interest
Unborrowed from the eye.—That time is past,
And all its aching joys are now no more,
And all its dizzy raptures.   Not for this
Faint I, nor mourn nor murmur ; other gifts
Have followed ; for such loss, I would believe,
Abundant recompence.   For I have learned
To look on Nature, not as in the hour
Of thoughtless youth ; but hearing oftentimes
The still, sad music of humanity,

Not harsh, nor grating, though of ample power
To chasten and subdue.   And I have felt
A presence that disturbs me with the joy
Of elevated thoughts ; a sense sublime
Of something far more deeply interfused,
Whose dwelling is the light of setting suns,
And the round ocean, and the living air,
And the blue sky, and in the mind of man ;
A motion and a spirit, that impels
All thinking things, all objects of all thought,
And rolls through all things.   Therefore am I still
A lover of the meadows and the woods,
And mountains, and of all that we behold
From this green earth ; of all the mighty world
Of eye, and ear,—both what they half create,
And what perceive ; well pleased to recognise
In Nature and the language of the sense,
The anchor of my purest thoughts, the nurse,
The guide, the guardian of my heart, and soul
Of all my moral being.
                    Nor perchance,
If I were not thus taught, should I the more
Suffer my genial spirits to decay :
For thou art with me here upon the banks
Of this fair river ; thou my dearest friend,
My dear, dear friend ; and in thy voice I catch
The language of my former heart, and read
My former pleasures in the shooting lights
Of thy wild eyes.   Oh ! yet a little while
May I behold in thee what I was once,
My dear, dear Sister ! and this prayer I make,
Knowing that Nature never did betray
The heart that loved her ; 'tis her privilege
Through all the years of this our life, to lead
From joy to joy ; for she can so inform
The mind that is within us, so impress
With quietness and beauty, and so feed
With lofty thoughts, that neither evil tongues,
Rash judgments, nor the sneers of selfish men,
Nor greetings where no kindness is, nor all
The dreary intercourse of daily life,
Shall e'er prevail against us, or disturb
Our cheerful faith, that all which we behold
Is full of blessings.   Therefore let the moon
Shine on thee in thy solitary walk ;
And let the misty mountain-winds be free

> To blow against thee : and, in after years,
> When these wild ecstasies shall be matured
> Into a sober pleasure ; when thy mind
> Shall be a mansion for all lovely forms,
> Thy memory be as a dwelling-place
> For all sweet sounds and harmonies ; oh ! then,
> If solitude, or fear, or pain, or grief,
> Should be thy portion, with what healing thoughts
> Of tender joy wilt thou remember me,
> And these my exhortations ! Nor, perchance,
> If I should be where I no more can hear
> Thy voice, nor catch from thy wild eyes these gleams
> Of past existence—wilt thou then forget
> That on the banks of this delightful stream
> We stood together ; and that I, so long
> A worshipper of Nature, hither came
> Unwearied in that service : rather say
> With warmer love—oh ! with far deeper zeal
> Of holier love. Nor wilt thou then forget,
> That after many wanderings, many years
> Of absence, these steep woods and lofty cliffs,
> And this green pastoral landscape, were to me
> More dear, both for themselves and for thy sake !"

This poem is characteristic of the loftiest side of Wordsworth's genius. In it he struck for the first time the sublime note that has drawn men after him as the prophet of a new delight, a full-voiced speaker of things that all feel dimly and vaguely, but which no poet before him had expressed with such force. But mark, as confirming what I have said about the gradual character of transitions in poetry, that both the rhythm of Wordsworth's lines and the feeling expressed are developments from Cowper. The level. Ouse flowed through a flatter landscape than the Derwent, and there was a fire and majesty in Wordsworth's stronger spirit that we look for in vain in the gentle Cowper. But the direction of their feelings was the same ; the rhythm of their verse had much in common ; Wordsworth's torch was kindled at Cowper's. " A great poet creates the taste by which he is enjoyed," Wordsworth said, and the saying is often repeated. But it is isolating him too much to say that he created the taste that enjoyed his Nature poetry. We can believe this only when we ignore all that happened in the half century between Pope's death and the appearance of the 'Lyrical Ballads.'

No : the current formula that Wordsworth created the taste by which he is enjoyed is only a half or a quarter truth. The currency that the saying has obtained is due chiefly to a vague impression, such as often arises when the facts of history are mingled together and fancifully rearrangd in the popular memory, —a vague impression that all Wordsworth's poetry was received with a howl of derision and ridicule when first submitted to the public. There were three veins in one volume—"Tintern Abbey Lines," "Guilt and Sorrow," and the 'Lyrical Ballads.' Now it was not against what is commonly understood by his Nature poetry, such poetry as I have quoted, that the storm was directed, but against some of his lyrical ballads, strictly so called,—"The Idiot Boy," "Goody Blake," and "The Thorn." And the storm did not become loud and long till Wordsworth not only defended these poems in his famous Preface, but with aggressive obstinacy maintained that all true poetry must be composed on the same principles. Further, though the storm against these poems has long since subsided into a calm, the taste for them has not yet been created. Even Mr Myers admits that "The Thorn," "The Idiot Boy," and "Goody Blake and Harry Gill," have been "justly blamed for triviality." As I am one of the few who do not agree with this verdict, having a natural taste for such grotesque mixtures of pathos and rough humour,— a taste not created by Wordsworth, but more probably by a bucolic upbringing,—I am all the less likely to be biassed in the admission that the taste is not general.

These lyrical ballads, which owed their origin to an accident, are certainly strange and original, fully coloured by the poet's individuality. The idea of writing them probably occurred to Wordsworth when he was conversing with Coleridge over the German imitations of Percy's old English ballads. The idea of writing the "Ancient Mariner" occurred in the course of the same companionship, and the difference between them and the "Mariner" represents the difference in individual character between Wordsworth and Coleridge. The two friends began writing the "Mariner" together, but their conceptions were so different that Wordsworth left Coleridge to finish it.

CHAPTER XIII.

WORDSWORTH—*continued.*

"THE IDIOT BOY"—PROSE *v.* POETRY—COLERIDGE ON WORDSWORTH.

IF you have read some of the lyrical ballads to which I directed you, you will not, I think, be surprised that they appeared trivial, absurd, and even repulsive to the generality of readers of poetry when first they made their appearance. The wonder rather is, that they found as many readers as they did; for though many mocked, a considerable number read them, as appears from the fact that a second edition was called for in 1800. This could hardly have been the case if the vein of sentiment had been altogether new in literature. Sensibility to the joys and sorrows of humble folk, a disposition never entirely absent from civilised communities, we may well believe, had been deliberately cultivated during the latter part of the eighteenth century as an artistic motive. A whole school of prose fiction ministered to this sentiment, the most prominent examples of which are Sterne's 'Tristram Shandy' and 'Sentimental Journey,' where the sentiment appears casually, and Mackenzie's 'Man of Feeling,' where it is the dominant feeling. Universal sympathy, tender interest in everything that lives and moves, was the note of this school. Burns wore out two copies of the 'Man of Feeling' carrying it about in his pocket; and it doubtless helped to awaken and foster in him the tenderness of heart that inspired his "Address to the Mouse." Sensibility, in fact, pervaded literature during the last forty years of the century; and the tender experiences of Betty Foy, the mother of the Idiot Boy, would have commended themselves from the mere force of literary custom to thousands of readers, if dressed to advantage in the familiar sentimental prose style. And although Wordsworth's style was not the familiar style, the taste for the kind of subject at least had been cultivated before his day.

The story of the accident that led Wordsworth to write ballads on subjects taken from common life is well known, and was put on record by himself in a note to "The Idiot Boy." In the spring of 1798, when he and Coleridge were near neighbours and close friends, they proposed making a walking tour together, and to meet the expense it occurred to them to write together a ballad by the way and send it to the 'New Monthly Magazine.' The poem of the "Ancient Mariner" was the result. Wordsworth made a few suggestions and contributed a few lines, but, as he says, "as we endeavoured to proceed conjointly (I speak of the same evening) our respective manners proved so different that it would have been quite presumptuous in me to do anything but separate from an undertaking upon which I could have been only a clog." He proceeded instead to write independently lyrical ballads "on natural subjects, taken from common life, but looked at, as far as might be, through an imaginative medium." The difference between the 'Lyrical Ballads' and the "Ancient Mariner" represents the difference in individual character and history between Coleridge and Wordsworth. Ideas work themselves out differently according to the minds in which they take root.

Wordsworth was country-bred, familiar only with the simple folk of the Northern dales till he was seventeen; and his experience of towns and townspeople did not evoke new sympathies to supplant the old. It was not merely the face of inanimate nature that had charms for him. He had the keenest sympathy with his humble country neighbours. The simple incidents of their lives interested him as much as they interested the humblest gossip in the hamlet or in the hillside cottage, though in a different way. His imagination fastened on these incidents, and transfigured them. Consider, for example, the incidents of "The Idiot Boy" as they would present themselves to an ordinary village gossip, and you

will understand Wordsworth's theory about the creative function
of the poet:—

> " Imagination needs must stir;
> Dear maid, this truth believe,
> Minds that have little to confer
> Find little to perceive."

Old Betty Foy, who lives in the same house with Susan Gale, has
an only child, Johnny, an idiot, whom she loves with all her heart.
Susan falls ill, and Betty mounts her poor boy on a pony and
sends him for the doctor. The boy does not return. Betty is
alarmed and goes in search of him; finds him after a long search
in a vale staring at the stars and listening to the hooting of the
owls, perfectly delighted with them and himself. Susan meantime, left alone, gets anxious in her turn, ceases to feel her ailments, gets up and hobbles after, and the two old women, delighted with the recovery of Johnny, forget all about the illness,
and bring him home in merry triumph. That is all the story of
the Idiot Boy. To most people it must always appear trivial, yet
when Wordsworth heard of the incident it haunted his imagination.
He pictured to himself the Idiot Boy's delight when he was put
on horseback, the mother's pride that he could be of some use, the
fears that came over her as hour after hour passed and neither he
nor the doctor came, her growing impatience, her wild agitated
search in the moonlight, and her overflowing joy when at last she
found the truant. Every stanza in the poem is a vivid picture of
simple human feeling, delightful if you have any interest in the
motherly feelings of such a poor old woman as Betty Foy. But
we cannot be surprised that so few entered into the spirit of
Wordsworth's imagination. Even now, when his fame is established, and it is customary to denounce the purblind critics who
ridiculed his first publication, we find " The Idiot Boy " generally
given up as a mistaken experiment. Wordsworth unintentionally
took a sweeping revenge on those early critics when he rearranged
his poems so that their chronological order cannot be followed
without some trouble; for many people now loathe and detest and
reprobate their memory who entirely agree with them. Mrs Oliphant—who, although she uses the now orthodox language against
the worthless critics who sneered at the 'Lyrical Ballads,'—the

literary gladiators who fleshed their swords upon Wordsworth's first efforts—condemns without knowing it the very poems that they condemned, and, in language equally strong, makes a comparison between "The Idiot Boy" and "John Gilpin," very much to the disadvantage of the former. "The choice of such colloquial familiarity of treatment," she says, "as suggests a jocular rather than a serious meaning, the absolute insignificance of the incident, and the absence of any attempt to give grace and dignity to the story, balked its effect completely as an exposition of nature, while the humour in it was too feeble, too diffuse, to give it a lively comic interest. Cowper had ventured to be quite as colloquial and realistic in 'John Gilpin,' with electrical effect." The comparison between "The Idiot Boy" and "John Gilpin" is not a happy one, for the two poems are in very different keys of humour: we are expected by the poet in the one case to smile with moist eyes and heart profoundly touched, and in the other to laugh heartily.

Mrs Oliphant complains of "the absolute insignificance of the incident," and "the absence of any attempt to give grace and dignity to the story." While such complaints are made by professed admirers of Wordsworth, who find no words too hard for the injustice done him by the contemporary critics of the 'Lyrical Ballads,' how can Wordsworth be said to have created the taste by which he is enjoyed? His admirers now repeat the same criticisms of the same works. It was in defence of himself against such complaints as are made by Mrs Oliphant and Mr Myers that Wordsworth wrote his celebrated Preface. There are two passages from this Preface that are very often repeated: one, that the language used in poetry should be the language really used by men; and the other, that poetry is the spontaneous overflow of powerful feeling,—that it takes its origin from emotion recollected in tranquillity. These two dicta have passed into literature as the quintessence of Wordsworth's poetical theory, and they fit in with the current conception of Wordsworth as the leader of the revolution against the poetical theories of the eighteenth century. But the Preface, as you will see if you read the whole of it, was much more limited in its purpose: it was apologetic and not constructive; it was really an elaborate justification of his own practice in the

case of the lyrical ballads, not the enunciation of a universally
binding poetic creed, although Wordsworth, not the meekest of
men, was inclined to take the aggressive against what his critics
considered good poetry. We must read the Preface along with
"The Idiot Boy," "The Thorn," "Goody Blake," "Peter Bell,"
and other ballads of the same class, if we would understand its
purport. As the meaning of the theory that the language of
poetry should be the language really used by men—a theory that
everybody has heard of that has ever heard of the name of Wordsworth—as the meaning of this theory is not very generally understood, it may be worth while to recall what Wordsworth actually
did say.

"The principal object proposed in these poems [the ' Lyrical Ballads ']
was to choose incidents and situations from common life, and to relate and
describe them, throughout, as far as was possible, in a *selection* of language
really used by men, and, at the same time, to *throw over them a certain colouring of imagination, whereby ordinary things should be presented to the
mind in an unusual aspect ;* and further, and above all, to make these incidents and associations interesting by tracing in them, truly though not
ostentatiously, the primary laws of our nature, chiefly as far as regards the
manner in which we associate ideas in a state of excitement."

It is commonly supposed that by the language really used by
men, Wordsworth meant colloquial language, above all, for poetic
purposes, the language of rustics ; and seeing that the vocabulary
of an ordinary peasant is extremely limited, the theory has been
laughed at as a preposterous limitation of poetry. But Wordsworth did not really propose anything so absurd as this. He did
indeed defend the choice for poetry of themes from rustic life and
language from rustic life, because "the essential passions of the
heart find a better soil in which they can attain their maturity,
are less under restraint, and speak a plainer and more emphatic
language"; and because peasants "hourly communicate with the
best objects from which the best part of language is originally
derived," and "from their rank in life, and the sameness and
narrow circle of their intercourse, being less under the influence of
social vanity, they convey their feelings and notions in simple and
unelaborated expressions." In this overstrained argument in his
own defence Wordsworth undoubtedly went too far, and exposed

himself to very obvious and easy ridicule. But even in this passage he did not commit himself to the theory that all poetry should be composed of such homely materials; he was only in a spirit of defiant paradox playing for a little with the idea that if a poet dealt only with the feelings of peasants, and used only words known to them, his poetry was likely to be more permanently intelligible and interesting. The paradox is arguable, but against it must be set the fact that the words of rustic dialects, though very persistent, do become obsolete and acquire new shades of meaning as much as the words of literature and cultivated speech; and the further fact, that as civilisation advances, the relations among individuals and the feelings thence arising become too complicated to be typified by the incidents of life in a country parish. This part of Wordsworth's theory may be dismissed. as overstrained and fantastic. Only it must be remembered, to do him justice, that he did not propose to use bare incidents without a colouring of imagination, and that the poet's words were to be a selection and a metrical arrangement, the selection dictated by the feeling to be expressed, and the feeling by the poet's sensibility.

The opinion in favour of rustic language was, however, but a part of Wordsworth's theory of poetic diction, a casual and detachable incident. The main thesis of his preface, of his apology for his own poetry, was that poetry has no special language distinct from that of ordinary life or of prose—that the language of passion, of powerful feeling, is the same whether in metre or not—that it is possible to write poetry without using any other words than such as are to be found in prose writing.

"If in a poem there should be found a series of lines, or even a single line, in which the language, though naturally arranged, and according to the strict laws of metre, does not differ from that of prose, there is a numerous class of critics who, when they stumble upon these prosaisms, as they call them, imagine that they have made a notable discovery, and exult over the poet as over a man ignorant of his own profession. Now these men would establish a canon of criticism which the reader will conclude he must utterly reject, if he wishes to be pleased with these volumes. And it would be a most easy task to prove to him that not only the language of a large portion of every good poem, even of the most elevated character, must necessarily, except with reference to the metre, in no respect differ from that of good prose, but likewise that some of the most interesting parts of the best poems will be found to be strictly the language of prose, when prose is well written."

And again :—

"It may be safely affirmed that there neither is, nor can be, any *essential* difference between the language of prose and metrical composition."

This was the gist of Wordsworth's theory of poetic diction, that in the best parts of the best poems no words are used that are special and peculiar to poetry, that would not be found in well-written prose. I might claim it, I think, as confirming the view I have expressed to you as to the influence of the prose literature of the eighteenth century in effecting the change that took place in poetry soon after the French Revolution. But, you may ask, was Wordsworth's theory correct? Surely, you will say, the order of the words, the construction of the sentences, is different in poetry? and the selection of the words is different? Coleridge, in his criticism of Wordsworth's theory in the 'Biographia Literaria,' perhaps the most suggestive and eloquent piece of critical writing in our language, urges both of these considerations as if Wordsworth had denied them. He will not believe that Wordsworth could have meant only that the words used in the best poetry must be such words as would excite no surprise if they appeared in good prose, because, he says, nobody who had enjoyed the slightest opportunity of understanding Wordsworth's mind and character would suspect him of proclaiming a truism. Therefore it must have been Wordsworth's intention to claim for the best poetry the same style as prose in the ordinary sense of the word style, having reference to the composition, the arrangement, or, as Coleridge says, the *ordonnance* of the words, and not the mere words themselves. And interpreting Wordsworth in this way, his friendly critic has no difficulty in showing that neither in his own poetry nor in any other poetry is the style identical with that of prose. "The true question must be, whether there are not modes of expression, a *construction*, and an *order* of sentences, which are in their fit and natural place in a serious prose composition, but would be disproportionate and heterogeneous in metrical poetry ; and *vice versa*, whether in the language of a serious poem there may not be an arrangement both of words and of sentences, and a use and a selection of (what are called) *figures of speech*, both as to their kind, their frequency, and their occasions, which on a subject of equal weight would be vicious and alien in correct and manly prose. I contend that in both cases, the unfitness of each for the place of the other frequently will and ought to exist."

Coleridge's interpretation of Wordsworth and his reply upon this interpretation have both been universally accepted since the 'Biographia Literaria' was published, Coleridge's early intimacy with Wordsworth lending authority to his interpretation, and common-sense lending sanction to his reply to the theory as interpreted. And yet it is impossible to read Wordsworth's preface through with care enough to group and put together his detached statements, concentration of dry thought not being one of his virtues as a writer, without feeling that he never meant to deny what Coleridge affirmed against him; that he abstained from insisting upon this difference between poetry and prose in point of arrangement only because he regarded it as a truism; and that when he spoke of there being no essential difference between the language of prose and metrical composition, he was thinking of the mere words, if by words we understand figurative words as well as plain literal words. His language again and again implies that the distinction between poetry and prose emphasised by Coleridge was present to his mind. He discusses at length and with great analytic skill how and why it is that metre adds to the reader's pleasure, speaking of the "continual and regular impulses of pleasurable surprise from the metrical arrangement." He indicates, in fact, the very theory of the origin and effect of metre that Coleridge develops more fully and presents as a qualification of Wordsworth's doctrine. It was no part of that doctrine that the poetic order of words must necessarily be the prose order, though he contended, in vindication of his own practice in the metrical ballads, that it might be the prose order, without losing any of the power peculiar to poetry. The point that Coleridge laboured most against Wordsworth, and established most brilliantly, was that there are figures of speech which, as regard kind, and

number, and occasion, would be in place in poetry and out of
place in correct and manly prose.   But I don't think that
Wordsworth had overlooked even this, though he did not guard
himself with sufficient care against being supposed to have overlooked it; for he says that "if the poet's subject be judiciously
chosen, it will naturally, and upon fit occasion, lead him to
passions the language of which, if selected truly and judiciously,
must necessarily be dignified and variegated, and alive with
metaphors and figures."   What he objected to was the "poet's intervening any foreign splendour of his own with that which the
passion naturally suggests."

That it was the words and the words only that Wordsworth
had in his mind when he maintained that the language of poetry
did not differ essentially from the language of prose, is further
shown by the example he quotes from Gray:—

> "In vain to me the smiling mornings shine,
> And reddening Phœbus lifts his golden fire :
> The birds in vain their amorous descant join,
> Or cheerful fields resume their green attire.
> These ears, alas ! for other notes repine ;
> *A different object do these eyes require ;*
> *My lonely anguish melts no heart but mine ;*
> *And in my breast the imperfect joys expire :*
> Yet morning smiles the busy race to cheer,
> And new-born pleasure brings to happier men ;
> The fields to all their wonted tribute bear ;
> To warm their little loves the birds complain.
> *I fruitless mourn to him that cannot hear,*
> *And weep the more because I weep in vain.*"

"It will easily be perceived," he goes on to say, "that the only
part of this sonnet which is of any value is the lines printed in
italics; it is equally obvious that, except in the rhyme, and in
the use of the single word 'fruitless' for fruitlessly, which is so
far a defect, the language of these lines does in no respect differ
from that of prose."

If Wordsworth's plain statements had not been sufficiently
explicit, his comments on this passage would have been sufficient
to show that what he really objected to was the habitual employment by poets of certain conventional figures of speech that

had dropped out of the prose style, and had come to be regarded as the exclusive colours of poetic diction. The expulsion of these conventionalities was all the revolution that he proposed in poetic style. The truth is, that in the heat of the moment, with all the arrogance and obstinacy of his nature, roused by the ridicule poured on his ballads, he exaggerated the difference between his own poetry and that of his predecessors. He told the public with lofty anger that the public taste was corrupt, and that if they wished to enjoy his poems, which were deliberately adapted to interest mankind permanently, they must give up much of what was ordinarily enjoyed. All this was provoked by the open contempt for his *prosaisms*. He carried the war into the enemy's country with the angry retort: "Cleanse yourselves of your gaudy, glossy, meaningless, conventional *poeticisms*, and then you will be able to enjoy my *prosaisms*." His special plea for the colloquial language of rustics was but a side-issue in his general poetic theory, intended only for the special defence of a few passages in the 'Lyrical Ballads,'—in "The Thorn," for example, and in "The Idiot Boy." A not uncommon impression is that Wordsworth advocated this as the only fitting language for poetry, and, upon this misunderstanding, readers naturally charge the poet with gross inconsistency between his theory and his practice; for if you open a volume of Wordsworth's poems anywhere, you will find abundance of words that are never to be heard in the mouth of an ordinary rustic. But you will not, I think, find many words that would be considered inadmissible in prose style, supposing always, what was part of his theory, that the prose-writer was in the same exalted key of feeling with the poet. You may say, as Coleridge said, that this is in fact an unreal and artificial supposition; that when feelings reach a certain pitch of intensity, they cannot as a matter of fact be expressed in prose so as to command the sympathy of the reader; that metrical language is the customary vehicle of intense feeling; that we expect to find a less impassioned strain in prose, and are consequently disposed to ridicule, as out of place, figures of speech in harmony with the strain, which from habit and association we regard as appropriate in poetry. That Wordsworth would have admitted this,

if it had been put to him, we have every reason to believe from
what he actually says, but when he wrote the Preface he was
in too aggressive a mood to be particular about stating his
doctrine with all the explicit qualifications needful to meet
obvious objections.   He did not care to present it in such a way
as to win instant acceptance from common-sense. · He was for
the moment wilfully, not to say arrogantly, paradoxical; and
while we recognise that he was misunderstood, we must admit
that he had himself to blame.

Another part of the poetic theory set forth in the preface has
received much less attention than his theory of poetic diction,
although it deserves more as a clue to Wordsworth's main point
of distinction from other poets.   It concerns his choice of subjects
and his mode of constructing his poems.   Perhaps evolving or developing is a better word to use than constructing, because on
principle the poet left his imagination more free than the artist
generally does to follow the impulses of the feelings aroused by
his subject.   Wordsworth's theory was put forward primarily to
defend himself against the charge of triviality and insignificance
in his choice of subjects and incidents, the charge that Mrs Oliphant repeats.   But it has a much wider bearing, and it is worth
taking some pains to understand his meaning for two reasons.   In
the first place, such poetry as Wordsworth's, as he himself pointed
out, cannot be thoroughly enjoyed unless you follow the course of
his imagination in composing it.   Mere passive reading will not
do ; the reader's imagination must exert itself to accompany the
poet's.   And in the second place, though this is an inferior motive,
there are several cant terms in contemporary criticism that have
grown out of Wordsworth's doctrine, and are often used—sometimes intelligently and sometimes not, but in one way or the
other often.   The fashionable word evolution, when rightly employed in poetic criticism, is employed in a sense defined by
Wordsworth's theory as to how a poet should proceed.

Accused of choosing trivial incidents in his lyrical ballads,
Wordsworth's reply was that " the feeling therein developed
gives importance to the action and situation, and not the action
and situation to the feeling."   " Poetry is the spontaneous overflow of powerful feeling."   The poet's business is to study " the

manner in which we associate ideas in a state of excitement," and
in proportion as the succession of ideas in his poetry obeys these
natural laws of association, follows this course of evolution, his
poetry is real poetry and not a rhetorical imitation. Closely interwoven with this doctrine, in Wordsworth's statement of it, was
another not strictly relevant, that people are too much accustomed
to the use of gross and violent stimulants in poetry ; that they
thirst for startling incidents, strange situations, violent passions,
the favourite objects of sensational and romantic fiction. This
charge against the public taste was part of Wordsworth's indignant and defiant retort upon his critics, and not, as I have said,
strictly relevant to his theory as to the right mode of poetic evolution out of powerful feeling. Strictly speaking, of course, the
mode of evolution is independent of the origin of the intense feeling that sets the imagination to work : we can only say that the
feeling must be there, no matter what the nature of the stimulant
that has given occasion to it. Still, this complaint about "the
degrading thirst for outrageous stimulation," as he calls it, has a
certain connection with Wordsworth's doctrine about the poet's
main business. For, the poet being bound to study "the manner
in which we associate ideas in a state of excitement," he can do
this only in his own mind ; he must study how his imagination is
affected by events within his own experience. Hence, while other
poets, as he pictured them, were ransacking history for good poetical subjects, such as were in their own nature extraordinary, and
might be tricked out by the fancy in such a way as to impress all
readers, he chose his subjects from incidents in familiar life that
had strongly impressed him and put his imagination in motion.
But there was another condition of good poetry. Not every image
that the excited mind conjures up is necessarily poetical. The poet
must select and modify for a particular purpose, that of giving immediate pleasure. "Nor let this necessity of producing immediate
pleasure," he cries, " be considered as a degradation of the poet's
art. It is far otherwise. It is an acknowledgment of the beauty
of the universe,—an acknowledgment the more sincere, because not
formal but indirect ; it is a task light and easy to him who looks
at the world in the spirit of love : further, it is a homage paid to
the native and naked dignity of man, to the grand elementary

principle of pleasure, by which he knows and feels and lives and moves."

The poet's choice of what his imagination evolves being thus restricted, how should he proceed in choosing his subjects ? When any incident excites him to intense feeling, he should study how his imagination works in raising that feeling to a higher pitch if it is pleasurable ; or if it is painful, throwing a veil over it or changing the light that falls upon it till it can be looked at with pathetic resignation. In every person the imagination is more or less active in this work of increase and consolation ; conjuring only images that reconcile us to sorrow and give a lovelier complexion to joy. The poet, with his keener sensibilities and more active imagination, does this more than other men. Wordsworth tried deliberately to be true to nature as a poet by putting into metrical language only the imagery that grew up in his mind under the impulse of intense feeling. If you read "The Thorn," you can trace how the imaginative structure was gradually reared that had its origin in a feeling of keen pity for the poor, outcast, suspected lunatic Martha Ray. The thought of this outcast, when he heard her story or saw her sitting by her thorn, haunted him. The poem really represents the fancies with which he soothed the disquiet of his own spirit at the existence of such miseries in the world, just as the poem of "The Idiot Boy" is composed of the fancies with which he heightened his enjoyment of the touching incident that was its foundation in fact.

It must further be added, and the fact explains the strength as well as the imperfections of Wordsworth's poetry, that writing on these principles, he wrote chiefly to please himself, "with his eye on the object," as he said, and without much regard to the effect to be produced on the reader. When the feelings stirred in him by what he saw or heard or read were satisfied by the work of his imagination, he had little solicitude about the best means of communicating the same satisfaction to his reader. The best means were the means that gave satisfaction to himself. And as his own life was peculiar, the life of a solitary student, or of a student moving within a narrow circle of interests, it was not to be expected that what interested him would interest everybody. Of this he was aware, but it did not influence his practice.

" I am sensible," he wrote, " that my associations must have sometimes been particular instead of general, and that, consequently, giving to things a false importance, I may sometimes have written upon unworthy subjects; but I am less apprehensive on this account, than that my language may frequently have suffered from those arbitrary connections of feelings and ideas with particular words and phrases, from which no man can altogether protect himself. Hence I have no doubt that, in some instances, feelings even of the ludicrous may be given to my readers by expressions which appeared to me tender and pathetic. Such faulty expressions, were I convinced they were faulty at present, and that they must necessarily continue to be so, I would willingly take all reasonable pains to correct. But it is dangerous to make these alterations on the simple authority of a few individuals, or even of certain classes of men ; for where the understanding of an author is not convinced, or his feelings altered, this cannot be done without great injury to himself: for his own feelings are his stay and support, and if he set them aside in one instance, he may be induced to repeat this act till his mind shall lose all confidence in itself, and become utterly debilitated."

We need go no further to understand the antagonism that Wordsworth provoked. It was no personal malignity. Controversy took a personal turn because he challenged comparison between his own feelings and those of others. It is the merit of such poetry that it is the expression of genuine feeling actually felt, and not of what the poet supposed that the world in general would feel in presence of certain objects.

CHAPTER XIV.

WORDSWORTH (*continued*)—COLERIDGE—SOUTHEY.

THE "ODE TO DUTY"—"THE SOLITARY REAPER"—THE LAKE SCHOOL.

You will be pleased to hear, I think, that I have abandoned the idea of trying to lecture you into an admiration of Wordsworth. I had intended to occupy this lecture with going over some of Wordsworth's poems, and pointing out their distinctive charms; but on mature consideration I have come to the conclusion that I should only be wasting your time, because those of you who are fitted by temperament to enjoy his poems will do so without any prompting, and those of you who are not would probably remain deaf to any rhetoric of mine in their favour. No poet is more unequal than Wordsworth, and I cannot forget the fact that when I was young myself, I had too intolerant an aversion to his prosy sermonising to have patience enough to approach in a sympathetic spirit what I now read with delight. It was this, indeed, that at first tempted me to think of picking out a few poems that might serve as an introduction to a sympathetic understanding of the man, but, on the whole, I think I had better leave that to the influence of time. It is characteristic of Wordsworth that his imagination was always set in motion by personal feelings; and unless you sympathise with the initiatory feeling, which you are not likely to do if you have not passed through something of the same experience, you cannot be expected to follow his imagination in its flight without an effort that is fatal to any real enjoyment of poetry. You can always be sure of finding in Wordsworth a genuine feeling of some kind, and if you have any delight in external nature, you will find that he awakens you, as no other poet can, to unsuspected aspects of familiar things, not merely fixing the eye on striking features that had escaped your observation but inspiring them with new suggestions. But preliminary sympathy with the poet's attitude is indispensable, and something more than a casual lecture is needed to give you that.

I shall content myself, therefore, in continuation and conclusion of what I said the other day, with referring to a few poems that may illustrate the relation between the imaginative structure and the emotional motive in his poetry. You remember my quoting his saying that true poetry has its origin in emotion: it is emotion that sets the imagination, the creative constructive faculty, at work; the imagination exerts itself to multiply and modify this initial feeling. You may call this, then, the emotional motive, while the fabric reared at the bidding of this motive, and conditioned through all its parts by the nature of this motive, may be called the imaginative structure, the temple reared as a fitting habitation for the feeling that commanded the poet's creative faculty to build a home for it. Now Wordsworth, as you will remember, held that poets generally worked under the influence of too outrageous emotional stimulants; their imaginations were not quick enough, not spontaneous enough, not sufficiently delighted with their own exercise, to be put in motion by slight and ordinary impulses; they remained still, dull, inert, except when visited by strong, violent, extraordinary excitements. His imagination was more excitable, more ready to stir; and besides, on moral grounds, he deliberately trained it to respond to slight impulses, and find its delight in its own exercise.

Hence arises what at first sight seems an anomaly in Wordsworth's poetry, as well as an apparent contradiction between his practice and some parts of his theory. Search his poems through, and you will find some that start from humbler, slighter themes than those of any other poet of high rank. But his poetry is not on that account simple. On the contrary, search his poems through, and you will find some, such as the famous odes to "Duty" and on the "Intimations of Immortality," that are as intricate, elaborate, and abstruse, as remote from the ordinary paths of thought, as ever poet's imagination created. The emotional motive is simple, the passion has almost always a simple origin, and often is of no great intensity; but the imaginative structure is generally elaborate, and when the poet is at his best, supremely splendid and gorgeous. No poet has built such magnificent palaces of rare material for the ordinary everyday homely human affections. And it is because he has invested our everyday principles of conduct, which are so apt to become threadbare, with such imperishable robes of finest texture and richest design, that Wordsworth holds so high a place among the great moralists of his race.

Take the greatest of his poems, the "Ode to Duty." The emotional motive to this is nothing more extraordinary than a quiet resolution, formed in no tempestuous moment of repentance, but in a placid stretch of even life, to make duty the rule of his conduct. But with what a splendour his imagination invests this! to what heights of ecstasy does he lift this simple feeling!—

> "Through no disturbance of my soul,
>   Or strong compunction in me wrought,
>   I supplicate for thy control;
>   But in the quietness of thought:
>   Me this unchartered freedom tires;
>   I feel the weight of chance-desires;
>   My hopes no more must change their name,
> I long for a repose that ever is the same.
>
>   Stern Lawgiver! yet thou dost wear
>   The Godhead's most benignant grace;
>   Nor know we anything so fair
>   As is the smile upon thy face:
>   Flowers laugh before thee on their beds,
>   And fragrance in thy footing treads;
>   Thou dost preserve the stars from wrong;
> And the most ancient heavens, through thee, are fresh and strong.
>
>   To humbler functions, awful Power!
>   I call thee: I myself commend
>   Unto thy guidance from this hour;
>   Oh, let my weakness have an end!
>   Give unto me, made lowly wise,
>   The spirit of self-sacrifice;
>   The confidence of reason give;
> And in the light of truth thy Bondman let me live!"

So simple is the motive often, that unless the path taken by the imagination is of itself delightful to you, unless you are caught up with it and transported, you are left at the end with a feeling as if there had been much ado about nothing. In illustration of this I would cite "The Solitary Reaper":—

> "Behold her, single in the field,
> Yon solitary Highland lass !
> Reaping and singing by herself ;
> Stop here, or gently pass !
> Alone she cuts and binds the grain,
> And sings a melancholy strain ;
> O listen ! for the Vale profound
> Is overflowing with the sound.
>
> No Nightingale did ever chaunt
> More welcome notes to weary bands
> Of travellers in some shady haunt,
> Among Arabian sands :
> A voice so thrilling ne'er was heard
> In spring-time from the Cuckoo-bird,
> Breaking the silence of the seas
> Among the farthest Hebrides.
>
> Will no one tell me what she sings ?—
> Perhaps the plaintive numbers flow
> For old, unhappy, far-off things,
> And battles long ago :
> Or is it some more humble lay,
> Familiar matter of to-day ?
> Some natural sorrow, loss, or pain,
> That has been, and may be again !
>
> Whate'er the theme, the Maiden sang
> As if her song could have no ending ;
> I saw her singing at her work,
> And o'er the sickle bending ;—
> I listened, motionless and still ;
> And, as I mounted up the hill,
> The music in my heart I bore,
> Long after it was heard no more."

Many of Wordsworth's imaginative flights, and these the most prized by his admirers, take their start from his delight in discovering some new aspect of Nature, or in the sudden flash upon his mind of some reflection that had never before inspired a poet. Wordsworth is sometimes called a nature-worshipper, but it would be more correct to call him a worshipper of the novelties of thought that occurred to him in the minute observation of nature. The mere delight of the eye, the glory of vision, had great charms for him, but greater still was the charm of the imaginative exercise to which new revelations inspired him. You remember the passage in which he describes what first moved him, as early as in his fourteenth year, to resolve to be a poet, the sudden conviction flashing upon him that there were many things in nature that poets had never observed? From that moment he kept in view, with the persistent obstinacy of will that was so marked a feature in his character, a definite purpose to supply the deficiency. And he carried out the purpose not merely by what might be irreverently called simile-hunting in nature, which many of his admirers in prose and verse have done to death, never allowing a leaf to cross their path, or a bird to sing within their hearing, without putting it on the rack to extract a moral from it, or treasuring it up in their memories, to be dragged in as after occasion might offer as a rhetorical embellishment. Wordsworth did, indeed, labour after new images from nature, and sometimes, though not often, used them as a rhetorician rather than a poet—that is to say, to tickle the fancy rather than touch the heart. But often when a new aspect of nature touched him, he allowed his imagination to dwell upon it, and circle round it, and weave for it a metrical body in which it might live among the permanent companions of the human spirit. Once, for example, as he stood in the twilight among his favourite hills, when the gathering gloom had covered over all traces of the handiwork of man, and even the transient features of the vegetation were dim and indistinct, nothing then being visible but the vague outlines of the valley, the soft gleam of the lake, and the shadowy masses of the mountains, the thought came to him that this was the spectacle that had met the eyes of men in all ages, had remained constant to human vision through all the changes that had passed over the face of nature. It was a solemn and affecting thought, and the poet's imagination

has provided for it a permanent dwelling-place in his sonnet to
Twilight :—

> " Hail, Twilight, sovereign of one peaceful hour !
>   Not dull art thou as undiscerning Night ;
>   But studious only to remove from sight
>   Day's mutable distinctions.—Ancient Power !
>   Thus did the waters gleam, the mountains lower,
>   To the rude Briton, when in wolf-skin vest
>   Here roving wild, he laid him down to rest
>   On the bare rock, or through a leafy bower
>   Looked ere his eyes were closed.   By him was seen
>   The self-same Vision which we now behold,
>   At thy meek bidding, Shadowy Power ! brought forth ;
>   These mighty barriers, and the gulf between ;
>   The flood, the stars,—a spectacle as old
>   As the beginning of the heavens and earth."

And it was not only in the solitude of hill and valley that such
thoughts came to him.   One of the best known of his sonnets is
that composed on Westminster Bridge.   If Wordsworth was not
the first poet to attempt to express the fact that a more profound
feeling of stillness and calm is experienced in cities before the rush
and roar of the day has begun than in the loneliest of mountain
solitudes, he has given such perfect expression to the truth that
he is entitled to all the honour of the discovery.

It is a distinctive feature in Wordsworth's nature-worship, one
that marks him off from lovers of less robust and healthy sentiment, that his conception of nature was wide enough to include
the works of man.   He held in theory that nothing was inharmoni-
ous in nature when seen through the right imaginative medium ;
and though, when the railway threatened his own Westmoreland
retreats, he hurled metrical thunderbolts at the invader, this was
in his later years, and before that time his imagination had been
able to reconcile the eye to what men of more confined range of
mental vision can only regard as discordant and unsightly.   When
we read his sonnet on Steamboats, Viaducts, and Railways, composed during the tour of 1833, we feel convinced that, if he had not
been disturbed from his natural balance by the projected Kendal
and Windermere Railway, he might have found the right imaginative medium through which to hear the whistle, and would not

have called upon the startled mountains, vales, and floods to share with him the passion of a just disdain. As this sonnet is not generally known, you will pardon me for quoting it :—

> "Motions and Means, on land and sea at war
> With old poetic feeling, not for this
> Shall ye by Poets even be judged amiss !
> Nor shall your presence, howsoe'er it mar
> The loveliness of Nature, prove a bar
> To the Mind's gaining that prophetic sense
> Of future change, that point of vision, whence
> May be discovered what in soul ye are.
> In spite of all that beauty may disown
> In your harsh features, Nature doth embrace
> Her lawful offspring in Man's art ; and Time,
> Pleased with your triumphs o'er his brother Space,
> Accepts from your bold hands the proffered crown
> Of hope, and smiles on you with cheer sublime."

Before passing from Wordsworth, I would recommend those who wish to give him a trial as a companion not to attempt "The Prelude" or "The Excursion" at first, but to search about among the shorter poems for some congenial spot in which sympathy and admiration may take root and develop into intimate enjoyment. Matthew Arnold made a selection from the poems, and wrote a preface to them. He is the writer to put you in sympathy with Wordsworth, if any human being can. It is a fashion to deride the "This will never do" with which Jeffrey opened his review of "The Excursion." But has it ever done ? I have never heard of or seen anybody prepared to say that "The Excursion" can be read with unflagging delight. It contains many splendid passages, but the bulk of it many of Wordsworth's most ardent admirers pass by with indifference, if not with actual repugnance. To take the case of Dean Church, for example, there is a manifest inconsistency between what he says of Jeffrey and his own comments on "The Excursion." At one place he tells us that the sneers of the 'Edinburgh Review' were in vain, and showed only that the poem was in advance of the times ; while again, referring to the poem itself, he admits that though many passages are majestic, we cannot speak so highly of their contents, and that the poet is at times both pompous and obscure. Jeffrey said nothing stronger against "The Excursion" than this, and the truth is that most of his criticism has been amply confirmed and justified.

And now for a short introduction to Coleridge and a shorter to Southey. It was owing to an extraneous accident, and not on the ground of any resemblance in their character or in their poetic principles, that they were spoken of in their lifetime as forming a school nicknamed the Lake Poets. Three men more dissimilar could not have been found,—Wordsworth absorbed in a definitely conceived poetic mission, living solely for it, day after day and year after year alternately opening his mind with wise passiveness till an inspiration should seize it, and working with strenuous vigour when the inspiration came; Coleridge, dreamy, speculative, aimless, rich in poetic and philosophic projects, but poor in perseverance, an inspired creator of splendid fragments, paving with good resolutions the way to slender achievement; Southey, a man of immense intellectual energy and copious literary faculty, but no distinctive genius, a ready and indefatigable writer, full of ambition and self-confidence writing epics for fame, reviewing articles and books for a livelihood, a professional man of letters who cheerfully resigned his youthful ambitions to follow a life of regular methodical production of such works as editors and booksellers would contract to receive and pay for on delivery, putting fame on one side except in so far as it was compatible with honest labour for the support of his household. The lives of the three ran in channels that diverged more and more as the streams lengthened. They were too different in character ever to have formed a school. Their poetic ideals were different. We may doubt whether Southey could have ever understood Wordsworth's conception of poetry as the imaginative embodiment of personal emotion; at any rate he went a very different way to work, ranging through history for subjects likely in themselves to impress his readers. It may have been that as a practical man, under the imperious necessity of producing what would sell, he felt that he could not afford to wait and watch for moments of inspiration, but must go in search of subjects capable of impressive treatment. This at least was what he did, and his poetry has not one quality in common with Wordsworth's. Rebellion against the tyranny of the couplet, it might be said, for Southey threw himself with presumptuous energy into metrical experiments, and his epics abound in irregular freaks of rhythm. But such vagaries were no part of Wordsworth's system, although at the time there is no doubt that, forming as they did the most superficially striking feature of Southey's "Thalaba," they confirmed the impression that he was leagued with Wordsworth and Coleridge in a conspiracy to propagate the heresies of the Preface to the 'Lyrical Ballads.'

It was in fact in a review of "Thalaba" in the first number of the 'Edinburgh Review' in 1802, that the existence of the Lake School was first proclaimed to the world. The reviewer had probably heard that all three poets were domiciled in the Lake country, and looking to the obtrusive irregularities of "Thalaba" and the startling paradoxes of Wordsworth's poetic gospel, it was natural perhaps that he should jump to the conclusion that this band of brothers had retired from the world to work out in secluded companionship the doctrines of the Preface. It was a circumstance in favour of a conclusion recommended by its dramatic effectiveness that, some years before, Southey and Coleridge had published a volume in conjunction, while Wordsworth and Coleridge were the joint authors of the 'Lyrical Ballads.' The truth was that Southey was not at the time a resident in the Lake country, though Coleridge was established there for the sake of Wordsworth's companionship, and Coleridge and Southey had married sisters, and Mrs Southey had spent some months with Mrs Coleridge while Southey, not yet settled down to his life-work as a man of letters, was wandering about in vague prospect of diplomatic employment. It was not till 1803 that Southey finally resolved to look to literature for a livelihood, and fixed his residence at Greta Hall near Keswick; and it was for domestic reasons rather than for the sake of Wordsworth's society that he chose this residence in the Lake country,—his acquaintance with Wordsworth being in fact slight, and his sympathy with Wordsworth's poetical theories far from intimate. The ordinary cares of this world had a paramount hold on Southey in those years, and his foremost anxiety was to find the means of reconciling them with his poetic ambition: far from his thoughts was any idea of sharing as a sworn confederate in another man's mission. It was chance, and not community of aim or community of sentiment, that brought the three poets together in their early manhood. There can be no confederacy without a leader, and these three were too strong in their energies and distinct in their individualities to submit one to another's purposes in life. The links between them were slight and transient, and had all been accidentally formed by Coleridge, the man of many projects and quickly kindled generous sympathy with the works of others, all the freer in its play that he had no very definite work of his own. But the contemporary 'Edinburgh Reviewer' could not be aware of these details which have been disclosed to posterity; and several superficial facts were in his favour when he coined the nickname of the Lake School.

Of the three, Coleridge and Wordsworth, though as different as possible in character, had most in common in their views of poetry. The doctrines of the Preface most probably took shape in Wordsworth's mind during those long walks and talks with Coleridge in the summer of 1797 to which I have before alluded. There can be no doubt that his friendship with Coleridge in their early manhood was a most important influence in the development of Wordsworth's mental and poetic life. There is a marked difference between what he wrote before and after. I would even go so far, arguing from the precision with which Wordsworth uses psychological terms in the Preface, that not a little of his theory was consciously or unconsciously derived from Coleridge. And the basis of my argument would be this—Wordsworth was not a reader of philosophy, and he professed to detest mental analysis; yet the analysis of the creative faculty in the Preface is at once profound and clear. Coleridge, on the other hand, had a passion for philosophy; his quick and subtle intellect revelled in its intricacies; it was his delight before poetry even when he was a schoolboy, and when he was an old man he could hardly be brought to converse on any other subject. Only the year before he sought the acquaintance of Wordsworth, the first son born to him, the ill-starred Hartley Coleridge, had been named after the English philosopher whose technical language is used throughout Wordsworth's Preface, not without the awkwardness and crabbedness that comes from want of familiarity. Coleridge was saturated

with Hartley's psychology when he and Wordsworth first met; and
when he was full of a subject his eloquence about it was un-
matchedly rich and full.   A new Plato would find admirable
subjects for imaginary dialogues in these conversations between
Coleridge and Wordsworth when they met almost daily for a
whole year.   Only Plato himself could hardly have done justice
to the abundance and eloquence, the wide discursiveness, of
Coleridge's talk.   Carlyle saw and heard him in his old age, and
has left a description that is often quoted :—

"I have heard Coleridge talk with eager musical energy two stricken
hours, his face radiant and moist, and communicate no meaning whatsoever
to any individual of his hearers, certain of whom, I for one, still kept eagerly
listening in hope: the most had long before given up, and formed, if the
room was large enough, secondary humming groups of their own. . . . You
swam and fluttered in the mistiest, wide, unintelligible deluge of things,
for most part in a rather profitless uncomfortable manner.   Glorious islets
too I have seen rise out of the haze, but they were few, and soon swallowed
in the general element again.   Balmy sunny islets, islets of the blest, and
the intelligible ;—on which occasions those secondary humming groups
would all cease humming and hang breathless upon the eloquent words, till
once your islet got wrapt in the mist again, and they would recommence
humming.   Eloquent, artistically expensive words, you had always; piercing
radiances of a most subtle insight came at intervals."

Part of this unintelligibility may have been due to the listener,
for Coleridge in his Highgate days spoke in what was to Carlyle
an unknown tongue—the philosophical dialect of modern Germany.
Those who knew him in his youth heard him converse on more
intelligible subjects, and speak of his eloquence as a marvel.
And that his eloquence quickened Wordsworth's whole poetic
nature, and set him thinking with new energy about poetry, I
have not the least doubt; and I think it highly probable that the
doctrines of the Preface shaped themselves in his mind as he
listened to Coleridge's ever-flowing talk.   In restating some of
these doctrines in the 'Biographia Literaria,' with such fulness of
illustration and such explanations and verbal corrections that they
have became part of the critical creed, Coleridge was probably
only reclaiming what had once been his own.   Why, then, you
may ask, did he not say so ?   To answer this question is to recall
the character of the man.   Absorbed in a subject one day, and

violently pouring out his thick - coming thoughts about it, he would have not the slightest remembrance of what he had said a short time afterwards, when another subject had taken possession of him. A verbatim report of his conversation one year might have been passed off on him next year as the production of another mind. He has been accused, and we must admit convicted, of extensive plagiarisms both in his poetry and his philosophy : if anybody had plagiarised from himself, he would never have detected the fact. He never paused to think what was his and what was not, but gave all his powers of memory and imagination to whatever was uppermost in his thoughts at the time. I do not say that Wordsworth plagiarised from him, but it seems to me impossible to overrate the quickening influence that Wordsworth owed to his contact with this wonderful enthusiast.

The debt was not all on one side. It was during the memorable year of his companionship with Wordsworth that Coleridge wrote nearly everything that now remains as a measure of his wonderful poetic gifts. "The Rime of the Ancient Mariner" and "Christabel" were both written in that year, besides most of the short poems that make up the small volume of his poetical works. The presence by his side of the steady resolute will of the Westmoreland dalesman seems to have for the time constrained his imagination from aimless wandering; and the lofty unwavering self-confidence of his friend inspired him with a similar energy. Away from Wordsworth after that year, he lost himself in visions of work to be done that always remained to be done. Coleridge had every poetic gift but one—the will for sustained and concentrated effort.

One cannot help lamenting that the gift of resolute will was wanting in Coleridge. And if we make the lament for him, it is well-founded, for all the second half of his life was made unhappy by vainly renewed repentances for wasted opportunities. There is not a more pathetic poem in the language, to those who know the two men, than the poem written by Coleridge when his heart was full after hearing Wordsworth recite to him "The Prelude"— on the growth of a poet's mind.

> "Ah, as I listened with a heart forlorn
> The pulses of my being beat anew ;
> And even as life returns upon the drown'd,

> Life's joy rekindling roused a throng of pains—
> Keen pangs of love, awakening as a babe
> Turbulent, with an outcry in the heart;
> And fears self-willed, that shunned the eye of hope;
> And hope that scarce would know itself from fear;
> Sense of past youth, and manhood come in vain;
> And genius given, and knowledge won in vain;
> And all which I had culled in wood-walks wild,
> And all which patient toil had reared, and all,
> Commune with thee had opened out—but flowers
> Strewed on my corse and borne upon my bier
> In the same coffin, for the self-same grave !
> That way no more ! and ill beseems it me,
> Who came a welcomer in herald's guise,
> Singing of glory and futurity,
> To wander back on such unhealthful road,
> Plucking the poisons of self-harm ! And ill
> Such intertwine beseems triumphal wreaths
> Strewed before thy advancing !
> .   .   .   .
>
> And when—O Friend ! my comforter and guide !
> Strong in thyself, and powerful to give strength,—
> Thy long-sustained song finally closed,
> And thy deep voice had ceased—yet thou thyself
> Wert still before my eyes, and round us both
> That happy vision of beloved faces—
> Scarce conscious, and yet conscious of its close
> I sate, my being blended in one thought
> (Thought was it ? or aspiration ? or resolve ?)
> Absorbed, yet hanging still upon the sound—
> And when I rose, I found myself in prayer."

The charm of Coleridge's poetry is the special and inalienable charm of the art, the delight of new and melodious combinations. When the poetry is not emanative, the movement of the thought is entirely governed by feeling. Christabel is a fragment of most wonderful quality, and exhibits another singular feature of Coleridge's poetry—his marvellous power of touching the sense of the supernatural.

It was through Coleridge that Wordsworth made the acquaintance of Southey, a man who had very little intellectual sympathy with either of the other two members of the supposed Triad of Lake Poets. He was a young man of twenty at Balliol College in

Oxford, when Coleridge, always craving for the company of congenial comrades, introduced himself. Coleridge, two years older, had just broken off a second period of keeping terms at Cambridge, and had already had several characteristic adventures, the most notable of which was the freak of enlisting as a dragoon. He had contracted some debts at Cambridge, and this was his mode of evading his responsibilities. He took the name of Silas Thompson Comberbatch, filling out his own initials S. T. C., and, according to the most authentic form of the story, was discovered to be something more than he seemed by writing a Latin quotation on the wall of the stable. When he was discovered his friends were communicated with, and he obtained his discharge; but he did not take kindly to Cambridge afterwards, and when he called upon Southey his head was full of a wild scheme for establishing a small community under a new form of government in some remote part of America. Pantisocracy was to be the name given to this new model of a happy state, and the essence of the plan was that the members of the small community, having purchased a tract of land, should raise with their own hands the necessaries of life, while their wives—marriage was indispensable for a Pantisocrat—should look after the household and the children. All goods were to be in common, and the plan differed from ordinary communism only in this, that the men were all to devote a large part of their time to the cultivation of literature. Half the day, Coleridge calculated, would suffice for the provision of simple food and clothes; the rest was to be given to high thinking and poetry. Though Coleridge afterwards became the leading mind among the philosophical Tories, and Southey a bitter and unscrupulous partisan on the same side, both were then enthusiastically stirred by the French Revolution. Such was the temper of the youth of the time, excited to a degree that we can hardly understand now by this startling event, that Coleridge and Southey together succeeded in beating up no less than five other recruits. We can imagine how Coleridge luxuriated in picturing all the advantages of this scheme, the heights to which poetry could be carried by minds rendered healthy by open-air exercise and freed from all cares by the simplicity of their wants; we can imagine how, priding himself on being above all things a practical man, he calculated in exact figures the yield of an average man's labour per hour, discussed the allowance to be made for the fertility of the virgin soil, compared the merits of different regions of the great continent, cited facts from the books of travellers, apportioned the duties of the different members of the community, and with eloquent ingenuity argued away every difficulty that could be started. But there was one difficulty that could not be argued away—the want of money. All the recruits of Pantisocracy were poor—in fact, absolutely impecunious. The enthusiasts, however, were fertile in resources for providing the necessary supply. They so impressed a Bristol bookseller, Cottle, a good-hearted, generous man in spite of his name, that he gave them money for their poems, and promised more. They gave public lectures in Bristol on literature, history, and politics, which drew crowded audiences, it is said, till one evening Coleridge failed to put in an appearance. But with all their efforts—and Coleridge's were probably greater in planning than in executing, for he had a rooted aversion to regular labour,—with all their efforts, the Pantisocrats never raised funds enough to give their system of government a chance in practice. Three of them, indeed, took one step towards realising it, by providing themselves with wives. There was a family of pretty and amiable sisters in Bristol, of the name of Fricker, and Lovell, Southey, and Coleridge married one each. Then an uncle of Southey's intervened, and carried him off to Portugal for a time. There the history of Pantisocracy ends. Southey returned from Portugal with other aims, and Coleridge, though angry at first at his desertion, soon drifted off contentedly into other engrossing occupations for his fertile imagination. His besetting sin of irresolution never left him, with the result that, on his death in 1834, he left behind him a great reputation, but only fragments to support it,—fragments, however, which fully justified the admiration of his contemporaries.

CHAPTER XV

CAMPBELL—MOORE.

CAMPBELL—"PLEASURES OF HOPE"—THOMAS MOORE—THE LAST OF THE JOCULATORS — MOORE'S SOCIAL ENVIRONMENT — HIS JOCOSE AND MAUDLIN VEINS.

THE great poets who made the beginning of the nineteenth century famous appeared above the horizon one after another in quick succession. In the same year in which the volume of 'Lyrical Ballads' was issued by a Bristol publisher, a poem was published in Edinburgh and received throughout the country with much less mixed approbation. This was the "Pleasures of Hope," the work of a still younger man than either Wordsworth or Coleridge, Thomas Campbell, a youth of one-and-twenty, uncertain at the time as to his career, and himself alternating so violently between despair and hope when he thought of the future that his friends were disposed at times to doubt his sanity. It is significant that both these publications of the dawn of a new period came from the provinces. In Campbell's work, which is known to every schoolboy and schoolgirl in lines and extracts, but which nobody reads now as a whole except under some other compulsion than the fascination of the poetry, there were no signs of a disposition to break with the past either in form or in choice of subject. Akenside, fifty years before, had sung the "Pleasures of the Imagination," and Samuel Rogers, following him, had in 1793 sung the "Pleasures of Memory," and the happy thought occurred to young Campbell, suggested apparently by a jocular passage in a friend's letter, of continuing the series. Hope was in like manner person-

ified, and apostrophised, and glorified as a beneficent principle,
with illustrations drawn from savage life and from civilised life,—
from the whole range of history and the whole circle of the arts
and the sciences. So far there was an intenser personal feeling at
the beginning of Campbell's poem, inasmuch as he had little
pleasure in life except the pleasure of hope when the subject
occurred to him; but this feeling had but little shaping influence
on the composition. The successive incidents in the poem do not
follow in any natural train of excited, impassioned reflection; they
might have been treated separately and fitted together by mechanical forces, the principle of arrangement being the rhetorical
principle of affording variety to the reader. The versification and
the diction imitated the most approved models of the eighteenth
century; there are passages that recall Goldsmith, and passages
that recall Pope. Darwin, the author of the "Botanic Garden,"
is generally regarded as having carried the style of Pope and
Goldsmith to ridiculous excess. There was sufficient freshness in
Campbell's work as a whole to save him from this reproach. The
whole work gives an impression of abundant intellectual power
and abundant poetic sensibility. Yet bits might be taken from
the "Botanic Garden" and bits from the "Pleasures of Hope,"
and when they were put side by side a reader familiar with both
writers would find it difficult to decide which was Campbell's and
which was Darwin's.

Campbell afterwards did much better work than the "Pleasures
of Hope"; and there is a story told of his state of mind just before
its publication that illustrates better than volumes of commentary
how this most approved style in which he wrote was beginning
to pall even on those who could not see their way to a better.
While he was engaged in revising the proofs of it, he one evening
entered the rooms of a friend of his, who has recorded the circumstance, sat down before the fire with a face of angry discontent,
and without speaking a word took up the poker and began tracing
figures in the soot on the back of the chimney. Presently he
turned round and addressed his astonished friend in the most insulting language. Not being answered according to his folly,
he turned after a time upon what proved to be the source of his
strange behaviour, his own poem. He had been reading the proofs

of it all day, mending and polishing the lines till all meaning seemed to have gone out of them, and the whole composition struck him as trash. "There are days," he went on, "when I can't abide to walk in the sunshine, and when I would almost rather be shot than come within the sight of any man, to be spoken to by any mortal. This has been one of those days. How heartily I wished for night." He spent the evening with his friend, and after some hours the fit of despondency was followed by a fit of wild mirth, in which he proclaimed his assurance that the poem would make him at once a great man, and gravely decided how and where he should live when this greatness was achieved.

It would be easy to make too much of such violent fluctuations of mood in a sensitive youth, unstrung and distempered by over-work as Campbell then was. But we may well contrast this sensitive uncertainty and the steady assured confidence with which about the same time Wordsworth and Coleridge were putting in execution their definitely conceived poetic ideals. One of them at least, the one who did most solid work, had no alternations between extravagant self-confidence and extravagant despair. With all allowance for Campbell's temperament and circumstances, I should be inclined to attribute a large part of his faltering and misgiving and impatience with his own work to his perceiving by fits and starts that this elaborately contrived fabric of finely orna-mented shreds and patches embodied an artificial sentiment, and did not express feelings to which he longed to give vent. He was a man of quick and strong feelings, but in his expression of them he was hampered by respect for the decayed gentility of literary tradition. He was afraid to move freely in the dress of elevated diction sanctioned by Pope's authority as *de rigueur* the poet's raiment; he was too self-conscious of it; the thought of how his feelings would look in it trammelled their natural movements.

The truth is, that beneath the smooth and glossy artificial Popian crust of the "Pleasures of Hope" there was more in it of the spirit of the French Revolution than we find either in Words-worth or in Coleridge. The literary revolution, of which they were recognised leaders, was a thing altogether apart from the political revolution, not in any direct way inspired by it — the result of a quite independent chain of causes; in fact, as I have tried to show, not, strictly speaking, a revolution at all, but a natural literary development, the roots of which lay chronologically behind the political revolution. But Campbell was directly influenced in the tone of the thoughts that he expressed in verse by the political circumstances of his time. His restless ambitious spirit, by turns discontented and sanguine, and at all times intensely sympathetic, had more in common with the spirit then acting on public affairs than either the hard self-contained Wordsworth or the dreamy and speculative Coleridge—of imagination and speculation all compact, and comparatively indifferent to the material on which his faculties worked. It is curious to trace the operation of two antagonistic forces in Campbell's mind,—the habit of elevated and elaborate expression, formed at the University, in accordance with the literary tradition of Pope, and the tempestuous energy of feeling fostered by the disturbed state of public affairs. He was quite a model student in the University of Glasgow, standing high as a scholar in his classes, and winning prizes for English verse with poems that were pronounced by the professors far superior to anything ever submitted in such competitions. He wrote an "Essay on the Origin of Evil" in the style of Pope's "Essay on Man" that was considered an incomparable imitation of the great original. But Campbell was also a leader in debating societies outside the regular University course; and there, as was natural, the principles of the political revolution found many enthusiastic supporters. You know, I daresay, that in the nineties of last century attempts to apply the doctrines of liberty, equality, and fraternity were suppressed in Scotland with extraordinary severity. Three gentlemen—Palmer, Gerald, and Muir—in whose memory a monument now stands in the Calton Burying-ground at Edinburgh, were transported to Botany Bay for an offence in the way of agitation which, under the English law, was punishable only with a short term of imprisonment. Campbell, when a boy of sixteen, walked all the way from Glasgow to hear one of these men, Gerald, a man of remarkable eloquence, defend himself on his trial. The speech and the subsequent conviction made a great impression on the sensitive youth,—so great an impression that his friends thought it had unsettled his reason, such was the passion with which he spoke against modern society and all its institutions.

Now underneath the smooth couplets and the dignified diction and imagery of the "Pleasures of Hope," it is not difficult to detect traces of this deep-seated passion, when we know the poet's early history, disguised though it is by the conventional splendour of the expression. There is, for example, the famous passage on the Russian subjugation of Poland, and another, not so familiar, at the close of Part I., where he denounces the plunder of India by Warren Hastings :—

> "Rich in the gems of India's gaudy zone,
> And plunder piled from kingdoms not their own,
> Degenerate trade ! thy minions could despise
> The heart-born anguish of a thousand cries ;
> Could lock with impious hands their teeming store,
> While famished nations died along the shore ;
> Could mock the groans of fellow-men, and bear
> The curse of kingdoms peopled with despair ;
> Could stamp disgrace on man's polluted name,
> And barter, with their gold, eternal shame ! "

Or, again, the following :—

> "Tyrants ! in vain ye trace the wizard ring ;
> In vain ye limit mind's unwearied spring :
> What ! can ye lull the winged winds asleep,
> Arrest the rolling world, or chain the deep ?
> No !—the wild wave contemns your sceptred hand ;
> It rolled not back when Canute gave command."

The literary quality of such verses is not high : in aiming at elevated diction, the young poet approaches perilously near to turgid bombast. Yet in these verses the spirit of the French Revolution speaks more plainly than in any of the productions of Wordsworth and Coleridge. They were disenchanted, disillusionised, before they wrote about the French Revolution. If we could recover any of Coleridge's lectures on Pantisocracy, we might find something like the above. Campbell, we must remember, was only twenty-one when he wrote the "Pleasures of Hope"; and though he pointed his moral specially against Russian tyranny in Poland, there shines through his verse unmistakable evidence of sympathy with the motives and aspirations of revolutionists elsewhere. The dress was the dress of Pope, but the voice was the voice of a later time.

To the force of the habit of expression in which he had been educated I should also be disposed to attribute Campbell's strange distrust of the poems that have been universally recognised as his best and most enduring work—"Ye Mariners of England," "Hohenlinden," "The Soldier's Dream," "The Battle of the Baltic," and a few others. He contributed these poems to the 'Morning Chronicle' after he had made a reputation by the "Pleasures of Hope," and before he settled in London to the more commonplace literary labour in which he spent the rest of his life. So doubtful was Campbell of the value of these lyrics, that he would not put his name to them, for fear of compromising the reputation of the author of the "Pleasures of Hope." Now I should say it was a result of the ideas of literary dignity in which he had been brought up that Campbell should have feared that "Hohenlinden" and "Ye Mariners of England" would appear too trifling for a poet of the rank that his first poem gave him. It was an example of the force of the same restraint of habit that kept Gray from "speaking out." Like Gray, Campbell lacked the courage of his imagination. The incubus of literary tradition lay heavy on him. He had a distrustful critic within, the creation of scholastic training, which clung to the skirts of his imagination and impeded its freedom of movement whenever it tried to burst away from the beaten track. His diffidence about "Hohenlinden" is sometimes quoted as an example of the saw that "genius is unconscious of its own excellence." But against this must be set the fact that late in life Campbell considered that "O'Connor's Child" was his best poem, and that in this he has the support of most people who are familiar with his poetry. It is unlike his popular lyrics in the fact that it takes more than one reading to appreciate, but it is worth the trouble of reading more than once. Some think that if "Gertrude of Wyoming" had been published before the "Pleasures of Hope," it might have ranked as his chief work, but the subject is too remote to have achieved any great amount of popularity.

The year after the publication of the "Pleasures of Hope," another young poetic adventurer, an Irishman, crossed St George's Channel with his bundle of MSS. in search of a publisher and subscribers in London. The MSS. in his case were only metrical translations from a Greek poet, Anacreon, artificial verses in praise of love and wine. Yet in a few months this adventurer, though he was only just out of his teens, and his father was nothing more eminent than a humble Dublin grocer in a small shop in a small street, became one of the lions of London society, and numbered the Prince of Wales among the subscribers to a sumptuous edition of his translations. From that time forward he held a place among the most popular poets of his generation. Publishers, whose business it is to gauge the public estimation of writers, furnish a sure test of popularity at least, however much that may be at variance with critical verdict, in the prices that they are willing to pay for poems. And even after Byron had appeared in the field, when Mr Perry, of the 'Morning Chronicle,' was negotiating as a friend with the Longmans the sale of a work by Thomas Moore, he was in a position to stipulate that the price should be as high as had ever been paid for a poem of the same length. The poem was not then written or even planned,—it was only understood that the subject should be oriental; and this was the rate of remuneration for which Moore's friend bargained. For so many lines, to be paid for on delivery, the poet was to receive £3000. Scott was paid this sum for 'Rokeby,' and Perry argued that Moore could not take less. The publishers assented, thereby showing that Moore at the time was, in their opinion, as popular with the buyers of poetry as Scott.

If we were to look for the secret of Moore's popularity in his poetry alone, we should be doing an injustice both to him and to the taste of the generation with whom he was such a favourite. He was personally popular; he impressed society otherwise than by his poems; these were but a part of his claims to admiring recognition. If we open a collection of his poems now, and read his " Odes of Anacreon," to which the Prince of Wales and other notabilities of rank subscribed, we desist after a time with something of the disgust we should feel at a profuse display of pretty, sham jewellery. The ample brimming bowls and goblets of wine, the wreaths and garlands of roses, the rich perfumes, the sparkling eyes, the golden tresses, and the snowy necks, are well enough in moderation, but some eighty odes of such materials pall for lack of variety. Any variety that there is lies within the narrowest

limits : now it is a bowl and now it is a goblet, now we drink and
now we quaff, now it is a bud and now it is a full-blown rose, now
a garland and now a cluster, now ringlets and now tresses; but it
is always wine and flower, with little variation of phrase.   We are
soon surfeited with such sentiment, and disposed to laugh at its
artificiality.   Moore's prettinesses, always expressed in soft and
melodious verse, were probably a pleasant surprise to a generation
weary of didactic poems; but if we have a liking for such things
now, we can find more genuine articles of the same kind, compounded with much higher art, in the poetry of the seventeenth
century, the volumes of Queen Henrietta's poets,—Lovelace, and
Carew, and Suckling, and, above all, Herrick.

Nor were his original poems, published soon after under the
pseudonym of Tom Little, in the least of higher quality.   They
were little poems, indeed, generally spun up to some glittering
conceit, as commonplace as it is glittering.   No poet of the eighteenth century, in the days when the great patrons of poetry were
connoisseurs of the art, would have dared to submit effusions so
very poor in thought and vulgar in sentiment.   There is a poem
on Variety, for example.   Variety is the great charm of nature.

> " Ask what prevailing, pleasing power,
>   Allures the sportive, wandering bee
>   To roam untired from flower to flower,—
>   He'll tell you 'tis variety.
>
>   Look Nature round, her features trace,
>   Her seasons, all her changes see ;
>   And own, upon Creation's face,
>   The greatest charm's variety."

Therefore, following nature's law, the poet will seek variety.   But
no: there is " the nymph he loves,"—this is " Patty "; he can
never be false to her.

> " For me, ye gracious Powers above !
>   Still let me roam, unfixed and free ;
>   In all things, but the nymph I love,
>   I'll change and taste variety.
>
>   But Patty, not a world of charms
>   Could e'er estrange my heart from thee ;
>   No, let me ever seek those arms :
>   There still I'll find variety."

What poor stuff is this, compared with Lovelace's " Paradox," of which it is a Brummagem imitation :—

> " 'Tis true the beauteous star
>   To which I first did bow
> Burnt quicker, brighter far,
>   Than that which leads me now,
>   Which shines with more delight,
>   For gazing on that light
>   So long, near lost my sight.
>
> Through foul, we follow fair.
>   For had the world one face,
> And earth been bright as air,
>   We had known neither place.
>   Indians smell not their nest,
>   A Swiss or Finn tastes best
>   The spices of the East.
>
> So from the glorious sun,
>   Who to his height hath got,
> With what delight we run
>   To some black cave or grot.
>   And, heavenly Sidney, you
>   Twice read, had rather view
>   Some odd romance, so new.
>
> The god that constant keeps
>   Unto his deities
> Is poor in joys, and sleeps
>   Imprisoned in the skies.
>   This knew the wisest, who
>   From Juno stole below
>   To love a bear or cow."

We have seen Moore in his jocosely sentimental vein; see him next in his maudlin love-sickness :—

> " Have you not seen the timid tear
>   Steal trembling from mine eye ?
> Have you not marked the flush of fear,
>   Or caught the murmured sigh ?
> And can you think my love is chill,
>   Nor fixed on you alone ?
> And can you rend by doubting still
>   A heart so much your own ?

> To you my soul's affections move
>   Devoutly, warmly true ;
> My life has been a task of love,
>   One long, long thought of you.
> If all your tender faith be o'er,
>   If still my truth you'll try ;
> Alas ! I know but *one* proof more,—
>   I'll bless your name and die."

Such are fair specimens of the poems of Tom Little, so famous in their day; and if we take them as they read, after making all allowance for the novelty of the strain when they appeared, and for the very slight interest in poetry and consequent want of discrimination in London society at the time, we cannot but be astonished that the author should have jumped at once into a foremost place, even although Wordsworth and Coleridge had so much against them as candidates for general favour, and Scott and Byron had not yet appeared on the scene. But the truth is, that it was as a writer of songs to be sung and not of poems to be read that Moore established his hold on the public mind; and he was greatly helped by his personal popularity in the circles where the fashion was set even in poetry. Many in those days would buy and admire even a volume of poetry when the name of the Prince of Wales appeared at the head of the list of subscribers. But how did Moore, who was not born in a palace but in a back street in Dublin, achieve such fashionable popularity that he secured the Prince's name for his literary venture ? It was chiefly his exquisite singing of his own songs that made him the rage. It is hardly an exaggeration to describe Moore as the last of the Troubadours, or, to be more precise, as the last of the Joglars, —of the men to whom Bishop Percy, by a slight historical error, gave the name of Minstrels. These were, as I daresay you have heard, a class of men in the middle ages who sometimes attached themselves to a court, and sometimes wandered from one feudal castle to another, welcome guests wherever they went on account of their skill in making and reciting or singing poems, and other entertaining qualities. When they were not gentlemen born and rich enough to amuse themselves as well as their hosts in this way, they owed their livelihood to the bounty of their patrons, after receiving valuable presents. They were entitled to be called Troubadours or Inventors, if their own poetry was excellent; and if they could only render the poetry of others, their professional name was Joglar or Joculator. The joglar added other entertaining resources to that of reciting poetry; he carried gossip from castle to castle, and sometimes was capable of amusing his audience with sleight-of-hand tricks. Of course the joglar might also be a troubadour. As civilisation developed and society became more complex, there was a natural division of labour; the poet was differentiated as such, and often received his reward and his means of livelihood in pensions from the public exchequer and sinecure posts in the public service. We see this differentiation in full force in the time of Chaucer. Now Moore might be called the last of the troubadours or the joglars in our country, partly because he made a poetic reputation by singing his own songs in fashionable drawing-rooms, and partly because he was the last eminent English poet who looked to his poetry as an indirect means of obtaining a provision for life through the public patronage of influential friends. In later life, when he wrote a fragment of autobiography, he speaks of his pen as having been his sole means of support throughout his life. It was his means of support from necessity and not from choice; it was so only after he had been disappointed in his expectations from another source; and even then, it was so only partially. For the first twelve years of his London life, Moore made comparatively little by his pen; indeed he wrote very little, only two small volumes of elegant and sparkling trifles. His chief steady source of income was an annuity of £500, paid him by the publisher Power for supplying words to Irish and other national melodies. Moore used to sing them in the drawing-rooms of his fashionable friends to give them a start. We must of course call the composition of these literary work, although many of them seem poor enough if they are read and not sung. Anyhow they were handsomely paid for, the poet receiving his annuity for them for twenty-seven years,—pleasant contrast to the melancholy case of Burns, who refused to take anything for a similar service to a Scotch publisher —the service, of course, not being really worth so much, seeing that Burns's songs were not fashionable songs, expensively pub-

lished.   But Moore had another source of income, in no way connected with his pen—a sinecure office in the Bermudas, which, after
the first year, he was able to discharge by a deputy.   He received
this appointment in 1803, and though it afterwards proved a
source of embarrassment to him, owing to the rascality of a deputy,
for whose embezzlements he was held responsible, it brought him
£400 a-year for eighteen years.   For twelve years Moore upon
these resources lived in London the life of a diner-out in the
greatest request, in expectation of some appointment more lucrative than his West India registrarship.   These expectations, and
his chagrin at their repeated postponement, and ultimate ruin in
1812, are very frankly confessed in his Diary.   Swift's saying
that great men never reward in a more substantial way those
whom they make the companions of their pleasures, was verified
in the case of Moore.   One of his earliest patrons, on whom he all
along built his best hopes, was Lord Moira, a scholarly peer,
of generous but hesitating and irresolute temper, munificent almost
to the point of ostentation, and specially willing to befriend men
of genius and learning.   He was in power in the Granville Administration of 1806, and again in the Liverpool Administration
of 1812, under which he went out as Governor-General to India;
but on neither occasion was he able to do anything for the poet.
It is somewhat comical now to read Moore's complaints of his
hard lines in not being promoted to some lucrative post, without
the slightest qualification for filling it.   He evidently regarded
himself as having been very badly used by his aristocratic friends,
and especially by Lord Moira, from whom he had expected better
things.   He repeats bitterly Lord Moira's constant assurance when
he gave any hint of impatience—"I am not oblivious of you.
Depend upon it, I am not oblivious of you."   The fact seems to
have been that Moira hesitated between posts that he considered
not good enough to offer to Moore, and posts for which, though
they were good enough, he was obviously unfitted; and thus Moore
in the end got the allowance of poor Mother Hubbard's dog—nothing, and was obliged to fall back on literature for a livelihood.

   "How it was," Mrs Oliphant says, "that the little Irishman
from Dublin, who came across the Channel with a few introductions and some translations from Anacreon in his pocket, scrambled

into good society, it is somewhat difficult to make out." It is difficult indeed, if we think only of the social interval between his father's little shop in Dublin, which the poet euphemistically calls a wine-store, and the fashionable drawing-rooms in which he so quickly became a favourite. But his fragment of autobiography, which ends with his introduction to London society, and looks as if it had been written to explain the paradox, shows him to us in intermediate stages, through which the transition was as easy and natural as any other process of evolution. Young Moore and his songs were the rage in the best society of Dublin before they were the rage in the best society in London, and there were links between the two along which the modern troubadour slid in the easiest manner possible, making good his footing in the new fields of social conquest by the same agreeable entertaining qualities that had served him in the city of his birth. "In anecdote, small-talk, and especially in singing, he was supreme—for many years he had been the most brilliant man in his company," says Henry Crabb Robinson of him in his famous London days. He had shown the same supremacy, and asserted it with the same good sense, modesty, and quiet dignity, before he left Dublin. But how did he acquire the tone of polite metropolitan society in anecdote, small-talk, and singing? Irishmen, from their geniality, frankness, love of fun, and general willingness to please and be pleased, are naturally agreeable companions; but what amuses in the back-parlour of a Dublin wine-store could not reasonably be expected to amuse a more fastidious audience with different interests and different ways of life. The autobiography, however, explains this puzzle also. Moore's mother was his presiding good genius, and it is one of the finest traits in a character that has many lovable features, that to the last he retained his affection for her, and among all his fine friends never lost an opportunity of making her life pleasant. "It was from the first," he says, "my poor mother's ambition, though with no undue aspirings for herself, to secure for her children an early footing in the better walks of society ; and to her constant attention to this object I owe both my taste for good company and the facility I afterwards found in adapting myself to that sphere." She was helped in this purpose by the religion of the family. They were Roman Catholics, and as always happens with a proscribed sect, there was a close union between their various ranks. We have seen how the same circumstance operated in the life of Pope. It was easier for Mrs Moore to get her children into the better walks of society than if she had been a Protestant. The future poet was a lively and precocious child, and social superiors began to covet his company at a very early age. Decayed gentlewomen, punctiliously correct in manners, yet gay and sprightly in conversation, as only Irish maiden ladies can be, made much of him as an engaging prodigy, and invited him to their tea-parties. He was sent to the best school in Dublin; and schoolfellows, whose fathers were richer than his own, invited him to spend the vacations at their homes. Although the conspiracy of the United Irishmen was being formed at the time in the Irish capital, there was no outward sign of discontent; life went merrily with singing-parties, dancing-parties, and supper-parties. There was a rage too at the time for private theatricals; and Moore's schoolmaster, as it happened, was a leader in such entertainments, managing the stage, writing prologues and epilogues, and giving lessons in elocution. In the art of recitation, Moore was his show-boy, and when he was eleven years old was selected to speak the epilogue in a performance of "Jane Shore" at the private theatre of a Lady Borrowes—the first of the many women of title who figure in the story of the poet's life. Then, fortunately for him, just as he was fourteen and ready for the University, the prohibition against Catholics was removed, and he was admitted to Trinity College. There he distinguished himself by his facility in writing English verse, and made more acquaintances in "the better walks of society." By this time too he had begun to write songs as well as to sing them; and as he always sang to his own accompaniment on the piano, and came, as he says, to be dependent on it, he was saved thereby from the solicitations of jolly good fellows to join companies where there was no such instrument, while he was all the greater an acquisition in the "better walks." He had also the run of a large library, where he acquired a great store of miscellaneous scholarship which secured him the attention of the Provost of the College. "The Provost's house," he says, "was the resort of the best society in Dublin, and his wife and daughters were lovely, literary, and fond of music." Thus it happened that before he left Dublin, at the age of nineteen, to enter at the Middle Temple in London and get his Anacreon published, Moore, though only the son of the keeper of a wine-store, had been expressly invited to dinner to meet no less a person than Lord Clare, the Chancellor of the University. He was coveted by the best society then, as afterwards, for his own qualities as an agreeable well-bred companion.

Of all his writings it is still to the songs that we must go to know him at his best. The oriental charms of "Lalla Rookh" become tiresome as we get older, and as we begin to look critically at the art of the composition. The poem was not composed in a poetic spirit, and there is very little poetry in it. It is rather an artificial putting together of words and imagery than real poetry, and it was felt as such by his contemporaries. They enlarged on the wonderful fidelity of his pictures to life, and, like Sir John Malcolm, could hardly believe that the poet had not been in the East. This is not, however, a strictly poetical quality. Moore deliberately set himself to read up his subject, and in the poem he used imagery only that would be intelligible to an oriental. Had he been writing poetry for orientals this would have been all right, but it is all wrong for us, and Moore had to burden his poem with explanatory notes.

The last years of his life were spent in writing a History of Ireland, now quite unknown. He persisted in this work, and this gives us a higher idea of his character. With all his apparent affectation he was a genuine patriot, an industrious worker, and a most exemplary son and husband, and there is no doubt that it was these qualities that helped to make him the darling of the London drawing-rooms.

CHAPTER XVI.

SCOTT.

INFLUENCE OF OLD BALLADS—SUMMARY OF LIFE—POEMS.

ALTHOUGH the French Revolution, in my opinion, had no influence on our poets, beyond perhaps making them feel a certain exaltation of energy as belonging to a time of great events,—an impulse that would carry nobody far except along a road on which he was prepared otherwise to travel, — it is worth noticing that all the eminent poets of the time had personal experience, more or less accidental, of the consequences of the Revolution.   The consequences, in fact, were so widespread throughout the length and breadth of the country, that it was difficult for anybody to avoid encountering them at one turn or another.   The adventure of Wordsworth and Coleridge was the most curious; but all were characteristic of the time of suspicion, espionage, conspiracy, prosecution, and preparation in self-defence brought upon this country by fears of a similar domestic revolution, and of invasion from our aggressive revolutionised neighbour.   Coleridge had rendered himself a suspicious character by his Pantisocracy and his 'Watchman'; and when he and Wordsworth were living near each other in Somersetshire in 1797, without any ostensible occupation or means of livelihood, a spy was sent to watch their movements, and dog them in their walks on the Quantock Hills.   This worthy, as might have been expected, could · make little of any conversation in which the metaphysical Coleridge had the lead; but one day, as the story goes, they were talking of Spinoza, and as the spy happened to have a very red nose, and laughter sometimes accompanied the mention of Spinoza's name, he thought they were poking fun at him, and reported accordingly. Campbell, we have seen, came across the consequences of the French Revolution in the trial of Gerard for trying to spread revolutionary principles in Scotland. Moore had personal experience of other consequences, more than one of his college friends in Dublin being concerned in the conspiracy of the United Irishmen,—a direct result of the establishment of the Republic in France. And Scott also felt the whiff and wind of the world-shaking event, though in a different way. In the year in which Wordsworth and Coleridge were holding their memorable conversations on the Quantock Hills (in 1797), Scott, a young Edinburgh lawyer, was enrolled as Quartermaster of the Royal Mid-Lothian Regiment of Cavalry,—a body of volunteers raised to defend the country when the new Republic began to give evidence of an aggressive disposition. At the very time when the two Lake poets were discussing the principles of ballad composition, and carrying them out each in his own way, Scott was galloping on the sands at Musselburgh, also intent on ballads, chanting fragments of old ballads to the rhythm of his horse's motion, and making new ballads as he plunged through the fresh sea - air, and re - enacting in imagination the feats of ancient chivalry.

There is much martial spirit in Scott's poetry, and it is likely, as he himself believed, that his battle-scenes owe something of their freshness and force to his experience in the saddle of the Mid-Lothian Yeomanry. When a glass of water is on the point of freezing, a touch with a wire will transform it, as if by magic, into a bundle of icy crystals; and it is possible that Scott was shaken into poetry by the warlike excitement of galloping about directing the manœuvres of his volunteers. But just as the crystallisation of the freezing water is determined by its previous condition, so was the direction of Scott's poetry determined before he had his interest in chivalry quickened by taking part in military manœuvres. It was this previous poetic education, in fact, that made him take such a keen delight in the mimicry of war, and amidst the bustle and galloping to and fro realise how the ancient knight felt when pricking on the plain in search of adventures, or spurring his horse into the thick of a battle.

When we find men so very different in character and circumstances as Coleridge, and Wordsworth, and Scott, men reared in London, in Westmoreland, in Edinburgh, all simultaneously interested in one kind of composition, we may be sure that it is somehow in the air. The interest in ballad literature in England was first made acute by the publication of Bishop Percy's 'Reliques.' I have already mentioned the date of this publication, 1765. Such things are the great events of literary history—they are to it what treaties and laws are to political history; and their dates must be remembered if we are to understand those great movements of which they mark the beginnings. Scott first got hold of this collection of ballads when he was a boy of thirteen, and he has described the effect produced upon him. "The summer day," he says, "sped onward so fast, that notwithstanding the sharp appetite of thirteen I forgot the hour of dinner, was sought for with anxiety, and was still found entranced in my intellectual banquet." How was the mental soil prepared for this enthusiastic reception? It is not every boy of thirteen that can become so absorbed in a book as to forget his dinner. Scott, it is needless to say, was not an ordinary boy. As a schoolboy he was not brilliant in the regular task-work. He seems to have obstinately refused to learn Greek, and, it is said, was nicknamed by an irritable master the Greek dunce; and his position in the Latin class is described by himself as having been meteoric, varying rapidly between top and bottom. It was not, indeed, till he reached the higher classes, where the master, Dr Adams, the author of the well-known book on Roman antiquities, taught something more than the mere syntax of the language, that Scott ever moved far from the less honourable position. He rose when questions were asked outside the prescribed lessons, and fell slowly and surely when the course of questioning returned to the grammar. The secret seems to have been that, owing to bad health, he had been rather irregularly educated, and at a very early age had formed habits of reading omnivorously for himself, and was too much absorbed in his own reading to have much interest or much memory to spare for the niceties of Latin construction. About the time when Percy's ballads fell in his way, he was confined to bed for several weeks by a serious illness, and one of the doctor's prescriptions for him was that he should be allowed to read as much as he liked, the consequence being that he read through the greater part of a circulating library in the neighbourhood,—novels, romances, books of travel, histories. The out-of-the-way knowledge got in this manner, and retained in a memory that was always singularly powerful, enabled him to occasionally delight the antiquarian rector of the High School, and redeem the disgrace incurred by the inexactness of his knowledge of the classical languages. The future novelist was in fact educating himself, unconsciously, but not the less assiduously and effectively, for his work in life. His appetite for ballads had been specially whetted before he fell to at Percy's 'Reliques' with such eagerness. His ancestors came from the great ballad country, the Borders; and some of them had furnished themes for the ballad-singer. His father was a Writer to the Signet in Edinburgh, and his mother the daughter of a Professor; but he was the lineal descendant of a Border chief, "Wat or Walter Scott of Harden, whose wife was celebrated in song as the Flower of Yarrow. She was the lady who, according to tradition, was in the habit of serving up at table, when provisions ran short, a dish of spurs,—a signal that he must take horse and borrow a few cattle and other eatables from English neighbours on the other side of the Border. The clan Scott occupied a prominent place in Border history, and numbered in its various ranks not a few heroes of the persuasion and calling of Robin Hood and Little John." One of Scott's earliest and favourite books was a history of this "right honourable clan," "gathered out of ancient chronicles, histories, and traditions of our fathers," by another Walter Scott, Scott of Satchell, "an old souldier," as he described himself, "and no scholler, and one that can write names, but just the letters of his name." The delicate boy's imagination had been fed on Border traditions, and one of the first-fruits of his delight with Percy was a resolution to collect such ballads as were to be found in circulation among the peasantry of his own country. How far the Latin dunce was from being a dunce at work within the range of his own interests, may be judged from the fact that at the age of fifteen he wrote a poem, which he modestly committed to the flames, on the Conquest of Granada.

After leaving the High School, Scott attended some classes at the University, but what they were is of no consequence. He went on educating himself widely and energetically in his own way and on his own lines, without any conscious purpose. In 1786, when he was fifteen years old—he was just one year younger than Wordsworth—he abandoned a fancy for the military profession, and was entered as an apprentice in his father's office. This circumstance was important in his education for two reasons. It trained him to business habits, for which he was remarkable throughout the whole of his busy life. He never neglected his own profession, though an early appointment to moderately lucrative posts withdrew him from practice at the bar; and he carried habits of regularity, method, and punctuality into his literary work. His immense power of memory, which enabled him to perform such wonders of rapid production in middle age, was greatly helped by systematic ways of storing his promiscuously acquired antiquarian and historical lore,—his arrangement of books, note-books, and references being always a model of precision. His employment in his father's office was of important service to him in another way. The collection of rents and other legal business took him into various parts of the country, and gave him opportunities not only of collecting ballads, which he did deliberately and of set purpose, but of observing and studying, which he did unconsciously, the oddities, humours, and serious sentiments of that society of which, in his novels, he afterwards drew so broad and truthful a picture.

Another cardinal circumstance in his education requires to be mentioned. It was a small circumstance in itself, but it had considerable consequences. A lecture on German Literature, delivered to the Edinburgh Philosophical Society by Henry Mackenzie, the " Man of Feeling," in 1788, seems to have roused a great enthusiasm for the study of German among the young men of Edinburgh. Scott, then a youth of seventeen, joined with some others in forming a class. According to his own account, he was told by their teacher that he would never learn the language, because he would not take pains to lay a stable foundation by means of grammatical exercises ; but he learnt enough to be able to get at the meaning, and his first publications were translations from Bürger and Goethe in 1796 and 1799, a few romantic ballads, and a chivalry-play. "How far," Carlyle says, "'Goetz von Berlichingen' actually affected Scott's literary destination, and whether without it the rhymed romances, and then the prose romances of the Author of 'Waverley,' would not have followed as they did, must remain a very obscure question—obscure and not important." Carlyle probably rather suggests the German influence on Scott when he speaks of Goetz as the parent of an innumerable progeny of "chivalry plays, feudal delineations, and poetico-antiquarian performances." What it probably did for him was to encourage him to persevere in the road along which he was already travelling. Before coming in contact with the modern ballads and feudal tales of Germany, he had exhausted everything of the kind to be found in our own literature, and had even mastered old French and Italian for the same purpose, reading through various collections of medieval romances, besides Dante, Boiardo, and Pulci, and "fastening like a tiger upon every collection of old songs which chance threw in his way." German literature attracted him as the first attempt in modern Europe to found a new literature on the old,—a literature inspired by an antiquarian spirit, a loving regard for old times, and antagonistic both in its mystical longings and in its literary forms to the clear precise vision and careful elaborate style of the school of Racine and Pope. Scott himself is reported to have said of Taylor's translation of "Leonore," "This was what made me a poet." He had heard Dugald Stewart recite the lines—

> " Tramp, tramp, across the land we go ;
> Splash, splash ! across the sea."

"I had several times," he said, "attempted the more regular kind of poetry without success; but here was something that I thought I could do." This was when he was a boy; and as soon as he knew German, one of his first tasks was a translation of this ballad under the title of "William and Helen." Now, although Scott made the remark about the influence of Taylor's translation to a friend of Taylor's—and he was a man who liked to say complimentary things at his own expense—it is possible that the fresh German literature gave him the first revelation of the natural bent of his powers. But the impulse he received from German literature would probably have died out if it had not been reinforced from other quarters. As Carlyle says, a question of the kind is necessarily obscure, and not important; only Scott's contact with German literature deserves to be mentioned as an incident in the story of his literary development.

At the time when he published his translations from the German, although he had reached his twenty-eighth year, nobody seems to have had a suspicion of the genius that was latent in him, or of the direction that it would take. To the outside world he appeared simply as a young lawyer likely to prosper in his profession, universally popular as a humorous boon companion, always in high spirits, rather affecting idleness, yet never behindhand with his work, with a certain reputation as a man of wide reading, taking an interest in literature and antiquities, but not suspected of any serious literary ambition. A casual stranger meeting Scott at this time, and hearing of him from his companions, would never have dreamt of regarding him as likely to become a more popular poet than Wordsworth, or Coleridge, or Campbell, or Moore. None of these young men thought of disguising their literary aspirations; they stood from the first in all men's eyes upon their character as poets. Yet somehow, with all his real or assumed indifference, Scott even then seems to have received rather more than the respect paid to the mere *dilettante*. When Campbell was negotiating the publication of his "Pleasures of Hope," he was somehow attracted to Scott, and in a letter that has been preserved, showed himself eminently pleased with the attention that Scott paid to him. It is the custom to speak of Scott as having stumbled, by accident as it were, into literary fame; but there are not wanting evidences that, although he did not allow literary ambition to absorb his energies, and kept this, like all other aspirations, under the control of a healthy practical will, he was not quite so indifferent as he appeared. He was not a man who

wore his heart upon his sleeve, and he liked to turn aside jestingly
any inquisition into his own serious feelings. In his farewell to
the Harp of the North, these lines occur:—

> " Much have I owed thy strains on life's long way,
>   Through secret woes the world has never known,
>   When on the weary night dawned wearier day,
>   And bitterer was the grief devour'd alone.
> That I o'erlived such woes, Enchantress ! is thine own."

After they were published, when the conversation between him
and a friend turned upon them, he dismissed the subject with a
comical look and smile, remarking, " Yes, as Master Stephen says,
they are very melancholy and gentlemanlike." In like manner,
he made light of his literary studies, and affected the air of a
trifling outsider, while in his large and genial being he found room
for an amount of literary labour, and steady preparation for labour,
as great as was practised by any professional man of letters in his
time. " Every step that I have gained in the world," he once
said, " has been hard won ; " and it is a mistake to look upon Scott
as a careless, good-humoured genius, who stepped into the lists
and carried off the prize for which so many other men had been
laboriously contending.

From a very early age the ambition to "found a poetical character," as he himself expressed it, had been a powerful motive in
his life, though not overpowering and all-absorbing ; and he had
been steadily accumulating the materials of which he made such
rapid use when, at last, the accident he had been waiting for
pointed a finger in the right direction. He possessed his soul in
patience, and, without hasting or resting, with tranquil industry
accumulated till the opportunity declared itself. Even when he
was in the thick of his novel-writing, and producing more work
than any other man of letters in his time—two or three novels a-
year—he was apparently so much occupied with professional, and
social, and other literary engagements, that James Ballantyne, who
was in the secret, could afford to treat as absurd the idea that he
could be the mysterious author of the Waverley novels. How
could a man who had to be in his place every day during business
hours as Clerk to the Court of Session, who was to be met at

parties in the evening when he lived in town, who had his house
full of visitors when he lived in the country, who did so much
miscellaneous literary work in his own name—how could such a
man possibly find time to write novels that were one of the wonders of the world. The reserve that he maintained about his
novels, with such plausibility he maintained equally well in his
earlier days, when he was gathering the materials that he afterwards wove into shape. 'Waverley,' the first of the long series of
his novels, was not published till 1814, but he did not then for the
first time conceive the idea of realising the daily life of people in
the old times. A dozen years before that, some remarks that he
made in a talk with Mr Gillies, whose 'Recollections of Sir Walter
Scott' is one of the most instructive books that have been written
about the great man, show that his imagination was then busy
picturing the details of ancient life. They are looking at the
ruins of Roslin Castle, and speaking of the traditions of the place,
when Scott said : " I wish we knew more than we are ever likely to
do of the powerful family that once owned this castle and chapel.
Doubtless there were beautiful damsels as well as belted knights
that now ' sleep the sleep that knows no waking' under these cold
stones. Anxious, of course, were the days and hours which they
spent within their castle walls ; intricate and hazardous the adventures in which they were engaged. A chronicle of Roslin or of any
other old castle of consideration—that is to say, a minute record
of the lives of its various inhabitants, how they fought and
caroused, loved and hated, worked and played—would be worth
more than all the mere romances that ever were penned, as a fund
of amusement and instruction. But we have only vague outlines ;
imagination must do the rest." And he went on to say : " On the
whole, how little more do we learn from history than that Sir
William lived and ruled at one time, and Sir John at another, while
of the fair dames little or nothing is said ! We find their names
in long lists, it is true, and as having assisted in certain public
occasions of war or pageantry. But the poet must either discover
or invent more than this. He requires to know their individual
habits of life, their wants, wishes, and springs of action. In truth,
we know far more about Major Weir and his enchanted staff than
about any of the Roslin barons and baronesses ; and if I were ever

to become a writer of prose romances, I think I would choose him, if not for my hero, at least for an agent and leading one in my production."

Carlyle overlooked such evidences of the zeal with which Scott in his younger days kept his imagination busy in reconstructing past life, and the thoroughness with which he ransacked history for facts to guide his imagination, when he sneered in his own contemptuous way at Scott's power of extempore writing, of producing "impromptu novels to buy farms with." "A word here," Carlyle says, "as to the extempore style of writing, which is getting much celebrated in these days. Scott seems to have been a high proficient in it. His rapidity was extreme; and the matter produced was excellent, considering that; the circumstances under which some of his novels, when he could not himself write, were dictated, are justly considered wonderful." But he goes on to say, "In the way of writing, no great thing was ever, or will ever be done with ease, but with difficulty. Let ready writers with any faculty in them lay this to heart. Is it with ease, or not with ease, that a man shall do his best in any shape; above all, in this shape justly named of 'soul's travail,' working in the deep fences of thought, embodying the True out of the Obscure and Possible, environed on all sides with the uncreated False? Not so, now or at any time. The experience of all men belies it; the nature of things contradicts it. Virgil and Tacitus, were they ready writers? The whole *Prophecies of Isaiah* are not equal in extent to this cobweb of a 'Review' article. Shakespeare we may fancy wrote with rapidity, but not till he had thought with intensity; long and sore had this man thought, as the seeing eye may discern well, and had dwelt and wrestled amid dark pains and throes—though his great soul is silent about all that. It was for him to write rapidly at fit intervals, being ready to do it. And herein truly lies the secret of the matter; such surprises of mere writing, after due energy of preparation, is doubtless the right method; the hot furnace having long worked and simmered, let the pure gold flow out at one gush. It was Shakespeare's plan; no easy writer he, or he had never been Shakespeare. Neither was Milton one of the mob of gentlemen who write with ease."

Sound doctrine this, no doubt, and particularly worthy to be kept in remembrance by an audience like this who will exercise a paramount daily and hourly influence on a new generation, and who may be tempted to encourage boys and young men in the silly conceit that they can do great things without labour and by sheer force of innate capacity. But sound as Carlyle is about the necessity of work, he is most unjust in his application of the doctrine to the case of Scott. His savage attack on Scott's impromptu manner of writing is an example of his strange inability, with all his piercing insight, to look fairly at the character of successful contemporaries. Carlyle's admirers are wont now to pass over all criticisms of his weak points, with the remark that it is the fashion now to run him down; but as I published twelve years ago the same opinion of him that I hold still, I may claim to speak without prejudice from recent revelations. His essay on Scott, though like all his other writings the work of a man of great critical genius, is throughout, whenever he refers to the main subject of it, prejudiced and unfair. Scott's novels were not impromptu, though written with unparalleled rapidity; in his case there had been great, furious energy of preparation, though he was as studiously secretive about the preparation as he was about the execution. He wrote rapidly because he wrote out of a fully stored mind. To read Carlyle's essay, one would suppose that Scott turned to prose romance with careless facility when he found that his metrical romances no longer sold, no longer commanded the ear of the public, Byron having supplanted him in popular favour. This, indeed, is a very common impression, encouraged by a sort of vulgar wonder at Scott's versatility, that he easily turned his energies to prose when he found that verse would no longer pay. But, to use Carlyle's phrase, "the seeing eye may discern well," if the seeing eye takes the facts of Scott's earlier life within the range of its vision, that though he did not begin to write romances in prose till he was past forty, a large part of his previous life, so wide-ranging in its energies, had been a most studious and even systematic preparation. The conversation which I have quoted to you, showing a bent towards prose romance as an outlet for the creations of his imagination, took place some years before he had written any of his metrical romances, and while he was still only known among his personal acquaintances as a moderately prosperous lawyer and extremely pleasant companion. In fact, viewing his life as a whole, we should say that his metrical romances were but a passing diversion from the main direction of his imaginative energies. And now to explain briefly how these metrical romances came to be written.

'The Lay of the Last Minstrel' was the first of them. He was engaged in preparing for the press his collection of Border Minstrelsy, the fruits of his search for Border ballads, when the subject and the form occurred to him. He was possessed at the time, as he tells us, with the ambition of "founding a poetical character," but both subject and form were suggested by accident. The subject grew in a remote way out of his soldiering. As Quartermaster of the Mid-Lothian Yeomanry, Scott made the acquaintance of the Duke of Buccleuch, the great head of the clan Scott. Feudal loyalty, such as a vassal was expected in medieval times to feel for his lord, was a real sentiment with the poet from his boyhood, and he would have considered it a duty to look upon the Duke as his feudal superior with respect and reverence. The duty was rendered a pleasure by the character of the man, which was frank, hearty, and generous. Something as near an intimacy as was possible in the circumstances sprang up between the poet and the Buccleuch family. The young Countess of Dalkeith, in particular, interested herself in his amusement and business of ballad-collecting, and in a few original ballads which he had composed himself for his forthcoming volume and for other collections. One day this lady suggested to Scott what she considered an excellent subject for a ballad. It was a legend which she had heard of as being current among the Border peasantry concerning one Gilpin Horner—a strange tricksy hobgoblin, which used to turn up unexpectedly in the haunts of men in the shape of an ugly little dwarf, and when excited was in the habit of muttering, "Tint! Tint! Tint." One sometimes hears the question asked why the goblin page in 'The Lay of the Last Minstrel' cries "Lost! Lost! Lost!" What or who was lost? The goblin himself it is that is lost, having strayed as it were from his supernatural master into human society; wandering off in a truant frolicsome mood, and being unable to find his way back. It is a pretty fancy, and Scott was delighted with it as a subject, as well as with the compliment of a suggestion from such a quarter. This was exactly what it ought to be, so like the good old times, when the gratified bard received a theme from his feudal lady. He bowed at once to the high command, and set to work to compose a ballad which might find a place in his proposed Border Minstrelsy. It was natural that he should think of connecting the goblin somehow with the house of Scott, considering who had given him the subject; and it was natural also that, thinking of this noble house in connection with such a subject, his thoughts should turn to a renowned lady of Buccleuch in the sixteenth century—Dame Janet Bethune, a woman of a learned family, with a reputation for her knowledge of magic, as well as for the vigour with which she had managed the affairs of her house during a long widowhood. In Scott's active imagination, the subject quickly took such dimensions that he began to feel that here at last he had lighted on a theme for a work of greater pretensions than a ballad,—a theme out of which might be developed a picture of Border manners such as he had long been ambitious of executing. His ambition for some time had soared higher than the ballad; he had become convinced· that a poetical character, such as he wished to establish, could not be founded on so narrow a basis. Once inspired with the thought that his opportunity had come at last, he quickly elaborated a simple plot on which to weave his picture of life on the Borders in the sixteenth century, of alert strongholds, fighting clans, gallant chieftains, sturdy and fearless retainers,— elevating it into the regions of romance with a deal of love and superstition. It is difficult for us to realise what an influence Scott had in changing the current conception of the borderers. They had long been looked upon as simply cattle-stealers, and yet Scott, by the force of his genius, convinced people that his way of looking on them was the right way.

From the time of Jeffrey till the 'Life of Scott' in the "English Men of Letters Series," it has been the custom to say that the plot machinery in 'The Lay of the Last Minstrel' is defective, and that the Goblin is a mere excrescence. It is argued that Scott failed to connect the superstitious machinery with the general course of the story, and that everything done by the Goblin's action might have been accomplished by natural means. That was the common criticism in Scott's time, and when it was mentioned to him he characteristically made a jest of it. He said he had meant him for a great personage, but he had slunk down to the kitchen. This criticism was made under the false idea that Scott composed carelessly and in haste. The truth is that the Goblin at every turn of the story has an influence on the action. Of course it is true enough that different means might have been adopted, but then the effect would have been different.

Jeffrey said that the young laird might have wandered into the wood by himself, but the effect produced on us by the Goblin enticing him out in a wicked frolic and eluding the sentinels by an assumed disguise is very different. The plot is more complex than this, and indeed is more compactly framed than is generally stated in formal criticisms of the work. The story opens with a feast in Branksome Hall, where the knights are in readiness to depart. While they are making merry the Lady retires to her bower, and overhears the spirits of the mountain and of the flood conversing about her daughter's fate. She hears them say that Branksome will never prosper till the Lady's pride be quelled and her daughter allowed to marry Lord Cranstoun, with whose family they are at feud. The Lady determines to defy fate, and sends William of Deloraine to Melrose Abbey for a mystical book that had long been buried in the tomb of "the wondrous Michael Scott." On returning with his treasure, William is attacked and wounded by Cranstoun and left to the care of the Earl's goblinpage. The Goblin sees the mystic book and sits down to unclasp it, but has scarcely done so when thunder is heard and a flash of lightning comes between him and the book—not, however, till the sprite has mastered certain magic spells.

By means of his newly acquired knowledge the Goblin conveys Deloraine into the castle and decoys the young heir into the woods, where the boy is caught by the English. Deloraine had committed some outrage on the English border, and Percy had entered Scotland to demand his surrender. The Lady will not give him up, but says that he will appear himself to fight the man who has brought the charge against him. But how can William do this, since he is seriously wounded? Here comes the important action of the Goblin. He uses the spell to bring Cranstoun into

Branksome, and Cranstoun dressed in Deloraine's armour proves victorious. The Lady then admits that fate is too strong for her, and allows him to marry her daughter. Thus the action of the Goblin page is a very essential one, and Scott had a deeper meaning in the story than appears on the surface. He further imitated medieval stories in making the 'Lay' a sort of allegory, in which the struggle between supernatural and human powers portrays the struggle between human will and fate. The means that the Lady takes to prevent what is destined from coming to pass become in the end the very means by which it happens.

As to the metre of the story, it is interesting to know that Scott received an important hint from Coleridge's "Christabel." We find the influence of Coleridge appearing everywhere in the early part of the nineteenth century, despite the fact that he wrote so little. "Christabel" was composed in 1797, although it was not published till 1816, and it so happened that a friend at Malta to whom he recited the poem had such a remarkable memory that he was able afterwards to recite it in turn to Scott. It was thus that Scott got the hint of a peculiar variety of the metre he used.

CHAPTER XVII.

BYRON.

SUMMARY OF LIFE—POPULAR IDENTIFICATION OF THE POET WITH HIS CREATIONS—"ENGLISH BARDS AND SCOTCH REVIEWERS."

THE year of the publication of 'Childe Harold'—the work that brought Byron's extraordinary personality before the world—was 1812. The day even is worth remembering, because it had probably been chosen with a superstitious preference and a fancy for singularity in the smallest things characteristic of the man. It was the 29th of February, a date in the calendar that comes only once in four years.

Like Scott, Byron leapt at once into fame. While Wordsworth and Coleridge and Southey and Campbell and Moore were known only to small circles and isolated admirers, the fame of Scott and Byron was European. 'The Lay of the Last Minstrel' was sold and read more widely than any poem ever had been before. It was followed by 'Marmion' and 'The Lady of the Lake,' and the applause grew louder and more general with each publication. 'The Vision of Don Roderick,' a slighter poem and in a different stanza, was received somewhat more coldly; but when 'Childe Harold' was published, Scott was engaged on another metrical romance, 'Rokeby,' for which he received a larger price than had ever before been paid for a poem,—a sign that, in the opinion of publishers at least, his popularity was still on the increase. Then Byron's turn came. 'Childe Harold' was received with an intense excitement beside which the rage for Scott's poetry appeared insignificant. Scott to this extent had prepared the way for Byron, that he had given an interest in poetry to thousands of readers to whom verse in any shape had been a thing to be avoided as dull and unintelligible. But no poet before Byron had commanded so wide an audience; the world had never seen so general a curiosity about a poet's next work.

Writers about Byron, from Moore to Mrs Oliphant, have puzzled themselves to account for the instantaneousness with which 'Childe Harold' took hold of the public mind, and have generally found the solution in the fascinating strangeness and romantic interest of the writer's character. This was part of the secret, no doubt, a large part; but it was not all. If each generation were not so busy with the moods of the moment as to be incapable without an effort of realising how people felt in the peculiar situations of past history, the fitness of Byron's first great work to the time in which it was produced could hardly have escaped observation. When we turn to 'Childe Harold' now, our interest is all in the poet, and we skip with comparative indifference the stanza after stanza of description and reflection to fasten on the autobiographical portions. But in the stanzas that we now skip, the readers of the writer of 1812 found powerful expression given to thoughts that were agitating their own minds, concerning scenes and events that had for them an intensity of interest such as men rarely feel except about their own personal concerns. Bear in mind the position of England and the state of Europe at the time, read the first two cantos of 'Childe Harold' in that connection, and you will find in stanza after stanza abundant evidence of one cause for the excitement with which the poem was received. Napoleon was then at the zenith of his career, master of Germany, and Austria, and Italy, and half-master of Spain. It seemed as if he was on the point of achieving his ambition of making the conquest of Europe. He was engaged in preparing for that huge expedition into Russia which proved his ruin, but there was no symptom of ruin then. His arms had hardly received a check, except from English troops in the Peninsula. Great Britain seemed the only Power capable of checking his course, and there was an intensity of excitement throughout our country such as had never been experienced before and has never been since. We were fighting for our national existence, fighting as the champions and leaders of all the kingdoms of Christendom, pouring subsidies into the hands of our Continental allies, raising armies by conscription. All eyes were turned at the moment upon Spain, where our troops under Wellington, after some doubtful victories, stood at bay within the lines of Torres Vedras, facing four French armies that were quartered in the Peninsula.

In the midst of this excitement, what were our poets doing to put themselves in sympathy with the national mood? Every one of them was quietly pursuing his own predetermined line of literary activity, inspired by no message to the troubled spirit of the age of force and distinction enough to command attention. Wordsworth had indeed issued from his Westmoreland retreat a commonplace prose tract on the Convention of Cintra, and some noble sonnets dedicated to Liberty and Independence. Some of these sonnets are among his masterpieces in point of literary form and loftiness of sentiment; but they have not the fire and directness of popular verse. Coleridge, his brief fit of poetic activity over, was lecturing on Shakespeare and expounding political philosophy in a periodical called the 'Friend.' Southey was writing review articles for the 'Quarterly,' and meditating a poem on the last of the Goths, in execution of his scheme of poems based on national mythologies. Moore was busy with a new number of his Irish Melodies, and speculating on the chances of a change of Government. Campbell, who had electrified the country twelve years earlier with his national songs, had revived the Spenserian stanza in "Gertrude of Wyoming," and was working hard at taskwork for the publishers. Scott had shown more inclination to follow the direction of popular interest. He had appealed to the spirits of the Mountains and the Torrents, who had inspired his minstrelsy before, to vouchsafe him inspiration for a loftier theme, the liberation of the Spaniards by Wellington; and in 'The Vision of Don Roderick' had celebrated the triumphs of our soldiers in the Peninsula with stirring martial ardour. There was much spirit in the strain, and three of the stanzas describing the soldiers of England, Scotland, and Ireland have become classical, and are still dear to every schoolboy. As a prophet of the warlike spirit of the time Scott was unmatched and unmatchable, but he harped only on one string, and high and stubborn as was the reso-

lution of the country at the moment, fixed as it was in its determination to fight, the national mind was crossed by other moods
in the pauses of the conflict, moods in which the equally tempered
Scott was incapable of giving expression. And these moods, natural in a time of great excitement and sustained suspense, found
an exponent of titanic force in the young poet who made his voice
heard in the pilgrimage of Childe Harold. Can it be matter for
astonishment that all ears were inclined to hear ?

The strain in which the new poet addressed the public was not
the most obviously opportune one of drum and trumpet ex-
hortation. It was full of irregular, almost capricious changes,
varying through many moods, from fierce delight in battle and
fiery enthusiasm for freedom to cynical mockery of ambition
and despondent meditation on the fleeting character of human
happiness and national greatness. It was the work of a distempered mind, and it spoke out with passionate sincerity what
was in that mind; and so doing, as the age itself was moody
and distempered with prolonged and feverish excitement, it was
a revelation to thousands of readers of their own inmost thoughts.
Macaulay in a well-known passage describes Byron as having
interpreted Wordsworth to the multitude. Looking at this—his
first production—purely from the literary point of view, there is
much truth in this, for the pilgrimage of Childe Harold was
undoubtedly the spontaneous overflow of powerful feeling; the
poem was evolved by the poet's imagination out of genuine
personal emotion; the satisfaction of this emotion was the motive
that set the imagination at work. Byron's poetry came from
the heart. In this respect, and also in the matter of poetic
diction, he may truly be said to have interpreted Wordsworth's
theories to the multitude. But he did more than this: he
interpreted the multitude to themselves; he showed them as
in a glass what they had been on the point of thinking.

The first stage of Childe Harold's pilgrimage lay through
Spain, on which at that moment the trembling hopes of Europe
were fixed as the theatre where Napoleon's fate was to be
determined,—where the last stake was being played for or against
him. The poet described the scenery where this thrilling drama
was in progress, and commented on the actors and the incidents.

We must remember this to understand the full force for his contemporaries of such lines as :—

> "By Heaven, it is a splendid sight to see
> (For one who hath no friend no brother there)
> Their rival scarfs of mixed embroidery,
> Their various arms that glitter in the air."

Or—

> "And must they fall? the young, the proud, the brave,
> To swell one bloated chief's unwholesome reign?
> No step between submission and a grave,
> The rise of rapine and the fall of Spain?"

Or—

> "No more beneath soft Eve's consenting star
> Fandango twirls his jocund castanet:
> Ah monarchs! could ye taste the mirth ye mar,
> Not in the toils of glory would ye fret;
> The hoarse dull drum would sleep, and man be happy yet!"

Or the stanza with which he takes farewell of Spain—

> "Nor yet, alas! the dreadful work is done;
> Fresh legions pour adown the Pyrenees:
> It deepens still, the work is scarce begun,
> Nor mortal eye the distant end foresees.
> Fall'n natives gaze on Spain: if freed, she frees
> More than her fell Pizarro once enchained."

In the second canto Byron conducted his pilgrim to Greece, to scenes of departed greatness, and his meditations there also struck a sympathetic chord in the hearts of a people who saw historic grandeurs trembling all round them, and knew not when the turn of their own empire would come. The half-hearted mirth with which the pilgrim, with his assumption of joyless cynicism and discontent produced by satiety, relieved the monotony of his gloomy meditations, his sudden changes of mood from ardent aspiration to bitter mockery, from impassioned delight in nature's beauties to scorn of men's deformities, were all in unison with the hysterical distracted state of the public temper. We must live over again the anxieties of those troubled years when the strain of resistance to Napoleon's ambition, sustained year after year, was becoming intolerable, and the sternest resolution was dashed at times by fears that the dreams of the man of destiny would be fulfilled, — we must do this to understand the instantaneous effect of 'Childe Harold.' The poet spoke the words that were on everybody's lips, spoke them with all the fire and intensity of genius. Intense susceptibility to the impressions of the moment was always a striking feature of Byron's character, and he "drew from his audience .in a vapour," to use once more Mr Gladstone's famous simile, "what he gave back to them in a flood." He professed indifference in the opening of his poem; spoke with a languid air of his reluctance to awake the weary Nine for so lowly a lay as his; but the fire of most of the subsequent stanzas gave the lie to this affectation.

This close harmony with the moods of the time is greatly left out of sight in attempts to explain the rapidity with which Byron gained the ear of his audience. Too much stress is laid in these explanations on the romantic character of the hero, driven into his pilgrimage by a strange unrest, satiated with pleasure, rendered joyless by the excess of it, prematurely penetrated by the conviction that all is vanity; a wanderer, not because he hopes for relief from change, but because change is an imperative necessity to him. It was not the character of Childe Harold that first drew attention to the poem; it was the interest in the poem that drew attention to the character of the poet, with whom the public, in spite of his protests, persisted in identifying him. We must not credit the readers of the first two cantos of 'Childe Harold' with knowing all that we can now learn about Byron, from works of which this first effort, with all its revelation power, was comparatively but a feeble and one-sided instalment. Their interest was principally in the poem itself, which enthralled them before they knew much or anything about the author; and if we try to look at it with their eyes, following its movement with the interest they naturally had in its incidents, we find abundant reason for their admiration in the impetuous vehemence with which the poet hurries from theme to theme, fixing one impression after another with a few powerful strokes, moving with the ease of a giant in the fetters of a difficult stanza, controlling the rhymes with a master's hand into the service of his fervent feeling, instead of allowing them to direct and check and hamper its flow as is the way with rhymesters of less resource. The interest of the public, once kindled in the poem, turned naturally to the poet, and they would have it that in his strange hero, a new character in poetry, he had drawn the picture of himself. Every striking publication sets the public speculating about the author, and there were several superficial circumstances that favoured this belief. Byron had himself passed through the scenes through which he conducted his pilgrim. True, he said in the preface that the pilgrim was only "a fictitious character introduced for the sake of giving some connection to the piece"; but the very disclaimer encouraged the public in the popular conviction. When they began inquiring about the author, they found that he was a young lord in his twenty-fifth year, who had for some time been his own master, and had led rather a dissolute life: why, if he did not mean to picture himself, should he choose so discreditable a fictitious character as a prematurely jaded voluptuary, stalking in joyless reverie through scenes in which all Europe at the time felt a living interest?

The mistake was natural perhaps, and yet none the less it was a mistake. Childe Harold's moods were only the darker moods of an intemperately sensitive and variable spirit, in which heights of joyous mirth were quite as frequent as depths of sombre melancholy. When Byron began the poem, his intention was, as he says in his preface, following the words of Dr Beattie, "to give full scope to his inclination, and be either droll or pathetic, descriptive or sentimental, tender or satirical, as the humour struck him." He had intended, in fact, what he afterwards accomplished in 'Don Juan.' And in his first drafts of the poem he had called the hero Childe Burun, the ancient name of his family. But as he went on and thought of making his pilgrim a fictitious character of certain stamp, a character, as he tells us, modelled on Dr Moore's 'Zeluco,' he altered the cast of the poem to correspond, and replaced more than one mirthful passage by others of a melancholy description. Thus only one side of his own character was represented in the poem, and the shades even of that were very much deepened.

To make this clear, let us run rapidly over his life before the

publication of 'Childe Harold.' We shall see that he had other
reasons for despondency and discontent than the fulness of satiety.
His life had been very different from that of most young members
of the peerage. He had succeeded to the title of Lord Byron at
the age of ten, by the death of an eccentric and violent grand-
uncle, who had never recognised his existence, or done anything
to help his mother in giving him an education suitable to his
future rank. The Byrons were one of the oldest families in
England, but for several generations before the birth of the poet
the family estates had been reduced and the family name disgraced
by turbulent, extravagant, and scandalous conduct. There were
honourable traditions in the family, but they belonged to a date
before its elevation to the peerage. Captain Byron, the poet's
father, was a profligate younger son, who added gaming to his
other vices. His first wife was the divorced wife of a peer, with
whom he had eloped, and who died soon after their marriage.
The Hon. Mrs Leigh, Byron's half-sister, was the only offspring of
this union. His second wife was Catherine Gordon, the heiress
of Gight. He married her for her money, and in less than two
years (1786-88) it was swallowed up in the payment of his debts.
Gight was sold, and she was left with only enough to yield her
the small pittance on which she educated her son. This son, the
poet, was born in London on 22d January 1788. Mrs Byron,
though passionately attached to her spendthrift husband, was a
woman of extremely violent temper; and life with her husband
proving impossible, she withdrew with her young son to Aberdeen
in 1790, two years after his birth. The father contrived to extort
from her narrow means a sum sufficient to take him to France,
and died there in the following year. Mrs Byron remained in
Aberdeen, domiciled in one flat after another in Queen Street,
Virginia Street, and Broad Street, till the death of the fourth
Lord Byron in 1798, in the poet's eleventh year, opened the way
to his succession, and the family removed South. With such a
mother, a woman of naturally ungovernable temper, exasperated
by her being dragged down from affluence to poverty, sometimes
fondling her child with extravagant affection, sometimes storming
at him as "a lame brat," and hurling things at him—the fire-irons

are said to have been her favourite weapons—a proud, sensitive, passionate child was not likely to learn self-control. Among other things, she probably exaggerated that sensitiveness about his lameness to which biographers and critics attach so much importance. He seems to have had one or both feet clubbed; and one of the first uses that his mother made of her larger command of money, when he became Lord Byron, was to consult physicians and quacks about the cure of this defect, and on their advice to apply painful remedies in vain. Her violent temper and capricious affection harmed him quite as much after his accession as before, for she kept incessantly interfering with himself and his teachers, and quarrelled so outrageously with his guardian, Lord Carlisle, and with everybody who came near her, that she was practically excluded from the society of people of her own rank. Thus it happened that when Byron came of age he had no friends except such as he had made for himself at Harrow and Cambridge. Brought up with very exalted ideas of his own rank, all the more vivid that he had not been born in it, he had no knowledge of the domestic life of families in that rank; he had no social acquaintance with them; and when he was of age to take his seat in the House of Lords, there was not a single member of that House whom he could ask as a personal friend to introduce him. There was some technical difficulty also about his taking his seat; at the last moment an impediment was discovered which could not be removed till a document had been hunted up somewhere in Cornwall. When Byron set out in 1809 on the travels which he has immortalised in Childe Harold's pilgrimage, he had no pleasant home to take leave of, no pleasant relations to break off with the class to which he belonged; he had bitter memories where other men have sweet and sad; and in his despondent moods it required no strong effort of imagination to picture himself as a joyless outcast, a scornful hater of his kind. Perhaps one reason for the readiness with which the public identified him with his gloomy hero was that they could not understand how a young lord could be unhappy from any other cause but a surfeit of the pleasures of life; they did not know at what a distance from the lap of luxury the titled author had spent his early years, otherwise the evidences of unhappiness and distemper of mind in his poetry might have been more intelligible to them.

The real Byron at this period, however, though he had his moods of passionate melancholy, was far from being habitually joyless and misanthropic, consumed by a mysterious sadness. He was prone to extremes, as might have been expected from the descendant of such ancestry. He came of turbulent kin on both sides. He was tempestuous in all his feelings, extreme in anger and extreme in affection, in melancholy and in mirth, but the pendulum swung as often to the one side as to the other. For every height there is a hollow. We hear of his fits of ungovernable temper in his childhood, of his silent, sullen rages, of his falling in love at the age of eight with such precocious intensity that years afterwards the mention of the marriage of the girl nearly choked him with jealous fury. But there is a brighter side to the picture, though that is not so often dwelt upon. Those who were set in authority over him, from his nurse, Mary Gray, to his tutor at Harrow, found him extremely sweet-tempered and affectionate when they treated him with kindness. He was by no means unruly when he was not crossed and thwarted and misunderstood in his playful advances, though he was then resentful enough. Like all people of extravagant sensibilities, he was exacting in his claims for a return of affection, and quick to take offence when the response was not as ardent as he thought he had a right to expect from the warmth of his overtures. It is not a good constitution of mind for happiness in this world, where individuals are not always ready to reciprocate; but it is as far removed as possible from the hard, sullen, misanthropic temperament that remains sealed up in its own moroseness, impervious to any touch of kindness. Byron is often described as a morbid egotist; but his egotism, if such it is to be called, took the form of an intense longing for sympathy: it was not, at least, a cold self-contained egotism, or an egotism that demands more than it is willing to give, but an intemperate craving for an interchange of kindly offices, apt, only as such feelings are, to be chilled and embittered when it meets with an irresponsive or hostile object. When we read the record of his school and college friendships, of which there are numerous and eloquent memorials in his first published poems, and compare this with the moods of Childe Harold, who described his friends as—

> "The flatterers of the festal hour,
>   The heartless parasites of present cheer,"

we can understand Byron's saying that he would not for all the world that his character were like his hero's. Some of his critics endeavour to give an unfavourable colour even to his friendships, by representing that he chose his friends from a rank beneath his own,—boys and youths who might flatter his vanity by their gratitude for his patronage. But all his school and college friends were not beneath him in rank. The critics forget this, and forget also that owing to Byron's early training he was likely to feel most at home with his poorer schoolfellows, and that from the same cause he was more likely to feel sympathy with poverty and be disposed to relieve it.

It was a necessary incident of Byron's high spirit and craving for love and friendship and admiration that he should be inordinately ambitious. If he had not been lame, he might, with his taste for an active life and the traditions of his family before him, have realised his boyish dream of raising and commanding a regiment. Failing this, his ambition seems at first to have been towards the distinction of an orator, and he was noted at school for his declamatory powers. He did not, in fact, abandon this ambition till "he awoke one morning and found himself famous" as a poet. Only two days before he had made his first speech in the House of Lords, and had achieved a decided success in that fastidious assemblage. But his school days fell in the time when one great poet after another was rising into fame, and, always sensitive to the influence of circumstances, he began to try his hand at verses. The applause of friends induced him to appeal to a wider audience, and in his nineteenth year he issued with memorable results a small volume entitled 'Hours of Idleness.' The preface to this is very characteristic. We can trace all through a curious struggle between modesty and pride, a disposition to be conciliatory and estimate his efforts modestly, crossed every now and then by a haughty consciousness of real power. There are several expressions peculiarly interesting in the light of his subsequent career. "I have

hazarded my reputation and feelings in publishing this volume,"
he said. "I have passed the Rubicon, and must stand or
fall by the cast of the die." This serious language, appropriate to an enterprise in the issue of which the writer was
deeply interested, is hardly in keeping with his protestations further
on of indifference, with his offer to submit without a murmur to
the verdict of the critics, or with the statements that poetry is not
his primary vocation, that he will be content with whatever credit
he may get from this volume, and that "it is highly improbable,
from his situation and pursuits hereafter, that he should obtrude
himself a second time upon the public." Upon one point he was
very explicit,—that he wished no consideration at the hands of
critics on the ground of his rank: he "would rather incur the
bitterest censure of anonymous criticism than triumph in honours
granted merely to a title." There was, however, a somewhat un-
generous comparison suggested between himself and bards who
lived in elevated residences in the close air of towns, and made
money by their writings; and this, combined with many references to his rank and his youth and the seats of his ancestors in
the poems themselves, was seized upon by the 'Edinburgh Review'
and made the theme of a very cutting article. "Whatever judgment," said the reviewer, who is generally supposed to have been
Lord Brougham, "may be passed on the poems of this noble minor,
it seems we must take them as we find them, and be content; for
they are the last we shall ever have from him. He is at best, he
says, but an intruder into the groves of Parnassus; he never lived
in a garret, like thoroughbred poets; and 'though he once roved a
careless mountaineer in the Highlands of Scotland,' he has not of
late enjoyed this advantage. Moreover, he expects no profit from
his publication; and whether it succeeds or not 'it is highly improbable, from his situation and pursuits hereafter,' that he should
again condescend to become an author. Therefore, let us take
what we get, and be thankful. What right have we poor devils
to be nice? We are well off to have got so much from a man of
this lord's station; who does not live in a garret, but has the sway
of Newstead Abbey. Again, we say, let us be thankful, and, with
honest Sancho, bid God bless the giver, nor look the gift-horse
in the mouth."

Byron writhed under this ridicule, all the more galling that it was accompanied by a contemptuous judgment that his poetry belonged to the class which neither gods nor men are said to approve, and that his effusions were spread over a dead flat, and could no more get above or below that level than if they were so much stagnant water. We need not pause to consider whether the criticism was just or unjust: the poems are of interest now only as throwing light on his character; and if they were mediocre, and neither particularly good nor particularly bad, the same fault could not be alleged against the productions to which this criticism led. The poet greatly misjudged himself when he promised submission without a murmur. He resolved instantly upon revenge. The common story ran, that immediately on reading the review he drank two bottles of claret, conceived the plan of a bitter satire on 'English Bards and Scotch Reviewers,' and sat down and wrote a hundred lines of it at a single sitting. It is possible that he did this; but it would seem, from a passage in Moore's Life, that long before the appearance of the article he had a satire of the kind lying by him, and that the attack only gave him a motive for remodelling and publishing it, and inspired some of the more bitter passages. It was fourteen months after the article that the satire in reply made its appearance, and it created a great sensation,—as well by its trenchant force as by the boldness and gallantry of the youth in tackling the 'Edinburgh Review,' then in the height of its formidable critical supremacy. It is possible that during the year and more that elapsed, Byron's wrath might have evaporated, and that he might have come to the conclusion, which he afterwards expressed, that it was "a miserable record of misplaced anger and indiscriminate acrimony," if the severity of the 'Edinburgh Review' had been counterbalanced by any warmth of recognition and appreciation from other quarters. If any of the poets of the time had protested against the injustice of the review, if his volume had opened the doors of society to him as 'Childe Harold' afterwards did, if his relative and guardian, Lord Carlisle, had given any recognition of his ability or shown any sympathy with his aspirations, Byron, always prompt to respond to kindness and affection, would certainly not have retaliated with indiscriminate acrimony, bringing within the sweep of his anger not merely the

Scotch reviewers who had attacked him, but the English bards who had received his adventure with silent indifference. He would not have had the same motive for making them disagreeably aware of his existence and of his power. But as it was, no recognition came to counteract the effect of the hostile criticism, and he made the resolution to pay off his score against the whole world of literature, and go abroad. The friendlessness of his position was, as I have said, brought still more painfully home to him by the circumstances attending his coming of age and his introduction to the House of Lords.

The study of Byron's life before he began the pilgrimage of Childe Harold thus shows us that he was a very different man from the pilgrim, who is represented as a youth who had been rendered misanthropic and scornfully indifferent to everything that poor human life could yield by an unbroken course of sycophantic flattery and unbridled self-indulgence. Though Byron took the incidents of the travels from his own experience, and put his own reflections into the mouth of the pilgrim, he undoubtedly, as he himself said, took the conception of the character from Dr John Moore's 'Zeluco.' All the same, the identification of the poet with his own creation laid firm hold of the public mind, and helped to strengthen the impression produced by the poem. The real Lord Byron, as we know him in Moore's Life, would have been a much less romantic and interesting character to the generality of readers.

From the winter of 1812 till his death in the spring of 1824, Byron kept his position as the foremost poet, the greatest literary force, of his generation, every year bringing some new revelation of his amazing power and fertility. At first the poet's popularity threatened to be fatal to the development of his genius. Society, which had received the productions of his nonage with indifference, and had applauded the spirit of his vindictive satire without exhibiting much curiosity about the author, opened its arms immediately to the powerful assault of the pilgrim. Congratulations and invitations were showered upon him from a fashionable world which had hitherto ignored the existence of the impoverished lord of Newstead Abbey, too proud and shy to push any claim to their acquaintance. He went everywhere as a lion, as the most interesting lion that had been on exhibition for many years, and he accepted this change in his circumstances with all the impressionable facility of his character. A certain contempt may have mingled with his pleasure in the sweet taste of social homage, a certain bitterness when he thought how he had been neglected before; but he had too much of the milk of human kindness in him not to be delighted with his popularity. There was only one drawback to his pleasure, an unconquerable shyness. He was not at his ease in mixed society. He had never in his life been accustomed to it, and his sudden introduction as an object of universal attention was not calculated to put him at his ease. But this constraint and embarrassment, which would probably have worn off in time, did not prevent him from deriving much enjoyment from his new position, and in the company of his familiars he threw off his reserve and gave free rein to his high spirits, while the public, deceived by an attitude due more to shyness than to pride, gave him credit for all the inward gloom and meditative joylessness of the hero of the pilgrimage. The idolising of Byron lasted for four years, and if it had lasted longer, his genius would probably have been stifled before it reached its maturity. He produced his least important work in those four years, as a result of accommodating himself to the spirit of the society which lavished flattery and admiration on him. He belonged to the not uncommon class of men who cannot exert their full powers without the stimulus of adversity and opposition. There was a rage at the time for oriental tales. It was in the year of Byron's entrance into fame and society, as you may remember, that Moore made his contract with the Longmans for a poem on an oriental subject. Byron had been in the East, and had been besides an omnivorous reader of Eastern history, and he set himself to supply the same fashionable demand, producing in marvellously quick succession 'The Giaour,' 'The Bride of Abydos,' 'The Corsair,' 'Lara,' and 'The Siege of Corinth.' The tales were full of life and colour, and their melodramatic heroes and incidents fairly eclipsed in popular favour Scott's medieval barons and nuns, Highland bandits and Lowland moss-troopers. But they belong to a much lower range of artistic creation than Byron's later work. Again the world paid him the equivocal compliment of identifying him with his gloomy, self-contained, man-defying heroes, even circulating the myth that he had himself been a remorseless pirate during his wanderings in the East; and he was vain enough, mainly I believe to cover with romantic mystery a reserved manner really due to shyness, to encourage rather than discourage the belief. The Nemesis for this masquerading soon overtook him, but we cannot regret it much, seeing that if he had continued an admired member of fashionable society, his work as a poet would never have reached the same depth and grandeur. "Society," as he afterwards felt and said, "is fatal to all great original undertakings;" it is certainly fatal to undertakings in the spirit of Byron's subsequent works. We have a measure of what satisfied the society of the Prince Regent's Court in Moore's 'Lalla Rookh' and Byron's own metrical tales.

It was in the consequences of an unfortunate marriage that Byron paid the penalty for the public conception of him as a monstrous Childe Harold or a Lara. I need not dwell upon the incidents of that brief union. He was married to Miss Milbanke on the 2d January 1815. A daughter was born on the 10th of December. On the 13th of January next, Lady Byron left home on a visit to her parents, and on the way wrote an affectionate letter to her husband beginning "Dear Duck," and ending "Your Pippin." A few days after, her father wrote to say that she could not return to him, and proceedings were at once commenced for a judicial separation. The reasons for this strange rupture must always remain a mystery and a subject for dispute. "The causes," Byron once said, "were too simple easily to be found out." There certainly is not the slightest foundation for the abominable calumny published some eighteen years ago by Mrs Beecher Stowe on Lady Byron's authority. As soon as that charge was made public, indisputable proofs were forthcoming, in the shape of affectionate letters, that Lady Byron remained on intimate terms with Mrs Leigh, and if she then entertained the suspicion which she afterwards communicated to Mrs Leigh, she deserves to go down to posterity as one of the worst specimens of her sex. At the time, with admirable self-control, she maintained impenetrable silence as to her reasons for deserting her husband, with the result that the British public, regarding Lord Byron as a Childe Harold or a Lara, imagined that the reasons must be too dreadful for publication, and made up for the lack of facts by the wildest creations of fancy. If the case is looked at calmly, a simple explanation is not difficult to find. A woman who could ask such a husband in a voice of provoking sweetness "when he meant to give up his bad habit of making verses," a woman who never lost her temper, never gave up her point, and inflicted the most malignant stabs in the tenderest places with angelic coolness, possessed the power of goading a sensitive impetuous man to frenzy. She had a maid, for example, to whom Byron entertained a violent aversion, because he suspected her of poisoning his wife's mind against him. Lady Byron listened to all his furious tirades with unruffled meekness, but never consented to send the woman away. She was quite as jealous of her dignity, quite as resentful of slights, real or supposed, as himself; and in their differences of opinion she had the inestimable advantage of a temper perfectly under control, and a command of all the sweet resignation of a martyr, combined with the most skilful ingenuity of provoking retort. Byron with his liability to fits of uncontrollable passion could never have been an easy man to live with; but if his wife had been a loving warmhearted woman, with the unconscious tact that such women have, the result would probably have been very different.

For a few weeks after Lady Byron left her husband, society was content with house-to-house rumour and comment; but presently the indiscretion of one of the poet's friends gave an opportunity for public remarks on the case, and Byron's character being prejudiced by the identification with the worst heroes of his poetry, that howl of indignation was set up which is so graphically described by Macaulay. Byron, in a tender and remorseful fit, had written a farewell to his wife. There was no reason to doubt the sincerity of his feelings; as we now know, the tears fell from his eyes on the paper as he wrote the lines. A friend to whom he showed this farewell, thinking that it might counteract the rumours that were in circulation against him, sent it to a newspaper. But the public regarded it as an attempt to prejudice them against the wife by representing her as harsh and unforgiving, while he on his

side was willing to be reconciled; and when it was followed soon
after by the scathing sketch of Mrs Clermont, the maid whom
he suspected of poisoning Lady Byron's mind against him, the
outcry became loud and indignant, and the poet, burning under
a sense of injustice, but roused at last to return scorn for scorn,
went off once more on a pilgrimage from England, vowing never
to return.

Once more, after his four years of sunshine, in revolt against
society, distempered,—

" Like sweet bells jangled, harsh and out of tune,"—

Byron became the exponent of the restlessness, the discontent, the
passionate longings of a time that was, like himself, "out of joint."
And the greatest of his works were written during the remaining
eight years of his life, before he perished in the Greek war of
independence, and the extent of these, quite apart from their
quality, is a standing sufficient answer to the exaggerated reports
that were circulated about him in the country from which he had
withdrawn.   I am glad to see that Mrs Oliphant, in her recent
work on 'English Literature from 1790 to 1825,' written with
most admirable judgment, breadth of sympathy, and easy mastery
of her materials, does not incline to a very prevalent impression
that Byron's reputation is on the wane.   In purely literary circles
no doubt it has been for a generation or more, because it is the
tendency now to judge poets mainly by their technical qualities,
and it is not in minute finish or exactly interpretative felicity that
Byron's strength lies.   His feeling was too deep, his thought too
impetuous, to admit of his being a great verbal artist, like Tennyson or like Carlyle.   We must take his achievement as a whole, if
we wish to give him his due rank in literature.   His singular
sensitiveness to the impressions of his own immediate surroundings
is against the permanence of his fame, because living as he did in
a time of unrest and conflict, and reflecting these characters in
his poetry, he is apt to appear hysterical, affected, and unreal to
people who look at him out of a calmer atmosphere.   On the other
hand, the superficial inconsistencies of his character must always
tempt critics who have a liking for difficult problems.   He is like

Hamlet in this respect, as I have elsewhere said before. In the desolation of his youth, in his moodiness, in his distempered variation between the extremes of laughter and tears, in his yearning for sympathy, his intensity of friendship, his fits of misanthropy, his habit of brooding over the mysteries of life, Byron unconsciously played the part of Hamlet with the world for his stage, and left a kindred problem for the wonder of mankind and the puzzled speculation of the curious in such matters.

CHAPTER XVIII.

NOVELISTS FROM MRS RADCLIFFE TO BULWER LYTTON.

STERNE—MISS EDGEWORTH—HANNAH MORE—JANE AUSTEN—'WAVERLEY'
—MISS MITFORD—MRS SHELLEY—'VIVIAN GREY'—'PELHAM.'

I MENTIONED in a previous lecture on novelists that in the half-century or more between Sterne—the last of the great group of novelists in the middle of the eighteenth century—and Scott, between 'Tristram Shandy' and 'Waverley,' the chief honours of novel-writing were carried off by women, Miss Burney, Mrs Radcliffe, Miss Edgeworth, and Miss Austen. These four names stand out above the crowd as being not imitators but writers of sufficient original genius and sufficiently fortunate in the novelty of their subjects to be ranked as leaders, as founders of schools or epochs in a small way. I have already spoken of the first two, whose triumphs lay within the eighteenth century; I shall now say a few words to indicate the historical position of Miss Edgeworth and Miss Austen.

Miss Edgeworth was about four years older than Scott, being born in 1767, but she had fourteen years the start of him in reputation as a novelist. Her first notable production was 'Castle Rackrent,' in the first year of the century, 1800, fourteen years before 'Waverley.' It broke ground in a new field, afterwards worked to excess by craftsmen and craftswomen of all degrees of merit: it was a story of Irish life, a revelation to the English novel-readers of a new condition of society, a new range of character and emotion. Scott afterwards said of Miss Edgeworth's Irish tales that they had done more to bind Irishmen and Englishmen together than the Union. She certainly elevated the character of the Irish peasantry in the interest of the world ; showing the good and amiable qualities that underlay the too obvious indolence and thriftlessness and squalor—the gaiety of heart, the readiness of wit, the tenacious steadfastness of attachment, the helpful generosity in distress. Miss Edgeworth was a realist, and she did not fail to put the unfavourable traits into her picture ; but she treated the failings of the Irish tenderly, as if she loved them on the whole. The Paddy of fiction and the stage is really her creation ; she is the author of his existence in literature, of the sly, ready-witted, fluent, faithful, and generous Paddy. Herself the daughter of an Irish landowner, Edgeworth of Edgeworthstown, she had not seen Ireland till she was sixteen, and was thus all the better fitted to be impressed with peculiarities that might have escaped her notice if she had lived among them from infancy. She was brought very closely in contact with the poor people of Ireland as well as with the landed families of various ranks, for her father, an enthusiastic man of progress, full of eighteenth-century philanthropic and educational theories, and ever ready to make ingenious experiments of his own, having resolved to reside on his Irish estates, resolved also to get rid of middlemen as the curse of the land system, and employed his daughter practically as his steward and factor. For years of her life she had every day to grant interviews to her father's tenants, hear excuses and grievances, settle disputes, answer petitions : and on rent-days more particularly her hands were full. Miss Edgeworth's knowledge of Irish life was thus most intimate, and she had a keen eye for the humorous side of it, while her observations were not permitted to degenerate into aimless caricature or disguised satire by good sense and real sympathy with the people. 'Castle Rackrent' is the story of an Irish landed family, put into the mouth of an old steward, who in his time had served several landlords of the stock in succession,—Sir Patrick, Sir Murtagh, Sir Kit, and Sir Condey, men of different character, but all agreeing in doing their best, whether by lavish expenditure, gambling, or avaricious litigation, to help on the ruin consummated by the last of the series. The faithful old retainer admires them all with all their faults, and seen through his indulgent eyes their crimes and their follies, their freaks of wild expenditure and their matter-of-course extortions from their tenantry, their love-making, their hospitality, their family quarrels, and the dealings all the time of the too-faithful steward with the artful tenants, excite in the reader an extraordinary mixture of laughter and pity.

Miss Edgeworth never surpassed this her first work of note, and in some respects did not again come up to it. She had been engaged before with her father in writing stories for children, stories with a moral and educational purpose. It was the age when Hannah More's tales, intended to counteract the influence of the French Revolution, and teach the common people to rely upon the virtues of content, sobriety, humility, industry, reverence for the British Constitution, trust in God, and in the kindness of the gentry, were circulating in thousands and hundreds of thousands. It was natural that moralists, in a generation distinguished for its philanthropic endeavour, all the more conspicuous that philanthropy was a new passion among the upper classes—it was natural that in a generation which produced Wilberforce and Clarkson, the agitation for the abolition of the slave-trade, and the impeachment of Warren Hastings for the oppression of the Hindus, moralists should try to press into their service the revived art of story-telling, for the productions of which the reading public were so clamorous. Miss Edgeworth is sometimes called the inventor of the novel with a purpose; but it was really the invention of the age, and I don't think she can claim the merit of being the first in the field. She was perhaps the first novelist with a purpose entitled to high rank on purely artistic grounds. It was her father apparently, between whom and herself there was the closest confidence, and who was from first to last her literary director, dictator, and censor—not wholly, it is supposed, to the advantage of her art—who insisted upon her devoting her talents to the purpose of moral education. The fact certainly is in support of this prevalent belief, that 'Castle Rackrent' was the only novel written by her without his superintendence. She eluded her director in this, and wrote it as a little surprise for him. And it is the only one of her novels that has no obvious and obtruded lesson. There is no harm even from the artistic point of view in writing novels

with a moral purpose.   Novelists, whether they intend it or not,
by the very fact that they represent human beings in action, and
so furnish examples that readers, consciously or unconsciously,
imitate, just as they imitate their own companions in real life,
must influence conduct; from the very nature of their art, they
cannot avoid influencing conduct; and it is desirable that they
should endeavour to influence conduct for the better and not for
the worse.   But they are apt to miss their aim as well as injure
their story by making the behaviour of their characters unnatural,
and the incidents that befall them impossible, if they allow the
deliberate enforcement of a moral to influence the probable evolution of a story out of given characters and given circumstances.
Miss Edgeworth fell into this error in several of her stories with a
purpose.   In 'Belinda,' for example, one of her tales of fashionable life, one of the most brilliantly drawn characters in fiction,
Lady Delacour, is converted by the force of circumstances from a
gay, heartless, daringly cynical leader of fashion into a model
wife, and that too after years of outrageous frivolity.   In another
story, 'Ennui,' Lord Glenthorne, a young nobleman so rich that he
has no interest in anything, and spends his time till he reaches
middle life in torpid vacuity and listless search for amusement, is
suddenly changed by the loss of his fortune into a model of industry, applying himself with indefatigable perseverance to the
most repulsive studies, and distancing every competitor in fields
to which they have given the application of all their lives and all
their abilities.   Such sudden revolutions of habits in middle life
are not true to nature; long-confirmed habits are not thrown off
by real human beings with such ease.   The novelist represents
them as taking place, not in her function of a painter of manners,
but in pursuance of a moral purpose.   Lady Delacour's conversion
is intended as an encouragement to ladies of fashion to abandon
heartless flirtation and vain display: they are supposed to be struck
with the greater happiness of the lady in her regenerate condition.
And Lord Glenthorne's conversion is intended as an incentive to
noble lords to discard unworthy amusement, and experience the
greater happiness of energies devoted to nobler pursuits.   Such is
the novelist's obvious intention; but whether such pictures are
likely to do more harm than good is not so clear, for the case with

which these interesting reprobates shake off their long-indulged habits is apt to encourage would-be imitators of their ultimate good conduct to defer the period of amendment till it is too late. I admit, however, that from the moralist's point of view, quite apart from strict adherence to human probabilities, there is something to be said on the other side, and that the delight taken by the converts in their altered course of conduct may be rendered more potent as an example, by the fact that they are represented as deriving no real pleasure from the pleasure-seeking of their unregenerate days. It would, however, give an entirely wrong idea of Miss Edgeworth's novels to lay much stress on their moral purpose. Apart from their purpose, they are most brilliant pictures of life. The moral is not constantly obtruded, as in Hannah More's celebrated 'Cœlebs in Search of a Wife,' published while Miss Edgeworth was in the height of her popularity. The reader, especially the young lady reader, is preached at from beginning to end of that excellent work; the only incidents in Mr Cœlebs's career are his visits to various families in the course of his deliberate search, the only surprises consist in the discovery of weak points in superficially pleasing young ladies and sterling qualities in the superficially unattractive. We are not led to feel the slightest interest in the issue of Mr Cœlebs's great enterprise; there is nothing shown in him to make us care whether he finds a woman worthy of his fastidious choice or not. Yet Hannah More was far from being a dull writer, and in the exposure of affectation and pretence and shallowness she showed a very fine sense of humour. Only, her book is not a story, but a string of journalistic social articles on the minor and the higher morals. Now, Miss Edgeworth is not so avowedly and obtrusively didactic as this. She is seldom so clear and decided in her purpose as, for example, Mr Wilkie Collins in 'Heart and Science,' or Mr Besant in 'All Sorts and Conditions of Men.' She took an interest, either for herself or at her father's instigation, in various social reforms, and did her best to advance them incidentally, as Dickens did in 'Nicholas Nickleby' or 'Dombey and Son.' The proportion of direct didactic in her writings is really comparatively small, while her pictures of life, as it was to be seen in fashionable society and on Irish estates, were as faithful and complete as they were animated, sensible, and humorous. Miss Edgeworth must certainly be pronounced to have gone out of fashion, seeing that Miss Broughton ran a tale through one of the magazines with the title of 'Belinda,' without anybody remarking, in print at least, that this was the title of one of Miss Edgeworth's most famous novels. Whether Miss Zimmern's pleasantly written biography in the "Eminent Women of Letters Series" will do anything to restore her faded popularity is doubtful; and yet novel-readers who have exhausted the novels of their own generation might do worse than give 'Belinda' or 'Castle Rackrent' a trial.

If I were to judge from my own experience, I should not recommend Miss Austen's 'Pride and Prejudice' or 'Sense and Sensibility,' still less 'Mansfield Park' or 'Emma,' with the same confidence to confirmed novel-readers of the present day. Nobody can read any of Miss Austen's works without admiring her wonderful closeness and keenness of humorous observation, the skill with which she displays every turn in the motives of commonplace character, and the exquisite quality of the ridicule with which her fancy dances round and round them as she holds them up to our inspection. If you once make the acquaintance of the Bennet family in 'Pride and Prejudice' you can never forget them, so distinctly is each individual marked, and so keen and exquisite is the revelation of their foibles. In mere art of humorous portraiture, in a quieter and less farcical style than Miss Burney's, Miss Austen is an expert of classical finish. But somehow, speaking for myself, I must confess to a certain want of interest in the characters themselves. Unless one is really interested in the subjects of such an elaborate art of portraiture, the gradual revelation of them, touch after touch, is apt to become tedious, however much one may enjoy for a time the quick and delicate play of the writer's gently malicious humour. But this want of interest in the characters of English middle-class provincial life is of course a personal defect. You will find that Mrs Oliphant writes with rapture about her great predecessor in fiction, and I daresay you have read somewhere Sir Walter Scott's often-quoted compliment to her. "Read again, and for the third time at least, Miss Austen's very finely written 'Pride and Prejudice,'" he entered in his Diary. "That young lady had a talent for describing the involvements and feelings and characters of ordinary life which is to me the most wonderful I ever met with. The big Bow-wow strain I can do myself, like any now going; but the exquisite touch which renders ordinary commonplace things and characters interesting from the truth of the description and the sentiment is denied to me. What a pity such a gifted creature died so early." Sir Walter also reviewed her novels in the 'Quarterly,' and helped to bring them into notice. In one respect she had a great and legitimate attraction for novel-readers of her own time that she no longer possesses. Her field of manners-painting was new: nobody before her had taken scenes and characters from the life of the provinces, though Miss Burney had had hosts of imitators in the description of fashionable life in the metropolis. And she had another distinction also, not so striking now, in the fact that when fiction was overrun with romantic sentiment and improbable incident, workers in the hackneyed paths having reached a despicable level when her first novel made its appearence in 1811, she restricted herself to ordinary everyday character, and never went beyond probability either in conduct or in incident. Miss Austen was the daughter of the rector of Steventon, a parish in Hampshire; and after her father's death, and before publishing her novels, she lived for some years with her mother at Southampton, and for some time at Bath. All the material of her novels is such as might have come within the range of her own limited personal experience, and she treats her characters, and comments on their conduct, very much as she and her family were in the habit of looking at and criticising the life of their own neighbourhood. Hence the vividness, the fresh air of reality, that is one of the secrets of her power as a novelist: her figures are not lay figures or creations of vacuous fancy, but real men and women, represented not in accordance with any merely conventional canons of art, but as such characters presented themselves to her in real life.

Another female novelist, who never took the classical rank accorded to Miss Edgeworth and Miss Austen, but who was a very conspicuous and much-discussed personage in her day, also achieved her first successes before the publication of 'Waverley.'

This was Miss Sydney Owenson, afterwards Lady Morgan. With the usual longevity of women of letters, to which Miss Austen was an exception, dying in 1817 at the comparatively early age of forty-two, Lady Morgan lived and continued to write till 1859, although she was an eminent author several years before Miss Austen emerged from the obscurity of Hampshire. Where she was born remained to the last a mystery, and her biographer, Mr Hepworth Dixon, respected her wishes on the point, and either did not attempt to discover, or if he did discover anything, kept the secret. Tolerably early in her career a great point was publicly made against her by one of her critics, Mr J. Wilson Croker, because she pretended to be younger than she really was, and this was probably the reason why she never would tell, and was unwilling that the little fact should be known after her death. Lady Morgan's age, brought into prominence by the ungallant man of dates Croker, who did not like her politics—Croker was the original of Rigby in Disraeli's 'Coningsby'—was a disputed point for nearly half a century. Writing to the 'Athenæum' in 1859 (January 22) *apropos* of some allusion to her age, the lively old lady made the following rhyme :—

> " Then talk not to me of my age ;
> I appeal from the phrase to the fact
> That I'm told in your own brilliant page
> I'm still young in fun, fancy, and tact."

She made her first appearance as a novelist in 1804 with 'St Clair,' and followed this up with ' The Novice of St Dominic ' and ' The Wild Irish Girl ' in 1806. According to her own account, she was still in her teens when she wrote ' The Wild Irish Girl,' which made her reputation, but the statistical Croker maintained that she was born in 1770. There is documentary evidence that she was at a boarding-school in Dublin in 1794, and at that time considered herself too old to sit on her father's knee ; but certainly twenty-four would be a mature age for a schoolgirl, so that Croker was for once out in his dates, though he pretended to have consulted a register. The lady, it is needless to say, paid the critic out : she made him sit for the portrait of one of her most odious, sycophantic, unscrupulous political adventurers, Con Crawley in

'Florence M'Carthy.' Croker must have had a thick skin if he felt none of the shafts that were levelled at him. Macaulay ridiculed him heartily in his essay on Boswell's Johnson, and Disraeli's Rigby is one of the most cutting of the satires of that master of the art. The beginning of Croker's dislike to Lady Morgan, whom he attacked with a virulent personality not uncommon at the time but long since out of fashion, was her politics. She followed Miss Edgeworth in choosing her subjects from her native country of Ireland ; but she was herself a different type of Irishwoman from that cool, sensible, impartially humorous lady— enthusiastic, romantic, inordinately fond of excitement and social notoriety.   She drew her ideal of her own character in 'The Wild Irish Girl' Glorvina.   Two of her Irish novels — 'Florence M'Carthy' (1818) and 'The O'Briens and the O'Flahertys' (1827)—may still be read with interest. The character of Florence M'Carthy is charming ; Phyllis French, in a recent novel by Frank Lee Benedict, 'The Price she Paid,' is an evident copy of her. Lady Morgan may have seen the original from which she drew in the earlier part of her life, for she was the daughter of an Irish actor, and had seen a good deal of Bohemian life before she acquired distinction as an authoress and was taken up by the Abercorn family, and married almost by stratagem to the family physician, Sir Charles Morgan.

Another Irish novelist deserves a word of mention, if only for the singularity of his career,—the Rev. Charles Maturin, curate of St Peter's in Dublin.   Maturin had the curious fortune to attract the attention of some of the greatest magnates of literature in his time, who were struck by the power of his writing and his conception of situation and character, and believed one after another that it was possible for him to cure himself of the wild rhapsodical extravagance by which his productions were disfigured. He followed up Lady Morgan's ' Wild Irish Girl ' with a ' Wild Irish Boy '; and a romance of his, ' The Family of Montoria, or, The Fatal Revenge,' fell into Scott's hands in 1810, and was reviewed by him in the ' Quarterly.' Maturin professed himself entirely convinced by the criticisms of his friends, acknowledged that his previous works were failures, and undertook to keep himself within the bounds of probability in the novel of 'Women, or, Pour et Contre.' His heroine Zaira was a great artist of unhappy domestic life, a study of the same kind as Madame de Staël's 'Corinne' or George Sand's 'Consuelo.' It is not an uncommon type in recent fiction; Miss Bertha Thomas's 'Violin-Player' is a recent example. Maturin had also a tragedy, 'Bertram,' produced at Drury Lane in 1818, through the influence of Lord Byron, which had the honour of being critically dissected by Coleridge. But he never overcame his tendency to absurd extravagance of expression and wild improbability, though we can understand why it was that the great critics of the time continued to hope that he would tone down.

Miss Edgeworth, Miss Austen, Miss Owenson, and the wild Irish boy Maturin were in full swing when 'Waverley' appeared in 1814, and was followed at short intervals by a series of novels received with an excitement to which there is hardly a parallel in our literature—no parallel at all, if we except the novels of Dickens. It would be absurd to attempt any criticism on the Waverley Novels in a fragment of a lecture, and the chief facts about the reception of them and the life of the great novelist during their composition are doubtless familiar to you all. I have already sketched for you how he laid the foundation for his extraordinary rapidity of production once he began to write novels. It was not, strictly speaking, *impromptu* writing, as Carlyle tauntingly described it,—not *impromptu* in the sense of being writing without any previous preparation; it was rapid in virtue of great previous enthusiasm and industry in the accumulation of materials. He could not in so short a space of time have painted the costumes and manners and characters of so many different periods, from the eleventh century to the eighteenth, in Scotland, in England, on the Continent, if his mind had not been full of them before he began to write, and that familiarity had been obtained by years of labour in regions dry as dust to all but the enthusiastic antiquary. Special students of the present day can point to a good many errors of detail in Scott's medievalism, though chiefly on trifling points; but we must compare his romances with other so-called historical romances before his time, if we are to do justice to the extraordinary range of his historical knowledge, quite apart from his genius in reviving the life of the past. Miss Jane Porter's 'Scottish Chiefs' was one of the first historical novels produced in this century, and the lady was always proud of having set the example to Scott; but there is very little real local colour in her account of the adventures of Wallace and Bruce—there is hardly an attempt made to keep to historical probability. You will find in the introductions which he wrote for his novels shortly before his death an account of the actual incidents that suggested the various plots; but he would have had to go back over his life to his boyhood, when he devoured every history he could lay his hands on, in order to trace the origin of the resources that enabled him to clothe with such richness of costume and incident the bare skeleton of story that served him as a starting-point. It would seem that it was almost an accident that he did not begin writing prose romances before his metrical tales; and he humorously observes in the introduction to 'Waverley' that if his readers were inclined to complain of his fertility in novel-writing, they had reason to congratulate themselves that he was comparatively advanced in life before he began. He did make two beginnings, one in 1800 and another in 1805, of which you will find an account in the introduction to 'Waverley'; but he threw them aside for one reason or another. It was the success of Miss Edgeworth's Irish tales, he tells us, that finally determined him to try to do for the people and scenery of Scotland what she had done for Ireland.

You all know the great calamity of Scott's life, the heroic courage with which he faced it, and the amazing power with which he laboured cheerfully to retrieve his misfortune. You know how he connected himself with the printing and publishing business of the Ballantynes and Constable; how in 1826, after earning unexampled sums by his novels, he found himself involved in liabilities to the amount of £170,000; and how he set himself to clear off this enormous load, toiling from morning till night till paralysis came upon him, and he broke down in the struggle,—not, however, till he had accomplished the object of his honourable determination. His ambition had been very different in his prosperous days, to found another great territorial family of Scotts; but he laboured for the five years that his powers lasted with even greater energy to redeem his name from the fancied disgrace of a debt that was not of his own contracting. You know also that he did not avow the authorship of the Waverley Novels till this misfortune overtook him.

At first he was afraid of his reputation as a poet, and afterwards he kept up the disguise from no definite reason, but simply because he liked it. He did not like to appear in society as a literary lion, and he delighted in having a secret all to himself, and in being the centre of a mystery. Carlyle's fierce criticism of the novels was that they were not profitable for doctrine, for reproof, for edification, for building up or elevating in any shape. Scott, as Carlyle said, certainly gave by his novels immense pleasure to indolent and languid readers, but he also brought all classes of readers together by his sympathetic delineations of characters in humble life. No novelist in any century has exercised a more healthy and beneficial influence.

Professor Masson has collected some curious statistics showing the enormous impulse given to novel-writing by the success of the Waverley Novels. In 1820, when they were at the height of their popularity, the number published, or received at the British Museum, was 26, an average of one every fortnight. Ten years later, when the series was nearly finished, in 1830, the number received was 101, nearly an average of two a-week. And it would appear from the British Museum Catalogue that the average has been pretty steadily maintained since. I doubt, however, whether the authorities of the Museum have always been careful to avail themselves of their rights, for in several cases, having occasion to see if possible the first editions of various novels, I have found, rather to my surprise, that a novel is represented there by an edition issued years after its first publication.

Among the host of novel-writers who made their first appearance in the ten years after the date of 'Waverley,' the three of most marked originality and distinction were women,—Miss Ferrier, Mrs Shelley, and Miss Mitford. Even after Scott, Miss Ferrier found something fresh in the humorous observation of Scottish character. We have seen how he compared his own bow-wow style with the more realistic modern art of Miss Austen, and envied her power of entering into the humour of ordinary respectable characters. Miss Ferrier had the gift which he lacked, and exercised it with great felicity in her novels of 'Marriage' and 'The Inheritance.'

Mrs Shelley, the daughter of William Godwin, himself a novelist of considerable repute at the end of the eighteenth century, wrote only one novel, but the conception was so original and unique that it is not likely to be soon forgotten. This was 'Frankenstein.' It appeared in 1818, and had the honour of being reviewed by Scott, who found time for all sorts of miscellaneous literary work even when his greatest novels were on the anvil. Mrs Shelley boldly accepted Horace Walpole's idea of taking the utmost licence as regarded probability of incident, concentrating her power upon imagining how her hero felt and acted in his supernatural circumstances. The hero was a German student who had by unwearied vigils discovered the secret of imparting life to inanimate matter ; and who constructed a gigantic monster and was terribly persecuted by his own creation.

Very different in character was the work of Miss Mitford, one of the most delightful and natural and genially humorous writers in the language. Her sketches of life in ' Our Village,' of the "Talking Lady," the "Talking Gentleman," of poachers, seamstresses, domestic servants, young men and old men of local note, remain, after half a century of imitations, as fresh as if they had been written yesterday. No human being ever had a cheerier or more sympathetic outlook on the world. Her sympathies, with a certain waywardness, turned rather towards characters that the respectable world frowns upon, with lawless good-hearted characters and coquettish beauties. She liked to show the good side of such beings to the world. Like Miss Edgeworth, she had a father, but a very different father from the energetic, inventive, philanthropic, restless squire of Edgeworthstown. Dr Mitford was an "awful dad," a scapegrace who spent his wife's fortune in a few years, ran rapidly through a lottery prize which his little girl had the good fortune to draw, and in his old age subsisted on the small remnant of his fortune and the proceeds of his daughter's literary industry. Yet his daughter adored him, and took infinite delight in his "friskings," as she called his little eccentricities, living in a small house that was a lesson in condensation, refusing all holiday invitations from her wealthy relations, never stopping in her literary work except to read the sporting newspaper to the graceless companion who called her his "mamma," and was the stay, support, and admiration of all the loafers in the neighbourhood. Miss Mitford's early ambition was to be "the greatest English poetess," and when she was little more than twenty her metrical tales were praised by Scott in the 'Quarterly,' while some years later tragedies from her pen were highly successful at Covent Garden. The short tales and sketches collected under the title of 'Our Village' were written originally for a magazine, purely for the supply of the household, and yet they brought her more enduring fame than her poetry. They had an influence on the early manner of Dickens, and may almost be said to have founded a school of periodical sketch-writing.

The natural result of the interest created in authorship by Scott and Byron in fashionable society was the rise of a school of fashionable novelists. This was the chief literary phenomenon of the last five years of the reign of George IV., the last five years of our period. Of the fashionable novels then in fresh repute only two are now much remembered, Disraeli's 'Vivian Grey' and Bulwer Lytton's 'Pelham.' But there was a large cluster of them, all with something of the same character, and that something new. The authors were men moving in the society which they attempted to describe. Up to that time fashionable life had been described by women; now the young dandies—sucking diplomatists, politicians, and statesmen—seized upon the novel as a dramatic vehicle for conveying their views on the manners of society and the affairs of the State. It is an interesting thing for the historian to have had the inner life of political society so copiously described before the Reform Bill, which produced such a change in the political power of the upper hundreds: we have vividly depicted in the pages of these novels the old state of things, and we are brought into immediate contact with the ardent fiery spirit of the young ambitions that were awakened by the prospect of change. 'Vivian Grey' and 'Pelham' have been kept alive by the subsequent reputation of their authors; but there were three other authors who fairly shared with them the applause of contemporaries. Mr Plumer Ward's 'Tremaine, or, The Man of Refinement,' was the first of the series; then followed Mr Lister's 'Granby'; then side by side Disraeli and Bulwer and Lord Normanby.

CHAPTER XIX.

SHELLEY AND KEATS.

SHELLEY—VARIOUS CONCEPTIONS OF THE POET—CHARACTER—KEATS—THE
REVIEWERS — CHARACTERISTICS OF HIS POETRY — " ENDYMION " AND
" HYPERION."

THE common judgment of Shelley, at least as expressed in literary
organs, has undergone a complete revolution since he was a living
man.   Nobody now would venture to publish an article about
Shelley without copious protestations of admiration for the poet,
whatever the opinion might be expressed about his conduct as a
man.   To acknowledge indifference to his poetry would be to set
one's self against an overwhelming weight of authoritative opinion.
To deny him equal rank with any poet of his generation would be
heresy.   Enjoyment of Shelley is often put forward as a test of
poetic sensibility : if Shelley does not delight you, you are set down
as not being capable of knowing what poetry is.   He is now *par
excellence* the poet's poet.

But it was otherwise when his poems first appeared.   He received
hardly a word of cordial recognition from any critical organ of
authority, except from his friend Leigh Hunt's journal the ' Examiner.'   The potentates and powers of criticism—the ' Quarterly,'
the ' Edinburgh Review,' ' Blackwood's,' and the ' Literary Gazette '
—were unanimous in derision and denunciation.   That such stuff
as " Alastor " and " The Revolt of Islam " should pretend to be
poetry was hailed as one of the most ludicrous pretensions in
an age fertile in ludicrous literary pretensions.   It was a mere
incoherent farce of meaningless imagery, a collection of lines

pretty enough in themselves, but the most hollow of emptinesses; more sound and fury, signifying nothing. In so far as any meaning was discernible through the iridescent vapour of words, the critics did not like it. The poet's designs, in so far as they could be made out, were immoral, anarchic, atheistic; whenever he deviated into intelligibility, it was to rave against all law and order, human and divine,—to rave with fierce shrill hysterical vituperation against all that other men held sacred. There were reports also, which the critics did not fail to publicly notice, about his private conduct, which accounted for his mad rebellion against established order. It was said that he was a young man who had been expelled from Oxford for an atheistic publication; that he had married a schoolgirl and deserted her, with the result that she committed suicide; and that he had persuaded another young girl of sixteen to run away with him while his first wife was still alive. In short, the poetry was effeminate, hysterical, and contemptible, in so far as it was not dangerous and unsettling; while the poet himself was a disreputable profligate, against whom all respectable persons should set their faces.

Such was the conception of Shelley which all readers of the leading organs of public opinion in his generation were invited to entertain. As far as his poetry was concerned, not a little of the animus against it was due to its strangeness, its novelty, its unlikeness to anything that had been published before in verse. Even if the circumstances had been favourable to its receiving a fair judgment as poetry, we may well doubt whether on its first appearance the critics would not have treated it as a flock of birds might treat a new-comer in gorgeous but unfamiliar plumage. We must remember, also, that Shelley's first noticeable works, "Alastor" and "The Revolt of Islam," were deficient in many of the great qualities of his later works, and were justly liable to the reproach of incoherent copiousness and obscurity. But there were accidental circumstances calculated to strengthen any prejudice that might be against Shelley's poetry, based on its own intrinsic defects and difficulties. The literary world was divided more sharply than at any time before or since into hostile factions, and provincial and political enmities were allowed to bias literary judgments to a degree of flagrancy now almost incredible. There was the 'Edinburgh Review' clique under the banner of Jeffrey, and the 'Blackwood' clique under the banner of Wilson, and the 'Quarterly' clique under the banner of Gifford, and the 'Examiner' clique under the banner of Leigh Hunt. Men like Scott and Byron, with their bold, direct, intelligible address to the great body of readers, swept past these guardians of the gates of the Temple of Fame straight to their destination. But if a poet was not easily understood by the multitude, if he needed an interpreter or a sponsor, or a kindly word of introduction, and had not friends in more than one camp, praise from one quarter was more than likely to awaken hostility in every other. There was a jealousy between Edinburgh and London, of which any new aspirant might be made the victim. Hard things were said in the London organs about the Scottish critics, and the Scottish critics, proud of the renown of Modern Athens, asserted themselves in violent denunciation of everything Cockney. No words were too bitterly contemptuous for the Cockney school of poetry : they had an ideal Cockney in their minds, compounded of vulgarity, bad taste, effusive sentimentality, affected prettiness,—and they poured the vials of their scornful mockery upon every poem published in London in which there was a suspicion of these qualities. Then there was a political jealousy between Tory, Whig, and Radical, in the interests of which a new poem was sharply scrutinised and cordially welcomed or denounced according to the creed of the reviewer. The 'Quarterly' and 'Blackwood's,' the champions of Toryism, and the 'Edinburgh,' the champion of Whiggery, had an almost equally keen scent for a revolutionary. Any discontent with the established order of things, beyond such discontent as was recognised in the Whig programme, was sure to draw down from the 'Quarterly' and 'Blackwood's' a charge of Jacobinism, atheism, and infidelity, and to ensure that the 'Edinburgh' should either join in the cry or pass over in silence the work in which the dangerous doctrines appeared. The situation was still further complicated by purely literary factions, factions based on difference of literary creed. By 1818, the reverence for the traditions of the eighteenth century had been rudely shaken ; but there were still among the critics a good many who shook their heads over modern innovations and sighed for the good old style. The new edition of

Pope had given an occasion for comparing the old with the new, and Gifford of the 'Quarterly' was a bigoted, hard, and vehement supporter of Pope, ever ready to launch out with all his energy of invective against unexpected novelties. Now Shelley had the misfortune to concentrate on his person the lightnings of no less than three great factions. Before he published "Alastor" he had connected himself publicly with Leigh Hunt, the leader and founder of the so-called Cockney school, so that Shelley, like Keats, who made his first essay about the same time, was regarded as a new development of Cockneyism. He spoke with daring disrespect of venerable institutions, and so incurred the wrath of all the literary organs of respectability. And in his method he departed more widely than any previous poet from the concise epigrammatic reasonable style of Pope, so that all who had leanings in that direction were doubly scandalised by his extravagances.

The fullest expression of Shelley's character is to be found, of course, in his poetry; but if that puzzles you, there is much that may be cleared up by a reference to his letters—*e.g.*, a selection of them recently published by Garnett; 'Essays and Letters from Abroad,' by Mrs Shelley; 'Memorials of Shelley,' by Lady Shelley; 'Records of Byron, Shelley, and his Contemporaries,' by Trelawney. The letters are masterpieces of expression, frank, candid, really letters, and yet so perfect in style that Mr Matthew Arnold expects the reputation of them to be even more enduring than his poetry.

The key-note of Shelley's character, his ruling motive, was an excessively sensitive hatred of everything in the shape of harshness, tyranny, injustice, carried to extremes that to an ordinary mind appears fantastic and insane. Such sensitiveness is not rare among men when their own interests are touched, but Shelley's resentment took a much wider range than a morbid instinct of self-defence. He could not bear the thought of the existence of oppression anywhere under the sun; the thought of such a thing maddened him, and kindled his energies to be up and doing at once for its extinction. In his youthful vehemence, he was a stranger to wise patience and slow deliberate calculation of ways and means, and his action, consequently, was not always the best action for the end in view; but such was his motive, a violent, furious dislike to wrong-doing. Himself one of the gentlest of creatures, playful, affectionate, beloved by all who knew him, he was capable, under this intolerable spur, of behaving with the fury of a demon. Nothing could be further from the truth than representing Shelley as inspired by a blind hatred of all law and order, a violent assailant of established institutions because they interfered with the pleasure of following his own will, because they interposed checks between him and the execution of wayward, capricious, whimsical impulses. It was the excesses committed in the name of law and order that he could not endure; the cruelties sanctioned by established institutions that drove him into revolt against them. Law and order and established institutions offended him, not by their spirit but by the delinquencies and transgressions of their accredited ministers, many of whom, in the history of the world, have not merely fallen short of ideal righteousness, but, under the protection of sacred names, have in small things and in great committed shameful offences against humanity. It was the defect of Shelley's temperament that he was almost insanely sensitive to harshness and cruelty of conduct, not with a shrinking sensitiveness but with the sensitiveness that flamed out in fiery indignation, the sensitiveness of a man who came of the high-spirited chivalrous race of the Sidneys. This spirit was the ruling principle of his conduct in small things as well as in great, and led him into some eccentricities that appear merely ludicrous to the ordinary mind, and into one eccentricity which, viewed in the light of its tragic consequences, has the appearance of a scandalous crime. For example, he would not drink tea with his sugar, because sugar was the produce of slave-labour; and he ate nothing but vegetable food, because he believed that man had no right to kill and eat the lower animals. When he was a boy at Eton he rebelled against the system of fagging, which was much abused by youthful bullies. To this he alludes in the often-quoted stanzas in the dedication of his "Revolt of Islam":—

" Thoughts of great deeds were mine, dear Friend, when first
The clouds which wrap this world from youth did pass.
I do remember well the hour which burst
My spirit's sleep : a fresh May-dawn it was,
When I walked forth upon the glittering grass,

> And wept, I knew not why ; until there rose
> From the near schoolroom, voices, that, alas !
> Were but an echo from the world of woes—
> The hard and grating strife of tyrants and of foes.
>
> And then I clasped my hands and looked around—
> But none was near to mock my streaming eyes,
> Which poured their warm drops on the sunny ground—
> So without shame I spake,—' I will be wise,
> And just, and free, and mild, if in me lies
> Such power, for I grow weary to behold
> The selfish and the strong still tyrannise
> Without reproach or check.'   I then controlled
> My tears ; my heart grew calm, and I was meek and bold."

It is a common statement that Shelley was expelled from Oxford—to which he was transferred from Eton at the age of nineteen, in 1811—for publishing a tract in defence of Atheism.   But
this would appear to be not strictly correct.   What he did was to
issue a tract containing certain propositions maintained by Atheists,
and to invite the Heads of College in Oxford to answer them,—
an invitation which they met, as De Quincey puts it, by "invit-
ing" the unpractical enthusiast to withdraw from the University.
Undoubtedly the great stain upon Shelley's life is his treatment of
his first wife, Harriet Westbrook.   There are papers in the hands
of the Shelley family that have not yet been published, but which
are said to reconcile his behaviour with the high and honourable
spirit that he showed in all other circumstances.   This much is
already clear, that it was his chivalrous generosity that first
connected him with the girl whose subsequent fate was so tragic.

Those who seek to defend Shelley's conduct to his wife on the
ground that he was an ethereal impulsive creature, a visionary
child too much wrapt up in his visions to be fit for ordinary human
duties or to be judged by any ordinary standard of right and
wrong, a being so good, so gentle, yet so fragile and so child-
ishly eccentric in his impulses, that the heart shrinks from holding
him responsible for the harmful consequences of impulses so devoid
of malicious intention, and judgment is suspended in wondering
pity—such defenders do great injustice to the fundamental
strength of the poet's character, and interpose an obstacle to
the understanding of his greater poems.   He was a visionary, in-

deed, but not an aimless and drifting visionary; the dreamer's eyes were fixed steadily, constantly upon one vision, the struggle between good and evil in the world, the vicissitudes of this struggle, and the final triumph of good. He read history; he observed life; but wherever he turned his eyes all the actions of mankind presented themselves as moves in the terrible game between these opposing principles. The centre of interest for him in the world-drama was the protracted duel between good and evil. This view of life was natural in a generation perplexed and disturbed by the staggering events of the French Revolution and the world-wide ambition of Napoleon. The great problems of human destiny were forced upon all the reflective minds of the time, and Shelley's nature was not merely profoundly meditative, but deeply interested in the issue, and passionately eager for a solution. A knowledge of his character and of his view of life is indispensable to the understanding of such poems as "Alastor," and "The Revolt of Islam," and "Prometheus Unbound." Without this simple key they must always appear meaningless rhapsodies, incoherent mazes of sweet sound and beautiful imagery, without beginning, middle, or end, capricious ethereal movements of fancy and imagination leading nowhere. You cannot open their pages anywhere without being enchanted with the wonderful melody and affluence of imagery, of which critics labour in vain to give any idea, by piling up all the epithets that belong to whatever is most charming in poetic creation. But this wonderful procession of forms to the music of most melodious verse is not so aimless as it appears at first to the dazzled senses; it has a meaning and a direction even in its most seemingly capricious movements. The poet does not address the senses but the understanding heart. Concerning "The Revolt of Islam," Shelley himself said, in answer to a letter from his friend Godwin censuring its exuberance: "The poem was pro-' duced by a series of thoughts which filled my mind with unbounded and sustained enthusiasm. I felt the precariousness of my life, and I resolved in this book to leave some records of myself. Much of what the volume contains was written with the same feeling, as real though not so prophetic, as the communications of a dying man. . . . I felt that it was in many respects a genuine picture of my own mind. I felt that the sentiments were true, not assumed; and in this I have long believed—that my power consists in sympathy, and that part of imagination which relates to sentiment and contemplation."

The lofty strain in which "Alastor" opens gives us an idea of the intense passion with which he composed his poetry:—

> " Earth, ocean, air, beloved brotherhood !
>   If our great Mother has imbued my soul
>   With aught of natural piety to feel
>   Your love, and recompense the boon with mine ;
>   If dewy morn, and odorous noon, and even,
>   With sunset and its gorgeous minsters,
>   And solemn midnight's tingling silentness ;
>   If autumn's hollow sighs in the sere wood,
>   And winter robing with pure snow and crowns
>   Of starry ice the grey grass and bare boughs ;
>   If spring's voluptuous pantings when she breathes
>   Her first sweet kisses, have been dear to me ;
>   If no bright bird, insect, or gentle beast
>   I consciously have injured, but still loved
>   And cherished these my kindred ;—then forgive
>   This boast, beloved brethren, and withdraw
>   No portion of your wonted favour now !"

The poem, in short, is an allegory.   Like all intricate allegories, it is difficult to interpret, and the difficulty is increased by the fact that the allegory is not, as in the case of Spenser's ' Faery Queen ' or Tennyson's Idylls, a separate stream of story, complete and intelligible in itself, but a stream that is often interposed with the realities that it is intended to represent.   Its full interpretation in every particular is perhaps impossible, because the poet was intent only upon the expression of his own thought and feeling, and to understand every turn of this we should have to read the histories that he read, see the sights that he saw, and track him through his study of the speculations of his time : but the general drift of the allegory is obvious enough, if we only recognise it as a vision of the vicissitudes of the struggle between good and evil, in which sometimes the apparent triumphs of good become the most terrible instruments of evil, and sometimes the triumphs of evil become beneficent instruments of good, while in the end the principle of good is victorious.   "Alastor," "The Revolt of Islam," and "Prometheus" are all poetic embodiments of the same view of the history of man and the same ardent hopes for his future.   I would remind you again of the Wordsworthian theory of poetry as the spontaneous overflow of powerful feelings, and of what I said as to the height and intricacy of the structure that the imagination may raise at the original bidding of the simplest of emotional motives.   If Byron interpreted Wordsworth to the multitude, Shelley may be said to have interpreted him to those who make poetry a study.

Among his shorter poems you will find some of the most exquisite poetry in the language,—the " Ode to the West Wind," for example, being held by many to be the finest English lyric. The " Stanzas written in Dejection " might be cited as another example, the concluding lines of which are exquisitely beautiful and pathetic :—

> " Alas ! I have nor hope, nor health,
>   Nor peace within, nor calm around,
>   Nor that content, surpassing wealth,
>   The sage in meditation found,
>   And walked with inward glory crowned—
>   Nor fame, nor power, nor love, nor leisure.
>   Others I see whom these surround—
>   Smiling they live and call life pleasure ;
> To me that cup has been dealt in another measure.
>
>   Yet now despair itself is mild,
>   Even as the winds and waters are ;
>   I could lie down like a tired child,
>   And weep away the life of care
>   Which I have borne and yet must bear,
>   Till death like sleep might steal on me,
>   And I might feel in the warm air
>   My cheek grow cold, and hear the sea
> Breathe o'er my dying brain its last monotony.
>
>   Some might lament that I were cold,
>   As I, when this sweet day is gone,
>   Which my lost heart, too soon grown old,
>   Insults with this untimely moan ;
>   They might lament—for I am one
>   Whom men love not—and yet regret,
>   Unlike this day, which, when the sun
>   Shall on its stainless glory set,
> Will linger, though enjoyed, like joy in memory yet."

You need not be frightened by occasional passages in Shelley's poetry of denunciation of things you admire. No true Christian need fear to read Shelley. He did not denounce the spirit of Christianity, but excesses committed in the course of the history of the Church and its connection with political creeds.

Shelley died young, before he had completed his thirtieth year; but Keats, who was three years his junior, died before him. The belief fixed in the public mind by Byron's line—

> "John Keats, who was cut off by one critique"—

is only a half-truth, if it is any portion of the truth at all. The disease to which he succumbed, pulmonary consumption, would probably have cut him off at an early age, whatever the reception of his poetry had been. Unfriendly criticism at the utmost only hastened his end. Certainly the criticism was very savage. Keats suffered from the same accidents in the literary situation as Shelley; he was a friend of Hunt's, and a Cockney, and a rebel against the traditions of Pope, and these facts intensified the bitterness of the 'Quarterly' and 'Blackwood's.' And his assailants had a taunt to level at him such as they could not use against the son of a baronet, connected by blood with some of the oldest noble families in England; "Johnny" Keats, as 'Blackwood's' delighted to call him, had been a surgeon's apprentice, and was the son of a livery-stable keeper. Keats had too much manliness in him to have been much affected by the truculence of his critics, if he had been a self-satisfied poet. But the effect was aggravated not only by ill-health and pecuniary embarrassments, but by his profound dissatisfaction with his own work. He said himself, and with every appearance of sincerity, that a sense of his shortcomings from the high ideal that he had set to himself gave him "pain without comparison beyond what 'Blackwood' or the 'Quarterly' could possibly inflict." "I have no cause to complain," he wrote. "I have no doubt that if I had written 'Othello' I should have been cheered. I shall go on with patience. . . . I know nothing; I have read nothing; and I mean to follow Solomon's directions, 'get learning, get understanding.' There is but one way for me. The road lies

through application, study, and thought.   I will pursue it."
These were the words of a young man of a very different fibre
from the affected, mawkish, puling sentimentalist pictured by
the critics of the time as the author of "Endymion." Keats
had but a short lease of life before him when he wrote thus,
but to the last he pursued earnestly his ideals of excellence,
and the world has arrived at a very different measure of the
worth of his performance from that formed by himself on his
death-bed, when he told his friend Severn to put on his grave-
stone the inscription, "*Here lies one whose name was writ in
water.*"

Keats is often coupled with Shelley as if they were poets of
kindred genius. But the connection between them was purely
accidental : beyond a certain profusion and fluency and richness
of imagery they had little in common, as little as any two poets
of the same generation. They both died young. They both
died in Italy, and their monuments stand in the same cemetery
at Rome. Both of them were cut off with much unfulfilled
promise of great things. When Shelley's body was recovered,
a copy of Keats's "Endymion" was found in his pocket. One
of Shelley's few popular poems is the lament for Keats under
the pastoral name of Adonais. These facts have associated the
two poets in the general memory. But their aims in art were
widely different. Keats had none of Shelley's fiery enthusiasm
for humanity ; and although he had an ample share of the poet's
peculiar gift of making new combinations, his combinations are
more sensuous—they have not the subtle intellectual flavour of
Shelley's. A poet of high rank is always his own best critic,
and just as Shelley most truly characterised himself when he
said that "his power consisted in sympathy and that part of
imagination which relates to sentiment and contemplation," so
Keats most truly characterised himself when he said that his
ruling principle was "a yearning passion for the beautiful."   " I
have loved the principle of beauty in all things," he wrote in
his last days. I am inclined to think that Mr Matthew Arnold,
a critic with whose judgments I rarely find myself in dissent,
makes a somewhat misleading remark when he insists that Keats's
master-passion was not the passion of the sensuous or sentimental

poet, but was an intellectual or spiritual passion. If the words
sensuous and sentimental were intended in an opprobrious sense,
the remark might be useful; but if they are used in the literal
meaning, and then contrasted with intellectual and spiritual,
their tendency is to withdraw the reader of Keats from the main
characteristic of his poetry. The beauty that Keats pursued,
whether or not we call that beauty "truth," was loveliness

"In shape and hue and colour and sweet sound,"—

to use the words of Shelley in the "Adonais." I imagine that
Mr Arnold's intention in drawing the distinction that I have
quoted was to lay stress on the fact that the loveliness on which
Keats's heart was set was not a meretricious loveliness, but a
loveliness that was great and noble and pure. Still it was a
sensuous loveliness in this meaning, that more than any other
poet he aimed at and succeeded in depicting in words the beauty
that painters put on canvas and sculptors chisel in marble. It
is peculiarly easy to trace the main external influences that
moulded Keats's poetry, because all his work was done in youth,
when the enthusiastic admirations of the artist are most marked
in endeavours to emulate what he admires. And it is a marked
peculiarity of Keats's poetry that its most vital moulding influences came not from the work of previous poets but from the
sister arts of painting and sculpture. Impassioned admiration
of Greek sculpture gave a more potent turn to Keats's poetry
than any other external influence. Byron recognised this when
he spoke of him as having

"Without Greek
Contrived to talk about the gods of late
Much as they might have been supposed to speak."

We see this influence not merely in his famous "Ode on a
Grecian Urn," where he deliberately seeks to interpret in words
what the artist had sought to design in visible lines, but all
through his poems—in "Endymion," in "Hyperion," in the "Eve
of St Agnes," in "Lamia," in "Isabella." If we wonder what the
surgeon's apprentice at Ealing could have known about Greek
sculpture and ceramic art, we must remember that the Elgin

Marbles were brought to this country and deposited at the British Museum when he was a boy. You know Byron's denunciation of the nobleman, with heart cold as the crags that guard his native coast, who had the shameless rapacity to plunder Athens of these masterpieces; but looking impartially at the act and its results, we recognise that they have had a much more vital and suggestive influence on the mind of Europe in London than they would have had in Athens, and they have given us much of what is most precious in the poetry of Keats. One of Keats's friends was the painter Haydon, who records in his autobiography the intoxicating effect produced on him by his first sight of Greek sculpture. " Endymion " and " Hyperion " make it certain that Keats shared his friend's enthusiasm. Let the meaning sink into the mind, and you will see a succession of pictures executed in the spirit of Greek plastic art. In " Endymion " Keats seems always to have had a succession of pictures and sculptures before his mind's eye, and his poetry seems to be the interpretation of the impression he receives. The opening of " Hyperion "—and also some of his other poems, such as the " Ode to the Nightingale " and " The Eve of St Agnes "—is like the description of a statue, with the repose and stillness of Greek sculpture, which is not a dead stillness but motion instantaneously arrested.

SUPPLEMENT

I.

MR COURTHOPE'S BIOGRAPHY OF POPE.

IT is thirty-five years, as every reviewer has remarked, since the edition undertaken by John Wilson Croker and now completed by Mr Courthope was announced; but the real beginning of the work that Mr Courthope brings to a close may be said to date from the papers by Mr Dilke, of which that announcement was the text. Mr Dilke's discovery of the Caryll letters may be said to have opened a new chapter in the history of Pope's reputation. By this lucky find, followed up with amazing acuteness and patience, Mr Dilke was able to clear up several incidents which had baffled all previous biographers; and his success and the piquancy of his discoveries gave an immense stimulus to research into the obscure particulars of Pope's life and the obscure allusions in his poetry. Pope's marvellous intellectual activity and ingenuity, and his persistent habit of mystification in everything relating to himself, made his life and works the best possible field for the exercise of detective skill. By all this the edition now completed has profited. But for Mr Dilke's researches, and the impulse they gave to investigation, it could never have been what it has become. Mr Elwin, Mr Courthope's predecessor, made the most ample acknowledgment of his debt to this enthusiastic volunteer from the outside; and now one of the main interests of the biography which it has fallen to Mr Courthope to execute is to see how he views Pope's character under the fierce light that has been thrown upon it. The new biographer is in the position of a judge hearing an important case reopened after the discovery and production of a vast and intricate mass of fresh evidence.

The importance of Mr Courthope's decision is considerable. The completeness of the new edition must make it the standard for a good while to come, and the accompanying biography has thus a position of great advantage for influencing the general judgment of Pope's character. It is just as well that the biography should have been delayed till the disturbing effects of the new discoveries had passed away, and that the task of judicially weighing and summing up should have fallen to one whose judgment has not been biassed by the first shock of damaging revelations, and whose temper has not been exasperated by the worry of tracking the man of many mysteries through the perplexing details of his subtle little plots and manœuvres. It is just as well that Mr Elwin's place was taken by Mr Courthope before the stage of passing final judgment was reached. Mr Elwin had great merits as a critic; it would be most unjust not to acknowledge the excellence of his editorial work. He spared no pains in research; he passed over no difficulty; and he took as much trouble to make his statements clear and concise as he did to make his information accurate. In his notes and introductions he gave a very fair and full representation of the commentaries of previous authorities. His own judgments on critical points were perhaps too uniformly hostile and unsympathetic; but they could never be accused of haste, and they were always backed by well considered and closely expressed reasons. Perhaps an unfair impression of his want of sympathy was given by his having to deal chiefly with Pope's earlier and more imperfect work : when he did admire, as in the case of "The Rape of the Lock," he expressed his admiration ungrudgingly. But in all that concerned the moral character of his subject Mr Elwin wrote too much as a righteously indignant avenger, as one who had been disgusted by the discoveries of Pope's double-dealings, and whose anger had been kept alive by having to track his tortuous courses through so many perplexing circumstances. Pope had endeavoured ·to pass off a sophisticated correspondence as genuine, and the interests of truth demanded that the deception should be exposed. "I do not pretend to think," Mr Elwin said, "that genius is an extenuation of rascality;" and it was as a rascal, a detected and discredited impostor, a gentleman who had stooped to the arts of a professional forger and swindler, that he pursued the poet through all his dealings with friends and enemies, publications and publishers. Pope cannot protest his goodwill to an acquaintance in the exaggerated fashion of his time without drawing down upon himself the comment, "At the age of twenty, when frankness usually preponderates, Pope already abounded in the ostentatious profession of sentiments he did not entertain." In the same letter Pope professes indifference to fame—a not uncommon profession, and one not often taken too seriously by the discerning. "In spite of his boasted apathy," Mr Elwin comments, "there cannot be found in the annals of the irritable race a more anxious, jealous, intriguing candidate for fame." And so on. One tires of it after a time, and begins to doubt whether it is generous, or even just, or at all proportioned to the offence.

No doubt when an intriguer is found out, it is well to make an example of him *pour encourager les autres.* But Mr Elwin carries it too far in the case of Pope. He strikes a note of excess, and a misleading note, when he speaks of Pope as "an intriguing candidate for fame." The intrigues in which Pope has been detected do not belong to the time when he can properly be said to have been a candidate for fame; they were engaged in long after his fame was established, partly to humiliate his enemies, and partly to gain credit for a universal benevolence and lofty equanimity of soul which he did not possess. He gained his fame originally by honest means enough, purely on his merits, in spite of the considerable disadvantages of obscure parentage and unpopular religion. Rascality and swindling are not excused by genius; deception is deception, and perfidy is perfidy. But what Mr Elwin seemed to forget was that there are degrees of moral turpitude. One may hold this without incurring any suspicion of Jesuitical ethics. Our righteous indignation does not rise to the same height against all offences that may be put in the same general category. Falsehood is falsehood, but there are degrees. A man who tries to swindle the world out of its good opinion, to make people believe him full of "the unclouded effulgence of universal benevolence and particular fondness," with no motive but sheer vanity and inordinate love of applause, cannot without violence to common sense be put on the same moral level with the professional forger. Nine people out of ten who read the full narrative of Pope's frauds are more disposed to laugh at the ingenuity and fatuity of his tricks than to denounce them in angry reprobation. They are inexcusable and disgraceful, but taken in all their circumstances, as incidents in the life of a man otherwise memorable, they are nearer peccadilloes than crimes. A year or two ago, in writing a short sketch of Pope's life for an encyclopædia, I hazarded the opinion that when all the new revelations of Pope's intriguing habits are fairly weighed, his character remains where Johnson left it, neither better nor worse. "In all this," Johnson remarks of one of Pope's manœuvres about "The Dunciad," "there was petulance and malignity enough, but I cannot think it very criminal." The remark might be extended to most of the fresh instances of double-dealing. In judging of them it is well to bear in mind the maxim which the great moralist quoted as one "that cannot be denied," that "moral obliquity is made more or less excusable by the motives that produce it." It is satisfactory to find that Mr Courthope approaches Pope in the spirit of Johnson rather than of Mr Elwin.

Mr Courthope does not try to extenuate or explain away Pope's moral delinquencies, but to put them in their proper place as parts of a very complex character. The result is that he brings us back to a judgment of Pope's moral character not substantially different from Johnson's. The space occupied by Mr Dilke and Mr Elwin in tracing with so much acumen the poet's mysterious ways, and the startling character of their revelations, have overloaded one side of the portrait, and Mr Courthope has been at pains to restore the right proportion. His judicial deliverance will carry none the less weight that all the time he is adducing extenuating circumstances he protests that he has no intention of excusing or extenuating Pope's misdoings, and that "from the moralist's point of view the case must go undefended." The apparent inconsistency is only superficial; it is merely a nice question of naming. Mr Courthope is quite right to say that he does not excuse or extenuate or defend from a moral point of view, if he thinks that the use

of such expressions would imply that we ought to approve in
Pope's case of conduct mean and contemptible in itself and unworthy of his fame. We need not quarrel about words, if a
biographer observes just proportions in his general estimate of the
man's moral nature as a whole, and if he allows due weight to
considerations· that prevent us from classing Pope morally with
"professional swindlers" and "'dirty animals' like Joseph Surface." This Mr Courthope does with great ability and fairness.
Throughout the biography he gives prominence to the ideal and
magnanimous strain in Pope's character as shown both in his
private life and in his writings. Since the recent discoveries
were made, Johnson has often been laughed at for speaking of
"the perpetual and unclouded effulgence of universal benevolence
and particular fondness" that shines out in Pope's letters. It
has been assumed that all this was mere hypocrisy and pretence,
because some of it was put in when he revised and redirected his
correspondence, and that there was no such element as benevolence
iu the malign little poet's disposition. Mr Courthope corrects
this. His narrative gives fair prominence to the instances of
kindly generosity to dependents and affectionate attachment to
friends with which Pope's life abounds. The new letters in the
correspondence, the letters that were not prepared for the public
eye, are not all to Pope's discredit. Though he did alienate
Bolingbroke by an inexplicable trick—it was, after all, a little
trick—he kept the love of most of his friends, and Arbuthnot, a
shrewd judge of men, credited him with "a noble disdain and
abhorrence of vice." And whatever casuistry may be applied to
the incidents of his life, it is not to be denied that the moral
standard of his Satires as a whole is high. His praise of the Man
of Ross, of Bathurst, of Allen, and of Barnard the Quaker must
bo set over against Sappho and Atossa, Sporus and Atticus; there
is no good reason to suppose that his admiration of the one was
less sincere than his hatred of the other. Mr Courthope seems to
me to fairly establish his contention that Pope was naturally of an
ardent, generous, and romantic temper, and that this strain was
never wholly lost amidst the bitter quarrels in which his later life
was involved.

A generous warmth of temperament, craving for affection as

well as admiration, craving for both intensely as necessities of a
very fragile constitution, and apt to intemperate vindictiveness
when they were withheld—this was the basis of Pope's nature.
His moral delinquencies are not put in a fair light unless they are
viewed as the defects of such a temperament, launched out of a
quiet, secluded, bookish youth into a world of roughly intriguing
cliques and factions,—"literature," as Mr Mark Pattison happily
puts it, "a mere arena of partisan warfare," and "the public
barbarised by the gladiatorial spectacle of politics." It was in
this school that Pope acquired his habit of plotting and double-
dealing. . Mr Courthope suggests that he may have owed the
habit to his Roman Catholic training. Equivocation was regarded
by them as an excusable weapon against penal laws, and what is
allowed in particular cases may easily be extended till it becomes
a general rule of life. It may well be that Pope was helped by
the casuistry of his Church in justifying his crooked ways to his
own conscience. There is a trace of this self-deception in the
words of his letter to Martha Blount: "I have not told a lie
(which we both abominate), but I think I have equivocated pretty
genteelly." But, in truth, Pope did not need to go to his persecuted co-religionists for lessons in the art of genteel equivocation
or hardier forms of duplicity. His political friends—and every
man about town was then a politician—Jacobite and Hanoverian
alike, were as accomplished in the art and as unscrupulous in the
practice of it as any Roman Catholic priest. It was a fierce
struggle for existence in the political world when the succession
was uncertain and the throne insecure, and straightforward
morality was not in fashion. Statesmen were fighting with life
and all that made it worth having in peril, and were ready to use
any means to win, whether of force or fraud. It is really by their
intellectual qualities, their ingenuity, their far-reaching subtlety,
their niceness of calculation, that Pope's intrigues are distinguished
—their intellectual qualities and the pettiness of their objects.
We must regard them as an imitation in his own private concerns
of the games for larger stakes that were going on round him in
the political field. There can be no doubt that Pope had great
natural gifts for intrigue, and that he took to it with great relish.
The pleasure of the sport, the employment that it offered to his

restless ingenuity, blinded him to its immorality, and the passion grew upon him till he could do nothing directly, but "played the politician about cabbages and turnips." The fact that a straight line is the shortest distance between two points was with him a reason for not taking it. It is impossible even now to follow him through the steps of any of the intricate plots which recent inquiry has unravelled with such patience without some motions of sympathy with the artist's delight in his contrivances, so ingenious were they, and out of all proportion to the advantage to be gained. Ingenuity, of course, is no palliation of fraud; but the amount of our indignation cannot but be affected by the impostor's motives, and the theory that finds in Pope's tortuous conduct nothing but mean and cowardly hypocrisy is simply imperfect analysis. This is just as indiscriminate as it is to find the animating spirit of his Satires in arrogant malignity and cruelty. Mr Courthope does good service in his chapter on "The War with the Dunces" in tracing the history of the quarrel, and showing that the most shady transactions of Pope's later years were really incidents in a protracted war in which he was not the original aggressor. Not to have struck the first blow in a quarrel which he conducted with so many discreditable artifices and such relentless cruelty, is not, perhaps, much to boast of. But wanton malignity is undoubtedly a less respectable motive than vindictiveness, if we are to admit degrees of wickedness and of moral reprobation; and it is something to have it established by a careful judicial examination that Pope was vindictive rather than malignant.

As a clear, well-arranged, and well-divided narrative of Pope's life, pervaded by a moderate and judicial estimate of his character, Mr Courthope's biography is admirable. But his large and massive method of handling, which yields such excellent results in the condensed narrative of intricate events, and the judicial summing up of the complicated cases of conscience, is seen to want flexibility and precision when applied to such a many-sided question as Pope's place in literature. Perspicuity of manner is gained at the expense of exactness of substance. Mr Courthope, indeed, places Pope with every appearance of exactness, with a bold geometrical simplicity, just at the point where lines representing Medievalism and the Classical Revival intersect; but he

is not so successful in his attempts to justify this simple diagram
as corresponding to historical facts.

The defects of the massive method of handling are that it in-
volves the omission of connecting links, and the assumption of
large and definite masses common to the understanding of writer
and reader. If the latter condition does not exist, the writer is
tempted to take it for granted, and to refer to periods and ten-
dencies on the large scale as if their characters were matters of
clear and common knowledge, or at least established acceptation
among critics. The result is that statements severally distinct,
confident, and sonorous, give rise to a good deal of trouble when
we try to reduce them to consistency for ourselves, or when the
writer undertakes the office for us, and attempts to supply the
links of connection. Thus Mr Courthope opens his biography by
presenting the date of Pope's birth as a time of unsettlement and
confusion, distracted by "opposing forces, Catholic and Protestant,
Whig and Tory, Aristotelian and Baconian, Medievalist and
Classicist." Having thus boldly described the situation, he passes
at once to his hero, as "the poet who learned to harmonise all
those conflicting principles in a form of versification so clear and
precise that for fully a hundred years after he began to write it
was accepted as the established standard of metrical music." It
is a masterful and imposing introduction; but when the dazzled
mind recovers, and asks in what sense Pope can be said to have
harmonised Catholicism and Protestantism, Whiggism and Toryism, Aristotelianism and Baconianism, Medievalism and Classicism, it is not so easy to find a clear answer. It is right to say at
once in fairness to Mr Courthope that this is only the opening
statement of his thesis, and that he does afterwards attempt,
partly at least, to make it good, and enable us to follow him intelligently in his bold transition from the general character of the
time to the personality of Pope and the distinctive character of
his work. But it is right also to say—and it illustrates the defects of the massive manner—that the reader would go very far
astray who should take in its most obvious and literal sense
Pope's harmonising of these mighty opposites. To see how
Pope harmonised Catholicism and Protestantism, one's first
impulse would be to turn to the Essay on Man; but it cannot

be there that the harmonisation of which Mr Courthope thinks is effected, for he calls it—not altogether justly—"a farrago of fallacies." So with Whiggism and Toryism. We recall the lines—

> "For forms of government let fools contest;
> Whate'er is best administered is best."

This cannot be the reconciliation spoken of, calling both parties equally fools. The truth, of course, is—if I rightly understand Mr Courthope—that he uses the words Whiggism and Toryism, Protestantism and Catholicism, &c., in a subtle sense to signify a certain indefinite central idea or animating principle. The reader who wishes to penetrate to his meaning must tackle two very perplexing chapters, one on the "Essay on Criticism" and a second on Pope's place in English Literature, where the same topic is resumed.

These chapters are the least satisfactory part of the book. Perhaps it is that Mr Courthope has tried to crowd too much into too little space. Seeing that he attempts to formulate the leading changes in the principles of poetic creation, from Aristotle to Wordsworth, with the "Essay on Criticism," as a central and turning point, this is likely enough. Perhaps it is that his ideas took shape as he wrote, and that while he continued to make large and definite statements, they were not originally so cast as to show their coherency. At any rate the result is perplexing enough. Mr Courthope at the end of the last chapter formulates certain conclusions about Pope's place in literature that one can at least understand, however much one may differ from some of them; but the discussion through which he reaches them is much less plain sailing, and it is not easy to follow the connection between some of the theories advanced in the course of it and the propositions to which we are finally conducted. Further, though the drift of the argument, so far as I can make it out, is paradoxical, it proceeds often by statements which are among the commonplaces of criticism, at least in words, and give it an air of plausibility till we see that it compels us, if we accept it as sound, to give them a special interpretation. The discussion would have been less intricate if Mr Courthope had tried to establish Pope's position inductively by an examination of his poetry and a comparison of it with what came before and after. It is, however, by way of abstract discussion of his critical principles as laid down in the Essay that he proceeds, and thus we are involved in a bewildering series of definitions of what is meant by Nature, Wit, True Wit and False Wit, Mediœval Methods, and Classical Methods and Modern Methods. Finally, although the gist of the argument seems to be that the central artistic principle of Pope and his school is the "direct imitation of Nature," and that the Essay, in virtue of its distinct enunciation of this principle, occupies a more important position in literature than is commonly assigned to it, I have searched in vain for any attempt to define what is meant by that very familiar but not very tangible phrase "imitation of Nature." At least as much turns upon the meaning of that as on the meaning of Nature, and the conceptions of Nature prevalent at different times. But I will try to disengage his main positions, and examine what they seem to me to imply.

The starting-point of Mr Courthope's dialectic, which has no lack of freshness and vigour if it is somewhat intricate, is the "Essay on Criticism," the place to be assigned to it in literature, and Mr Leslie Stephen's disparaging description of it as a "coining of aphorisms out of commonplace." This Mr Courthope challenges, and maintains in effect that its critical principles were not commonplace to Pope's own generation, but that, on the contrary, when the Essay is taken in relation to the course of literature from Aristotle down through the Middle Ages to the time of Queen Anne, it is seen to mark an epoch. And the main significance of this epoch is, as I understand Mr Courthope, the return after a long interval to a conception of the relations between Nature and Art identical with Aristotle's. According to Aristotle, poetry is "a direct imitation of Nature"; and Pope brought Poetry back from Medievalism to this conception when he counselled poets to

> "First follow Nature, and your judgment frame
> By her just standard, which is still the same."

Mr Stephen says that "Follow Nature" is a maxim "common to all generations of critics." Against this Mr Courthope develops a theory of the essence of Medievalism as consisting in the imposition of subjective and metaphysical conceptions on Nature, and contends that the significance of Pope's advice was the clear and definite repudiation of this practice; that Pope in effect said, "Imitate Nature directly," and that this is the distinctive feature in his critical principles.   He even seems to hold that it was in this that Pope's much discussed "correctness" consisted, and not in stricter attention to the rules of metre and grammar and rhetoric.

All this is comparatively simple, whether or not we agree with it.   Perplexity arises when we begin to ask wherein Pope's adherence to the standard of Nature distinguishes him from our great poets before him and our great poets after him.   We understand at once that Mr Courthope's doctrine is opposed to the common habit in our century of speaking of Pope's poetry as "artificial."   So far I am, for one, in complete sympathy with him.   But does he mean that Pope was the first poet in our literature to set up the just standard of Nature?   His exposition here and there would seem to imply this, as well as the large importance that he claims for the Essay; but he expressly says that this is not his meaning.   He expressly mentions Chaucer and Shakespeare among the poets who have imitated Nature directly.   But if this direct imitation of Nature is the distinctive feature of Pope's principles, and the ground on which his school is called "classical," why are not Chaucer and Shakespeare also called "classical"?   When we ask this we find ourselves not far off from Mr Stephen's position that the following of Nature is a common maxim.   Mr Courthope's paradox would seem then only to amount to saying that great poets are all of one school.   What, then, was distinctive in Pope's following of Nature?

Mr Courthope would answer this in effect by saying that in Pope's mind Nature was opposed to the "false wit," the metaphors, conceits, fantastic allusions, and mystic symbolism of what Johnson called the "Metaphysical School" of the seventeenth century, Donne and Cowley, and the earlier work of Dryden.   If he had not gone beyond this, and his serviceable illustration of the European prevalence of this false wit for more than a century, everybody would have understood him and agreed with him.   It is tolerably obvious that abstinence from false wit in this sense is one of the items of Pope's correctness; he expressly particularises it himself.   Whether or not it is warrantable to describe Pope's

method generally as a reaction against this false wit, as if it constituted the whole of his correctness, is another question.   But Mr
Courthope does not stop here.   He goes on to connect false wit
with Medievalism generally, the subtleties of Scholastic Philosophy, Thomas Aquinas, the Provençal poets, Dante and Petrarch,
and the allegorical and symbolical presentation of Nature.   Here
again we admit the connection,—anybody would : there is an obvious affinity between the keen, far-reaching, beautifully ingenious
analogies of Donne and the analytic triumphs of the Schoolmen,
of whom indeed Donne was at one time a close student.   We admit
the connection ; but we pause when we are asked to jump from
this admission to the conclusion that Pope's lines—

> "True wit is Nature to advantage dressed,
>   What oft was thought but ne'er so well expressed "—

were a formal renunciation not merely of the conceits of the poetry
of the seventeenth century, but of Medievalism generally, as false
wit, and a return to Aristotle and the standard of Nature.

It certainly is a most ingenious argument.   If Mr Courthope
may claim to rank with Johnson as a judge of Pope's morality, he
may equally claim to rank with Warburton as an interpreter of
Pope's meaning.   His interpretation of Pope's Classicism as opposed to Medievalism carries with it the relation of the Essay to
Whiggism and Toryism, Protestantism and Catholicism, Baconianism and Aristotelianism.   Up to the time of the Revolution, which
seated a Protestant on the throne, the Court had a leaning to
Catholicism, and thereby encouraged Medievalism, and the Tories
were the party of the Court.   Thus, although Pope himself was
a Catholic and a personal friend of the leading Tories, the "Essay
on Criticism," in virtue of its protest against Medievalism in
poetry, falls into line with the anti-medieval spirit of Whiggism
and Protestantism.   By Aristotelianism as opposed to Baconianism Mr Courthope must mean the philosophy of Aristotle as
developed by the Schoolmen, for it is part of his theory that
Pope used the word Nature in the same sense as Bacon, and
consequently in the same sense as Aristotle.   One is still left
wondering what exactly he meant by saying that Pope "harmonised" all those opposing forces, seeing that the Essay is

held to have signalised the final triumph of one class of them. But it is a most ingenious theory, certainly "witty" according to the definition of wit that Mr Courthope quotes from Locke, whether we are to reckon it as true wit or the opposite.

Mr Courthope's theory about the place of Pope's "Essay on Criticism" is so far sound that it maintains, in a very abstract and metaphysical manner, the tolerably plain fact that the Essay was part of the general and gradual emancipation of the English mind from medieval habits of thought. Beyond this he does not seem to me to establish his case. Pope got less than his deserts from the critics of the last two generations : the fashion of taste had gone against him ; but we should go as far wrong in the opposite direction if we argued that the advent of Pope in poetry was an event comparable to the advent of Newton in physical science, or to the advent of Locke in philosophy. Even if we admit that "True wit is Nature to advantage dressed" did mean in Pope's mind "True poetry is Nature directly imitated," how can a method which Pope had in common with Chaucer and Shakespeare, Ariosto and Cervantes, be said to be so distinctive of a school as to warrant the title of "classical" ? Personally I do not think that the *differentia* of the so-called "classical" school is to be found in formal critical principles ; it seems to me to lie rather, as I have indicated before in this magazine, in unconscious habits of expression. It has obtained the name "classical" on more superficial grounds, namely, that translations of Latin and Greek masterpieces and imitations of leading classical forms were among its most conspicuous productions, and that its critics, in the earlier period of the school, professed great deference for the ancient authorities. Certainly directness cannot be said to have been a prominent feature of its imitations of Nature, if direct imitation is the opposite of allusive, allegorical, and abstract presentation. We may pass "The Rape of the Lock" as direct, if we get a definition of Nature that includes sylphs and gnomes ; but what shall we say of "The Dunciad" ? And what shall we say of the countless odes to and descriptions of personified Seasons, Passions, Institutions, Conditions, Faculties, which held the field till the last years of the century ? These were at least as much indirect imitations as the "Roman de la Rose," the great medieval example of allegory, and yet they form the bulk of the work of the "classical" school.

Mr Courthope has not proved his paradox about Pope's relation to his predecessors, and he makes out a still less plausible case for a still bolder paradox about Pope's relation to Wordsworth. There is such a refreshing novelty about a theory which upholds Pope as distinctively the poet of Nature, and Wordsworth as a reactionary ally of "false wit," that one could wish it were not so manifestly strained and perverse. It is to be regretted too for another reason, that just as there is justice in Mr Courthope's defence of Pope against the charge of being peculiarly artificial, he does lay stress upon a feature in Wordsworth's theory of poetry that is very often overlooked. Wordsworth, though he is commonly called the poet of Nature, claims supremacy for the imagination in poetic work :—

> " Imagination needs must stir.   .   .   .
> Minds that have nothing to confer
> Find little to perceive."

Coleridge says the same thing in the familiar lines :—

> " Dear Lady, we receive but what we give,
> And in our life alone does Nature live."

There is no antagonism between this and adherence to the just standard of Nature, unless Nature is taken in a very limited sense ; but it gives Mr Courthope an opening for connecting the modern poets with the false wits whom Pope superseded, and developing and pointing against them a new interpretation of the line—

> " What oft was thought, but ne'er so well expressed."

"Pope, the antagonist of the metaphysical school, had taught that the essence of poetry was the presentation, in a perfect form, of imaginative materials common to the poet and the reader—

> " What oft was thought, but ne'er so well expressed."

Wordsworth maintained, on the contrary, that matter not in itself stimulating to the general imagination might become a proper subject for poetry if glorified by the imagination of the poet. There is an obvious analogy between this method of composition and the wit, or *discordia concors*, which was the aim of the seventeenth century poet."

This would have been true enough if it had been part of Wordsworth's theory that a poet's imagination may give poetic value to anything—a broomstick, for instance—irrespective of the ordinary laws of feeling. It is only by taking this as Wordsworth's meaning that Mr Courthope is able to give a semblance of plausibility to his case, and starting with a little misunderstanding he goes on to enlarge this till we find him taking it as a condition of poetic work on Wordsworth's theory that the poet should "burn the bridge of connection between himself and his readers;" that is, should consult only his own feelings, and pay no regard to the manner in which other men think and feel. In answer to this, it is sufficient to point out that the opposite of this is repeatedly asserted to be a poet's duty in the preface to the "Lyrical Ballads," a document to which Mr Courthope refers as an "animated rhetorical treatise," but which, judging from his extraordinary perversions of its leading doctrines, he cannot have studied very attentively. How can he reconcile the following extract from the preface with what he says of Wordsworth's theory :—

"The Poet is chiefly distinguished from other men by a greater promptness to think and feel without immediate external excitement, a greater power in expressing such thoughts and feelings as are produced in him in that manner. *But these passions and thoughts and feelings are the general passions and thoughts and feelings of men.*"

The truth is that Wordsworth's quarrel with artificial poetic diction was that it was not intelligible to men in general as the appropriate expression of the feelings described. "The poet thinks and feels," he said, "in the spirit of human passions. How then can his language differ from that of all other men who feel vividly and see clearly?" Wordsworth was very far indeed from ignoring, even in theory, the need of "imaginative materials common to the poet and the reader," and he was fully alive to the danger of yielding to what he called "particular associations" as distinguished from such as were general; but, as he explains, he was obliged to trust his own judgment as to what would be intelligible to his readers. What other judgment than his own would Mr Courthope suggest for the poet's guidance? How can the poet reach the common heart or the common mind except through his own heart and mind? Where else can he find his imaginative materials? But it is not easy to make out what function Mr Courthope assigns to the imagination in poetry. "In every great epic or dramatic poem," he says, "the action or fable, in every great lyric poem, the passion is not imagined and discovered by the poet, *but* [what is the point of the antithesis?] is shared by the poet with his audience: the element contributed by a poet singly is the conception and form of the poem." "The imaginative materials are common to the poet and the audience." Mr Courthope seems to mean that unless a poet chooses subjects—fables, situations, characters, passions—that are easily and widely intelligible, and intrinsically interesting, he must be content with a limited audience. But why should this be said in words which appear to deny the creative character of the imagination, as if Shakespeare had not "imagined" the passion of Hamlet and Othello, or Milton had not "imagined" the bearing, the despair, and the defiant hatred of his rebel angels in the fiery pit?

On his title-page Mr Courtney quotes the saying of Horace, "*Difficile est proprie communia dicere.*" It is difficult; but one often feels in reading his critical chapters that he has succeeded. One could wish that his exposition of his paradoxes had been as successful as his disguise of his endoxes, for it is a gallant and vigorous attempt to give new life to an old controversy.

II.

THE SUPPOSED TYRANNY OF POPE.

THERE is one notable change in Pope's position since the last centenary of his birth. His manner is now old enough to bear revival. A clever writer of epigrammatic couplets, with something much less exquisite than Pope's mastery of his favourite stave, and much less strong and keen than his wit,—a passably clever imitator, in short,—would be certain now of a wide and cordial welcome. Of course a certain discretion would have to be shown in the line of imitation: not all the master's subjects would serve equally well for the modern disciple. We should probably find little to admire in a new "Windsor Forest"; even a new "Essay on Man," with all our recent modern developments in philosophy and religion thrown in, might not attract as wide a circle of readers as 'Robert Elsmere'; but it may safely be said that the time is ripe for new "Imitations of Horace" if only the man were ready. As for a new "Dunciad," that is a more delicate subject to hint at, as nobody knows what might happen, and it would not be a comfortable experience to be hitched into the rhyme if the new satirist had as sharp a tooth as his great original. It is better to let sleeping cynics lie. But certainly it is a wonder that in these days of "New" things—New Lucians, New Republics, New Plutarchs, and so forth—nobody should have essayed to give us a New Dunciad. Is it that in this age of universal cleverness we have no Dunces, or that Pope's form is not quite so easy to imitate as it was the fashion fifty years ago to say?

Or is it that we are all so very good-natured that the "airy malevolence" of the great satirist would not be tolerated?

This much at least is certain, that if we had material, and a satirist, and if our satirist were dexterous enough to evade the law of libel—another barrier to the imitator of Pope—the form of epigrammatic couplets would now have all the charm of novelty, whereas a hundred years ago the public ear was tired of them. From the first of these propositions we imagine there will be no dissent; but as regards the second a very general impression to the contrary prevails. In spite of the labours of such accurate historians of literature as the late Mr Mark Pattison and Mr Stopford Brooke, Pope's relations to the poetry of the latter half of the eighteenth century are still very generally misunderstood. If the average educated man, with some knowledge of the broad outlines of literary history but no special interest in its details, were asked as a question pertinent to the recent celebration, what would have been the probable reception of a poem in Pope's manner when last his centenary came round, he would probably answer out of a vague impression that in the year 1788 a poem in any other manner would have been promptly extinguished by the critics. The general notion is that the authority of Pope was supreme throughout the eighteenth century, and that it remained unshaken till the advent of the new potentates, Wordsworth, Coleridge, Scott, and Byron. It is supposed that the public taste was so devoted to Pope and what is called the "classical school" that no departure from its principles of composition would have been received with patience; that even Milton and the great Elizabethans were decried and neglected; and that long and determined efforts were needed before the public could be brought back to a higher standard of poetic excellence. This indeed is commonly given as the explanation of the utter decay of poetry in the eighteenth century, that people lived in slavish subjection to narrow and exclusive rules of art; that all who felt an impulse to write in verse were intimidated into taking artificial standards as their guide rather than Nature; that genius was stifled by timid and laborious endeavour after correctness. And Pope's name was the bugbear used to frighten unruly genius into submission.

Such was the view of the poetry of the eighteenth century proclaimed with authority some fifty years ago, and still, after a good many years of sober contradiction, very extensively held. An opinion backed by the confident and brilliant rhetoric of Macaulay is not easily dislodged. The reaction against the critical school that set in with the great poetic expansion at the beginning of this century was definitely established by Macaulay's article on Moore's 'Life of Byron' in the 'Edinburgh Review.' It gave articulate expression to the effect produced on the public mind by the destructive criticism of which Wordsworth, Coleridge, and Bowles were the leading exponents. Their tone of course was much more judicial, but since they laid stress on the defects of Pope, and the public had been accustomed for two or three generations to hear chiefly of his merits, the general impression produced was that his poetry was essentially and radically vicious; that he was, as it were, an impostor who had long deceived the people, but had been detected and exposed at last. This exaggerated condemnation was not the fault of the new critics, but it was the natural result of their saying what they said at the time when they said it. That happened in Pope's case which happens in the progress of all conceptions towards exact qualification. Thinking on any subject is generally done by halves or by bits, each of which as it comes into prominence fills the area of the whole truth. As long as the public mind was dazzled by certain splendid qualities in Pope's verse, these qualities virtually represented the sum of poetic excellence: he was simply a poet: there was no question of defects or limitations. There came a time when the defects were loudly insisted upon, and the public mind was occupied in the same exclusive manner with poetic excellence of a different type which had yet to undergo its process of qualification. Pope was then simply no poet: he was the complete antithesis of poetic excellence. Pope's reputation followed the ordinary law in passing through those two violent stages on its way towards a more fixed and definite formation: it may safely be said to have now reached a further stage in which merits and defects are no longer in mutually destructive antagonism, and Pope is recognised as a great poet, to be admired, enjoyed, and studied for what he was, without being despised or neglected for what he was not.

We speak of the conception of Pope's poetry in that vague but none the less real receptacle of ideas, the general mind, to the fluctuations and advances of which it is not easy to obtain a definite index. Perhaps one of the most satisfactory gauges of public opinion, whether of men or of measures, is to be found in the attitude of moderate critics. If modern critics are apologetic and conciliatory in hinting at blemishes, the man or the measure, we may be sure, stands high in public estimation. In the case of Pope, we find that in the eighteenth century, before his poetry had passed through the crucible of the Wordsworthian school, such a moderate critic as Joseph Warton had to be cautious in pointing out Pope's limitations; whereas thirty years ago such a temperate admirer as Mr Carruthers had to guard himself carefully against the charge of putting Pope's merits too high. More recently Mr Elwin's elaborate criticism of Pope has been received with some impatience on account of its hostile and unsympathetic tone; and the remarks made about him within the last two months have shown a disposition to make amends for the violence of previous disparagement.

While there has been this oscillation concerning Pope's merits in the general mind, following in its own way the movements of critical dialectic, there has been comparatively little substantial difference of opinion among the few who, in Wordsworth's language, make "a serious study of poetry." Although critics of the Wordsworthian school discredited Pope so much that it became among their more foolish adherents a mark of corrupt taste to find a word to say in favour of anything written in the eighteenth century, the leaders themselves, especially Coleridge and Bowles, were by no means insensible to Pope's unrivalled brilliancy within his own limits. On the other hand, it is a mistake to suppose that the critics of the eighteenth century, even in the generation immediately after Pope's own, were unconscious of those limits, although they had more complete sympathy with the poet's merits and were more ungrudging in their praise. Too many of us still see even the criticism of the eighteenth century through the spectacles of reactionaries who were in too violent a

heat to see clearly. The admiration of Pope was not an unqualified and unreasoning idolatry among the critics of the eighteenth
century. Even Bowles's main contention, over which there was
so much discussion at the beginning of this century, that satiric
and ethic poetry are necessarily from their subject-matter inferior
species, and cannot entitle a poet to the first rank however masterly in execution, was put forward in substance by Joseph Warton as early as 1756. It was put forward in substance though
with a slight difference, Warton's exact position being that wit
and satire are transitory and perishable, while nature and passion
are eternal. And ten years earlier this same ambitious youth,
having just taken his degree at Oxford, issued a volume of odes,
in the preface to which he expressed a modest hope that they
"would be looked upon as an attempt to bring poetry back into
its right channel," his opinion being that "invention and imagination are the chief faculties of a poet," and that "the fashion of
moralising in verse had been carried too far." This was in 1746,
within three years of Pope's death, and the bold venture was so
far successful that a second edition was at once called for. The
Odes of Warton's schoolfellow and friend, Collins, who wrote in
the same independent spirit, but with infinitely greater genius,
were published at the same time: they had indeed intended at
first to publish together. The poetry of Collins was of a much
less simple, commonplace, and popular cast, and his volume of
Odes remained unsold; but it opened the door to an intimacy
with Thomson and Johnson, an evidence that such critical authorities were far from being disposed to stifle genius that did not
accommodate itself to the manner of Pope. But it may be said
that Warton's free criticism of Pope was only an impotent heresy,
an individual eccentricity serving only to make more marked the
general drift of opinion. Was it not the case that he kept back
the second part of his essay for more than a quarter of a century,
and that Johnson supposed the reason for this to be "disappoint-
ment at not having been able to persuade the world to be of his
opinion as to Pope"? Yes; but the "opinion" to which Johnson referred was the opinion that Pope's reputation in the future
would rest upon his "Windsor Forest," his "Eloisa to Abelard,"
and his "Rape of the Lock," rather than upon his moral and

satirical poems. Of Warton's essay itself—or rather of the first part, for the second part was not published till a year or two before his death—the great critic repeatedly wrote and spoke in terms of the highest praise. It was this essay that he described as "a book which teaches how the brow of Criticism may be smoothed, and how she may be enabled, with all her severity, to attract and delight." No man was ever less disposed than Johnson to suppress independent criticism, however paradoxical this may seem to those who have been taught to regard him as the inflexible administrator of narrow and arbitrary critical laws. He was punctiliously conscientious in always giving a reason for his critical decisions. Lord Mansfield's famous advice to the judge who knew no law would have been abhorrent to one who prided himself on his knowledge of critical law, and who held that all critical laws worthy of respect were founded in reason. "Reason wants not Horace to support it," was one of his characteristic maxims. That his reasons were always valid would be too much to claim; but they were always, except when thrown off in the caprice of conversation, the result of profound and penetrating thought, and he would be a very presumptuous critic that should lightly set them aside.

"Temporary arrest of poetic expansion" would be a fairer description of what took place in the eighteenth century than "utter decay of poetry"; and to assign as the explanation of this arrest the overbearing force of Pope's example, or the chilling influence of Johnson's precepts, or slavish subservience to arbitrary rules, is, to put it soberly, not to give a sufficient explanation. It is not quite fair to criticism to regard it as if its main function were to direct and nourish its poetry of the period, and to argue that it stands condemned as necessarily unsound if the contemporary poetical crop is poor and scanty. It has been too much the habit of literary historians to look upon the poverty of the poetry as the main literary phenomenon of the eighteenth century. If the idea had occurred—and it is at least worthy of examination—that possibly the critical school of which Johnson was the master helped to lay a foundation for the splendid outburst of poetic production in a subsequent generation, the critical principles of the eighteenth century would have had a fairer chance of being judged upon their merits. Johnson was certainly no champion of narrow and exclusive tenets. There were certain obvious and definite qualities in Pope, smooth melodious rhythm, clear sense, elegance or refinement of phrase and idea, on which he frequently dwelt as high poetic merits. "Here," he exclaimed of Pope's "Eloisa," "is particularly observable the *curiosa felicitas,* a fruitful soil and careful cultivation. Here is no crudeness of sense, no asperity of language." But highly as he admired such qualities, and although he probably did not feel with sufficient force the danger of buying them at too great a sacrifice, the absence of them did not blind him to other merits. He appreciated the power of Collins, though he did find fault with his occasional obscurity and his "harsh clusters of consonants." He found harshness and barbarity in the diction of Milton, but that did not prevent him from speaking of Milton as "that poet whose works may possibly be read when every other monument of British greatness is obliterated"; or from saying that "such is the power of his poetry that his call is obeyed without resistance, the reader feels himself in captivity to a higher and a nobler mind, and criticism sinks in admiration." With all his love for Pope, he found passages in Dryden "drawn from a profundity that Pope could never reach." He criticised Shakespeare, as he said, "without curious malignity or superstitious veneration," but whoever thinks that he measured Shakespeare by cold and formal notions of correctness should read his noble preface. "The work of a correct and regular writer is a garden accurately formed and diligently planted, varied with shades and scented with flowers; the composition of Shakespeare is a forest, in which oaks extend their branches, and pines tower in the air, interspersed sometimes with weeds and brambles, and sometimes giving shelter to myrtles and roses; filling the eye with awful pomp, and gratifying the mind with endless diversity." This is not the language of a narrow and exclusive critic with a single eye to correctness of an artificial kind.

The poetic barrenness certainly cannot be explained by the predominance of narrow and exclusive critical theories. Exclusive admiration of Pope and the classical school, contented acquiescence in its methods and subjects as the perfection of art, inability to feel and enjoy excellence of any other kind, cannot be charged against the critics of the time.   Pope himself was by no means insensible to the greatness of his great predecessors, Chaucer, Spenser, Shakespeare, and Milton.   His conversations with Spence afford abundant evidence of his catholicity as well as his delicacy of judgment.   And if we pass from Pope to his successors in the eighteenth century, we find that we cannot number disrespect for Shakespeare among the causes of their poetic incompetence, and that Nature was often in their heads, if not in their hearts, as the great original from which the poet ought to draw.   The Winchester schoolboys, Warton and Collins, were perhaps singular in their enthusiasm for Spenser.   But the cult of Shakespeare was universal.   Edition followed edition, and commentary commentary, while Garrick in Shakespearian parts was the delight of the town. When Akenside, in the last year of Pope's life, extolled with much applause "The Pleasures of the Imagination," he began by invoking the aid of "Fancy," as the Spirit of Poetry—

> "From the fruitful banks
> Of Avon, whence thy rosy fingers cull
> Fresh flowers and dews to sprinkle on the turf
> Where Shakespeare lies."

A few years later, in 1749, when a company of French players acted by subscription at the Theatre-Royal, Akenside's enthusiasm was such that he treated their visit as an insult to Shakespeare, and put the following "Remonstrance" into the mouth of the outraged dramatist :—

> "What though the footsteps of my devious Muse
> The measured walks of Grecian art refuse ?
> Or though the frankness of my hardy style
> Mock the nice touches of the critic's file ?
> Yet what my age and climate held to view
> Impartial I surveyed and fearless drew.
> And say, ye skilful in the human heart,
> Who know to prize a poet's noblest part,
> What age, what clime, could e'er an ampler field
> For lofty thought, for daring fancy yield ?"

The same note was struck by Churchill in the first year of the reign of George III. :—

> "May not some great extensive genius raise
>   The name of Britain 'bove Athenian praise ? . . .
>   There may—there hath—and Shakespeare's muse aspires
>   Beyond the reach of Greece : with native fires
>   Mounting aloft, he wings his daring flight,
>   Whilst Sophocles below stands trembling at his height.
>   Why should we then abroad for judges roam,
>   When abler judges we may find at home ?
>   Happy in tragic and in comic powers
>   Have we not Shakespeare ? is not Jonson ours ? "

We have quoted enough to show that the poets of the eighteenth century, from beginning to end of what has been called the darkest period of the century, were not, in principle at least, enamoured of tameness and trimness in art, and that they did not of set choice and with deliberate acquiescence confine themselves to a low range of imaginative effort. Rather they seem to have been striving and straining with turbulent ambition after higher things—after things too high for their powers. Gray, who had more right to speak than any of those whom we have quoted, seems to have been conscious of this impotence, this disproportion between desire and achievement.

> "But not to one in this benighted age
>   Is that diviner inspiration given
>   That burns in Shakespeare's and in Milton's page,
>   The pomp and prodigality of heaven."

The difficulty would be to find the critics whose authority the minor poets resented and considered it necessary to abjure. Rymer, who is sometimes referred to as if he had been a representative critic of the period, was at least as much laughed at in his own generation as he has ever been since, and represented only a perverse and splenetic opposition to the general strain.

The inability of the period to fulfil its aspirations after a larger and bolder style of poetry, with more of life and passion in it, would be almost pathetic if it were really required of every generation to be great in poetry, and it were to be held dishonour to come short of greatness in the divine art. The tyrannical authority of a critical school cannot be held responsible for this dishonour to the generation after Pope, if dishonour it be. The only respect in which criticism may have had a discouraging influence was this, that there was so much of it. Under the lead of Johnson, the great aim of criticism was to discover how the heart was reached, to detect by analysis of an impressive passage what helped and what hindered the effect. "You must show how terror is impressed on the human heart," he said, in speaking with his friends of what a critic ought to do in considering the use made of a ghost in a play: this was the only kind of criticism that he would call real criticism, "showing the beauty of thought as formed on the workings of the human heart." Now when an artist begins to consider too curiously how an effect is produced, he is apt to be hampered and, it may be, paralysed if he has not energy enough to transcend the consciously or painfully analytic stage, or to perform his analysis with such swiftness and sureness of perception that he proceeds at once and as if by instinct to the required combination. The amount of poetic production in the generation after Pope may have been lessened by excess of the critical spirit and the multiplication of negative conditions, but this could have affected only the minor poets or men of poetic talent, because the man of poetic genius will not and needs not consider his ways and means too curiously.

How are we to account for the arrest of poetry in the eighteenth century, if it was not due to the chilling influence of critics imbued with artificial principles? Burke's aphorism that "the march of the human mind is slow," is a part of the explanation that should not be lost sight of in the search for minute causes. Leaps and bounds of poetic expansion are not to be expected in every generation. Slow progress is the normal law, and we need not torture ourselves to discover reasons for a particular case of slow progress as if it were something exceptional. After all, there was some progress even in poetry itself, besides what may have been done in the way of suggestion and collection of material for the poetry of the future. Collins and Gray are great names, though not of the first rank; and even in the darkest period such minor bards as the Wartons, Shenstone, and Beattie did not merely grind old tunes but sounded a distinctive note, however humble. Collins, in especial, added an ever-living branch to the tree of our literature: his Odes are not mere dry twigs on that tree. Of the peculiar form in which he expressed the rapture of learned meditation, gathering together the most moving incidents of human experience under abstractions conceived as living forces, Collins is the one great master. He is essentially a scholarly or academic poet, and could never be popular in the wide sense, his subjects being historical and his mode of expression such that he cannot be followed without some intellectual effort; but the effort is worth making, because he had deep and genuine feeling to put into his verse, and the power to transmit that feeling, whole and harmonious, to the reader. One of Wordsworth's central qualities, his attitude towards Nature, is a natural and easy transition from the spirit in which Collins conceived the pageant of history.

Great bursts of poetic activity come but seldom. They are exceptional facts; and those anxious *rerum cognoscere causas* should first endeavour to determine the causes or leading conditions of those departures from the normal law. It should be an easier task, and should conduce to the understanding of the comparative inactivity of other periods. If we take the works of the leaders of the great poetic revival of this century—Wordsworth, Scott, and Byron—we find that they differ in certain broad respects from all the works of the eighteenth century. We find something like the origination of new species or new varieties in poetry. The form, in a large sense of the word, is new, and the vein of feeling is new. New themes are treated in a new way, and with a new spirit. Consider the mere form of the 'Lay of the Last Minstrel,' the first genuinely popular poem, interesting to all classes, of the new era—a metrical romance regularly constructed, with perfect unity of action, incidents all helping forward the progress of the story through various complications to a catastrophe. No such poem had ever been written before; it was a new form in poetry—classical regularity of form combined with romantic freedom of accident. The precepts of the classical school, reiterating how an epic, the vain ambition of the poets of the eighteenth century, ought to be constructed, were not thrown away upon Scott, although he made a free use of them. Then the spirit of the poem—the serious epic treatment of the necromancing Ladye of Branksome Hall, the Wizard, the Goblin Page, and the bold Mosstrooper. We have nothing like this in the eighteenth century. In Pope's time such personages would either have been burlesqued or treated with affected respect, such as a grown-up person would use towards fairies and hobgoblins in telling stories about them to a child. They might have figured in an Ode to Superstition, but an artist would hardly have dared to narrate their doings with the air of a serious believer, and without taking the polite reader into his confidence. Taken altogether, in form and spirit, the 'Lay' was a new thing in literature, a new species of poem. The same may be said of "Childe Harold." Here also we find a new species of epic, such as the formal writers on epic poetry had never contemplated—the hero of which is not a mythical king like Arthur, or a personified Virtue moving in Faeryland like Spenser's Red Cross Knight, or Guyon, or Britomart, but a modern man moving in modern scenes. Wordsworth also is new in form as well as in spirit. No poet before him had dared to shut himself up in the country and choose as the subject of his verse, without any reference to his fine friends in town, his own personal feelings and reflections as aroused by the moving spectacle of sky and hill and glen, and the homely life of rustic neighbours. He wrote a species of pastoral poetry that had not been legislated for by the technical lawgivers of the art, though the want of it had been vaguely felt by Walsh when he wrote wistfully of a Golden Age in which "the shepherds were men of learning and refinement."

Whether or not these are the main characters of the new poetry, the vital principles underlying smaller differences, it is in such large new features that we must seek the secret of the great expansion rather than in little changes of artistic aim or conscious repudiation of definite critical theories. The fetters that had to be broken were nothing so palpable as formal rules of critical authority. They were bonds from which emancipation is much less easy, the restraints of unformulated, undogmatic, inarticulate custom. It was habits of feeling that had to be changed, not rules of art. And the reason of the comparative poverty of the poetry of the eighteenth century was that no poet was born or bred with sufficient force of personality to effect this change. Probably it could not have been effected without the invention of forms of poetry that had the broad characters of new species, so inveterately were the old habits of feeling associated with the old forms, drama, epic, descriptive poem, ode, elegy, and sonnet, each having its established unwritten standard of poetic elegance or refinement. It is only when some distinctively new kind of thing is reached by happy inspiration that creative energy is exalted to the pitch that results in a great period of poetry.

The eighteenth century, possibly because the time was not ripe, had not inventive energy enough in poetry to strike out new lines, but it contributed in many ways to make expansion easier for those that came after. Especially did the rich and varied development of prose in essay and fiction prepare the way for the subsequent emancipation. The influence of this prose as a solvent of established poetic customs has not been sufficiently remarked. Fifty years ago the popular conception of this revolution was that it was a literary echo of the French Revolution; that throughout the eighteenth century poets had bent submissively under the yoke of Pope and the classical school, but that catching the heat of the political ferment they were emboldened to raise the standard of rebellion and throw the rules of their tyrant to the winds. But the example of freedom from traditional standards of dignity set by prose works of imagination and prose comments on life had much more to do with the poetic revolution than the contemporary political excitement, though this also may have been a factor in the result. The serious Muse sat in stiff and starched propriety while her nimbler sister revelled in the enjoyment of freedom, but she tired at last of nursing her dignity, and unbent. Prose writers had familiarised the world with the subjects and sentiments of the new poetry for a generation or two before they attained the intensity that seeks expression in verse. The emancipating influence of the prose literature becomes obvious when, disregarding their individualities, we look at the general strain of the pioneers and the leaders of the poetic revolution. Cowper might be described with general truth as an essayist in verse. Wordsworth deliberately and articulately claimed liberty to use in verse the same diction that might be used for the expression of the same feelings in prose; and incidents such as he made the subjects of his lyrical ballads had for long been considered admissible material for the novelist. Characters and incidents similar in kind to those in Scott's metrical romances had made their appearance before in prose romance. Byron's "Childe Harold" was avowedly suggested by a character in prose fiction: he intended his hero, he said, to be a kind of poetical Zeluco. Prose thus led the way to greater freedom of subject and sentiment in poetry, and matured the ideas to which poetry gave the higher artistic expression.

It is of some importance that we should understand the real nature of the last poetic revival, and see that there was more in it than a revolt against established poetic diction and artificial critical rules. This opprobrious word artificial has been allowed too long to create a false prejudice against the poetry of the eighteenth century. It may be doubted whether in any important sense of the word the best poetry of the eighteenth century was more artificial than the best poetry of the nineteenth. The undiscriminating contempt that at one time sought to justify itself by this vague term of reproach, and that was natural enough in the exultation of a new movement, has now all but passed away, and has given place to a feeling that after all the poets of the eighteenth century may be worthy of study by those ambitious of still further developments. And who knows but that in this once-despised period inventive genius may yet find a hint and a starting-point for fresh triumphs?

III.

THE HISTORICAL RELATIONSHIPS OF BURNS.

THE old conception of the Ayrshire ploughman-poet undoubtedly was that his poetry had no historical connection; that it stands apart as a unique phenomenon, entirely unconnected with the main stream of English poetry; that the peasant-poet owed everything to nature, and nothing to books; that he was a high-priest of poetry, without literary father or mother, raised up by nature herself *ab initio* amidst the most disadvantageous circumstances, as if to put to shame man's feeble calculations of means to ends in literary culture. This was the old conception, people finding it difficult to understand how a ploughman could have trained himself to be a great poet. I do not know how far this conception still prevails; but as something very like it is to be found in the famous essay on Burns by another great Scotchman of genius, Thomas Carlyle, and as it harmonises with our natural desire to have an element of the miraculous in our saints and heroes, it has probably survived all the plain facts set forth by the poet's biographers. There is in the conception this much obvious truth that Burns owed little to school and nothing to college; but when it is said that nature, and nature only, was his schoolmaster (unless the word is used in a sense sufficiently wide to include the works of man, and among them that work of man called literature), the theory does injustice to Burns as an artist, and is at variance with the plain facts of his life.

Supreme excellence in poetry is never attained by a sudden

leap up from the level of common ideas and common speech, whether a man's everyday neighbours are rustics, or men and women of art and fashion and culture. The world in which his imagination moves is never entirely of his own creation. The great poet must have had pioneers from whom he derived some of the ideas and resources of his craft—enough, at least, to feed and stimulate and direct his own inborn energy. Burns, in truth, was a self-taught genius only in the sense in which all great artists are so; those who see in the Ayrshire ploughman's mastery of the poetic art any rarer miracle than this are those only who attach an exaggerated importance to what schools and colleges can do in furthering the highest efforts of human genius. Beyond a certain point, as we all know, every man must be his own schoolmaster; in this sense, nature was the schoolmaster of Burns. But, all the same, his poetry is not an isolated creation, entirely disconnected from the main body of literature. It has its own individuality, as the work of all great artists must have; but it had a literary origin, as much as the poetry of Chaucer or Shakespeare, or even Pope. When nature has done her work, and the unexpected has happened, it is generally easy to find something very natural in the means she has used to bring the unexpected to pass; and the very circumstances that seemed at first sight to be disadvantageous to Burns are now seen to have favoured him in the fulfilment of his mission.

For a work of genius we require first of all a man of genius; but there are conditions that render the exercise of his genius possible, and there are influences that modify the character and the direction of his work. And, in the case of literary work, these conditions and influences are generally found in antecedent literature, though not necessarily in the literature of the language in which the artist works—literature having really an international unity. The course of literature is mainly self-contained; and, in reading its history, the impulse to great work in one generation may often be traced back to dimly-conceived aims and blind and imperfect performances in a previous generation. Nature begins her preparations for the advent of a great man long before he makes his appearance.

It is interesting, and it strengthens our sense of the unity of literature from generation to generation, to trace back in this way the movement that culminated in the poetry of Burns to a very humble episode in the English poetry of Queen Anne's time—a passing fashion for writing what is called pastoral poetry, and a quarrel on the subject among the more celebrated wits of the day. The fashion had prevailed for some time before in France; in England the starting-point was Dryden's translation of Virgil's eclogues. To this translation was prefixed an elegant discourse on pastoral poetry in general by William Walsh, Esq., a gentleman of wit and fashion, who wrote in a very neat and pointed style, subjected the views of the Frenchman, Fontenelle, to delicate and polite ridicule, and submitted to the public with great spirit and elegance his own views of what pastoral poetry ought to be. Mr Walsh's ideal was of the most artificial kind, his poetical shepherds being men of a golden age, when grazing was the chief industry, and shepherds were, as he put it, men of learning and refinement; and his chief rules being that an air of piety should pervade the pastoral poem, that the characters should represent the ancient innocent and un-practised plainness of the golden age, and that the scenery should be truly pastoral—a beautiful landscape, and shepherds, with their flocks round them, piping under wide-spreading beech-trees. Pastoral poetry, as conceived by Mr Walsh, who spoke the taste of his age, was a species of elegant trifling, something like the recent fancy for old French forms of verse (ballades, rondeaus, villanelles, and so forth), and nothing might have come of it; but it so happened that Mr Walsh was the earliest literary friend and counsellor of young Mr Pope, who was persuaded to make his first essay as a poet in pastorals, written in strict accordance with Walsh's principles, and of that came important consequences. Pope published in 1709, in a miscellany of Dodsley's; in the same volume appeared also pastorals from the pen of Ambrose Philips. Philips, known as "Namby Pamby," belonged to the coterie of Addison and Steele. Between that coterie and Pope arose jealousy and strife; hence, when four years later Pope produced his "Windsor Forest," there appeared in the 'Guardian,' the organ of the coterie (April 1713 is the date), a series of articles on pastoral poetry, in which Steele incidentally gave a roll to the log of friend Namby Pamby, who was named as the equal of Theocritus and Virgil, and ridiculed, by

implication, in a polite Queen-Anne manner, the pastoral poems of
young Mr Pope, without mentioning his name. This at least was
the construction put upon the matter by Pope, who took a clever
and amusing revenge of a kind to cause a great deal of talk about
the 'Guardian' articles. It was an amusing literary quarrel;
but Steele's theory of pastoral poetry, thus occasionally produced,
had more fruitful results. The numbers of the 'Guardian' really
set forth for the first time a fresh theory for that kind of composition, to the effect that in English pastoral poetry the characters
should be not classical shepherds and shepherdesses—Corydon and
Phyllis, Tityrus and Amaryllis—but real English rustics; that the
scenery should be real English scenery; and that the manners and
superstitions should be such as are to be found in English rural
life.

Nothing was done to realise this theory in England till the
time of Crabbe and Wordsworth (Gay merely burlesqued it in
his "Shepherd's Week"), but it so happened that it was taken
seriously in Scotland. At the time when the 'Guardian' articles
appeared there was a social club in Edinburgh, named The Easy
Club, which followed the literary movements of London with
keen interest; and of this club Allan Ramsay was poet-laureate.
Allan also wrote pastoral elegies *à la mode*, neither better nor
worse than the artificial stuff then in fashion; but in a happy
hour he thought of trying his hand at the real pastoral, as conceived by Steele, and produced 'The Gentle Shepherd.' Thus,
out of a passing literary fashion and a literary quarrel came the
original impulse to the composition of a work that must be
numbered among the conditions that made the poetry of Burns
possible. For no less honour than this can be claimed for
Ramsay's pastoral comedy. Carlyle says somewhere that a man
of genius is always impossible until he appears. This is quite
true, but it is only a half-truth; and the other half is that a man
of genius must always be possible before he appears. Favourable
conditions for the exercise of his genius will not produce the man;
but if the favourable conditions are not there when he appears,
his genius will be stifled, and he will remain mute and inglorious.

Ramsay's 'Gentle Shepherd' became, in the generation before
Burns, one of the most popular books among the peasantry of

Scotland, finding a place, it is said, beside the Bible in every ploughman's cottage and shepherd's shieling; and it may be said to have created the atmosphere in which the genius of Burns thrived and grew to such proportions. It did this by idealising rural life in Scotland, by giving the ploughman a status in the world of the imagination. It enabled him, as it were, to hold his head higher among his fellow-creatures, and opened his eyes to the elements of poetry in his hard, earth-stained, and weather-beaten existence. "His rustic friend," Carlyle says, in speaking of Burns and the boundless love that was in him, "his nut-brown maiden, are no longer mean and homely, but a hero and a queen, to be ranked with the paragons of earth." But it was Ramsay who first threw the golden light of poetry on the peasant lads and lasses of Scotland, and made heroes and heroines of Patie and Roger and Jenny and Peggy, and who thus created the atmosphere through which Burns saw them. No more striking proof of the power of literature to transform life can be given than the fact that half a century before the advent of Burns he was pre-ceded by an ideal prototype in the 'Gentle Shepherd.' Ramsay's description of his hero might pass for a description of the real Burns, only that nature asserted her supremacy by making the reality more astonishing than anything that the imagination of Ramsay, governed as it was by the genteel spirit of the time, had dared to put into verse.

Burns owed much to Allan Ramsay, and something also to another Scottish poet to whom he erected a memorial stone in Canongate churchyard, Edinburgh—the ill-fated Fergusson; but to say, with Carlyle, that he had "for his only standard of beauty the rhymes of Ramsay and Fergusson," is to miss altogether his true relation to the main body of English literature. His only standard of beauty! This is indeed to underrate the extent of the ploughman's self-education. I need hardly remind you of the studious habits of the Burns family, upon which all his biographers dwell; how their severe rule of bodily labour was combined with a rule of mental labour, no less strictly and strenuously observed because it was voluntary; how they carried books in their pockets to read whenever their hands were free from farm-work; how neighbours found them at their meals with spoon in one hand and book in the other. There is nothing, indeed, that impresses us more with a sense of the gigantic force of the personality of Burns and the breadth of his manhood than the thought that with all the strength of his youthful passion for reading, tending, as it did, to detach him from his unlettered neighbours, it should not have converted him into a self-opinionated prig or a snarling pedant. What saved him from this fate was, that he absorbed books, and was not absorbed by them; he was saved, probably, by that craving for distinction, of which he spoke more than once as his ruling passion, that thirst for admiring sympathy of living men and living women which made him appropriate and turn to his own uses what he found in books. That, probably, saved him from having "loads of learned lumber in his head." However this may be, the actual result was that Burns in those early years of intense and devouring study, ranging far beyond Ramsay and Fergusson, trained himself to be a great artist by mastering and rendering to harmonious practice the best critical ideas of his century.

The secret of Burns's enduring and still growing fame is, that he was the greatest poetic artist of his century; and I would submit the proposition that he was so, not because he stood outside the main current of his century, and drew his inspiration solely from nature, meaning by nature untutored impulse, but because he took into his mind from books, and succeeded by the force of his genius and the happy accident of his position in reconciling two elementary principles of poetry that weaker intellects cannot keep from drifting into antagonism and mutual injury. One of these principles is that with which we are familiar in eighteenth-century literature, under the name of "correctness," which is only another name for perfection of expression, in so far as that can be attained by laborious self-criticism. When Pope began to write, he was advised by his friend Walsh, to whom I have already referred, to aim at correctness: the ancients had said everything, and there was nothing left for the modern poet but to improve upon their manner of saying it. In his "Essay on Criticism," Pope embodied this idea in a couplet:—

> "True wit is nature to advantage dressed,
> What oft was thought, but ne'er so well expressed."

This is one principle; the other is that art must follow nature. It is a common opinion that the eighteenth-century poets were alive only to the first of these principles. But this will not bear examination; the sovereignty of nature was formally proclaimed by Pope, as well as the artistic doctrine of dressing her to advantage :—

> " First follow nature, and your judgment frame
> By her just standard, which is still the same :
> Unerring nature, still divinely bright,
> One clear, unchanged, and universal light,
> Life, force, and beauty, must to all impart,
> At once the source, and end, and test of art."

This was Pope's theory, and in the generation between Pope and Burns the importance of following nature and the vanity of artificial rules were insisted on with untiring enthusiasm by poets and critics alike. But till Burns arose, no poetic aspirant was found, with the doubtful exception of Collins, capable of reconciling the conflicting claims of nature and art in practice. Gray was stifled by too fastidious a desire for correctness : Thomson, Akenside, Shenstone, and the Wartons, had abundant enthusiasm for nature, but insufficient art. It was not, indeed, their poetic principles that undid the correct school, it was rather the artificial taste, the fear of vulgarity, the liking for something elevated above the vulgar style, among the audience for which they wrote ; . and this led them into what was really a violation of Pope's principle of aiming at what oft was thought, induced them to search for what seldom was thought, and to avoid what was never expressed in polite society. Burns was more fortunate in his audience, although he worked on the same principles, and found both warrant and guidance in Pope's " Essay on Criticism."

At first sight it might seem that Burns was all on the side of the naturalists :—

> " Gie me ae touch o' nature's fire,
> That's a' the learning I desire."

This aspiration is sometimes quoted as if it distinguished Burns from his artificial eighteenth-century predecessors, and as if it were the secret of his greatness; but really there is nothing singular in it : it might be paralleled from every poet and poetaster between Pope and himself. We are all willing to throw upon nature the labour that nature requires from us. It was not the touch of nature's fire alone that made Burns the great artist he was: it was the happy combination of this with an indomitable effort after perfection of expression. That Burns had natural fire there is no question; everybody feels it in his poetry, and everybody allows that the touch of nature's fire is indispensable. But Burns had courage enough to recognise that the possession of natural fire did not absolve him from the necessity of resolute artistic discipline; and his distinction lies in this, that he had strength enough to undergo the discipline without losing his hold on nature. How many of his songs fulfil in substance Pope's ideal—

"What oft was thought, but ne'er so well expressed"—

"Auld Lang Syne," "Ye Banks and Braes," "Scots wha hae," "John Anderson," "Tam Glen," "Duncan Gray." And if we either look at his poems in relation to the works of his predecessors, or study his recorded habits of composition, it is easy to see that it was not by trusting to natural impulse alone that he attained this perfection of expression. "It is an excellent method in a poet," he says in one of his letters, "and what I believe every poet does, to place some favourite classic author, in his walks of study and composition, before him as a model." This was obviously his own practice. For almost every one of his poems he had a precedent in general form as well as in metre: for "The Twa Dogs" and "Tam o' Shanter," Allan Ramsay's fables, the "Twa Books" and "The Three Bonnets"; for "Hallowe'en," Fergusson's "Hallow Fair"; for "The Cottar's Saturday Night," Fergusson's "Farmer's Ingle," and so on. Even for his interchange of rhyming epistles with brother bards, which were dashed, as he said, "clean aff loof," he had the precedent of Fergusson's correspondence with J. S. It would almost seem as if he never wrote except with some precedent in his eye, therein approving himself the genuine child of the critical principles and practice of Pope. Not, be it remembered, that he kept his precedent before him for servile imitation: it was before his mind rather as a stimulating rival, to be beaten on its own ground by superior natural force, higher art, or happier choice of theme. There is no better way of reviving our sense of the force of Burns's genius, if it should happen to get blunted by too prolonged familiarity, than putting his work alongside the precedent with which it competes. He did not waste his strength in searching for new types or strange topics, he tried to improve upon the old. "I have no doubt," he wrote to Dr Moore (in 1789), "but the knack, the aptitude, to learn the Muses' trade, is a gift bestowed by Him 'who forms the secret bias of the soul'; but I as firmly believe that *excellence* in the profession is the fruit of industry, labour, attention, and pains." And a description by himself of his habits at the age of sixteen gives us some idea of the kind of pains that he took, from a very early period, in his self-education to the office of poet: "A collection of English songs was my *vade mecum.* I pored over them driving my cart, or walking to labour, song by song, verse by verse; carefully noting the true, tender, or sublime, from affectation or fustian." There we see the artist at work, laboriously building up for himself a standard of perfection in expression, and boldly applying nature as the test of art.

Ten years later, at the age of twenty-six, in the winter of 1785, stimulated by the intention of "appearing in the public character of an author," Burns poured forth poem after poem with marvellous rapidity; and seeing that much of his best work was produced then, his easy impetuous speed has been contrasted with the laborious care of his eighteenth-century predecessors, and it has been supposed that this speed was the secret of his success. But those who argue thus forget the long previous years of discipline to which the poet, with all his ardour of imagination, had had the strength of will to subject himself. In the same way we are apt to marvel at the ease and certainty of touch of a rapid painter, and forget the pains that it took him to acquire such mastery. There are few remains of Burns's apprentice work, because most of it was done in his head as he followed the plough or walked beside his cart, or strolled or lay in his scanty leisure on banks and braes.

But it is possible sometimes to trace a succession of tries with a favourite idea, till at last he found a perfectly satisfactory setting for it. The line—

"But seas between us braid hae roared"—

is perfectly balanced in its place in " Auld Lang Syne " against
the companion line—

> " We twa hae paidl't in the burn."

But the ocean's roar had done duty in more than one of his earlier and less perfect poems before it was happily settled in its
present connection.   At that desperate crisis in his life when he
proposed to expatriate himself, and took a passage to the West
Indies, he addressed the following lines to Jean Armour :—

> " Though mountains rise and deserts howl,
>   And oceans roar between,
> Yet dearer than my deathless soul
>   Still will I love my Jean."

We find the same idea in another poem of the same date :—

> " Will ye go to the Indies, my Mary,
>   And leave auld Scotia's shore ?
> Will ye go to the Indies, my Mary,
>   Across the Atlantic's roar ? "

The idea occurs in still another poem, also written about the same
time :—

> " From thee, Eliza, I must go,
>   And from my native shore ;
> The cruel fates between us throw
>   A boundless ocean's roar ;
>
> " But boundless oceans, roaring wide,
>   Between my love and me,
> They never, never can divide
>   My heart and soul from thee."

I am afraid these quotations illustrate rather more than the
poet's artistic practice ; but they show at least that he was very
constant as an artist, if not as a man.

Burns not only studied his art in books, and measured himself
against established masters with resolute emulation and, we may
well believe, a glorious joy in his own powers, but, living as he
did in his youth from morning till night, day after day, in a world
of the imagination, with books for his constant companions, he
seems to have been influenced by books as few men have been in
his whole attitude towards life and his leading poetic themes.

He carried into his daily intercourse with plain country-folk, who were his neighbours under the real sky, ideals derived from this artificial world : from it he drew his sustenance ; it was the source of the strength that lay behind the outward man. Mr Robert Louis Stevenson, in one of his "Familiar Studies of Men and Books," draws an artistically harmonious and carefully finished picture of Burns as Rab the Ranter, imagining him as a rustic Don Juan or an Ayrshire Théophile Gautier. It is recorded that the farmer's son of Lochlea had, when a youth of twenty-one, the only tied hair in the parish of Tarbolton, and wore a plaid of a particular colour, arranged in a particular manner round his shoulders. This little peculiarity Mr Stevenson happily interprets as a sign of the poet's kinship in temperament with the self-reliant artist, who is not averse to public attention, but rather wishes to force his personality on the world. The comparison with Gautier is so far happy and suggestive that it puts proper emphasis on the artistic side of the poet's nature ; it keeps us from forgetting that the Ayrshire ploughman was, above everything, an artist, and, by force of artistic temperament and habit, not a little of a poser. Mr Stevenson's diagnosis of the tied hair and the particular plaid, as artistic symptoms, is good, and one could wish, in his review of Burns's love affairs and love-letters, to have had more of the same happy vein of interpretation—to have had more of the artist brought into prominence and less of the professional Don Juan. But the truth is, that any comparison of Burns to Don Juan or the magnificent leaders of the romantic movement in France is anachronistic, and, so far, misleading. Though these had something in common with Burns, they were later developments, with marked modifications of race and circumstances ; and if we go further back we shall find not merely parallels but prototypes, that had a direct influence in making Burns what he was. Rab the Ranter, the "rantin' rovin'" boy that was born of the poet's imagination in Kyle, and was the "worser spirit" of his conduct, was the lineal descendant of the roaring boys of the Elizabethan time and the swaggering wits and beaux of the days of King Charles II. ; but his nearest relations are to be found in the poetry and fiction that held the literary field when Burns was young. Rab the Ranter is first cousin to Tom Jones and Roderick

Random and Charles Surface, and was probably acquainted with
his relations; his own immediate parent was, as I have already indicated, the hero of Allan Ramsay's pastoral comedy, the 'Gentle
Shepherd' Patie, a rattleskull,

> "A very deil that aye maun hae his will,"

a king among his fellows by virtue of a natural air of superiority,
a rhymer and a singer, bold of address, glib of tongue, an adept in
chaffing the lasses, irresistible in his arts of courtship, but, with
all this, a student, "reading fell books that teach him meikle
skill," familiar with Shakespeare and Ben Jonson, with poems,
histories, and plays—"reading," as Ramsay says in his homely
phrase—

> "Reading such books as raise a peasant's mind
> Above a lord's that is not so inclined."

All the roaring boys of eighteenth-century poetry and fiction are
distinguished by a certain goodness of heart, and an active scorn
of meanness and hypocrisy; they have strong natural affections;
they are full of compunction for the victims of their warm-blooded
recklessness.   In short, they are all believers in "Rab's" ethical
creed:—

> "The heart aye's the part aye
> That makes us richt or wrang."

In so far as the poet was a rantin' rovin' Robin, this was his
literary lineage and consanguinity. But the real Burns had a
strain in him that would not permit him to be a light-hearted
roaring boy. Rab the Ranter represented only one of his moods
—a mood indulged rather in a spirit of defiance than with
thorough enjoyment, as in one to the manner born. Burns was
the son of the pious cottar whose Saturday night he celebrated,
and he could not remain long at ease in the Zion of the ranters,
however heartily he let himself go, and however splendid his
powers of expression were when he was in the vein. He was the
author of the addresses "To a Mouse" and "To a Mountain
Daisy," as well as of "Tam o' Shanter" and "The Jolly Beggars";
he was the "Man of Feeling," as well as "Rab the Ranter."
One of his most marked qualities is that which Carlyle expresses

with such eloquence of admiration, his large-hearted sensibility,
his boundless love of mankind, his warm· and ready sympathy for
poor outcast defenceless creatures exposed to misfortune's bitter
blast, a sympathy generous enough to embrace and make allowance
for even the enemies of the well-conducted animal world—the
prowling wolf and the devil himself.   Herein, also, Burns was not
singular; here, also, we find him the poet of

"What oft was thought, but ne'er so well expressed"

in his time.   When Burns wrote, sensibility or sentimentality—
tenderness for the woes of the unfortunate, especially for sufferings
that could not be relieved, or for which no relief was possible but
a compassionate tear — was, and had been for several years, a
ruling fashion in literature.   Sensibility was a favourite virtue in
the heroines, and even in the heroes, of the romances of the time.
Sterne's 'Sentimental Journey,' and Mackenzie's 'Man of Feeling,'
still stand out among the numerous contemporary writings in the
same vein.   "Dear sensibility!" cries Sterne, "source inexhausted
of all that is precious in our joys or costly in our sorrows! . . .
Thou givest a portion of it sometimes to the roughest peasant who
traverses the bleakest mountains.   He finds the lacerated lamb of
another's flock.   This moment I behold him, leaning with his head
against his crook, with piteous inclination, looking down upon it!
'Oh, had I come one moment sooner!'"   Sterne and Mackenzie
were favourite authors with Burns; he wore out two copies of
'The Man of Feeling,' carrying it about in his pocket to read at
odd times.

But the reader may ask, Am I not reducing Burns, the child of
nature, the heaven - taught poet, to a mere creature of books?
Would the lad that was born in Kyle not have been a "rantin'
rovin'" boy all the same if there had been no such character in
literature to catch his imagination and sway his conduct?   Would
he not have been a "man of feeling" if Sterne and Mackenzie had
never written a line?   Possibly; all that I suggest is that, apart
from any question of what might have been, books did, as a
matter of fact, influence both his character and his choice of
poetical themes.   The nature, of course, must have been there

before he could have been thus influenced, the natural affinity with what he absorbed from books, the germ that the "potency of life" in them, to use Milton's phrase, quickened and expanded. That Burns would have felt pity for the poor mouse whose dwelling had been ruined by his fell ploughshare, even if he had been absolutely illiterate, we can well believe; but that he would have written a poetic address to the mouse if he had not been steeped in the literature of sensibility is open to question. I merely afford an illustration of the truth expressed in Fletcher of Saltoun's famous saying: "Let me make the ballads of a nation, and I care not who makes its laws." Only Fletcher spoke of popular music-hall songs, and the remark admits of a much wider application—an application as wide as Milton gave it in his "Essay on the Liberty of Unlicensed Printing": "For books are not absolutely dead things, but doe contain a potencie of life in them to be as active as that soule was whose progeny they are; nay, they do preserve as in a violl the purest efficacie and extraction of that living intellect that bred them. . . . As good almost kill a man as kill a good book."

I do not mean that Burns owed everything to books. In virtue of his artistic temperament, he was peculiarly susceptible to influences of all kinds—to ideas current in the minds of living men, as well as to ideas preserved in books; but books exercised a paramount influence upon him, because as a poet or artist in words he, more than the generality of men, lived and moved and had his being in the atmosphere of books. We have his own direct testimony to this, even if it was not to be divined from his artistic temperament, and the study of his works in relation to his contemporaries.

Take an example or two. We find him at a time when things were not going well with him writing as follows to his friend, Robert Ainslie :—

"Let me quote you my two favourite passages, which, *though I have repeated them ten thousand times*, still they rouse my manhood and steel my resolution like inspiration :—

'On Reason build resolve,
That column of true majesty in man.'
—(YOUNG.)

> ' Here, Alfred, hero of the State,
>   Thy genius heavens high will declare ;
> The triumph of the truly great
>   Is never, never to despair !
>   Is never to despair !' "
>
> —(THOMSON, " Masque of Alfred.")

For many men,—most men, perhaps,—such high-sounding phrases are hollow and pointless, brass sounds and nothing more : for Burns they obviously had " a potency of life."   A letter to Murdoch earlier in his career is still more significant of the support he received from books, turning poetry to the use that the late Mr Matthew Arnold was never weary of recommending :—

" My favourite authors are of the sentimental kind, such as Shenstone, particularly his ' Elegies ' ; Thomson ; ' Man of Feeling,' a book I prize next to the Bible ; ' Man of the World ' ; Sterne, especially his ' Sentimental Journey ' ; Macpherson's ' Ossian,' &c.   These are the *glorious models after which I endeavour to form my conduct ;* and 'tis incongruous, 'tis absurd to suppose that the man whose mind glows with sentiments lighted up at their sacred flame —the man whose heart distends with benevolence to all the human race, he ' who can soar above this little scene of things '—can he descend to mind the paltry concerns about which the terræ-filial race fret and fume and vex themselves !   O, how the glorious triumph swells my heart !   I forget that I am a poor, insignificant devil, unnoticed and unknown, stalking up and down fairs and markets, when I happen to be in them, reading a page or two of mankind, and ' catching the manners living as they rise,' whilst the men of business jostle me on every side as an idle incumbrance in their way."

Through that frank letter we can look as through an open window into the heart of Burns, as it was at the age of twenty-four, and it helps us to understand why he failed as a farmer and why he succeeded as a poet, because it shows us how resolutely his heart was set on one ambition and how entirely his mind was occupied with the world of the imagination.   At that date the ranter strain in Burns's character was but very partially developed ; we can see that the " man of feeling " was then uppermost ; and we can note, also, the working in his mind of another favourite ideal of the time—a favourite ideal among artists at all times —that of the *spectator*, the *observer*, who comes down from his world of dreams and meditations to read in the great book of mankind.

Anything that I have said would lead very far from my mean-

ing if it conveyed the impression that Burns neglected to study
either man or nature from the life. My theory, if anything so
obvious can be dignified with the name of theory, only is, that it
was from literature that his genius received the original impulse
and bent to that study by which literature was so much enriched.
His poetry is not a mere freak of nature, a thing *sui generis*, but
an organic part of the body of English literature, with its attach-
ments or points of connection only slightly disguised by difference
of dialect. It drew its inspiration from literature, and it became
in its turn a fruitful source of inspiration to two great poets of
the next generation, Wordsworth and Byron. One main secret
of Byron's fascination was the frank sincerity with which he laid
bare his own personal feelings to the world, abandoning the timid
reserve, the polite reticence about self that had been the ruling
tradition of the eighteenth century; and it may be doubted
whether, with all his impetuous strength and defiant pride,
Byron would have broken so completely with this tradition if
Burns had not led the way. It is with the " nobly pensive " side
of Burns, with Burns as the "man of feeling," that Wordsworth
connects himself; and it may be doubted whether Wordsworth
would have reached the conviction which is the root and source
of so much of his best work, that—

> " Nature for all conditions wants not power
> To consecrate, if we have eyes to see
> The outside of her creatures, and to breathe
> Grandeur upon the very humblest face
> Of human life ; "—

it may be doubted whether Wordsworth would have reached this
conviction as an inspiring principle of fresh poetic work if Burns
had not first taught him, to use his own words in acknowledging
the obligation,

> " How verse may build a princely throne
> On humble truth."

Carlyle, in his celebrated essay on Burns, in which, with all its
eloquence, he seems to me to speak far too disparagingly of
Burns's actual achievement as a poet, regrets that his father's
circumstances did not permit him to reach the university, and

conjectures that he might then have "come forth not as a rustic wonder, but as a regular well-trained intellectual workman, and changed the whole course of English literature." But after all, as it was, Burns did something like this. I do not myself believe in the possibility of revolutionary changes in literature; the history of literature is the history of a gradual development, advancing often, no doubt, by leaps and bounds, but always by natural transition from one stage to another. I doubt, therefore, whether Burns would have "changed the whole course of English literature" if he had gone to a university; but, as it was, he exercised an important influence on that literature, and it is at least probable that he would rather have been hindered with than helped in that mission if his education had been different from what it was. He might have been a happier man otherwise, but it may be doubted whether he would have been a greater poet.

INDEX.

THE END.